INTIMATE INTEGRATION

Review 400 words
July 14, 2022
Great Plains
Quarterly

STUDIES IN GENDER AND HISTORY
General Editors: Franca Iacovetta and Karen Dubinsky

Intimate Integration

A History of the Sixties Scoop and the Colonization of Indigenous Kinship

ALLYSON D. STEVENSON

UNIVERSITY OF TORONTO PRESS
Toronto Buffalo London

© University of Toronto Press 2021
Toronto Buffalo London
utorontopress.com
Printed in Canada

ISBN 978-1-4875-0064-1 (cloth)   ISBN 978-1-4875-1152-4 (EPUB)
ISBN 978-1-4875-2045-8 (paper)   ISBN 978-1-4875-1151-7 (PDF)

Library and Archives Canada Cataloguing in Publication

Title: Intimate integration : a history of the Sixties Scoop
and the colonization of Indigenous kinship / Allyson D. Stevenson.
Names: Stevenson, Allyson D., 1976– author.
Series: Studies in gender and history ; 51.
Description: Series statement: Studies in gender and history ; 51 |
Includes bibliographical references and index.
Identifiers: Canadiana (print) 20200195956 |
Canadiana (ebook) 20200196006 | ISBN 9781487500641 (cloth) |
ISBN 9781487520458 (paper) | ISBN 9781487511524 (EPUB) |
ISBN 9781487511517 (PDF)
Subjects: LCSH: Canada. Indian Act. | LCSH: Interracial adoption – Canada. |
LCSH: Child welfare – Canada. | CSH: Native children – Canada – Social conditions. | CSH: Native
peoples – Kinship – Canada. | CSH: Native peoples – Relocation –
Canada. | CSH: Native peoples – Canada – Government relations.
Classification: LCC HV875.7.C2 S74 2020 | DDC 362.734089/97071–dc23

Cover illustration: *Maashkowishiiw She is strong*, Sherry Farrell Racette, 2015, acrylic on canvas. A
story painted from a story told of a story heard – a child's memory through an elder's voice – a
woman's courage as she faces aggressive men who threaten her family. She flees up into the hills
and watches as her house burns. She makes her way to Manitoba where she rebuilds and raises her
children. Not a victim. A warrior-mother. This painting is from the project *From Here: Story Gatherings
from Regina and the Qu'Appelle Valley*, a series of paintings based on conversations with Métis elders,
commissioned by the Gabriel Dumont Institute.

This book has been published with the help of a grant from the Federation
for the Humanities and Social Sciences, through the Awards to Scholarly
Publications Program, using funds provided by the Social Sciences and
Humanities Research Council of Canada.

University of Toronto Press acknowledges the financial assistance to its
publishing program of the Canada Council for the Arts and the Ontario Arts
Council, an agency of the Government of Ontario.

 Canada Council **Conseil des Arts**
for the Arts **du Canada**

ONTARIO ARTS COUNCIL
CONSEIL DES ARTS DE L'ONTARIO
an Ontario government agency
un organisme du gouvernement de l'Ontario

Funded by the   Financé par le
Government   gouvernement
of Canada   du Canada | Canadä

 MIX
Paper from
responsible sources
FSC® C016245

Contents

Acknowledgments

I first acknowledge the lands in Treaty 6 territory where I live, and Treaty 4 territory where I work. I am grateful to raise my children in the original homeland of the Métis people, our ancestors, with the knowledge of their kinship relations and their connection to our homeland.

This project originated with a question that bubbled up while I was working on my MA on Métis interpreters of the numbered treaties. As a student of Dr Jim Miller, whose work on the residential schools transformed Canadian historical scholarship, I wondered about Indigenous experiences of child welfare and adoption. With only a dim understanding of this potential question, I put it off until a much later date. In 2002 few people had connected child welfare, adoption, and government policy as a policy of Indigenous assimilation. In the time that has elapsed, at the insistence of survivors, the Sixties Scoop has emerged alongside the residential schools as another government-orchestrated policy of Indigenous elimination. I am grateful to the elders, survivors, and leaders who have shared their stories with me and continue to pursue justice for families affected.

My deep gratitude goes out to my early professors in the Department of History at the University of Saskatchewan, especially Dr Jim Miller and Dr Martha Smith-Norris, who were the first to see potential in me as an undergraduate student. My PhD supervisor, Valerie Korinek, demonstrated her confidence in me, and through her deep and abiding belief in the power of women supporting women, I was able to navigate through motherhood and PhD life and thrive. I will always value the time she invested in supporting me and my research. I am also grateful for the encouragement of Karen Dubinsky, my external PhD examiner, who insisted that I submit a manuscript to the Gender and History Series. My post-doctoral supervisor, Dr Catherine Carstairs, enthusiastically embraced me at the University of Guelph, read over the early manuscript, and offered much helpful advice. Kim Anderson and her family were gracious hosts while I was in Guelph, providing me with a friendly space and great conversation.

I am especially grateful for all the support from the University of Toronto Press, and the warm conversations with Len Husband. From the outset, this process has been made much more enjoyable with the supportive and always engaging editors. I am very thankful for the staff of the Provincial Archives of Saskatchewan, formerly the Saskatchewan Archives Board, especially Bonnie Dahl, Christine Charmbury, Tim Novak, Nadine Charabin, and all those behind the scenes who photocopied countless memos, digitized images, and undertook the tedious task of redacting files for the countless restricted access files I requested.

I am especially thankful for the important meeting and ceremony with Elder and Knowledge Keeper Peter Nippi at Kinisin First Nation at the very start of my research. It was his valuable insight into the importance of kinship upon which I framed this research and writing. Along the way I have benefited from intellectual conversations with Brenda Macdougall, who first alerted me to the collection of Adopt Indian and Métis commercials in the archives, and was an early external on my PhD committee. I was directed to pursue research on Indigenous children following the presentation by Sherry Farrel Racette at Congress 2007 at the University of Saskatchewan. Tara Turner and Cheryl Troupe of the Métis Nation-Saskatchewan also were instrumental in facilitating connections in the Métis community. My panel at the Berks Conference of Women's Historians with Margaret Jacobs, Amy Lonetree, Erica Newman, Shurlee Swain, Katrina Jagodinsky, Denise Cuthbert, Tara Briggs, and Karen Dubinsky all assisted in developing my analysis of transracial adoption and the Sixties Scoop. The staff and elders at the Marguerite Riel Centre, especially Director Joanne Yakowec, have always had an open door for me to visit, and learn.

From when I began this research until now, one constant has been the love and support of my family. We have all changed profoundly since this project first began as my children grew from little kids to adults, and my babies went from toddlers to teens. Without their love, this could never have been possible. Their patience and kindness provided me with the strength to carry on when I thought it was just too difficult. My husband, Tyler, has been by my side the whole way through, encouraging me and supporting me as I grappled with all the demands of a gruelling academic career and the personal struggles of being an adoptee. My in-laws Merrill and Carol Stevenson always saw the importance of this research and spent many hours looking after children, driving kids to hockey and music lessons, picking people up from school, and providing endless amounts of love and support. They gave up much of their time and leisure hours so I could publish this research and pursue my dreams. My parents were the first to plant the seeds of aiming high and always pursuing my passion. I know that they often wondered what I was doing and where this was all going. I knew from a young age that I could be whatever I wanted to be. While the journey home has been both fraught and deeply satisfying, it has enabled me to connect with my family of origin and homeland.

This book has been in the making for several years. I am deeply grateful for everyone I encountered on the way: friends, family, and colleagues, who inspired me, kept me going, helped me see the big picture, and kept me grounded. If I have missed anyone, I am very sorry. Any errors or omissions are my responsibility.

Maarsii

Prologue

The following history of Indigenous transracial adoption in Canada interested me on an academic and personal level. While I am an academically trained historian, I am also a Métis adoptee. I carry a strong sense of responsibility to ensure that the history I recount is an ethical, historically accurate rendering that enables scholars, individuals, and communities to understand the historical roots of the Indigenous child welfare crisis in Canada. I have chosen to include a portion of my coming home story in the beginning, as well as at the end of this book. As a Métis academic, I am weaving my *âcimisowin* together with my historical research and writing.[1] I have adopted the approach used by Nêhiýaw/Saulteaux scholar Margaret Kovach and placed important elements of my story in the prologue and the epilogue. As a space for "relational work" Kovach states, "Within Indigenous writing, a prologue structures space for introductions while serving a bridging function for non-Indigenous readers. It is a precursory signal to the careful reader that woven throughout the varied forms of our writing – analytical, reflective, expository – there will be story, for our story is who we are."[2] While it was challenging for me to bring my own experience into my academic work, it was also necessary.[3]

My adoptive family has always supported me in my search for my biological family, as well as in my academic work. I remember my mother, Helen Lawrence, telling me that I could be whatever I wanted. While neither of my adoptive parents attended university, I was always encouraged and expected to attend. Education was very highly valued by my parents and especially by my grandparents. I feel very privileged to have this opportunity to do work that brings me such satisfaction and often think of my grandmother Barbara Lawrence, the daughter of German immigrants who was forced to leave school in Grade 8 to work cleaning homes to support their large family. My grandparents, parents, and brother Alan are profoundly important to me as I navigate through this work, and through this world. As an adoptee, I am connected to my adoptive family and my biological families in both tangible and intangible ways.

Like many adoptees, for my first nineteen years, I yearned to know where I came from and who I was. I have since discovered that for many Indigenous peoples in Canada, this loss of connection and knowledge is all too common. Maria Campbell shared a teaching she received from elder Peter O'Chiese about the impact of colonization on Indigenous societies. He likened it to a shattered puzzle, with the scattered pieces being histories, teachings, stories, and knowledge. With some stories found in ethnographers notebooks, museums, and archives, she was encouraged to seek out all the places where we might find the pieces in order to put the puzzle back together for future generations. "That's what happened to our wahkotowin and to our stuff," he said. "Our kinships, our lives, and our teachings are all over the place."[4] Like these scattered teachings, knowledge of my personal and collective history as a Métis adoptee is scattered through government files, newspaper articles, community history books, and stories told to me. As I put together these pieces, I found that it was important for me to include my own adoption story for two reasons. First, I felt that there are many others like me who may never have the opportunity to speak about or hear experiences of adoption. Second, I wanted to begin integrating my historical training and my Métis background in my work in concrete and innovative ways, historicizing and theorizing a decolonial approach informed by my experience of coming home.

I was born in Saskatoon in 1976 and raised in Regina, Saskatchewan. As an adult, I learned that my biological families both came from Kinistino, Saskatchewan, a small town approximately seventy-five kilometres east of Prince Albert. On my eighteenth birthday I began a search for my biological family by registering for Saskatchewan's Post-Adoption Registry. My biological mother was interested in meeting me and provided her contact information in the event I should begin a search. In one of my first conversations with my biological mother, she informed me that my biological father had disappeared in 1980. He was the second son in his family of four boys. I found this information to be very devastating, and I mourned for a father I had never met. In 1998 I married Tyler Stevenson and moved from Saskatoon to his family farm near Kinistino in the Rural Municipality of Flett's Springs. With this move, I came home in ways I did not completely understand until I began this particular research. When I began to investigate the early homestead records and scrip applications of my ancestors for my genealogical research, I discovered that our farm includes land that my Métis ancestors homesteaded at the turn of the century. My husband, Tyler Stevenson, and his father farmed the Fidler field on the NE quarter section 2-44-21 W2, since the mid-1940s. This quarter section was first homesteaded by my great-great-great-grandparents James Edward Fidler and Sarah Ann Swain in 1903.[5]

When I met my families of origin for the first time in 1996 at the age of 20, I had had no knowledge of my original family. As part of the closed adoption practice of the 1970s, all identifying information was sealed, and children were issued a new birth certificate with their adoptive parents' names. Non-identifying information was provided for adoptive parents to share with children at the "appropriate time." While this was not shared with me until I was in my mid-twenties, throughout my childhood my adoptive parents explained to me was that my biological mother was young and unmarried and not able to care for me in the way she wished. While this is a profound oversimplification of a deeply complex and individual experience, their explanation was supported by the adoption documents I have since seen and my biological mother's rendering of her experience. In the non-identifying information packet provided to my adoptive parents, my mother is described in glowing terms, and my father is briefly mentioned as a twenty-year-old young man of Irish descent who was very attractive, with average to above-average intelligence. It continued to state that while they had been in a relationship for about a year and a half, they did not want to continue their relationship.[6] My father's background as a twenty-six-year old English-Métis was erased from the non-identifying information. Without my biological father's story, I have tried to fill these gaps through my research. Like many adoption stories, mine is both strikingly common yet also deeply personal.

"Coming home" is grounded in my lived experience as a Métis adoptee affected by the child welfare system, both as an adoptee and later as a foster child, seen through the lens of critical Indigenous methodologies to illuminate historic Métis experiences of erasure and what I call insistence. As an adoptee it was necessary to piece together my kinship relationships through witnessing the Métis migration, replacing and dispersal, using official archival records that were often created in order to manage and racialize Indigenous peoples. I have come to know, through my own genealogical reconstruction and historical research, how my ancestors have engaged in this struggle to remain connected to each other and to the lands in each of their respective time periods. By searching for my own story, and by re-establishing my family connections, I simultaneously tapped into a sense of Métis historical consciousness. I am contributing to this resistance/insistence through utilizing historical reconstruction to resist the settler colonial sundering of my kinship connections, land connections, and Métis identity, and insist upon reclaiming my Métis identity and place on the land.

Themes of exile and coming home figure prominently in Indigenous storytelling. Métis writer and artist Gregory Scofield's *Thunder through My Veins: Memories of a Métis Childhood* articulates his experiences growing up without knowledge of his Métis ancestry or understanding of Métis history. In his chapter "Pekwew, Pekewe (Come Home, Come Home)" Scofield recalls his first encounter with Métis culture and history at Back to Batoche Days. After his challenging childhood and youth in British Columbia, he finally found a place where he felt he belonged. He recalled, "As we left Batoche I felt my heart sink into the very landscape, my spirit joining those of my ancestors in the empty ravines and coulees. I had searched so long for a place of belonging, and now I had found it.... Never again would I search for a place of belonging. This place, Batoche, would always be 'home,' my home."[7] Neal McLeod devotes a chapter in *Cree Narrative Memory: From Treaties to Contemporary Times* to Indigenous experiences of spatial and spiritual exile, as well as interrogating the meaning and significance of coming home for Indigenous peoples. He argues that removal of people from their lands, and either confined to reserves, removed to colonies, or displaced to cities is a form of spatial exile. Spiritual exile is the consequence of disrupting transmission of Indigenous languages, songs, and stories. Indigenous people, through the colonization, removal to residential schools, as well as fostering in alien environments hostile to Indigenous peoples, experience both.[8]

As a Métis adoptee, coming home is an ongoing process and not a destination. It can be experienced in a singular moment, as well as through an evolving sense of groundedness in place, family, and community. My earliest experience of coming home occurred on the first Christmas I spent with my biological father's family. There, at my aunt and uncle's house, a homemade quilt waited for me under the Christmas tree. My great-grandmother made each of her grandsons a quilt that they received on their wedding day. Since my father never married and disappeared in 1980, the quilt was passed on to me once I returned home. This quilt, which my family uses each summer on the beach to bring us all together, has deep meaning for me and connects me to my father and his family in a very loving and tangible way. Because I did not have the opportunity to meet my father, grandfather, or great-grandmother, the scraps of material, gathered over time, lovingly stitched together by my great-grandmother's hands, provides a connection through time and space.

Through this writing I have also experienced the process of coming home as I delved further into the policies and legislation that structured adoption in the mid-twentieth century. It was my intention to make legible the invisible decisions that determined my life and the lives of so many others. With increased attention to the fallout of the Sixties Scoop, I hope that this work will be useful for those seeking the history of Indigenous child welfare in Canada.

INTIMATE INTEGRATION

Introduction

Saskatchewan/*Kisiskâciwan* is the heart of Canada's colonial enterprise. *Kisiskâciwan* is a Cree term for "it flows fast" and also the name of the river *Kisiskâciwani-sîpiy* that bisects the contemporary province.[1] The north and south branches join at the forks, east of the city of Prince Albert, flowing north-easterly through Cumberland House and into Manitoba. The Cree people call North America "*Iyiniwi-ministik*" (the People's Island), and elders say that First Nations have been on this land from time immemorial. First Nations elders in Saskatchewan explain that they were placed here by the Creator.[2] Archaeological evidence of human habitation from sites around the province date back 11,000 years.[3] European interest in the region first emerged in the late seventeenth century, and in the years that followed French, British, and Canadian fur traders sought Cree, Assiniboine, and Dene furs for European markets. These interactions between European men and Indigenous women in the north-western interior led to the ethnogenesis of a unique people that culminated in the birth a new nation, the Métis, who developed a unique Indigenous culture, language, and political identity rooted in a storied landscape.

The legacies and practices of settler colonialism resonate uniquely in Saskatchewan, and, from its earliest days, Indigenous elimination in Canada has been rendered most violently here.[4] It is out of this particular history, of this particular place, that the policies of removing Indigenous children in the second half of the twentieth century are situated.[5]

In the unilateral application of child welfare laws to First Nations and Métis peoples in Canada, a multitude of well-meaning and not so well-meaning Canadians developed a consensus on Indigenous suffering. In doing so, social workers and social scientists in the post-war period diagnosed the enacting of Indigenous familial roles and responsibilities and the material deprivations derived from the multiplying effects of colonization as a lack of adjustment to Euro-Canadian middle-class norms. However, in their new drive for legitimacy as secular saviours, social workers, social scientists, and politicians employed the logic that had long animated state-based approaches to solving the "Indian problem": the removal of Indigenous children from the influence of their families, communities, and cultures.

Beginning in the 1950s, First Nations and Métis peoples across Canada experienced an increase in interventions by child protection workers who apprehended Indigenous children and placed them in foster and adoptive homes for their purported protection. The abrupt and seemingly dramatic increase in apprehensions and adoptions by the 1960s has led to this complex set of logics being called "the Sixties Scoop." The term originated in a passage found in Patrick Johnston's *Native Children and the Child Welfare System*, who attributed the over-representation of Indigenous children in the child welfare system to the ethnocentrism of individual social workers. A former B.C. social worker reflecting on her time working in an Indigenous community "admitted that the provincial social workers would, quite literally, scoop children from reserves on the slightest pretext. She also made it clear, however, that she and her colleagues sincerely believed that what they were doing was in the best interests of the children. They felt that the apprehension of Indian children from reserves would save them from the effects of crushing poverty, unsanitary health conditions, poor housing and malnutrition, which were facts of life on many reserves."[6]

On one hand, this quotation points to the benevolent intent of individual social workers who sought to rescue children from the devastating material conditions they faced, but were unable to acknowledge the historical factors that led to those conditions. Indeed, placing the focus on frontline social workers obscures the larger legal and political history of Canada's Indigenous peoples. This settler colonial intrusion into the intimate realm of Indigenous families not only failed to produce the intended outcome of assimilated individualized non-Indians, but rather compounded loss and suffering that it purported to alleviate. Benevolent justifications to enact the cultural genocide of Indigenous peoples through removing children is the bleeding heart of settler colonialism.[7]

In Saskatchewan, First Nations and Métis elders, leaders, and communities did not remain silent in the face of these threats to the integrity of Indigenous nations. For Indigenous women, the historic colonial experience has had a distinctly gendered component. As such, some women have developed a politics of decolonization that takes into account the historic and gendered effects of colonization.[8] Initially First Nations and Métis women sought to work interdependently with government to care for families and children facing hardship. The Saskatchewan Native Women's Movement (SNWM) was a radical grassroots Indigenous women's group that worked to organize women and create Indigenous solutions to poverty and family breakdown. SNWM emerged as Saskatchewan's most vocal opponent of Indigenous child removal and transracial adoption, and worked to create Indigenous solutions for Indigenous families. They proposed an Indigenous feminist approach to address the impact of colonization in the lives of First Nations and Métis women in Saskatchewan. For example, they became involved in providing education and support to teen mothers to support their children, and they opened the first Native-run day care centre in downtown Regina in 1973. Their voices are an important alternative to the dominance of experts who were constructing the "problem of Indian child welfare" in the 1980s.[9]

However, in time, both Métis and First Nations peoples sought to create separate Indigenous systems of caring that better reflected the needs of families and communities affected by colonization and living in a society that regarded Indigenous culture and peoples as inferior. The provincial First Nations' political organization, the Federation of Saskatchewan Indian Nations (FSIN), crafted "Taking Control of Indian Child Welfare" and lobbied to end Indigenous transracial adoption. Indigenous peoples argued that when children were removed, adopted, and renamed by Euro-Canadian families, kinship systems, stories, and language transmission were interrupted. Compounding these losses has been the Euro-Canadian cultural justifications that further marginalized Indigenous peoples as poor parents, further feeding negative stereotypes of the lazy Indian, the drunken Indian, the dissolute squaw, and the backwardness of elders. The Sixties Scoop continues as the "Millennium Scoop," and the logics that animated the scoop persist.[10]

Maria Campbell, Saskatchewan Métis author of the ground-breaking autobiography *Halfbreed*, published stories told to her by Métis and First Nations elders. *Stories of the Road Allowance People* contains oral histories of meaningful, poignant, and sometimes funny Métis stories. One provides a useful starting place to reflect on the ways in which removing children from their families and communities has had lasting impacts on Indigenous peoples individually and collectively:

Excerpt from "Jacob"

Sometimes me / I tink dats dah reason why we have such a hard time / us peoples. / Our roots dey gets broken so many times. / Hees hard to be strong you know / when you don got far to look back for help.

Dah whitemans / he can look back for thousands of years / cause him / he write everyting down. / But us peoples / we use the membering / an we pass it on by telling stories an singing songs. / Sometimes we even dance dah membering. / But all dis trouble you know / he start after we get dah new names / he come a new language an a new way of living. / Once a long time ago / I could'ave told you dah story of granfawder Kannap / an all his peoples but no more. / All I can tell you now is bout Jim Boy / an hees story hees not very ole.

Well my granmudder Mistupuch / he never gets a whitemans name an him / he knowed lots of stories / Dat ole lady / he even knowed dah songs. / He always use to tell me / one bout an ole man call Jacob.

Dat ole man you know / he don live too far from here. / Well hees gone now / but dis story he was about him when he was alive. Jacob him / he gets one of dem new names when dey put him in dah / residential school. / He was jus a small boy when he go / an he don come home for twelve years.

Twelve years! / dats a long time to be gone from your peoples. / He can come home you know / cause dah school he was danm near two hundred miles / away. / His mommy an Daddy dey can go an see him / cause deres no roads in dem days / an dah Indians dey don gots many horses / 'specially to travel dat far. ...

Well Jacob him / he stay in dat school all dem years an when he come / home he was a man. / While he was gone / his Mommy an Daddy dey die so he gots nobody. / An on top of dat / nobody knowed him cause he gots a new name. / My Granmudder / he say dat ole man he have a hell of a time. / No body he can understand dat / unless he happen to him.

Dem peoples dat go away to dem schools / an come back you know dey really suffer. / No matter how many stories we tell / we'll never be able to tell what dem schools dey done to dah peoples / an all dere relations.

Well anyways / Jacob he was jus plain pitiful. / He can talk his own language. / He don know how to live in dah bush. / It's a good ting da peoples dey was kine / cause dey help him dah very bes dey can. / Well a couple of summers later / he meet dis girl / an dey gets married.[11]

Jacob and his wife had a son, adopted two daughters, and lived a good life together. One day the priest arrived at the reserve to take the children of the community to the residential school. There was great sorrow among the community, and Jacob demanded that the children remain. The priest insisted that the children must attend and reminded Jacob that he received a good education at the school. Jacob replied, "Yes I go to dah school / an dats why I don wan my kids to go. / All dere is in dat place is suffering."[12] The priest responded that Jesus suffered, and so must everyone else. Jacob further stated that Jesus knew his mother and his father, and he didn't have to lose his language and leave his home. He even told the priest that he didn't even know his own name since he'd been given the Christian name Jacob at the residential school. "'Your Dad hees Indian name was Awchak' dah prees he say / 'I tink dat means Star in your language.' / He never gets a new name cause he never become a Christian."[13] Once the priest told Jacob his name, his wife left in tears. She had discovered that they were brother and sister, since her father was Awchak also. Jacob later discovered that his wife had committed suicide.

Jacob he say / dah ole womans / dey stay wit him for a long time /
an dey sing healing songs and dey try to help him / but he say he
can feel nutting. Maybe if he did / he would have done dah same
ting.

For many years Jacob was like dat / just dead inside.[14]

One day, once his children were grown, his daughter returned home
with his granddaughter.

Jacob he say / he look at dat lil baby / an he start to cry an he
can stop. / he cry for himself an his wife / an den he cry for his
Mommy and his Daddy. / When he was done / he sing dah healing songs dah ole woman / dey sing to him a long time ago.

Well you know / Jacob he die when he was an ole ole man. / An
all hees life / he write in a big book / dah Indian names of all had
Mommies an Daddies. / An beside dem / he write dah old names
and dah new names of all dere kids.

An for dah res of hees life / he fight dah government to build
schools on the / reservation. / "The good God he wouldn of make
babies come / from Mommies an Daddies," / he use to say, / "if
he didn wan dem to stay home / an learn dere language / an dere
Indian ways."

You know / dat ole man was right. / Nobody he can do dat. /
Take all dah babies away. Hees jus not right. / Long time ago / dah
ole peoples dey use to do dah naming / an dey do dah teaching
too. / If dah parents dey have troubles / den dah aunties an dah
uncles / or somebody in had family / he held out til dah parents
dey gets dere life work / out. / But no one / no one / he ever take
dah babies away from dere peoples.

Saskatchewan continues to "take dah babies away from dere peoples," as do provincial and First Nations child-caring agencies across
Canada. Statistics point to high numbers of children who live out of
their homes, cared for by substitutes paid by provinces or First Nations
Child and Family Service Agencies. In Saskatchewan, Indigenous children make up over 80 per cent of children in the care of the Ministry of
Social Services, one of the highest rates in Canada. Meanwhile, Indigenous children make up 25 per cent of the total child population. Next

door, 90 per cent of children in care in Manitoba are Indigenous.[15] Scholars have found that the over-representation of Indigenous children due to child neglect is rooted in factors that include poverty, poor housing, domestic violence, and substance abuse.[16] In addition, the federal government has underfunded on-reserve child and family service agencies for decades. In 2016 the Canadian Human Rights Tribunal found the government of Canada in violation of the Canadian Human Rights Act for failing to provide the same rates of funding for on-reserve child and family services as provinces provide for off-reserve families and children in need. The impact of the decades-long funding gap led to children being removed from their family homes and communities, living indefinitely in foster care – an outcome that mirrors the disgraced residential schools system of years past.[17] Recently the federal minister of Indigenous services, Jane Philpott, characterized this over-representation as a national "humanitarian crisis" and vowed to devote increased resources to prevent apprehensions of Indigenous children.[18]

While long recognized as problematic by First Nations and Métis peoples, among non-Indigenous Canadians, academic attention turned to Indigenous over-representation in child welfare systems across Canada in 1983. Patrick Johnston's *Native Children and the Child Welfare System* revealed that the proportion of Saskatchewan's Indigenous children in the child welfare system was the highest of all the provinces. First Nations and Métis children made up approximately 63 per cent of all children in the care of social services.[19] By comparison, Native children made up 42 per cent of child welfare cases in Alberta, and 50 per cent in Manitoba.[20] Almost twenty-five years later, little progress had been made. In 2007, Saskatchewan's Child Welfare Review Panel released *For the Good of Our Children and Youth: A New Vision, A New Direction*. The report revealed that numbers of Indigenous children in care rapidly escalated between 2000 and 2009 from 2,470 to 4,382.[21] Contributing to the increasing number of children living outside their family homes were poverty and the historic relations between Indigenous peoples and the state. One significant historical contributor in particular was the past practice of Indigenous transracial adoption, now called "the Sixties Scoop."[22]

The Child Welfare Review Panel voiced concerns similar to those of social workers and bureaucrats in the early 1960s. The 2007 report determined that part of the reason for the rapid increase in numbers of children was workers' inability to plan for "permanent" homes for Indigenous children. The broken trust between Indigenous peoples as a result of the Sixties Scoop and transracial adoption policies had culminated in a political and social work climate that saw transracial adoption as untenable. In 1963 a lack of public interest in adopting non-white children drove a campaign to expand adoption for children in care. In an annual meeting of the federal Canadian Welfare Council, provincial child welfare directors discussed the adoption problems they experienced and the need to expand the public's notion of "adoptability."[23] Directors from the western provinces with larger Indian and Métis populations spoke of the high numbers of Indigenous children in their care and sought to work together to "solve what is a national problem of finding homes for Indian, Métis and Negroes, and other children who are difficult to adopt because of physical handicaps."[24] Saskatchewan's Director of Child Welfare, Mildred Battel, lamented, "It's always much easier to find homes for fair-haired, blue-eyed babies.... [I]t's the mixed-race children that represent the hard, unadoptable group." She felt that "the answer must be found in a reflection of public opinion." Alberta's welfare director suggested that advertising was an "expensive but efficient means to dispel old wives tales about adoption."[25] In 1965, twenty Indigenous children were adopted into white homes in Saskatchewan, but that was but a small fraction of potential adoptees, since over one-third of children in permanent care were Indigenous.[26]

The problem of placing Indigenous children was transferred to the Saskatchewan public when in 1967, under the direction of Frank Dornstauder, the Department of Social Welfare piloted the project Adopt Indian and Métis, later known as Aim. The idea was to educate Saskatchewan families – through radio, television, and guest speaker appearances at clubs and churches across the province – that Indigenous children were in need of permanent adoptive homes and families. Adopt Indian and Métis stimulated transracial adoption in Saskatchewan. It was the only targeted Indigenous transracial adoption program in Canada. The "Sixties Scoop" – taking Indigenous Canadian children out of their communities and placing them for adoption in non-Indigenous homes – lasted well into the next decade, with the social work field pushing transracial adoption as an ideal solution to the problem of increasing numbers of children leaving the care of their parents and communities.[27]

Saskatchewan's review of the Family Services Act (1973) in the second half of 1983 was part of a country-wide movement to address problems that beset provincial governments providing child welfare services to Indigenous peoples and to bring legislation in line with the cultural and legal changes that had taken place over the past decade.[28] The Saskatchewan public review offered an explanation and presented recommendations to address the high proportion of Indigenous children in care and the lack of preventative care for families. These explanations didn't satisfy Indigenous leaders or activists who had sought full control and recognition of their rights to determine the futures of their children. It also provided a public forum to air grievances, as well as raise awareness about these issues in the greater community. In the decade since the Métis Society and the Native Women's Movement first articulated a challenge to the child removal logic of the Department of Social Services, Indigenous peoples in North America had grown increasingly vocal in protesting the government policies that led to the breakdown of the Indian family, whether for education or protection. Beginning with decolonization movements in both Canada and the United States, control of the provision of child and family services to Indigenous children occupied a central position in discussions of self-determination. Ending transracial adoption symbolized ending the unequal and unilateral policies of integration that had emerged in the years following the Second World War.

Disruption and dispossession figure prominently in the colonization of Indigenous kinship. The main argument of this book concerns the centrality of Indigenous kinship, (*wáhkôhtowin* in Cree), not only for a sense of family relationships, but as the organizing principle from which Indigenous identity and political sovereignty emerge, hence the ongoing effort to eliminate this essential configuration. Neal McLeod explains that "kinship, *wáhkôhtowin*, grounds the collective narrative memory within *nêhiyâwiwin* (Cree language). There are important relationships not only among human beings, but also with the rest of creation… [W]*áhkôhtowin* keeps narrative memory grounded and embedded within an individual's life stories. It also grounds the transmission of Cree narrative memory; people tell stories to other people who are part of the stories and assume the moral responsibility to remember."[29] Respected Indigenous legal scholar James Youngblood Henderson argues that Indigenous kinship forms a critical pillar for

Indigenous legal orders. "The First Nations law of the relationship *(wâhkôhtowin)* embraces general concepts of nationhood, society, culture and communities. The law is not entertained as ideals of doctrines, but as relationship or attitudes that generate particular behaviours, as a spirit or mentality, which establishes its central beliefs and unifying teachings."[30] At the outset of this research on Indigenous transracial adoption, it was important to situate the policy history within an Indigenous framework rooted in local understandings of kinship, and attend to local Indigenous expressions of political engagement in resisting child removal.

This study began with three key avenues of inquiry for analysis of historic Indigenous transracial adoption policies in Saskatchewan. First, I sought to explore the relationship between historic federal and provincial First Nations and Métis policies and the emergence of Indigenous transracial adoption when viewed through the lenses of gender and race. Second, I examined the intersection of racial, gender, and social hierarchies in the 1960s through the 1980s in Saskatchewan as it pertained to child removal and transracial adoption. Finally, I explored Indigenous interactions with child welfare authorities and perceptions of transracial adoption.

This book responds to these three avenues by excavating the cultural and legal origins of Indigenous transracial adoption and key theoretical and historical issues of race, kinship, gender, and family in Indigenous and non-Indigenous societies. Chapter 1 establishes the theoretical framework and historical context with which to understand the particular logic of Indigenous transracial adoption in the Canadian context. Chapter 2 provides an ethnohistory of adoption and kinship in Indigenous societies. By examining cases of Indigenous adoptions in the pre-war period, this book argues that Indigenous people attempted to utilize the Euro-Canadian legal system to validate Indigenous family-making and adoption. The indigenizing of the child welfare law with its potential for expanding Indian nationhood and sovereignty came to abrupt halt in 1951 with the revisions to the Indian Act, which made reserves subject to provincial law and adoption of non-Indian children by Indians untenable. Chapter 3 explores Saskatchewan's provincial policies surrounding Métis rehabilitation, gender, and child welfare legislation with an eye towards locating the origins of Indigenous over-representation in the system between 1944 and 1965. Chapter 4 provides a case study of the CCF Métis policies and the operation of the Green Lake Children's home. Chapter 5 traces the conflicts between federal law and provincial law surrounding the legal status of illegitimate Indian children from 1951 to 1973, and the outcome of the jurisdictional disputes. It illustrates the rise of professional social workers who sought to adjust "problematic" Indigenous families and communities. Chapter 6 centres on the creation of Adopt Indian and Métis in 1967 in Saskatchewan, and incorporates voices of Indigenous adoptees. It also highlights the use of compelling images of individual Indigenous children in print and televised media first used in the American Indian Adoption Project (IAP), then later in Saskatchewan's Adopt Indian and Métis program, that enabled non-Aboriginal people to consider adopting an Indigenous child or children. The lineage of using emotional renderings of children had its origins in the child rescue movement of Britain that was embraced by the early adoption reformers in Canada and the United States. Such advertisements appealed to the public by drawing on emotional and heart-rending tropes of child rescue.[31] Chapter 7 explains the emergence of local Indigenous resistance to Indigenous transracial adoption by the Saskatchewan Métis Society, followed by the Saskatchewan Native Women's Movement. Chapter 8 then evaluates the North American Native American and Indigenous movements for self-determination and the restoration of Indigenous family caring. It also historicizes the role of social scientists and local activists joining forces to critique the logic of Indigenous child removal. It draws together historical and theoretical insights into gender, kinship, and citizenship to explore the politicized discourses around child welfare in the 1980s that led First Nations and Métis leaders to characterize transracial adoption as a form of genocide.

1

The Bleeding Heart of Settler Colonialism

Dere's lots of moving in dah stories of our peoples. Hees a good ting dat dah ole blood hees strong cause udderwise he would be easy to forget who we are. Dats why hees important for us to know dah names of dah places where we was born and growed up cause dem names and dem stories dey keep us hooked up and from dere we can go any place and we always knowed who we are. When we gets unhooked dats when it becomes dangerous.

— John (Dan) Campbell, *Stories of the Road Allowance People*, 1995

In the fall of 2018 the government of Saskatchewan, in partnership with the Sixties Scoop Indigenous Society of Saskatchewan (SSISS), held sharing circles in Meadow Lake, North Battleford, Prince Albert, Saskatoon, Fort Qu'Appelle, and Regina for Sixties Scoop survivors and family members to share their stories. The information gathered in the sharing circles was used to help inform the government's apology that took place on 7 January 2019 at the Legislative Buildings in Regina.[1] Four years earlier, in June 2015 Saskatchewan Premier Brad Wall promised a government apology for removing Indigenous children through programs such as Adopt Indian and Métis in the 1960s and 1970s but made clear that there would be no provincial compensation attached.[2] This announcement followed Manitoba Premier Greg Selinger's apology earlier in the month for the province's role in the Sixties Scoop. He acknowledged, "It was a practice that has left intergenerational scars and cultural loss. With these words of apology and regret, I hope all Canadians will join me in recognizing this historic injustice. I hope they will join me in acknowledging the pain of suffering of thousands of children who were taken from their homes."[3] In May 2018 the province of Alberta formally apologized to families and children affected by the Sixties Scoop after consultations with Indigenous communities around the province. Along with the apology, Alberta Premier Rachel Notley promised to work with Indigenous families and communities to "find a path to true reconciliation."[4]

Recent apologies by Prairie provincial governments come in response to class action lawsuits from survivors demanding recognition and compensation for the loss of family, culture, and connection, as well as abuse that these policies produced. Regina lawyer Tony Merchant has filed several class action lawsuits against the provinces for the harms of the Sixties Scoop, and in Saskatchewan, for the Indian and Métis adoption program.[5] Merchant is well known for representing thousands of residential school survivors in their class action against the government of Canada. A federal Sixties Scoop class action that originated in Ontario was settled on 6 October 2017 when Minister of Crown-Indigenous Relations and Northern Affairs, Carolyn Bennett, and Chief Marcia Brown Martel announced that an agreement-in-principle had been reached to settle the claims of Indigenous children removed during the 1960s and 1970s. Status Indian and Inuit children from across Canada who had been removed between 1951 and 1991 were eligible for compensation from the federal government for the loss of their culture during the time they spent in non-Indigenous foster and adoptive homes. While the initial class action lawsuit pertained only to on-reserve Indian children removed in Ontario between 1965 and 1984, the final agreement included all provinces and territories, and a broader time period. What was striking about the agreement was the lack of recognition of Métis children with similar experiences. The $500–$800 million settlement left out claims of Métis children, causing an immediate reaction from the Métis adoptees and foster children who similarly experienced a loss of culture, family connection, and sense of belonging. The government asserted that during this period it was the provinces that were responsible for the Métis, not the federal government.[6] Despite the recent apologies by provincial premiers, and the settlement agreement for the federal class action, the issue of the Sixties Scoop lacks broad public understanding. Unlike the Residential School Settlement Agreement, the Sixties Scoop Settlement Agreement did not require a formal statement gathering process or truth commission similar to the Truth and Reconciliation Commission (TRC). This striking difference leaves many survivors and communities without the opportunity to share their stories, and Canadians without the opportunity to understand the legacy of these policies.

This policy history of the Sixties Scoop draws on a generation of historical work on residential schooling and government Indian policy. Native-newcomer historiography in Canada has detailed the significance of policy and education in shaping relations between First Nations and the state. J.R. Miller has termed policy of the Department of Indian Affairs for Indian assimilation carried out from the late nineteenth century until the end of the Second World War "the policy of the bible and the plough."[7] These policies were embodied in church-run residential schools, reserves, and heavy-handed tactics of cultural and spiritual repression. Taken together, these all aimed to break down communal land-holding on the prairies, with the goal being eventual absorption of First Nations into the body politic. Miller's later work on residential schools looked specifically at those schools from the perspective of church, First Nations, and government, highlighting the role of the schools in shaping gender identities of Indian children through clothing, work regimes, and curriculum.[8]

More than merely educational facilities, Miller points to the importance of the residential aspect of the schooling, which had children live away from parents and communities for a significant portion of the year. Miller demonstrates that, from early contact onward, Europeans expressed a desire to socialize Indian children in the European context. An experiment began with the first Recollect boarding school, which opened in 1620 in the colony of New France. Four of the eight original pupils sent off eventually ended up in the care of the French. Their European instructors found it difficult to "curb the Indian youths' freedom loving ways."[9] The initial experiment failed but was followed shortly by the Jesuit experiment. The instructors found that removing children from the parents prevented parental interference, stating, "We would not be annoyed and distracted by the fathers while instructing the children."[10] Later, in 1635 Champlain observed that children also played a larger political purpose in establishing relations between the two groups. In exchange for the promises of European goods, Christianity, and military support, the Huron were asked to "next year bring many of their little boys, whom we will lodge comfortably, and will feed, instruct and cherish as if they were our little Brothers." Miller notes that, indeed, some First Nations groups did surrender children to the French boarding schools in 1636, and also First Nations people requested schooling from officials and in treaties.

From the origins of contact, the acquisition of Indigenous children has served both political and assimilatory purpose. The early experiment in residential schooling was replicated by Anglican missionaries. And by Confederation, boarding schools run by missionary societies were spread through the former British colonies. The schools that were established between 1883 and the turn of the century were part of the federal Indian policy, operated by the missionary bodies.[11] John Milloy also explores the residential school system, connecting it with the increasingly coercive post-Confederation colonization regime. Milloy states, "In the vision of education developed by both the church and the state in the final decades of the 19th century, it was the residential school experience that would lead children most effectively out of the 'savage' communities into 'higher civilization' and 'full citizenship.'"[12] The system suffered from chronic underfunding, and in 1920 revisions to the Indian Act made attendance compulsory, to bolster attendance to secure greater per capita funding.[13] Despite the lack of success and the high death rates, schools became routine from 1923 to 1946.

Milloy also finds that after 1946, the department began closing schools in response to the push for Indigenous integration and a desire to wind down the system. However, churches fought to maintain the schools. He notes that after 1951, the schools were less for the purpose of education, and increasingly filled the gap as child welfare institutions: "Those [neglected children] had become in the post war years, a significant portion of the residential school population, giving a new purpose to the schools as elements of an expanding post-war welfare state. That purpose prolonged the life of the residential school system."[14] Orphaned or "illegitimate" Indian children became inmates in the residential schools, masking the social conditions troubling families and communities in this period.

Studies in comparative Canada-U.S. policy history demonstrate that both countries have drawn upon their British legacy founded on the Royal Proclamation of 1763 when formulating post-colonial Indian policy. Roger Nichols points to the importance of the Royal Proclamation for establishing future treaty-making that called for the separation of Crown and Indian lands. Indigenous people retained their title to their lands, and although the British Crown ultimately held the title, Indian people were permitted to use and occupy those lands.[15] Following the American War of Independence, Americans abandoned their colonial agreements, sending Indians on the east coast west of the Mississippi in its removal policy. At that time Canada began to establish its civilization policy, based on the establishment of missions with schools, farming, and political status of wardship.[16] In both countries, wardship was the legal designation given to Indigenous peoples. In the United States it was based on the 1831 *Cherokee Nation vs Georgia* case, in which Chief Justice John Marshall determined that Indians were "domestic dependent nations," and their dependency was formally established in law.[17] In Canada, after the 1841 Act of Union and the Bagot Report of 1844, greater emphasis was placed on reducing government expenditures on Indians by encouraging individual assimilation. The Bagot Commission established that the past use of day schools had been unsuccessful, suggesting removal of children from parents to "manual labour schools" run by Christian missionaries and funded by the government as a solution.[18] Nichols found that in both countries, boarding schools became the primary means of securing assimilation, through the use of removal, isolation, and education of Indigenous children.[19]

David Wallace Adams's *Education for Extinction: American Indians and the Boarding School Experience, 1875–1928* discusses the importance of the boarding school education within the larger project of nation building in the United States. The idea of social evolution, drawn from the research of anthropologist and social theorist Lewis Henry Morgan's *Ancient Society: Or How Researches in the Lines of Human Progress from Savagery to Barbarism to Civilization* provided the intellectual framework for the system. Based on the belief in education for the uplift of Indian peoples from the low status of "upper savagery" or "lower barbarism," schools sought to offer children the opportunity to advance from the barbarism of their homes and families to the lower rungs of Western civilization. While earlier policies of removal and military conquest had been deemed untenable, assimilation of children replaced it. Wallace states, "After all this, the white man had concluded that the only way to save Indians was to destroy them, that the last great Indian war should be waged against children."[20] Two key ideas driving the schools were, first, to educate children on the importance of the nuclear family for property, inheritance, and moral respectability; and second, inculcation of the importance of private property, on which rested the entire edifice of civilization.[21] The goals of the system were to provide the rudiments of academics, the creation of individuals, and Christianization, while establishing proper gender roles and sexual mores.[22]

Margaret Jacobs builds on Wallace's insights by assessing the contribution of middle-class women to schooling offered by the state to Indigenous children in the United States and in Australia. She situates women's participation in the context of nineteenth-century maternal feminism. At this time, middle-class women gained legitimacy in the public realm through providing "uplift" to Indian children in schools. Drawing upon the insights of Sylvia Van Kirk into the connection between colonialism and gender, Jacobs traces the close relationships that developed between women responsible for transforming Indigenous bodies of children and homes, as an outcome of their close proximity in the schools.[23] Early in the U.S. boarding school programs, white women reformers played an integral role in implementing child removal. Over the course of their involvement as missionaries, teachers, and matrons, they began to question colonial policies, leading them to organize with Indigenous women against the removal campaigns by the 1920s.[24] Jacobs finds that the contradiction in employing white women as maternal agents of the state was, in fact, the intimacy that the boarding school experience engendered. Intimacy led the women to challenge the goals of the Indian Bureau and to demand that children be raised by parents in their homes and concluded that poverty, rather than culture, created the "Indian problem."[25]

Along with education, historians who have studied the impact of government policy on Indigenous peoples have connected colonization and ill health. Maureen K. Lux demonstrates, in *Medicine that Walks*, that disease became a function of race in the late nineteenth and early twentieth centuries.[26] Politicians and doctors saw ill health as a racial condition rather than recognizing that poverty and hunger lay at the root of most illness in Indian communities. The turn-of-the-century

Plains people faced both bacteriological invasions and economic marginalization. This work demonstrates how the racial construction of ill health functioned as an excuse to deny medical care and proper rations promised in treaties, but most damningly, to deny children in residential schools proper care or to finance improvements. The racialized discourse of Indigenous diseases created a climate where poverty and medical care were denied; likewise because of the neglect, settler populations developed the perception that reserves were "repositories of disease." In response to demands from white residents, governments imposed harsh measures such as quarantines that prevented already hungry people from either working or obtaining food. Thus, elimination took the guise of racialized discourses of ill health in the post-treaty era.

Mary-Ellen Kelm's *Colonizing Bodies: Aboriginal Health and Healing in British Columbia, 1900–1950* also challenges the contention that poor health is a necessary consequence of contact, by demonstrating that there are also political, social, biological, and cultural causes of ill health. Kelm looks at Aboriginal health not only through policies for Euro-Canadian medical care provided by authorities, but as a larger issue related to the loss of land in British Columbia, an inability to access adequate resources, and the transition from being autonomous entities to becoming imprisoned on reserves. Residential schools were an important element of this period, and ill health dominated the schools. She dismantles the political rationale used to justify the schools, that they were necessary to save children from their homes, and particularly their unassimilated mothers whom, it was believed, failed to understand Anglo-Canadian standards of hygiene. Residential schools, in keeping with her analysis of the construction of Aboriginal bodies, were meant to violently "re-form" children's bodies through adoption of Euro-Canadian hygienic practices and appearances. The second half of the book illustrates the simultaneous persistence of traditional Aboriginal healing and emergence of the medical profession as the front line in early twentieth century colonialism. In this case, the "combination of a sense of obligation with the notion that cultural change for the First Nations was essential to their physical well-being created a compelling argument for providing First Nations with medical care."[27] Medical care and missionary evangelization often went hand in hand to control and reform Indigenous bodies.

Historians have identified the post-war era as a watershed in the history of Native-newcomer relations. U.S. historian Donald L. Fixico's *Termination and Relocation: Federal Indian Policy, 1945–1960* traces the development of Indian Affairs policies aimed at terminating tribal land holdings and collective Indian identity. Under President Harry Truman, termination policies attempted the integration of Indians into the American melting pot. The answer to Indian poverty and illness was believed to be equality of opportunity.[28] Hugh Shewell's history of relief provision by Indian Affairs likewise identified the post-war period in Canada as shifting Indian policy toward integration after the revisions of the Indian Act in 1951. While his work is focused primarily on the origins of welfare dependency, he identifies the post-war period of integration and citizenship as a new assimilation scheme. Indian Affairs Branch (IAB) employed a discursive shift from *assimilation* to *integration* to consciously signal a rupture with earlier policies of assimilation. Shewell argues, "Beginning in the 1950's, Indian social policy and social assistance programs increasingly reflected the broad objectives of citizenship and integration. For some time, the Welfare Division was central to these objectives, and was the dominant division within the IAB."[29] The role of the state shifted from that of a protective position to a developmental function. The new secular focus on Indigenous integration through citizenship utilized the research of social scientists through improvements in living conditions and health standards.[30] According to Shewell, two obstacles that prevented the success of the new integration model were a lack of desire by First Nations peoples and a lack of acceptance by other Canadians. While Shewell provides an important start, there is no mention of child welfare, there is a lack of attention to gender, and the study ignores Saskatchewan.

Liberalism and the individualizing tendencies of the federal Indian policies is the focus of Jessa Chupik-Hall's master's thesis, "Good Families Do Not Just Happen." In it, she makes an important connection between integration and the increasing overrepresentation of Aboriginal children in child welfare systems across Canada.[31] First, she documents the absence of preventative family support by IAB. Rather, the IAB utilized its nationwide system of residential schools primarily after the Second World War as child welfare institutions for Indian children whose families were unable to care for them. This system masked the increasing difficulties facing Indian families in the post-war period.

Likewise, the application of equality rhetoric, embodied in "They are not Indians, they are just people,"[32] served to justify the extension of provincial services, while further accomplishing the goal of integration. While equality rhetoric was portrayed as noble, in fact children did not receive equal treatment because of the lack of in-home preventative services that non-Indian children and families routinely received.[33]

John Lutz's work on wage labour and relief in British Columbia adopts the approach of relationality. Lutz argues, "The state was not a single entity, but rather a hydra-headed being that pursued many different policies at once, some of which were at odds with others, and some of which, at least on particular issues, supported Aboriginal people."[34] He places Indigenous voices in the history, because in doing so, "integrating Aboriginal voices with non-Aboriginal voices turns history into a dialogue."[35] Unlike economist Helen Buckley and Hugh Shewell, he contends that the state did not willingly embrace "welfare colonialism." Lutz argues that the Indian Affairs Branch paid relief to Indigenous people primarily because the regulations of other provincial agencies limited Aboriginal access to both the subsistence and cash economies. Indigenous peoples, for a variety of factors, were squeezed out of the developing economies of agriculture, fishing, harvesting, etc., and relief became its replacement.[36] His study ends in 1970, and he concludes that "welfare has ensured that Aboriginal people did not starve and that they continue to have an alternative to wage work – but at a very high price."[37]

Buckley traces the failure of IAB policy to bring prosperity to western Canadian reserve residents, and, like Shewell, is interested in locating the origins of welfare dependency among First Nations people. She begins by insisting on the distinctness of Prairie First Nations from those in the east or British Columbia. In the prairie provinces, First Nations experienced the disastrous demise of the buffalo economy, followed by a stalling in reserve agriculture, while northern communities dependent on the trapline experienced economic decline with reductions in trapline incomes later in the twentieth century. She points out that reserve conditions worsened as white prosperity increased.[38] In the mid-twentieth century in western Canada, there was a collapse of the reserve economy, predicated by government policies aimed at making subsistence farmers out of First Nations people, and of economic development that relied on renting out reserve lands to white farmers. Out of this collapse came the contemporary origins of poverty, exacerbated by state-delivered income supplements. Mothers' allowances came at a time when traplines were circumscribed by CCF policies. Buckley alerts readers to the gendered effects of state policies on families – policies that undermined the role of men as women and children moved into villages and towns for children to attend school. Some men, unwilling to trap without their families, were no longer able to play a provider role. In large part, the purpose of the Native family underwent a profound shift with new sedentary lifestyle in the northern villages.[39]

Like elsewhere in Canada, Saskatchewan's provincial government, the Co-operative Commonwealth Federation (CCF), recognized that Indigenous peoples after the Second World War were no longer a dying race and crafted policies aimed at the eventual integration and citizenship of First Nations and Métis peoples through equal access to health and social services.[40] Previous historical study of CCF Native policy has been approached from traditional topics of political organization and government relations and neglected to fully interrogate the role of the Department of Social Welfare and Rehabilitation in the overall policy of Aboriginal integration. Jim Pitsula has looked at the CCF government liberal ideology of Indian integration, and its three-pronged approach to integration, of which the creation of a single voice for the treaty Indians in Saskatchewan in the Federation of Saskatchewan Indians was but a part.[41] Historian Laurie Barron challenged Pistula's characterization of the CCF's liberal democratic individualizing strategy when documenting the Native policies of the CCF. In *Walking in Indian Moccasins*, Barron argues that the CCF recognized the collective identity of Aboriginal political organizations, whether farmer or Native group, and were sympathetic to aims of the group. He believes that "concern for native community was generated both by the administrative dictates of the day, and by a socialist philosophy predicated on the notion of government assistance to the disadvantaged."[42] He argues that Saskatchewan politicians and bureaucrats saw problems faced by Métis and First Nations as similar, stemming from the belief that poverty and marginalization could be overcome through reform and rehabilitation policies that would eventually lead to integration into provincial services.[43]

In a prior article, Barron focused on the brief development of Métis farm colonies jointly undertaken with the Catholic Church in Willow

Bunch, Lebret, and Green Lake. In attempting to explain the logic of establishing the Métis colonies, Barron refers back to the CCF Social Gospel base, which was "premised on the doctrine of love and it proclaims the sanctity of cooperation as opposed to competition, hence it represents an explicit rejection of the 'survival of the fittest' ethos."[44] As part of the Métis rehabilitation policy, colonies, like Indian reserves, would enable the Métis to gradually assimilate and become competitive in mainstream society. The colonies were intended to be temporary, perhaps one generation; in actual fact they lasted a little over a decade.[45] With schooling and farm instruction, co-operatives, and oversight, colonies were meant to enable the Métis to develop the necessary skills and competencies to enter non-Indigenous society. Inherited from the Patterson government, they were under the direction of the Department of Social Welfare and Rehabilitation and were eventually abandoned by 1960 as a viable response to Métis integration, after which the government sought to integrate Métis people individually as they became part of the urban landscape.[46]

While Barron depicts the CCF colony scheme in the southern portion of the province as unproblematic, other historians have been more critical in their analysis. Despite the lofty goals initially envisioned by the CCF, scholars have documented the failure of the CCF Native policy in the colonies and in the north, and the development of Native dependency and increased poverty. While the government provided aspects of protection, such as through health and education, paternalism pervaded the provision of these services.[47] Despite the rhetoric of rehabilitation, Murray Dobbin and, later, historian David Quiring both argue that the CCF maintained a colonial relationship with the Indigenous people, failing to develop northern resources or a meaningful economic strategy that could bring the First Nations and Métis inhabitants into the economy.[48] Meetings with communities and the establishment of co-operatives are examples of the reforms pursued in the early days of the CCF in the north.[49] Once the policy was judged a failure by 1948, Dobbin argues, the government went "into a full retreat in the area of Native rehabilitation."[50] What he has characterized as Native rehabilitation was, in fact, not rehabilitation but support of self-determination and, in fact, what took place after this retreat was an oppressive variant of rehabilitation.

After 1950 the combined effects of the policy of centralization, introduction of a cash-based economy in the North, and implementation of the fur-marketing system devastated the Indigenous families who had previously been self-sufficient, semi-nomadic trappers and fishers. Gender roles, which had been stable and equitable prior to these changes, dramatically shifted, with men increasingly unable to provide for their large families.[51] Dobbin finds that it "was clear that the government was made aware from various sources, of the crisis that native people were facing and measures needed to halt and reverse the process, and it consciously chose to reject such measures."[52] The reason Dobbin gives for this clear example of CCF failure was its ideological and political background. With the CCF roots in agrarian social democracy and populist character, Social Gospel, and egalitarian focus, Indigenous needs did not fit into any paradigm.[53] Primarily, the CCF and the Saskatchewan electorate perceived the Métis as impediments to the progress of the province. Dobbin concludes that the CCF party that grew out of the settler colonial project, and its leadership, reflected the concerns of the farmers and small businesses that helped it win its first majority. Quiring attributes the failure of the CCF socialist policies in the North in part vaguely to the white politicians and bureaucrats' "various non-socialist and non-political beliefs and attitudes," indicating that the socialist CCF behaved in ways that were similar to other non-socialist governments elsewhere in Canada.[54]

Missing from the historical accounts of CCF Native policy are experiences of Indigenous women, hampering historians' abilities to fully comprehend gender and racial implications for rehabilitation policies for Indian and Métis people in the province. In the west, historians have demonstrated that as Euro-Canadian settler society emerged after the Northwest Resistance of 1885, racial and gender boundaries became more rigidly enforced, especially for First Nations and Métis women.[55] During the early settlement period, prairie Indian women were confined to reserves, and Métis women largely became invisible in the rural and urban settlements. After 1945 Indigenous women once again became visible in settler society. The disciplining gaze of the state turned on Métis women who were not conforming to the proper maternal role. With the introduction of mother's allowances in 1945, which encouraged settlement in villages and small communities so children could attend school, social workers and anthropologists evaluated Aboriginal women's domestic and maternal abilities through the bodies of Métis children.

While settler colonialism has its focus on ensuring the settler/Indigenous dichotomy, Métis people are a troubling exception to this binary. Excluded from Indian Act legislation and considered outside pioneer and settler society, Saskatchewan's Métis occupied an increasingly marginalized space in the urban and rural prairie landscape.[56] Emma LaRocque's writing has awakened scholars to the lived experiences of Métis women to challenge neat timelines or idealized versions of Indigenous culture.[57] The impact of racist and sexist stereotypes on the day-to-day lives of Métis women who experienced violence both inside and outside Indigenous society forms an important element when considering child welfare, especially when it was women who were left with child-rearing responsibilities the majority of the time. In *Halfbreed* Maria Campbell tells her powerful story of growing up in post-war Saskatchewan and the impact of racism, poverty, and sexism in her life, as well as her perception of child welfare workers.[58] For these two women, decolonization has meant defending themselves against racism as well as sexism. Stereotypes that emerged at the outset of permanent Euro-Canadian settlement on the prairies have persisted, depicting women as "dissolute, dangerous, and sinister as compared with their fragile and vulnerable pure-white counterparts."[59] Métis women experienced a distinctive version of discrimination that effectively segregated them socially and economically from both Indian and white society.

Intimate Integration seeks to fill in the gaps in the current historiography to enlarge both scholarly and public knowledge of the "Sixties Scoop." It draws on several disciplinary streams for its methodological and theoretical framing. It is first a work grounded in feminist ethnohistorical methodology, emerging from the strong historical foundation built by scholars of Native-newcomer relations and western Canadian history, and influenced by Indigenous historians and post-colonial scholars.[60] *Intimate Integration* situates Indigenous transracial adoption in a matrix of gendered, raced, and class relations between post-war settler society and First Nations and Métis women and families. As scholars of empire have pointed out, histories of childhood are implicated in racial and colonial politics.[61] In addition, feminist historians have long pointed to the relationship between gender and empire, and British colonialism in particular.[62] Sylvia Van Kirk and subsequent feminist historians of imperialism and colonization have identified the significance of intimacy in forging "tense and tender ties" in colonial contexts, as well as demonstrating the centrality of Indigenous women and women's experiences to histories of colonization. Van Kirk's insights into the intersection of gender, race, class, and imperialism through a historical interrogation of the role of gender in colonization stimulated scholars to trace the social construction of difference and the production of social categories.[63]

Drawing on Van Kirk's research, Ann Laura Stoler urges scholars to attend to the practices of comparison of colonial governments in the intimate frontiers of empires, drawing on post-colonial studies and histories of North America.[64] Her work has demonstrated that colonial authority depends on shaping affect, severing some bonds, and establishing others. Through intimate colonial practices, policies such as child welfare and transracial adoption helped create new types of bodies and structures of feeling, developing new habits of heart and mind.[65] Integral to assessing Indigenous transracial adoption as a colonial technique of control are the critical interventions of Michel Foucault's notion of "biopower" or the management of populations by state-sanctioned actors to regulate and discipline both individual bodies and population bodies.[66] The increasing surveillance and regulation of Indigenous families, termed here as "technologies of helping," represent increasing power of the state over the very intimate aspects of Indigenous family life, the birthing and rearing of Indigenous children. By harnessing the opportunities of modern state-controlled adoption, social workers and government agents enabled Indigenous children to be recast, not as members of a doomed and dying race, but as future citizens reared by proper families.

The transformation of Indigenous children after the Second World War, seen through the discourses utilized in the Adopt Indian and Métis Project campaigns by the Saskatchewan Department of Social Services, drew "normal" everyday white families into the business of integration through appeals to their sense of civic duty and the timeless visual appeal of needy children, while simultaneously undermining Indigenous families, nations, and systems of kinship. According to Ann Laura Stoler, "The welding of biopower to racism confers on racism its most virulent form."[67] The creation of sexual "others" to be policed through legislation or policy, affirms the superiority of the ruling elites and the degeneracy of Indigenous "others."[68] Couched often in language of benevolence, the legacies of the moralizing missions of the imperial interventions are evident in mid-twentieth-century adoption advertising that relied on humanitarian justifications and crisis management. The very policies that made Indigenous families vulnerable are erased and mystified. Stoler notes, "A broader view of imperial practice does not merely underscore that social reform and racism went hand in hand, or that 19th century liberalism and empire were complementary projects, as Uday Mehta and I each insisted early on. The humanitarian 'good works' of empire were part of this very durable architecture – with exacting exclusions and inequities structured through them."[69] This "bleeding heart" of settler colonialism is formative and deeply embedded within the national settler identity.

In addition to contributing to a critical historical analysis of Indigenous transracial adoption, *Intimate Integration* offers a decolonial history of Indigenous resistance and resurgence. As Linda Tuhiwai Smith argues, "*Coming to know the past* has been part of the critical pedagogy of decolonization. To hold alternative histories is to hold alternative knowledges."[70] It draws inspiration from critical Métis scholars Howard Adams, Maria Campbell, and Kim Anderson who forged a path for decolonial writing in Canada. In part, it provides an ethnohistorical account of Saskatchewan Métis and Cree adoption and kinship informed by oral history conducted with Indigenous elders, adoptees, and leadership. This provided critical insight into the lived experience of Indigenous transracial adoption and provincial child welfare removal policies in the 1960s and 1970s.[71] For this study, I conducted nine interviews in accordance with the ethical and privacy guidelines laid out in the "Tri-Council Policy Statement on Ethical Conduct for Research Involving Humans."[72]

Conceiving of Indigenous transracial adoption as a field of historical inquiry requires a thorough consideration of the ethical issues surrounding design, research, and distribution of findings from this project. At the outset, I sought out direction from an elder and leader recognized as knowledgeable about Indigenous practices and contemporary challenges First Nations people face. Midway through my research, I then established a relationship with Métis Nation of Saskatchewan, who also encouraged me on. They put me in touch with Métis elders who would be willing to share their knowledge with me, particularly their involvement with the Saskatchewan Native Women's Movement. I interviewed several of the original members of the SNWM.

I have been guided by the Six Principles of Métis Health Research when conducting interviews with Métis participants. These are, first, this importance of building reciprocal relationships that promote equality between the research and the Métis community. The second principle stresses the importance of respect for the individual as well as the collectivity. The third principle ensures that I provide a safe and inclusive environment for the participants. The fourth principle is to respect the diversity of the Métis people in their world views and beliefs. This concern is based on the recognition of diversity among the Métis and on the understanding that Métis identity can be situated anywhere on a continuum from contemporary to very traditional. The fifth principle stipulates that research should be relevant to those involved, that it should benefit evenly both the researcher and the community. Finally, the sixth principle requires that researchers should be knowledgeable about Métis history and the Métis cultural context.[73] I believe that I adhered to each of these principles to the best of my ability. As a Métis adoptee, I feel deeply committed to my community and aspire to have this research reach a wide and diverse audience.

Documents in provincial, federal, and private archives in Canada and the United States supplied the bulk of the material on government policies and individual adoptions. Archivists reluctantly allowed access to documents containing private and sensitive information.[74] Reading against the archival grain of policy documents and newspaper articles has shed light on the cultural, social, historical, and political forces that brought adoption to the forefront of discussions over citizenship and integration. Indigenous women's experiences predominated in the case files. As a researcher, I was mindful that considering Indigenous women's choice is fraught with difficulties. One must be careful to avoid oversimplification and alert to the limitations of such colonial sources. Provincial privacy legislation prevented access to provincial adoption case records, but since First Nations people fall under federal jurisdiction, several Indian Affairs case files have been used to explore transracial adoption and child welfare service to First Nations. Evidence indicates that in some cases Indigenous mothers sought welfare services such as adoption to secure homes for children they felt would otherwise suffer deprivations. It is important to acknowledge that for some Indigenous families, adoption provided an important child-caring option among a limited range of opportunities in a social and political climate that was hostile to Indigenous mothers and children.[75] The historically specific and varied responses by First Nations and Métis women in mid- to late twentieth-century Saskatchewan point to the need to take into account changes in gender relations in Indigenous communities. By looking comparatively at transracial adoption in Canada and the United States, as well as the transnational Indigenous resistance it engendered, the following narrative of the Sixties Scoop seeks to find the heart of colonial politics through the management of affective ties and attempts to explain changing national identities that transracial adoption sought to create.

Whether accomplished through residential schooling, child welfare policies, or legal means such as loss of status through Indian Act provisions, Indigenous child removal has a long and sordid history in settler colonial nations such as Canada, the United States, Australia, and New Zealand.[76] American historian Margaret Jacobs' transnational history of Indigenous child welfare, *A Generation Removed*, illustrates the settler-colonial origins of Indigenous child removal. The late Haudenosaunee scholar Patricia Monture confronted the systemic racism of the child welfare system and courts and reproached the system of committing genocide. In "'A Vicious Cycle'" she argues that "removing children from their homes weakens the entire community. Removing First Nations children from their culture and placing them in a foreign culture is an act of genocide."[77] Like the criminal justice system, the child welfare system removed people from communities. Using the rationale of "best interests of the child" she exposed racism and white privilege. Legal scholar Marlee Kline published a series of articles that explored Aboriginal child welfare law from a critical feminist theoretical approach. In the first article, "Complicating the Ideology of Motherhood: Child Welfare, Law and First Nation Women," Kline identified the cultural bias inherent in child welfare practice and application of child welfare law. Kline critiques the Euro-Canadian understanding of motherhood to expose the cultural norms of the nuclear family and white middle-class standards that denigrated Aboriginal extended families and community standards, utilizing the judgments from recent court cases.[78] In a following article, Kline exposed the ideological processes that lead discrimination against First Nations children and families in the courts. Kline deconstructs the "best interests of the child" concept that guides each element of child welfare decision-making.

She identified how liberalism has structured racism, and the use of the best interests of the child ideology has "created apprehensions as natural, necessary and legitimate rather than coercive and destructive."[79] Courts and social workers have not viewed children's identity or culture as an area worthy consideration when determining how best to protect children, since the use of nineteenth-century liberal tenets of individualism, abstraction, universalism, and impartiality eliminate such a possibility.[80] She identified the origins of the system in a new discourse of integration, with the goal of "economic assimilation of Indians into the body politic."[81] Kline differentiates the era of integration from the earlier period of assimilation and claims, "The result of the extension of provincial social welfare law on reserve was the further colonization of First Nations and the erosion of the political and social structures."[82] Kline's critical intellectual history of hegemonic notions of family and protection provides a useful starting point for exploring transracial adoption policies in the West.

Adult adoptees and survivors of the Sixties Scoop have generated a significant portion of the current publications on Indigenous child welfare in both academic research and popular media. These personal accounts reveal the human component missing in academic publications.[83] Ernie Crey, activist and a survivor of the foster care system in British Columbia, links the emergence of the child welfare system to the impact of residential schools on Aboriginal families.[84] First-hand experiences of adoption shed light on the complexities and contradictions that run through the lives of Indigenous people who have been made wards of the state.[85] Adult survivors of child welfare policies seek to make sense of their often individualized experience by writing and researching on adoption and connecting with others who have also been through the system. Though remaining in thesis or dissertation form, much of the recent graduate work has focused primarily on identity and adoption.[86] Adoptee Jeannine Carrière and co-authors have written extensively on transracial adoption in Canada.[87] Her dissertation looks at the impact of child removal (adoption) on the health and personalities of the Aboriginal adoptee. Carrière applies both the Western theoretical framework of human ecology and grounded theory alongside Aboriginal scientific theory to better understand the interconnections between adoption and well-being for Aboriginal children. She is especially interested in the spiritual aspect of transracial adoption. She concludes that children removed from their parents and communities suffer from profound loss, on an emotional as well as spiritual level.[88] Raven Sinclair's PhD dissertation from the University of Calgary, entitled "All My Relations," locates the history of transracial adoption within the framework of colonization. A First Nations adoptee from Saskatchewan, she conducted interviews with adoptees to examine the impact of transracial adoption on the development of Indian identity.

There is no historical study of the Sixties Scoop in Canada in print.[89] However, Joyce Timpson's PhD dissertation in social work examined the increased apprehension in Northern Ontario in the 1960s and 1970s, using oral histories from Indigenous peoples, CAS workers, and government employees.[90] She took a broad approach to the topic of family breakdown and subsequent intervention, concluding that child apprehensions increased due to "serious cultural trauma following relocation, loss of independent means of support, and the new educational systems that were incompatible with their traditional beliefs and lifestyles. These stressors revealed themselves in the high rate of alcohol abuse precipitating incidents involving the child protection agency."[91]

She identified three factors in creation of the child welfare crisis in Northern Ontario: the equality ideology, ignorance about First Nations people, and lack of systemic flexibility for applying different approaches. Her study addressed three factors that shaped disproportionate rates: child welfare policy and programs, the socio-economic context of Native communities, and the response of the Children's Aid Societies.[92] Her use of geographical, historical, and cultural specificity enabled readers to grasp the complex and multilayered elements that have contributed to the issue of Indigenous child welfare. Her research also revealed the interrelationship between relocation schemes and the impact on families and communities.

In recent years Canadian historians have published histories of adoption, moving the topic beyond the confines of those involved in social work and locating the issue in the larger cultural and historical context, adding further nuance and complexity to the often emotionally fraught topic.[93] Karen Balcom's *The Traffic in Babies* looked at the development of sound adoption practice in Canada through attempts to stem the illegal cross-border black market adoptions between 1930 and 1972.[94] Veronica Strong-Boag's *Finding Families, Finding Ourselves* brings to light the dilemma that Aboriginal birth mothers face when Indigenous priorities conflict with legal options.[95] Karen Dubinsky's *Babies without Borders: Adoption and Migration across the Americas* moves beyond the confrontational dichotomy between rescue or kidnap framework that has dominated discussion on transracial, transnational adoption. She correctly points to the deeply historic symbolism of children as "bearers, but never makers, of social meaning."[96] Her analysis ranges from Cuba, to Canada, then to Guatemala, pointing to the interlocking global issues of economic deprivation, colonialism, and sentimentalized childhood. Her discussion of the Canadian experience utilizes a comparative approach between the relatively successful adoptions of Black children from a Montreal adoption agency and the primarily unsuccessful adoptions of Indigenous children based on readings from adoption files in Manitoba and Montreal. In pointing to the continued over-representation of Indigenous children in the welfare system, Dubinsky's work challenges scholars working in the area of child welfare, particularly that of Indigenous children, of the dangers in constructing arguments around the use of symbolic children.[97]

This history of the Sixties Scoop in Saskatchewan situates the history of Indigenous transracial adoption in earlier Indigenous children removal policies that functioned in large measure as a primary mode of Indigenous assimilation and elimination. Indigenous transracial adoption, or the intimate integration of Indigenous children in settler families, reflected newly emerging technologies to substitute Indigenous affective ties with those bound to Euro-Canadian lifeways and nation. Through socialization in the intimate setting of families scrutinized by social workers, Indigenous children's properly modern upbringing – loving, educated, and modelled by the ideal nuclear families – would succeed where past attempts had failed. Whereas First Nations peoples had been subject to legal and geographic separation, integration sought to selectively eliminate such boundaries, and thereby eliminate Indigenous subjectivities, kinship, and nations.

Previous boundaries erected between Indigenous people and settlers relied on a complex combination of state-based legal, and spatial separation, as well as pseudoscientific theories of racial difference and cultural beliefs of inferiority.[98] At the end of the nineteenth and the beginning of the early twentieth century, the expanding Canadian state enforced the exclusion of First Nations and Métis peoples in the developing market economy. This form of exclusionary liberalism relied on the dispossession and containment of First Nations, as well as the creation of a web of surveillance that enabled politicians and policymakers a means to know "Indians" while also controlling and segregating them on reserves. Keith Smith argues, "The ways in which imperial powers came to know colonized peoples allowed the creation and maintenance of boundaries and oppositions that were formed in the process of colonization and at the same time justified colonial encroachment."[99] The historically specific conditions of the expanding and modernizing agricultural west, secured for future prosperity of Anglo-Celtic Protestant Canadians, entailed enforcing a strict racial segregation through the pass system, federal and provincial legal statutes, residential schools, and enfranchisement policies.[100]

State-based legal and political separations between Indigenous peoples and settler Canadians were ideologically maintained by print and news media, academic historians, and government bureaucracies using racial binaries that framed Canadian Indian policy as benevolent, and paternalistic control as justified. The mainstream press historically perpetuated colonial representations of Indigenous peoples to support expansionist colonial policies relying on three stereotypes about Aboriginal peoples: Indigenous depravity, innate inferiority, and stubborn resistance to progress and development.[101] In the 1870s and 1880s negative assessments of Indigenous peoples held by incoming Euro-Canadian settlers emerged out of the expansionist movement. Expanding the Canadian nation state westward, incorporating Indigenous societies, and creating an agricultural frontier dependent on British Canadian migration relied on images of unlimited plenty, a gendered and racialized "Eden" that would provide limitless potential for prosperity for Anglo-Celtic farmers.[102] First Nations and Métis peoples, many of whom had undertaken farming prior to the acquisition by Canada, likewise sought to prosper in the emerging economy by engaging in agriculture and learning Euro-Canadian methods of business. In the settlement period, negative accounts of Indigenous peoples circulated to rationalize government policies of segregation. In addition, newspapers and government officials relied on pre-existing racial characterizations of the lazy drunken Indian and the slovenly Indian woman as a handy way to deflect attention from the failure to implement the treaty promises and draw attention away from disastrous government policies.[103]

Ian McKay's "Liberal Order Framework" provides a useful context for examining the efforts to assimilate Indigenous peoples. Explaining the arc of Canadian history as an ever unfolding process of liberal rule, he argues that we should "imagine 'Canada' simultaneously as an *extensive* projection of liberal rule across a large territory and an *intensive process of subjectification*, whereby liberal assumptions are internalized and 'normalized' within the dominion's subjects."[104] Incorporating newcomers and extending the nation state across the continent, the liberal order is an ideological formation committed to the "belief in the epistemological and ontological primacy of the category of the 'individual' and an attempt to plan and nurture, in somewhat unlikely soil, the philosophical assumptions, and related political and economic practices of a liberal order."[105] Three tenets uphold the liberal order: the primacy of liberty, equality, and private property. In the liberal order framework, the body politic is made up of free and unencumbered individuals, who act independently of external obligations to family, religion, or natural condition. Excluded from its original conception were women, other races, workers, Catholics, and collectivist Indigenous peoples in particular.[106] Key importance was attached to the function of private property.[107] McKay points out that the initial consolidation of the Canadian project required a massive extension of the state and its institutions that were an essential component in the individualization of the citizenry. To liberalize social relations first required the build-up of immense government institutions, often before the development of classes.[108] One example of the extension of the liberal order framework entails the efforts to settle Indigenous peoples permanently on reserves and remove them from their lands in order to repopulate the West with European and Euro-Canadian individual agriculturalists. The remapping of the West with the homestead grid and the creation of "free homesteads" was part of the process by which the common land and resources in the West were violently transformed to private property through a form of "colonial alchemy."[109] Placed on reserves and under the surveillance of Indian agents and priests, Indigenous peoples were subjected to efforts to remake them into what Thomas Biolsi has called "the minimum definition of the modern individual."[110]

With the expansion of the settlement frontier into the West and the creation of Canada as a nation spanning sea to sea, Canada's myth of two founding peoples – the French and English – elided the critical

Indigenous contribution to the county.[111] The historic rupture relegated First Peoples to a racialized "other" that would either vanish under the inevitable march of progress or be forced to surrender their land, language, and spirituality to assimilate.[112] Patrick Wolfe termed this structure "settler colonialism," and as distinct from colonialism, it has both positive and negative dimensions. On one hand, it seeks to dissolve Indigenous societies through government policies and, in its place, establish a new society based on European social and political institutions indigenized so as to appear natural. Wolfe termed this process the "logic of elimination" and pointed to the assimilatory government policies of enfranchisement, whether voluntary or involuntary, child removal policies, allotment schemes, replacing Indigenous forms of kinship and genealogy as the key expressions of this process.[113] As he put it, "Settler colonizers came to stay so invasion is a structure; not an event."[114] Since settler colonialism has been driven by the "logic of elimination," it continually attempts to remove distinctions between groups, ideally achieving its full expression when Indians and Métis cease to exist as a distinct legal and social group. Thus, for the Indigenous people, the struggle against settler colonialism is to maintain cultural and political distinctiveness, keeping the settler–Indigenous relationship going.[115]

Gender and sexuality are intrinsic to settler colonization and the proliferation of the modern nation state. Scott Morgensen argues that theories of settler colonization must also interrogate how the "political and economic formation is constituted by gendered and sexual power."[116] Morgensen further argues that "gendered and sexual power relations appear to be so intrinsic to procedures of indigenous elimination and settler indigenization that these processes will not be fully understood until sexuality and gender are centered in their analysis."[117] Drawing on settler-colonial studies, this analysis is rooted in an exploration of the impact of the settler-colonial law on race and gender relations, and in particular, the emergence of Indigenous transracial adoption. Indian status has been defined and regulated in an attempt to create uniformity across the nation, ordering the differences between the multitudes of Indigenous belief systems. Morgensen argues that the Indian Act and the settler colonial ideology that underpinned it has, in effect, racialized kinship, thus contradicting "traditional definitions of indigenous nationhood based on genealogy, which may include adoption as well as biological descent, and without making race a determinant of degree of relationship."[118] Applying the law into spaces normally privileged as private, such as the home and family, illustrates the unequal power relationship.[119]

While Indigenous elimination is at the heart of settler colonial efforts of regulation and intervention, Indigenous peoples have resisted and evaded the law, indigenized adoption laws and policy, and accessed services to supplement or replace lost kinship and social support. Indigenous families responded to material deprivation, unplanned pregnancies, loss of spouses, or eviction from homes in a variety ways. Individual case histories point to a wide array of efforts to ensure support for children in difficult circumstances. The emergence of Indigenous women's political movements in the 1960s such as the Saskatchewan Native Women's Movement sought to reassert and reclaim Indigenous women's roles in ensuring the health of community, opening day care centres and women's shelters, and demanding an end to coercive transracial adoptions.

INDIGENOUS LEGAL ORDERS AND THE INDIAN ACT

Two legal mechanisms were primarily responsible for ordering relations between Indian nations and the Canadian state until the repatriation of the Constitution in 1982: treaties and the federal Indian Act. While some Indigenous peoples in the Northwest demanded that the incoming Canadians sign treaties to establish relations and secure guarantees for future security, Canadian treaty parties followed the procedures established by the Royal Proclamation of 1763 to obtain Aboriginal title to the lands for settlement.[120] The newly formed Canadian government signed treaties with Western First Nations between 1871 and 1877. These treaties also set out the future relationship with the Crown. In 1868 the Canadian government began to incorporate all previous legislation pertaining to Indian people into one body of laws. The principles of Canada's Indian policy had been established in the colonial period, prior to Confederation. The three principles that guided pre-Confederation Indian policy – protection, civilization, and assimilation – were incorporated in 1868 into the legislation, entitled "An Act Providing for the Organization of the Department of Secretary of State of Canada, and for the Management of Indian and Ordinance Land," which became the legislation guiding the administration of the federal Department of Indian Affairs.[121] Indigenous kinship and gender systems were increasingly targeted by the legislation as marriage and the reproductive choices of Indian men and women came under the purview of legislators and Indian agents.

While the gendering of legal Indian status had been a feature of colonial Indian legislation from 1857 onward, greater emphasis was placed on male political involvement as well as patrilineage in the nation-building period after Canadian Confederation in 1867.[122] Laws made in 1869 stripped women of the right to vote in band elections – a landmark moment for gender discrimination in Indigenous communities. That legislation also mentioned the consequences for women marrying non-Indians for the first time, revised in section 6: "Provided always that any Indian woman marrying any other than an Indian shall cease to be an Indian within the meaning of this Act, nor shall the children issue of such a marriage be considered Indians within the meaning of this Act."[123] For their choice in husbands, women and their children could be ejected from reserves. Indian agents had a number of tools at their disposal to enforce conformity to Euro-Canadian ideals of femininity and domesticity. For example, women considered disobedient had their rations withheld or children removed to residential schools by local Indian agents.[124]

Colonizing kinship itself was recognized as fundamental to remaking Indigenous peoples; at the same time, repatterning Indigenous communities to fit with the newly independent nation was an elusive yet essential project for defining what was Canadian. In 1876 the Dominion of Canada passed the Indian Act, for the administration of reserve lands and "Indians" in all provinces and the Northwest Territories. It defined the collectivity who resided on "reserves" – bands – and who was entitled to be included for the sake of the Act – "Indians." This Act sought to reconfigure Indigenous membership orders, governance, and kinship systems by dictating the terms of belonging and regulating reserve habitation.[125] Monitored by Indian agents empowered with the ability to dismember bands and criminalize dissidents, the Indian Act instituted a bureaucratic regime that depoliticized Indigenous nationhood.[126] In the Indian Act, 1876, section 3, "Indian" was defined first as any male person of Indian blood, reputed to belong to a particular band; second, any child of such person; and third, any woman who is or was lawfully married to such person. In section 3 (a) illegitimate children could be ejected from band membership after two years. Section 3 (c) stipulated that women who married anyone other than an "Indian" would no longer be an "Indian" but would retain her treaty annuities and become effectively enfranchised. Section 61 established the system of band governance on reserves with an elected chief and council. Supervised by the superintendent-general or Indian agent, males over the age of twenty-one could cast a vote, the majority of which would decide upon leaders and the matters of local concern that band councils oversaw.[127]

Historians have illustrated that in nation-building periods, marriage takes on additional significance, since the composition and reproduction of the populace occurs within the family unit. By incriminating some marriages, such as Indigenous marriages outside of the church and Indian women marrying non-Indian men, the state defined what types of sexual relations and which families were legitimate.[128] Feminist scholar Julia Emberley's work on the Aboriginal family reveals how the Indian Act legislation was utilized to shift gender allegiances and Indigenous political forms. Early Indian Act polices consistently drove to impose an ideology of patriarchal descent, described as the "disentitling of Aboriginal women from indigenous governance, accomplished by establishing fraternal links between Aboriginal men, created fissures within Aboriginal families along gender lines."[129] Gendered discrimination served a twofold purpose: attempting to universalize the Euro-Canadian family model and reconstituting the Indigenous family to reflect it, as well as removing Indigenous women from political influence. Public policy and legislation are thus critical for family formation, racial definitions, and nation building.[130] Indian status has been defined and regulated in an attempt to create uniformity across the nation, ordering the differences between the multitudes of Indigenous citizenship orders, kinship and legal systems, and genders.

FROM *WÁHKÔHTOWIN* TO TRANSRACIAL ADOPTION

In Indigenous societies, kinship determines both Indigenous modes of governance and forms of land tenure.[131] Marital patterns, child rearing, and kinship relations become the purview of the modern state precisely because they structure society and culture. In Indigenous societies kinship is an active principle of peoplehood, going beyond reproductive and familial connections. The colonization of kinship violently sundered not only intimate and familial ties but also the geopolitical connections that extend beyond human relationships to encompass the ties to land, animals, and ancestors that make up Indigenous identity. Anishinaabe/Ojibway legal scholar John Borrows eloquently articulates how Indigenous identity is rooted in kinship, in "'Landed' Citizenship: An Indigenous Declaration of Interdependence." He observed, "My grandfather was born in 1901 on the western shores of Georgian Bay, at the Cape Croker Indian reserve. Generations before him were born on that same soil. Our births, lives and deaths on this site have brought us into citizenship with the land. We participate in its renewal, have responsibilities for its continuation, and grieve for its losses. As citizens with this land, we also feel the presence of our ancestors and strive with them to ensure that the relationships of our polity are respected. Our loyalties, allegiance, and affection are related to the land."[132]

Indigenous citizenship belongs simultaneously to a political body and to a geographical/landed space. This identity takes shape through the kinship relations expressed through not only biological ancestral connections, but also to places that are claimed through generations. Cree and Métis people share the belief that kinship is of central importance for individual and collective identity and is inseparable from land, home, community, or family.[133] Where the Indian Act's sexual and gendered modes of elimination defined and regulated racial status, *wâhkôhtowin* (the Cree legal orders of kinship and other indigenous kinship systems) were based on obligations and relationships – genealogical and biological, but also adoptive.[134]

The civilizing logic of the Department of Indian Affairs (DIA) Indian policy not only targeted Indigenous marital practices in an effort to sever kinship ties but also sought ideological Indian elimination through socialization and education of children in isolated residential schools. Both the churches and government shared the goal of assimilating the Canadian Indian population through child removal policies, a common practice in settler colonial nations.[135] Churches targeted children because, on the basis of earlier experiences with missionary activities, they considered adults unsuited to the total physical, mental, and moral transformation required for Indians to take their place in the Canadian nation. The origins of the logic of child removal to residential schools stemmed from the belief that only through separating children from their parents could they be effectively assimilated.[136] The federal government and the churches considered the on-reserve day schools a failure in the efforts to rapidly assimilate Indian children. Families continued to engage in the Indigenous seasonal activities of gathering and hunting, and children's school attendance was sporadic. Other justifications included the poor state of the clothing of the children who attended school, and lack of a school lunches.[137] Schools were often purposely located in remote and inaccessible locations, since visits from families were seen to be disruptive to the civilizing process. Orphans remained the preferred students.[138]

A shift in approach occurred after the Second World War that culminated in growing numbers of children permanently removed from First Nations and Métis families and placed for adoption and in foster homes. While in some respects this points to evidence of a radical readjustment in racial boundaries, in fact much of the logics underlying Canadian Indian policy remained the same. Like past efforts at assimilation, the intimate integration of children initiated by social work professionals and supported by a federal bureaucracy armed with revised legislation and methods sought a reduction in expenditures in Indian Affairs. Between 1950 and the 1980s, when citizenship and integration became the focus of Indian assimilation, Indigenous transracial adoption rose to prominence as a key solution to the "Indian problem." Social workers asserted their expertise in not only adjusting the personal deficiencies of Indian and Métis clients, but also enacting integration, one child at a time. Beginning in Saskatchewan as a pilot project with the Métis in Green Lake in the early 1950s, transracial adoption peaked in the early 1980s.

In 1951, with additional legal changes to the Indian Act, kinship relations underwent a heightened form of colonization. The application, in particular, of child welfare and adoption legislation to Indian people became an opportunity to secure the intimate integration of Indigenous children outside their communities of origin. Canadian Indian policy between the 1951 Indian Act and the White Paper of 1969 pursued a unilateral direction, that of removing the distinctions between Indian people in Canada and other Canadians, by incorporating them into the education, health, and welfare systems from which they had previously been excluded. While writing on this period has seen this process primarily from the vantage point of the political goals, integration played out in the personal lives of individuals through fostering and adoption policies, particularly once Indian people became citizens of the Canadian nation after 1960. The transracial adoption of individual children was the intimate expression of the larger administrative and political goals: integration and elimination. In this period the Euro-Canadian home and the intimate domain of the nuclear family was enlisted as a site for establishing new methods of shifting affective sensibilities through the colonization of Indigenous kinship.

The variant of Indigenous transracial adoption that emerged between 1967 and 1984 in Saskatchewan differed significantly from that of typical Anglo-Canadian infant adoption. The narrative of white infant adoption typically begins with a young mother with an unplanned pregnancy who seeks to provide a secure family for her infant while she can continue with her future plans. The child, surrendered voluntarily by the mother at the hospital, then becomes a wanted child in a new family, hand-picked by social service experts trained in the management of proper kin relations.[139] Privacy legislation in Saskatchewan prevents researchers from undertaking qualitative or quantitative research on adoption files. One must rely on statistics compiled by social scientists for evidence for a study of transracial adoption. According to statistics compiled by Phillip Hepworth in 1979, Indigenous mothers rarely relinquished children voluntarily. Hepworth identified that a high proportion of native children were "illegitimate," but, unlike white "illegitimate babies," very few were relinquished for adoption after birth.[140] Hepworth found that the primary reason that Indian and Métis children came into care were for reasons of protection due to neglect. In 1973–74 the numbers varied between 94 and 96 per cent, while for non-Aboriginal children, that number was between 68 and 73 per cent. Thus a "typical adoption" involving an Indigenous infant took place only between 4 and 6 per cent of the time.[141] This suggests that the majority of Indigenous mothers attempted to parent children despite economic and social challenges and rarely sought adoption as a voluntary solution. The numbers suggest that Indigenous children came into care primarily through apprehensions, rather than through unmarried parents' legislation. In other words, the children were "scooped."

After Phillip Hepworth published *Foster Care and Adoption in Canada* in 1980, it was undeniable that a worrisome number of First Nations and Métis children in Canada did not live in their family homes. In 1977 over half of Saskatchewan children in care were First Nations, Metis, or non-status, yet they made up only 20 per cent of the child population.[142] Rather than diminishing, the figure climbed to 67 per cent in 1979.[143] In the years examined by Hepworth, 25 per cent of children coming into care were First Nations, and 25 per cent Métis. Of those children who became enmeshed in the provincial child care system, adoption was the outcome for only 3–4 per cent of Aboriginal children. Hepworth observed, "The available evidence suggests that native children once apprehended are less likely to be adopted and more likely to stay in care. The question then becomes whether the care child welfare services can provide is likely to be more beneficial than care provided in the child's original home environment."[144] A small number returned to their families, but the majority remained foster children in white foster homes, or moving between families. Analysing the phenomenon of transracial adoption, historian Karen Dubinsky asserts that "numbers provide part of the answer; overrepresentation is simply the racialization of poverty. But so too are the historical interactions of colonialism, which have consistently produced infantilized relations between Aboriginals and the Canadian state."[145] Adoption of Indian children into non-Indigenous legal families in some cases masked issues that were essentially matters of poverty and colonization. Cross-cultural analysis of adoption through ethnohistorical research will reveal how transracial adoption has become the dominant paradigm through which to discuss Indigenous child welfare despite its statistically rare occurrence.

Saskatchewan led the county in these intervention efforts, with social workers involved at every twist and turn of this decades-long saga of disenfranchising and, more recently, trying to do better by Indigenous families and children. This is the story of a country and a province making policies to address problems without having the courage to name or face the root of the problem: the settler colonialism that undermined the very fabric of Indigenous societies. For First Nations and Métis children, adoption seldom provided a winning solution to the twin problems of illegitimacy and unmarried motherhood. Social workers identified the newly developing social problem of the "unmarried

Indian mother" in the 1960s and the illegitimate Indian child, to which the solution was fostering and adoption in non-Native homes.[146] These policies and programs were justified by social workers as they argued that adoption saved state welfare agencies money and privatized the solution to the "Indian problem."

These combined impositions had deleterious effects on the mental, emotional, and spiritual health of Aboriginal people, individually and collectively. The Cree concept of *mino pimatisiwin*, meaning "living a good life," encompasses the social and spiritual aspects of health and well-being within Cree societies. According to Maria Campbell, part of that good life includes kinship relations, how people live with and interact with one another.[147] The good life and health are based on how relations are managed and include all of one's relations. Children had responsibilities to the community. Strong relationships between elders and children were considered critical for maintaining the strength and continuity of the people.[148] For Indigenous peoples, child removal is likened to the violence of warfare leading to the shattering of *wâhkôh-towin*, the system that connected each member to "all our relations."[149] Despite these interventions, persistence and survival of Indigenous teachings have endured. Through the examples of adoption that follow, Indigenous families continued to find methods to care for children that reflected Indigenous kinship systems, sometimes aided by Canadian law, other times in spite of Canadian law.

2

Adoptive Kinship and Belonging[1]

In 1949 grandparents on a Saskatchewan First Nations reserve wrote to the provincial Department of Social Welfare to explore the possibility of adopting four grandchildren, ranging in age from eight to fifteen.[2] Following their daughter's death in 1941, the family had followed the proper channels in order to adopt the children and have them enrolled as band members. In 1942 the Indian band council passed a resolution accepting the children. After forwarding the changes to his supervisor, the Indian agent received the following: "In reply, I am returning the signed Resolution to you as I am fully aware of the stand the department will take in this matter, that is they will be against the admission of these children because their mother married an outsider and the children are not considered as Indian under the interpretation of the Indian Act, I am not submitting this to Ottawa."[3]

The admission was not approved, and the children remained in a state of legal limbo on reserve, cared for by relatives. In 1949, when the family attempted to secure the children's adoption through the Department of Social Services, they were again denied, on the basis of Indian Act provisions.

While supportive of the inter-family adoption, the social worker involved was confronted by the federal Indian Affairs Branch's legalistic interpretation of the children's situation. In her letter of reply, she pointed out that Indian Act legislation contradicted child welfare practice that attempted to ensure the legal and social protection of children:

"The children are receiving good care in the respective homes and the younger ones at least would have no recollection of any other home. It would be desirable to give them security of adoption if it is possible."[4] The Indian agent likewise supported the adoption. However, the reply to this request was consistent with the Indian Affairs Branch position that rigidly enforced the Indian Act membership provisions: "For your information I should point out that, generally speaking, I am not much in favour of the adoption by Indians of non-treaty children, as we run into many different kinds of difficulty with regard to education medical cost, etc., and in this particular case, it would appear to me that our department is expected to be saddled with the responsibility of three children while their father is alive and apparently able to re-marry and support a second family."[5]

The Indian agent and social worker acknowledged the children's relationship with their community and kin, but department policy was clear that no white people (their terminology) were to be admitted to the band membership. The Indian agent was chastised for his role in advocating the adoption of the children. The director reminded him, "You are, surely, aware that it is the policy of this branch to not admit any person of white status to Indian membership and as adoption would not change the status of the children they could not be admitted to membership and should not be permitted to reside on reserve."[6] Fortunately, despite the intended policy to remove the children and relocate them, they remained on the reserve among their kin.

The persistence of the children's grandparents and community ensured that children in this case managed to remain with their kin. However, with the 1951 revisions to the Indian Act, Indigenous children increasingly left the care of family. In Saskatchewan, Indigenous transracial adoption, or the adoption of Saskatchewan's First Nations, Métis, and non-status children permanently into Euro-Canadian families, dramatically increased by the 1970s. The Adopt Indian and Métis ad campaign focused on children apprehended by social workers with Saskatchewan's Department of Social Welfare and Rehabilitation who had become permanent wards. The case above foreshadows many of the changes that gave rise to Indigenous transracial adoption in the 1960s and 1970s. First, the gendered Indian Act status provisions created legal barriers between families who sought to fulfil responsibilities for child caring and support. Without status, women and children were

unable to return to their communities in the event of a death or separation with their spouse. Indigenous children of mothers who'd lost status could not regain their status through adoption or live with relatives
on reserve. Second, the vexing jurisdictional ambiguity of Indigenous
children is evident. Child welfare was a provincial responsibility, while
"Indians and lands reserved for Indians" fell under federal jurisdiction.
Provincial child welfare policy and legislation and the Indian policy,
each with differing goals, remained at odds and unresolved from 1944
to 1984. Finally, the bonds of family and belonging among Indigenous
peoples, expressed through marriage, adoption, and child caring, faced
a new type of attack as provincial laws became applicable to Indian
people after 1951, replacing community sanction with social worker
professionals, and provincial adoption law.

Adoption in Indigenous societies has created familial relations where
there had been none before, ensuring that family lineages continued,
collective memories were passed down, children were cared for, and
strangers were transformed into kin. More than a method of providing
childless couples with the opportunity to parent, or orphaned children
with the security of a permanent home, Indigenous adoption created
and perpetuated Indigenous kinship systems. Cree and Métis people
shared the belief that kinship is of central importance for individual
and collective identity and is inseparable from land, home, community, or family.[7] Adoption in Anishinaabe citizenship orders is a family-
making practice that "seeks to continually renew the nation indefinitely
into the future."[8]

Adoption served several functions in Prairies Indigenous societies. It ensured vulnerable members were provided with care through
familial relationships in the case of abandoned or orphaned children.
It was used to replace children who had been lost through illness or in
battle. In addition, it could fulfil political goals such as securing peace
between warring groups. In each case, adoption enlarged the kinship
circle, enabling individuals and groups to secure material and affective support. Poundmaker's adoption illustrates the multiplicity of
functions that Indigenous adoption supplied. In 1873 Blackfoot Chief
Crowfoot adopted a Cree young man named Poundmaker. One of
Crowfoot's wives pled with the chief to adopt Poundmaker into their
family after seeing how he resembled her recently deceased son. Upon
being adopted, Poundmaker acquired a new Blackfoot name, wealth,

resources, and large Blackfoot family. In his Cree tribe, he also was given special status because of his new relationship with the powerful chief and former enemy.[9] The young Cree warrior would eventually become an influential Cree chief and vocal critic of the Canadian government Indian policy. The adoption benefitted Poundmaker personally and western First Nations as a whole. Anthropologist Mary Rogers-Black observed in her work among the Swampy Cree, "Sometimes these adoptions took place within the context of sustained trading and merger relations, but they often occurred in relations dominated by hostilities."[10] In this case, adoption came at the insistence of Crowfoot's wife, suggesting that women played an important function in adoption. Through adoption, Poundmaker was integrated into Crowfoot's kinship and social networks and was a recognized member of both Cree and Blackfoot societies.

Ethnographer David Mandelbaum observed adoption while working among the Cree in 1934 and 1935. The Indigenous practice of adopting an individual who resembled a lost relative was still in effect. His informant Fine-Day had adopted a young man from another reserve to replace his eldest son, who had passed away. "I took a man from Pelican Lake for a son because he resembles my eldest boy who is dead. He comes here every once in a while and I generally have a horse for him. Sometimes he brings me moose hides and meat in the winter. When I first took him for a son, I told him and gave him a horse. I didn't expect anything in return. If he is poor he doesn't have to give me anything. I am getting old and cannot do everything for myself. When I built that stable he helped me."[11]

Parent–child relationships entailed more than sentimental attachments. Obligations for care and assistance in times of need were created through adoption, since the family was responsible for providing for needy loved ones in the absence of alternative caring facilities. Elderly people were also adopted if their children had died. Mandelbaum also observed that when an elderly couple had no adult children to assist them, the chief took them to his house to care for them and treated them as his parents.[12]

Anthropologists and Indigenous scholars point to the importance of kinship as an organizing category within Indigenous communities.[13] As anthropologist Raymond DeMallie stated, "The kinship system itself provided the foundation for social unity and moral order. The norms of kinship were the most basic cultural structures patterning the social system; they formed a network that potentially embraced all members of society and related them as well to the sacred powers of the world at large."[14] Whereas children and adults have been made kin in Indigenous societies as a method to create obligations and relationships in pre- and post-contact periods, adoption in North American society is viewed as a legal parent–child relationship meant to approximate the biological nuclear family.[15]

Adoption expresses the values of Indigenous kinship, called *wáhkôh-towin* in Cree, or *Inewedensowen* in Saulteaux.[16] The Indigenous world view draws its inspiration from the interconnectedness expressed through the familial relationship.[17] Kinship embodied the obligations and responsibilities that both describe and prescribe proper relations between kin and non-kin. Métis scholar Brenda Macdougall explains, "The Métis family structure that emerged in the northwest was rooted in the history and culture of the Cree and Dene progenitors, and therefore in a worldview that privileged relatedness to land, people (living, ancestral, and those to come), the spirit world, and creatures inhabiting the space. In short, this worldview, wahcootowin, is predicated upon a specific Indigenous notion and definition of family as a broadly conceived sense of relatedness with all beings, human and non-human, living and dead, physical and spiritual."[18]

As such, belonging in the complex web of expanding relationships entailed obligations for support, knowledge of the protocols, the passing down of community memories, teachings, and ensuring the transmission from generation to generation. Cree scholar Neal McLeod states, "Kinship, *wáhkôhtowin*, grounds the collective narrative memory within the *nehiyawiwin* [Cree people]."[19]

Brenda Macdougall's history of the ethnogenesis of the Métis community at Île à la Crosse reconstructs the methods by which the kinship system was expanded. Adoption was an important element in the operation of *wáhkôhtowin*. Expanding the boundaries of family by bringing additional people into the group increased the total number of relatives an individual could look to for support.[20] Macdougall observed, "Adoption of young children by other family members, particularly after the death of their biological parents, was an important social institution that ensured the perpetuation of 'wahcootowin' because it allowed a family to survive death."[21] Adoptions were public and private displays of familial behaviours and beliefs. Macdougall found instances of interfamily adoption from scrip applications, but primarily adoptions of children by grandparents. Adoption of grandchildren not only provided continuity for children who'd lost their parents, but was also a benefit to the older person who passed down "wahcootowin" through sharing memories, protocols, and lifeways with children.[22]

GENDER AND FAMILY LIFE IN CREE MÉTIS SASKATCHEWAN

Oral histories collected from Indigenous elders in Saskatchewan about experiences and cultural beliefs about gender and reproduction indicate that there was a period of transition between the 1930s and the 1950s.[23] While older marriage traditions remained operative in the 1950s, Christian churches and residential schools had begun to influence how marriage was understood and lived. Marriage was ideally lifelong with one partner. However, while infrequent, divorce and separation could take place if the couple were incompatible. One partner could simply leave. After marriage, young women continued to be mentored by older women.[24] Saulteaux men would come and live with the woman's family for one year after the marriage, hunting and trapping for their in-laws. As Kim Anderson has related from oral histories with Prairie elders, "Marriage was as much about strengthening the female bonds of kinship and family as it was about a union between a man and a woman."[25] Both matrilocal and patrilocal arrangements have been recorded among the Cree, Anishinaabe, and Métis. When young women moved in with their husband's family they continued to be under the tutelage of mothers-in-law. Older women were authority figures in the households, with young women entering into a circle of women's kinship.

Indigenous women-centred approaches toward birth and reproduction continued to be practised openly from the 1930s until the 1950s, after which Western male doctors took over pregnancy, birth, and postpartum care.[26] Previously, women in the community had managed these aspects of health. The midwives were older women who were highly regarded in their communities, as Anderson again points out: "Their significant role in catching incoming life and managing a transition into community is a demonstration of a uniquely feminine power, a power that allowed women to be a conduit between the spirit and earthly worlds."[27] The declining opportunity for older women to play a role in birthing practices likely altered cultural and community relationships based on generational and gendered roles.

Likewise, family planning was a community affair, and older women, often midwives, sought to help young women of childbearing age manage fertility so that they could be strong to care for their children. Older women cared for new mothers who became weak after childbirth, preparing medicines for them until they were strong enough to have the next child. It was widely understood that a mother's death would harm her children, and communities sought to prevent that as best they could. Indigenous families looked after the health of their members by planning for births on a seasonal basis, ideally having babies born in the temperate months of May and June, rather than the harsh winter months when food was scarce and frigid temperatures made survival difficult. Like many cultural adaptations to the harsh subarctic climate faced by Prairie Indigenous peoples, "family planning was undertaken to ensure the survival of the people."[28]

The distinctive cultural practices and gender relations in Indigenous societies have been used to justify coercion and assimilation. The greater freedom of women and children threatened Euro-Canadian definitions of the nuclear family. This level of coercion was couched in the language of protection and linked to the national body.[29] Historian Joan Sangster observed in her study of women's incarceration in Ontario, "The creation of moral families, based on Western (Anglo) middle-class notions of sexual purity, marital monogamy, and distinct gender roles of the female homemaker and male breadwinner was an important means of creating moral and responsible citizens, the 'bedrock of the nation,' as legal authorities never tired of saying."[30] The law has been the method by which women and gendered norms have been colonized in Indigenous societies. Gendering Indian status and political participation that replicate Euro-Canadian societies has severed female kinship circles among women. The impact of these laws made women and children vulnerable to poverty and abuse.[31]

As in earlier periods, Indigenous women and communities responded in a variety of ways to attempts to realign Indigenous kinship. The multiplicity of responses suggests that Indigenous peoples have interpreted the opportunities afforded by law, policy, legislation, and social welfare services on the basis of perceived advantages and historical experiences. In all cultures, kinship is part of the social and cultural management of reproduction and is interwoven with gender.[32] The persistence into contemporary times of Indigenous adoption ceremonies, and Indigenous resistance to modern transracial adoption policies suggests the central importance and contested nature of kinship to the narrative of colonial relations.[33]

THE EMERGENCE OF THE EURO-CANADIAN ADOPTION PARADIGM

According to American anthropologist David Schneider, the underlying and unspoken basis of Euro-American kinship is predicated on what he terms "shared biogenetic substance," or the blood relationship, and is unique to European and North American cultures. There are two aspects to the kinship system: "the order of nature," meaning the reproduction of the biological family, and "the order of law," or the creation of rules, regulations, and traditions, such as adoption and marriage.[34] North American kinship is also distinctive for its "common sense" belief in the superiority of the ideal nuclear family: man, woman, and children, which is believed to have been formed according to the laws of nature and been given legal sanction.[35] In viewing transracial adoption cross-culturally through the lens of kinship, this chapter traces the origins of Euro-Canadian child removal policies alongside the Indigenous people's participation in remaking adoption to conform to their own cultural expression of kinship.

For Euro-Canadian settler populations, adoption was a New World development that reflected an optimistic belief in the power of the environment to shape individuals and the role of the family to nurture future citizens. Like European settlers who left behind pasts and kinship connections, moving to their adopted countries for a brighter future, infant adoption likewise offered the promise of new beginnings for both unwed mothers and orphaned or illegitimate children.[36] Massachusetts had the first recorded reference to adoption as the legal transfer of parental rights in 1851.[37] This law has been considered a watershed in the history of American family and society as well as a model for future adoption laws. The parent–child relationship was no longer considered strictly defined by blood ties.[38] Judges utilized the "best interests of the child standard" to evaluate whether parents were "fit and proper."[39] New Brunswick enacted the first adoption law Canada in 1873, but Saskatchewan did not pass adoption legislation until 1922. If children needed care, few families used legal adoption to formalize kinship prior to the 1950s. Beyond being prohibitively complicated and expensive, many other methods were available, including informal adoption, orphanages, foster homes, and boarding schools, to name a few.[40]

North American adoption emerged out of early twentieth-century reform movements, but rose to prominence only in the period following the Second World War when the idealized nuclear family was widely promulgated by psychologists and social workers.[41] Prior to the advent of professional social workers, late nineteenth-century Protestant benevolent societies believed in keeping white mothers with their infants. These reformists glorified biological motherhood and focused their efforts on keeping families together, and unwed mothers with their children.[42] In part, changing definitions of good motherhood contributed to the increasing popularity of adoption, but also changes in government policy. The rise of the maternalist welfare state and provision of mothers' allowances enabled financially strapped women to parent children, reducing the necessity of relinquishing children when male breadwinners left through death and desertion.[43] Direct state financial support to mothers reduced the likelihood that children would be institutionalized or adopted.

Prior to the First World War, child welfare organizations rarely recommended children for adoption, since the majority continued to believe that personality, intelligence, criminal tendencies, feeblemindedness, and promiscuity were inherited. These beliefs were supported by law and science of the times.[44] Likewise, adoption was considered an unappealing option for childless families who feared biological kin may return to retrieve youngsters, and to a lesser extent, had eugenic fears over the possibility of children inheriting their parents' "tainted blood."[45] Thus, in the early North American adoption era, adoptive children were doubly burdened, first socially because of illegitimacy, and second medically through being perceived as defective due to eugenic beliefs. To reflect the triumph of adoption as a new beginning and a major development in the history of "modern adoption," laws were passed that removed the term *illegitimate* from the child's birth certificate and issued a new name and birth certificate.

Three conditions altered the role of North American adoption in family making. First, the recession of eugenic thinking after the Second World War; second, the rapid increase in out-of-wedlock births; and finally, increased interest by potential adoptive parents.[46] To reduce the perceived risks inherent in accepting unrelated kin, professional social workers crafted policies and procedures to ensure safer, legal adoptions. Early adoption was meant primarily for childless white families seeking to adopt white children, and the matching of class, appearance, and intelligence enabled adoption to mirror the natural family. Social workers developed a scientific attitude toward matching, employing intelligence testing and taking detailed case histories of each individual involved in order to ensure the best possible outcome. This legacy of eugenics movement reflected ongoing fears of unknown hereditary conditions lurking in children's backgrounds.

The struggle to professionalize adoption reflected the struggle to professionalize social work in general, and over the first part of the twentieth century, commercial and benevolent adoptions were replaced by professional adoptions designed using exacting standards and regularized procedures.[47] While each step taken in professionalizing adoption brought it closer in appearance to the biological family, society failed to accept the legitimacy of the adoptive family on the same footing as the biological family. Laws passed intended to benefit the adoptive family against the power of blood ties and provide children an opportunity for social mobility.[48] In this effort, "social workers attempted to create adoptive families that not only mirrored biological families, but also reflected an idealized version of them."[49]

Social workers who had worked to make adoption more scientific did so in an attempt to overcome the Euro-American cultural belief that adoptive bonds between children and parents were inferior to biological relationships.[50] Provincial adoption law enshrined the adoptive relation as being as strong as a biological connection. Courts issued adoptive children new birth certificates and ensured that adoptive children received the same inheritance and legal rights as a natural child. Likewise, records of birth parents were sealed to ensure privacy for all involved.[51] In both Canada and the United States, scientific adoption promised to overcome disadvantages of birth, provide social mobility to illegitimate children, and importantly provide childless couples with the opportunity to parent, while eliminating the uncertainly that birth families might attempt to retrieve youngsters once their situations improved. Adoption offered permanence and stability in a hand-picked, "normal" family chosen especially for their adherence to the ideal. Social workers tried to replicate the biological family as well as possible by matching intelligence, appearance, and economic status. The legal kinship ties created through adoption, up to the emergence of transracial adoption, consistently came closer and closer to mirroring the "normal" Euro-Canadian biologically based nuclear family through both legislation and policy directives. For all intents and purposes, adopted children became legally similar to a child born to the adopting parents in lawful wedlock.[52]

INDIGENOUS ADOPTION AND EURO-CANADIAN LAW

Long before adoption gained widespread acceptance and popularity in Euro-Canadian and Euro-American society, Indigenous peoples used tradition and law for the care of needy youngsters. Examples of legal adoption from the Indian Affairs records in the first part of the twentieth century illustrate the formalization of kinship relations in the absence of oversight by professional social workers. Because the Department of Indian Affairs had control over matters of Indian status, and adoption entailed a change in legal status and family name, or perhaps band membership, families needed to obtain departmental permission before securing adoptions. In each of the following cases, the department had no objection to the parent-initiated adoptions. The adoption process followed a common pattern. First, the surviving parent selected the adopting family for the children, after which the band leadership was consulted. It appears that the majority of the adoptions took place between relatives, but it is not always clear. The primary reason that parents sought adoption for their children prior to 1940 was the death of either mother or father. Subsequently the band leaders of the adoptive family met and agreed whether to accept the child as a new member.

Ottawa's policy for adoptions between legally Indian people took shape in these early cases, which predate official adoption laws in some Canadian provinces.[53] Assistant Deputy and Secretary in the

Department of Indian Affairs J.D. McLean wrote to Indian Agent Walton McLean on 24 July 1913, "Secure from Indian agents the financial standing, and general character of persons who agree to adopt the children. If the recommendations are favorable the matter must be laid before the respective Indian bands and a resolution obtained in each case to accept the children into membership. It should be made clear in each case that amount at the children's credit in the Capital funds of the Alnwick band will be transferred to the band or bands into which they are admitted provided the Department approves the transfers."[54]

On 28 November 1913 Indian Agent Walton McLean informed his superior in Ottawa that he had obtained good reports of the adopting families, meaning they had "satisfactory characters and financial standing" enabling them to care for the children. He recommended the adoption be carried out with the approval of the bands into which the children would be transferred. Through this case, the elements of "modern adoption" intermingle with Anishinaabe adoption.[55] The children's mother had accessed her kinship networks with their protocol of obligations to seek out substitute care. The leadership of both communities was consulted and agreed to the adoptions. The language of the agreement clearly outlines the new relationship between the adoptive family and the children, removing the obligations for care from the children's mother. The community involvement and oversight ensure that each of the parties would fulfil their responsibilities set out through the adoption for the duration of the child's life.

Residential schools and adoption co-existed for Indigenous families who required additional support. Indigenous children who were too small to place in residential schools could be placed for adoption. Peter S—— applied to have his young son adopted after the child's mother died in childbirth. The four-year-old child was too young to be placed in residential school like his older siblings, and his father, Peter, had found an adoptive family that would be willing to care for him. It is unclear from the archival record whether Mrs W—— was a relative of his or of his deceased wife. Mrs Jimmy W—— of the Enoch Band was found to be an acceptable choice as adoptive mother by the Department of Indian Affairs, but prior to securing the adoption, the band first had to accept the transfer of membership from the Saddle Lake Band to the Enoch Band.[56] In response, the department recognized the band's jurisdiction over membership by deferring to their decision: "If Enoch's

band passes a resolution agreeing to the transfer of the boy from Blue
Quill's Band to Enoch's band, no objection will be made by the Department, providing that the father, Peter S—— agrees in writing to the
transfer and adoption of the boy by Mrs Jimmy W."[57] From the written
archival evidence, it appears that parents exercise greater autonomy
over children than in later periods, and band jurisdiction over members
demonstrates some degree of self-determination.

When potential adoptions challenged the legal regime established
by the Indian Act, kinship systems came under attack. The case of an
attempted Indigenous adoption in the same period draws attention to
the racialized and gendered regime established by the Indian Act as
it played out in the lives of women and children. In Saskatchewan on
12 July 1918, Robert B—— of James Smith Reserve sought permission
from the department to adopt the children of a widow, Ellen S——,
known formerly as Elena B——, of the Okemases Band. She had married Thomas S——, an Englishman, and as a result, lost her Indian status and had been unable to pass Indian status along to her children.
In 1909 Mr S—— enlisted with the Canadian Expeditionary Force in
Prince Albert but died before going overseas, leaving a widow and
three children. Mrs S——, while in Prince Albert, sought to find families
to place her children. Mr B——, a young man married to Eliza S——,
had been childless but had adopted the illegitimate child of his wife's
sister. In reply to this request, an official rejected the adoption: "I do not
recommend allowing B—— to adopt the S—— children and bring them
on the reserve as they are non-treaty. If Mrs S—— will not keep them,
the department of neglected children for the province of Saskatchewan
should look after them. I beg to enquire whether the Department can
forbid Indians adopting half-breeds, or white children and bringing
them on reserve. I beg to ask for instructions in the case."[58] While officials acknowledged that the adoption was a private decision to be made
between both parties, realistically they felt that there was no possibility
that the adoption could work since the children would not be allowed
to live on the reserve with their adoptive family. "I beg to state that
the Department is opposed to Indians adopting halfbreeds or white
children and bringing them into the reserve and cannot approve of the
agreement submitted and sanction the adoption of the children, as they
would be brought on the reserve."[59] The mother, Mrs S——, had lost
her Indian status with her marriage to a non-Indian and been forced to

leave her reserve and sever her kinship ties. One difficulty for women and children that came as a result of the Indian Act was that none of her kin who retained their Indian status would be able to adopt her children. Since her husband had come from England, it was unlikely she could look to his family for assistance. Kinship in North American settler society, viewed as the blood-based nuclear family, proved unstable when trouble arose. When this broke down through death or desertion, the state and churches stepped in to supply the needed care for children and vulnerable mothers. Settler society, particularly in areas recently settled, such as Saskatchewan and Alberta, lacked the deeply rooted extended families and institutions that more established areas would have. Indigenous women and children who'd lost Indian status faced few options outside of their kinship networks.[60]

The Frances T—— adoption case reveals the illogic of the racial and gendered definitions that define who is and who is not an Indian through the Indian Act, as well as the conflicts between federal and provincial legal regimes over the care of children. [61] In this potentially precedent-setting legal case, the Indian Affairs Branch attempted to set aside an order of adoption that had been granted by a provincial court judge in Alberta. Two years after the original adoption, the Indian Affairs Branch secured the assistance of lawyer, C.E. Gariepy of Edmonton Alberta, to overturn the adoption of Frances G. T—— by Joseph C—— and wife on 15 February 1937. Frances T——, a young mixed-ancestry child with a Métis mother and white father, had been legally adopted by an Indian couple of the Fort Chipewyan Band in Alberta.

On 21 February 1939 the Indian Affairs Branch, under the Department of Mines and Resources, submitted a request to the Department of Justice that an attorney be obtained to overturn an adoption order for Frances G. T—— in Alberta on 15 February 1937. At issue was the child's lack of Indian status prior to her adoption, and subsequent confusion about her legal status after her adoption by a status Indian couple. The department solicitor raised the issue first as a test case to determine whether Indian status could be conferred through adoption. Through Indian Act legislation, non-Indian women could legally become Indian through marriage; thus, it was probable that legal adoption could confer Indian status to children. The question put forward by the Indian Affairs Branch was whether provincial child welfare legislation could do the same. With the increasing acceptance of adoption across Canada as well as longstanding customary practice in Indigenous society, it was probable that Indian families would seek to adopt children without Indian status, thereby increasing federal obligations. Unlike earlier examples, the Indian Affairs Branch had not been consulted on this matter and thus was unable to prevent the adoption from taking place. There was concern that since no explicit legislation barred adopted children from Indian status, adoption could potentially reverse the goals of reducing the Indian population in Canada. This development proved troublesome to the Branch, whose mandate for over half a century had been to reduce the number of Indian people under its control. To accept this adoption could potentially set a precedent that non-Indian children could become Indians through adoption in defiance of the Indian Act's logic of elimination. The department sought to set aside the adoption and reassert its control over Indian status.

The Branch obtained the services of Edouard Gariepy, an Edmonton lawyer, to look into having the adoption order overturned on the basis of section 30 of the Indian Act, to determine if adoption gave the child a claim against the trust fund administered by the Crown.[62] Gariepy replied that he would give the matter consideration and consult with the provincial attorney general about the matter. Since considerable time had elapsed since the adoption was formalized, the Attorney General did not believe it could be successful. However, Gariepy thought that the order could be overturned on the basis of the inability of the ward (in this case, Mr.——, as an "Indian" was considered a ward) to take on contractual obligations without the written consent of the superintendent general, based on sections 34 (2) and 90 (2) of the Indian Act. In addition, Gariepy inserted his personal opinion that in the interest of the child herself, she, "only being [of] limited Indian blood, should not remain and be raised in the Indian fashion."[63] He agreed to pursue the matter on the basis of the absence of department consent to the adoption.

At issue were deeper matters of blood-based understandings of race and degeneration. The possibility that adoption could confer Indian status on non-Indian children disturbed white officials, who were perhaps well aware of the poor state of care they offered their Indian charges. To potentially allow a white child to suffer the indignities of Indian status and all that entailed challenged the binary thinking that enabled department officials, and the public at large, to justify and rationalize poverty and poor health on Indian reserves across the country. Also at issue was who had control over the matter. Indian people utilizing provincial legislation could potentially restore members lost to enfranchisement legislation, calling into question the gendered and racialized parameters used to restrict band membership and Indian status.

The background information provided for Frances reveals a complex Métis identity that officials continually sought to discipline into manageable Euro-Canadian definitions of either Indian or white. Frances's mother, Jennie (LaR) T—— had been born in 1896 in Red Deer, Alberta, to Métis parents. Her first marriage in 1914 was to Métis Henry N——, who was killed in action overseas. In August 1915 she married William T——, a white man who died in 1927. Frances was born in 1927, and in June 1935 she was left in the care of Alex A——, chief of the Cree Band of Riviere Que Barre, Alberta, after which the children came to the attention of child welfare officials. The case file on the adoption states, "Mrs C at this point states she arranged to take the child in question from Alex A——, her brother, and got the child June 1935. Through questioning, Gertrude (a sister to Frances) T—— states the mother was of Indian blood and her father a white man, further that she believes the mother was a relation to Chief Harry C—— who now resides at Anzac."[64] This genealogy of relations alludes to some type of family relationship between Frances's Métis mother and the C—— family, although it remains unclear.

D.B. Mackenzie, the provincial attorney general for Alberta, refused to consider setting the order of adoption aside. In reply to the federal department he stated, "From information obtained in that department I gather that no great hardship will be done to anyone if the adoption is now ratified by the proper official of the Indian Department."[65] He cited past practice of allowing adoption of half-Indian children and asked officials to leave Frances where she had happily lived for two years.[66] Unlike federal officials, Mackenzie appealed to common decency and importance of the familial relationship that had been established between the child and parents.

The ongoing bureaucratic fascination with the race of Frances T—— race and their refusal to concede her adoption was legitimate reveal a preoccupation with patrilineal descent and fears of racial degeneration. After this mild rebuke by Mackenzie, officials at the Department of Indian Affairs stated emphatically, "Frances T—— is not a half-breed but a white girl, and to recognize the adoption of a white child by Indians and the consequent Indian status of such child, would be out of the question from the view point of this branch."[67] In response, lawyer Gariepy countered, "For the purpose of the application, it was sufficient to show that this child was not the daughter of Indian parents, that she could not be considered Indian."[68] However, Gariepy was not as paranoid about racial implications in his grasp of the matter: "As a matter of fact from inquiries made by the Indian Agent and the RCMP, it is clear that she is the daughter of a half-breed mother and a white father. This could make her a quarter breed Indian."[69] Strictly on the basis of objective facts, he felt the adoption unwise: "To accept the adoption order, as to for instance that fact the C—— couple are treaty Indians, are destitute etc., would be a very bad precedent, as apparently the Department here to do child welfare would be very pleased to have Indian affairs branch take care of any half breed or child being part white and part half breed."[70] In addition to racial fears, adoption provided the opportunity to find families for problematic mixed-race children; the provincial departments struggled to find homes for children within white society.

Local doctor P.W. Head of Fort Chipewyan was familiar with the First Nations people of the area, and on 26 May 1939 he echoed the fears of the department officials: "This girl who has never known much of a proper home is taken fairly well to the Indian mode of life, but I do not consider it a suitable life for her as her views are very likely to change as she gets older. Moreover the aspects of schooling and general welfare will diminish rather than increase with the ageing of her foster parents. Personally I do not like the idea of a three quarter white child being made a treaty Indian."[71] Like the case of unredeemed captive Eunice Williams, adopted into a Mohawk family at Kahnawake in 1704, Frances represented reverse boundary crossing that troubled the settler colonial imagination. At the age of seven after a raid on Deerfield, Massachusetts, Eunice Williams was marched north to Canada and for all intents and purposes became Mohawk, speaking the language to the point of forgetting English, marrying, and having children. Despite attempts to induce her to return, she refused to go back to her Anglo-American family and remained an unredeemed captive.[72] As Sarah Carter has found regarding sensational captivity narratives in the early settlement period, "Assumptions about the 'wretched fate' that awaited these girls once they grew up both promoted and confirmed the negative images of Indigenous women that were firmly embellished in the colonial imagination."[73]

After lawyer Edouard Gariepy was unable to have the order overturned, the department referred the matter to the Deputy Minister of Justice E. Miall for his legal opinion, who provided the final word. On 19 July 1940, on the basis of a reading of the Indian Act, child welfare law, and how the term *child* has been defined in past cases, Miall stated clearly and unequivocally that Indian status could be created through adoption.[74] Deputy Minister of Justice Miall looked to the Indian Act to answer the questions of status, since section 2(d)(ii) the Indian Act defined *Indian* as the child of "any male person of Indian blood reputed to belong to a particular band."[75] Since at the time the Act did not cover the issue of adoption, it was then necessary to define the meaning of *child*. He then looked to both provincial and federal legislation. The Alberta Adoption of Infants Act, section 45(i), stated, "An order of adoption shall b) make such child, for the purposes of the custody of the person and filial and paternal duties and rights, to all intents and purposes the child of the adopting parent; c) give the child the same rights to claim for nurture, maintenance and education upon his adopting parent that he would have were the adopting parent his natural parent."[76] On the basis of the legally established parent–child relationship created through adoption legislation, Miall concluded that section 45(10) provides that "a person who has been adopted in accordance with the provisions of this Part shall, upon the intestacy of an adopting parent, take the same share of property which the adopting parent could dispose of by will as he would have taken if born to such parent in lawful wedlock and he shall stand, in regard to the legal descendants but to other kindred of such adopting parent, in the same position as if he had been born to him."[77]

Thus, on the basis of a reading of both the definition of *Indian* in the Indian Act and *child* in the Alberta Adoption of Infants Act, Frances had become an Indian through the powerfully worded legal protections that adoption legislation defined.

Adoption proved to be a unique mechanism for providing vulnerable children with social and legal belonging, and potentially affirmed Indigenous kinship systems. Miall was also careful to indicate, "Frances

Gertrude T—— is to be considered as the child of Joseph and Angelique
C – I surmise that the interest of the IAB is in the status of this girl has
to do with the distribution of moneys or potential inheritance within
the Band of an interest in the Band property and is not directed to the
proportion of Indian blood. By section 14 an Indian woman, marrying
a person other than an Indian, ceases in every respect within the meaning of the Act to be an Indian, and I am therefore not putting forward
any suggestion that the girl's status as an Indian derives otherwise than
from the adoption."[78]

Miall pointed out the relative unimportance of race and Indian blood
quantum in the past administration of the Act by referring to Treaty
8, signed in 1899 with the Chipewyan Indians and the promise to pay
every family head five dollars. He inferred that this clause had contemporary significance to the Indian family: "I suggest that effect can only
be given to this promise if payment be made to the head of the family
in respect of each person who, in the eyes of the law, is a member of this
family. I submit, therefore, that the effect of the adoption is to confer full
Indian status upon Frances Gertrude T——, the child in question."[79]
Using the text of Treaty 8, Miall defined the Indian family as being made
up of all members who were legally recognized as under the authority
of the head of the family. Thus, race played no role in determining who
became an "Indian" under this legal definition utilized by the treaty.
As such, adoption, by conferring a legal parent–child relationship, fell
under the same category. Despite the clear legal argument made by the
deputy minister, the department refused to recognize the logic of his
argument, which essentially rendered the gendered colonizing (il)logic
of the Indian Act and the Branch null and void when he determined
that neither blood nor race, but rather Indigenous kinship, played a role
in deciding who qualified as Indian.[80]

Despite the apparent hegemony of the Indian Act, this early example
may indicate that indigenization of adoption laws began to emerge as
Indian people utilized the protections of legal adoption offered by provincial legislation to support kinship obligations in the face of oppressive control by the department, day-to-day struggles of poverty and
isolation, illness, and death. However, Indian status conferred by adoption posed the risk of flaunting the irrational nature of the status logics
in the legal construction of Indian identity while advancing Indigenous
citizenship orders based on systems of Indigenous kinship rather than

patriarchy. Closing this subversive adoption loophole maintained set-tler-colonial government control over Indian status, and tightening the grip on Indigenous communities and families. In response, the branch sought to impose its own narrow definition of who could and could not qualify as Indian and to restrict the ability of Indian people to define adoption according to their own notions of family and kinship outside the legalized definition of Indian.

This case is significant in that it provides an early example of the ten-sions that emerged when federal attempts to reduce and legally elimi-nate Indian women and children conflicted with the provincial child welfare prerogative. The prerogative of social work practices and the developing provincial child welfare systems sought legislation and policies that were "in the best interests of the child," and legal adoption attempted to ensure the permanent care of children in families. The con-flict between provincial adoption laws and the federally defined Indian status as created by the Indian Act became more pronounced over time. This was especially true after the revisions to the Indian Act in 1951 made provincial laws applicable to Indian people on reserves and in cities, and explicitly racialized adoption to apply to "Indian" children only.[81] Frances T——'s Indigenous adoption offers a counter-narrative of colonization on kinship, race, gender, and legal status. When looking at the communication between highly placed government bureaucrats about the case, one witnesses the primary objectives of the Indian Act: reducing the number of those who counted as "Indian," minimizing the legal and financial responsibility for Indians, and ultimately eliminat-ing "Indians" altogether.[82] Officials furthered these objectives not only through restrictive laws designed to manage relations between Indian and non-Indian peoples, but also through the redefinition of "Indian child" in 1951.

3

Rehabilitating the "Subnormal [Métis] Family" in Saskatchewan

"At the zone of contact the scene is confused and turbulent."
— *1954 Report*, Native Welfare Policy, Department of
Natural Resources[1]

Between 1944, when the Co-operative Commonwealth Federation (CCF) came to power, and 1962, the Social Democratic CCF government in Saskatchewan undertook a shift in Métis policy from one that was premised on racial difference to that of colour-blind integration. The competing logics at work in this undertaking came about initially in response to settlers' demands for removal of Indigenous presence in their midst, followed by the application of CCF's distinctive ethos of rationalizing and individualizing Indigenous peoples. CCF policies of integration not only secured lands and resources from Indigenous peoples, but also attempted to alter subjectivities by rehabilitating the hearts and minds of Métis peoples to embrace the Canadian way of upward mobility, nuclear families, and urbanization. By analysing Premier Tommy Douglas's Métis removal and relocation policies, one can witness a sequence of overlapping and conflicting logics at work indicating a paradigm shift underway soon after the war in Canada. This era is a critical chapter in the history of social work, when Canadian society moved from embracing the promises of eugenics to rehabilitation. The introduction of the Métis colony scheme reflected a logic rooted in the biological/racialized nineteenth and early twentieth century, which then shifted toward a new and insidious form of welfare colonialism. Like other well-intentioned schemes to improve the human condition, these policies ended up inflicting more harm than good on the communities they sought to help.[2] The modernist effort to socially engineer Métis peoples to embrace the values of middle-class Canadians was tainted by conflicting settler-colonial objectives that racialized Métis peoples and recast their political efforts to secure a land base as a welfare problem in need of a welfare solution.

The unique historical context in post–Second World War Saskatchewan provides historical context for an essential aspect of the origins of Indigenous transracial adoption. In June 1944 T.C. Douglas and the CCF came to power in the provincial election, winning forty-seven out of fifty-three ridings and making it the first social democratic party to be elected in North America. From the outset, the impoverished Métis and Indian communities in Saskatchewan were an area of personal concern for the premier. Bolstered by its overwhelming majority, Douglas's CCF undertook sweeping reforms in child welfare legislation and Métis rehabilitation. From 1944 onward, the party grappled with developing a Métis and Indian policy that would fit with its social democratic ethos of "humanity first." The philosophy was an all-encompassing ethos that sought to integrate all Saskatchewan citizens into society by equalizing access to education, health, and welfare. However, this policy was at odds with fulfilling the ongoing imperatives of a white settler-colonial hinterland.[3] These conflicting objectives affected the direction undertaken and certainly the outcomes of Native policies, particularly in child welfare. This chapter explores the little-known history of the CCF Métis rehabilitation policy in Saskatchewan. It argues that the focus of rehabilitation gradually shifted from rehabilitating Métis families and male heads of households to rehabilitating women and children. Through child welfare legislation and the provision of child welfare services such as fostering and transracial adoption, Saskatchewan's child welfare system incorporated the Métis children of its failed rehabilitation attempts. The process has obscured the impact of racialized poverty and loss of land. Instead, the CCF strove to demonstrate an image of cultural superiority and benevolent generosity.

Métis people in Saskatchewan did not disappear after 1885. Instead, during the critical years from 1900 to 1950 the contemporary political and national identity was formed.[4] Métis communities continued to exist in both the northern and southern portion of the province. For Métis, the years after 1885 were difficult and formative. Like the Métis in Manitoba and Alberta, poverty, lack of economic opportunities, aggressive pursuit of Métis lands by rural municipalities, and poor crop years meant that Métis who did obtain lands in exchange for scrip ended up landless. In Saskatchewan, many Métis moved to the edges of Crown lands, forming communities that were known as road allowance communities.[5] Physically and metaphorically on the margins of Prairie society, the Métis road allowance communities reflected Métis kinship patterns and enabled a form of political and cultural autonomy. Métis men worked as seasonal labourers for local farmers, clearing roots, picking rocks, and helping at harvest time.[6] Since they did not own their property, they did not pay taxes and, as a result, were prohibited from sending children to local schools or accessing adequate medical care. Despite the marginalization, Métis men's labour provided an essential component of the rural economy prior to large-scale mechanization after the Second World War. With lands cleared and with mechanization underway, Euro-Canadian farmers deemed Métis labour unnecessary and increasingly perceived the Métis road allowance communities as "embarrassments" and demanded their removal.

The virulent racism directed toward the Métis had existed in unvarnished form since 1885.[7] In this period, Maria Campbell and Howard Adams have poignantly recounted the dehumanizing racism directed at Métis in Saskatchewan.[8] White residents feared the Métis posed a health threat to white communities in close proximity to Métis road allowance communities. Writing to the provincial government in 1943, concerned citizen Antoinette Draftenza felt that the government should intervene, at least for the sake of the children. She believed that "the children are intelligent and could be taught to become respected citizens."[9] She likened the Métis to biohazard: "If we know that animals are roaming at large spreading dangerous diseases, every effort would be made to check them, yet our Métis come into our business offices and stores, mop our counters with their trachoma and otherwise infected rags and handle foods which other unsuspecting people must touch or purchase. They eat out of garbage cans; not from choice but because they are hungry. What a pity any Canadian child should have to grow up to an existence like that."[10]

She proposed the government provide health care and education to the children. Draftenza saw the potential for education and health care to instruct the Métis in embracing Euro-Canadian standards of living through which Métis bodies could be reformed and made healthy prior to integration. Through proper education, the children "would also be inspired with a desire to improve their standards of living, and their parents through them. This in turn would give them confidence in their ability to make good and work shoulder to shoulder with the rest of us."[11] Draftenza saw the Métis, educated and healthy, as sharing in the future prosperity of the province.

Increasingly white citizens of Saskatchewan placed the responsibility for Métis rehabilitation on the provincial government. Prior to integrating Métis people into the social fabric of the province, white residents agreed that the Métis "standards of living" had to be improved. The strong tone and language of this letter reflects a simultaneous revulsion and fear of contamination, as well as a desire for the uplift and integration of Métis children. It was believed that education would prepare children for their role as future citizens and enable them to educate their parents about the Euro-Canadian ideals of cleanliness and proper living.

Community leaders among the Métis organized politically to address their position in rural society. The Métis Society was established in 1938 to address outstanding Métis land claims. Locals spread throughout the province to represent them. When it reported on the Métis Society in 1939, the *Leader Post* attributed Métis poverty to the early turn of the century when Métis had obtained scrip instead of treaties for their Indigenous title.[12] The Métis Society argued, "Scrip issued at a time when land had so little value, and for the most part, as soon as this scrip was issued, it was bought up by rapacious speculators at prices that often amounted to little more than a few cents per acre."[13] Métis leaders acknowledged the precarious position of Métis in the province and sought to secure a land base similar to what had been obtained by the Alberta Métis for future generations. The society wrote to Métis politician and activist Joe Dion of Bonnyville, Alberta, and invited him to their convention in Saskatoon on 25–7 June 1940. Dion was a founding member, organizer, and president of the Métis Association of Alberta from 1932 to 1940. During this time the Métis successfully lobbied the Alberta government for an inquiry into the Métis lands issue in Alberta. The Ewing Commission was struck in 1936 and recommended

the establishment of Métis colonies where they could become re-estab-
lished on tracts of land held in common.[14]

To address the concerns of the Métis for land and livelihood, the
Saskatchewan Liberal Party established the Métis settlement of Green
Lake in 1940. The government Local Improvement District (LID), which
administered areas without municipalities, operated the settlement.[15]
Green Lake's remote location and proximity to the forest fringe enabled
residents to combine agriculture with hunting, trapping, fishing, and
animal husbandry.[16] Initially, 100–150 Métis families had resided there,
but the arrival of white settlers had left the Métis destitute. With the
establishment of the colony, white settlers were bought out, and six
townships were set aside for the exclusive use of the Métis. Families
obtained forty-acre plots with ninety-nine-year leases that had title held
by the Crown. Schools were established by Catholic sisters after a lay
teacher could not be secured. Reporting on Green Lake, Commissioner
G. Matte indicated that "this condition existed at Green Lake, but we
were able to arrange with a certain RC [Roman Catholic] sisterhood to
provide not only schooling but nursing and hygienic facilities as well,
as the health condition of these people was very poor."[17] In addition,
other community buildings were constructed, including a central farm,
cannery, flourmill, and new homes. In 1941 Commissioner Matte was
optimistic when he said, "This project is still in its infancy, but the cooperation given by the Métis people themselves augers [sic] well for
success."[18] Provision for Métis education and health by the nuns meant
government expenditures were minimal.

At the CCF Party Convention in 1944, the beginnings of a Métis policy took shape on two issues of concern for local white populations: the
need for health care and for education of Métis peoples in Saskatchewan.
Since municipalities were responsible for providing financial support
for health care for those too poor to afford insurance, those municipalities with large Métis populations struggled. The CCF resolved to seek
out an alternative arrangement where the province provided heath care
for the Métis.[19] First Nations people in the province had federally provided health and education and a constitutionally protected land base.
Indigent Métis residents became the responsibility for rural municipalities, who issued relief and hospital cards.

Unsatisfied with long-range efforts to reform the Métis, municipalities with road allowance communities put political pressure on the

government to remove and relocate the Métis. Local residents no longer had any need for Métis labour.[20] In the late 1940s a growing chorus of citizen groups vocally demanded that the province assume responsibility for the care of the Métis.[21] Another resolution passed by the Saskatchewan Rural Municipality (SARM) representatives requested that the government locate Métis in districts where they could become self-supporting from their own efforts and become responsible citizens. SARM delegates argued that the Métis should be a responsibility of the whole province, not a burden on a few municipalities. The resolution suggested that they could be self-sufficient if located in surroundings "natural to them," or away from productive, agricultural lands coveted by white settlers.

Encouraged by the success of the formation of the Union of Saskatchewan Indians by Douglas and the CCF in 1945, the government hoped to replicate its success with the Métis. A conference was held 30 July 1946 in Regina to seek the input of provincial Métis groups on the future direction of Métis policy. Forty-two Métis representatives attended from across the province. Premier Douglas and Minister of Social Welfare and Rehabilitation O.W. Valleau were present on behalf of the government, as well as Department of Social Welfare and Rehabilitation (DSWR) bureaucrats J.S. White and K.F. Forster. The meeting was chaired by Morris Schumiatcher, who was also legal counsel for the Executive Council and a "trouble-shooter concerning Indian and Métis affairs."[22] Premier Douglas had requested that representatives of all Métis people gather in Regina to bring these issues to government attention. Chairman Morris C. Shumiatcher referred to Douglas's success in bringing the Indian people together under the single voice of the Union of Saskatchewan Indians. He began, "Now the problems of the Métis are every bit as great as those of the Indians, if anything they are greater. You have all the white man's problems and some of the Indian's problems as well, so that together that makes a very formidable set of obstacles which must be overcome in order to bring to you a reasonably good share of the good things in life."[23] The policy of the government was to assist marginalized groups to obtain health, welfare, and education. The chairman explained that the government felt itself responsible to ensure that each segment of society had the same access to the "good things in life." As well, it was hoped to create a single voice, as had been done for the Indian people, for all Métis in the province.

The negotiation between the political representatives of the Métis and the government took place through the Department of Social Welfare: "Our Department of Social Welfare hopes to be able to meet and consult with you, that together we may work out some method of assisting you with your problems. We do not believe in simple handouts, and we know that you do not believe in handouts of charity."[24] Prior to the meeting, the government had determined that the solution to Métis needs would be channelled through the Department of Social Welfare and Rehabilitation. While the stated intention was to assist in forming a Métis political organization, it was more likely that the department would introduce a policy for rehabilitating individual Métis rather than address political grievances. During the conference, those gathered heard the Métis policy take shape from Premier Douglas and Minister O.W. Valleau, the minister of social welfare.

The pressing issues for the meeting included the creation of a new Métis organization, welfare, education, health and veterans affairs. Addressing the crowd, Douglas stated, "We feel that the time has come now when we ought to face up to the whole problem of the Métis people, because of the fact the Métis people will affect other groups of people in the Province, and in particular communities where the Métis people live. Now that attitude of the government I can put in a very few simple words.... What we feel is that any group of people in our province, given an opportunity, given a proper chance, can do for themselves if only they are given a chance. In other words, our idea is not so much to help a group of people as to help them to help themselves."[25]

This statement illustrates significant conflict about the government's purpose and goals for the Métis. Nevertheless, the intended approach emphasized that the Métis would be integrated as individuals, not as a collective.

Many of the Métis from the agricultural communities came with suggestions for settlement and housing assistance from the government. Those in the northern areas sought to obtain reassurances that their communities would not be disturbed. While the intention was for the government to hear Métis input, Minister of Social Welfare Valleau indicated his lack of enthusiasm for a collective approach to resolving land issues: "I am not at all sure myself that the idea of group settlements is the wisest thing. You see you people are not a definite race apart. The *ultimate solution will be absorption* into the general population. I don't think there is any doubt about that."[26] The government was unwilling to purchase land for the Métis. They aimed to assist with uplift, albeit ambiguously: "With your help we can give you people a certain pride in yourselves, and you can't have that pride in yourselves until you are really proud of yourselves."[27] There was much disagreement throughout the conference amongst the Métis about the future of the provincial organization; however, many agreed about the need for secure land. Their historic experience of dislocation proved the value of a secure land base. The meeting ended without a clear articulation of the issues or their solutions.

The ongoing and conflicted public outcry for government intervention stimulated an interprovincial meeting to find a solution. Chaired by J.H. Sturdy, Saskatchewan's minister of health and welfare (who had replaced Valleau after the election in 1948), the government hosted an interprovincial conference to seek out possible solutions to the Métis situation. Inviting other welfare directors from Prairie provinces, Sturdy outlined his view of the problem, saying that the Métis fell "short of the economic and cultural level of the white population" and accordingly had "a higher incidence of illiteracy, destitution, illegitimacy and other social problems."[28] He believed that their living standards and "cultural level" needed to be improved. He believed that they misused family allowances and public assistance by not purchasing the proper foods and essentials and condemned Métis parents for failing to seek regular employment. He recognized that the growth of mechanical farming had eliminated much of the need for farm labour, and that many of the communities were isolated from employment opportunities. Finally, Minister Sturdy lamented that, despite the assistance being given to the Métis, the situation was worsening.[29]

The conference recommended approaching Métis and Indian rehabilitation with the assistance of the federal government.[30] Difficulties faced by Indigenous residents of the province were seen primarily as lack of adjustment to the Euro-Canadian nuclear family model and the inability to integrate into the modernizing economy and society in the West.[31] Not surprisingly, the solution was increasing social welfare interventions. While the long-term plan to address the growing social distance between white and Indigenous communities in the province was a comprehensive, federally supported Indian and Métis welfare response, the provincial government moved forward with its program of rehabilitation and relocation.

The term *rehabilitation* was increasingly employed by CCF officials to describe the process by which the Métis people would embrace the value system of the surrounding Euro-Canadian settler communities and cease to require government assistance and support. After the Second World War there was renewed interest in resource development and government intervention, particularly in the north, which led to fundamental changes to the Indigenous fur and fishing economy. This tension led to what one observer termed a confused and turbulent contact zone. The primary outcome was family breakdown and intergenerational conflict.[32] In the south, poverty and loss of land had pushed the Métis into a tenuous existence dependent on seasonal employment and government relief. From the point of view of government officials, the high birth rate exacerbated these problems. "It would appear that this process of change is giving rise to a problem from the point of view of the government in that budgetary appropriations on behalf of these people have increased in recent years."[33] Government rehabilitation policy, established in the early years of the CCF government, strove toward "the gradual integration under which the Métis ultimately are encouraged to develop into a mature, independent and self-sufficient group of people able to conduct their own enterprises and to solve their particular problems without excessive reference to government or other agencies."[34] Rehabilitation sought to educate Métis families to adopt the work ethic, dress, language, land tenure, aspirations, family structure, and political outlook of the majority Anglo-Canadian Saskatchewan residents. The virulent racism that flourished among the settler population in the post-war period was left unaddressed and unacknowledged.[35]

Tenets of the Social Gospel and moral purity were deeply embedded within the social and political identity of Tommy Douglas and the CCF party. During the CCF years in power, the state shaped the subjectivities of provincial citizens through the aegis of reform efforts in education and modernization of social welfare programs.[36] While, unlike Indian wards of the federal government, the Métis did not experience a distinctive legal regime dictating their relationship to the state, integration came through the legal and political structure of the province.[37] As Joan Sangster points out, "Even if 'race' as a legal category was not articulated in Canadian statues, racist ideology and operations resonated through the articulation of the law."[38] That Métis children went from being a fraction of the child welfare cases to the predominant number over the two decades under discussion illustrates how welfare legislation was articulated in the lives of Métis women and children.

Many of Tommy Douglas's accomplishments as premier of Saskatchewan and an MP in Parliament have been well documented. In fact, Canadians voted Douglas the greatest Canadian of all time, over Terry Fox, Pierre Trudeau, and Frederick Banting in a 2004 CBC poll.[39] However, there is a dearth of information in standard biographies on relations with First Nations and Métis peoples. The traditional historical accounts of the CCF and biographies of Douglas lack meaningful analysis of his view on Native issues. With the exception of Laurie Barron's *Walking in Indian Moccasins*, a book devoted explicitly to these policies, biographers have focused their discussion of Indian Affairs and Métis issue to a few paragraphs, with special mention of Douglas being made honorary chief, We-a-ga-sha, in 1945.[40]

Several historic events shaped Douglas's intellectual, spiritual, and political development.[41] The widespread and indiscriminate devastation of the Depression on the Prairies played a critical role in his reformist outlook. According to biographers McLeod and McLeod, "The spectre of poverty, in the city and in the countryside, challenged the youthful pastor to rededicate himself to the social gospel."[42] Douglas followed a route similar route to that of J.S. Woodsworth, his intellectual and political mentor, mixing ministry with sociological inquiry, eventually abandoning both for provincial and national politics.[43]

Another impact of the Depression on Douglas was his advocacy of eugenic solutions, most notably in his MA thesis.[44] Biographers have explained this anomaly as further evidence of Douglas's faith in the role of the expert and as part of a misdirected but not uncommon belief in the pseudo-scientific promise of eugenics in the interwar period.[45] When Nazi Germany began to sterilize its opponents, many on the Left grew disillusioned with eugenics. Douglas came to realize that the Nuremburg Race Laws of 1935 led to the slaughter of millions in Eastern Europe, and he dropped his support for eugenics. As evidence of his disavowal of eugenic solutions, while premier, Douglas soundly rejected any attempt to initiate eugenics as part of the public health-care system.[46] Unlike Alberta and British Columbia, Saskatchewan did not politically or legally develop sterilization laws targeting specific populations.[47] Douglas and the CCF embraced a social rather than biological

Tommy Douglas (R-A57294)

solution to criminality and illegitimacy, out of their left-of-centre belief
in government involvement in the conduct and reform of society.[48]

Even though Douglas's master's thesis in sociology from McMaster
University, "The Problems of the Subnormal Family," did propose
eugenic solutions, it was interested primarily in sociological interventions.[49] The disorderly "subnormal families," according to Douglas, had
a detrimental impact on the local community and society in general.

While the families that Douglas studied were non-Indigenous, his overall recommendations to rehabilitate the "subnormal" class bore a striking resemblance to early CCF Métis policy. Because of the apparent danger of "subnormals" to the surrounding community and their ongoing need for financial support, Douglas argued that this class should legitimately be subject to the intervention and regulation of the state. For Douglas and other social reformers, first, in order to be disciplined, the "subnormals" would have to be represented. This legitimized the invasive surveys and intellectual queries into the private lives of citizens.[50] Through his voyeuristic enumeration of the impoverished residents in Weyburn, Saskatchewan, Douglas shared an outlook similar to that of other middle-class reformer men who ventured into the working-class areas and homes in the name of scholarship or social intervention. In later years, many dispossessed and impoverished Métis people fit the criteria Douglas utilized to categorize those who were "subnormal." Surveys were conducted among the Métis to obtain demographic and personal information.

According to Douglas, "The subnormal family presents the most appalling of all family problems."[51] In addition to containing members who appeared mentally deficient, families were seen as falling below accepted moral standards, "subject to social disease, and finally so improvident as to be a public charge."[52] Douglas proposed a new solution for the social worker, legislator, and educator "to a problem long neglected, too long placed in the category of unmentionables."[53] Douglas's concerns hinged on the unbridled sexuality and perceived irresponsible reproduction of the women, the evidence of which was their large families. "Surely the policy of allowing the subnormal family to bring into the world large numbers of individuals to fill our jails and mental institutions, and to live upon charity, is one of consummate folly,"[54] Douglas lamented. Not only was the impact felt in the economic cost to society, but also in the contamination of the surrounding "normal" community. Having the "subnormal" live amongst the normal led to three interrelated social outcomes with which Douglas was concerned. First was the danger of sexual and medical contamination.[55] Second, there was a degeneration of academic standards in the classrooms, where he feared that "a large number of subnormal children in the community cannot but have a detrimental effect on the mental standards and intellectual attainments of the community."[56] Finally, there were the moral effects of the female "sexual delinquents" who were responsible for lowering the moral standards of those they contacted. Unlike the "normal" young women, these women lacked a sense of shame for unwed pregnancies, clear evidence according to the thinking of the time that they were mentally defective. "At the same time some of these girls become illegal mothers and much of the stigma has been removed."[57] The high economic needs of the "subnormal family" increased the taxes for the whole community through expenses of medical bills, dental bills, charity, and education. With their children cared for in orphanages or on relief, Douglas stated, "Instead of having the upkeep of 12 women, the city now has the cost of 175 individuals on its hands."[58] Douglas focused his attention on women's reproductive abilities and their moral guidance/instruction within their families. On both counts, he judged the women harshly and deficiently, while he demonstrated they were a clear threat to provincial society.

The environment was implicated in the moral state of the families. However, Douglas was at a loss on whether it was the cause or the effect. Moral and physical qualities intertwined in the "filth, squalor and unwholesome conditions." For example, "Case no. 1 where two entire families are living in a three room shack. Privacy is of course impossible, and despite the fact that the children are normal, there are unmistakable signs of moral degeneration, because of the home influence."[59] The subnormal social environment encouraged the lack of adherence to decent moral codes accepted in the larger society as the families in general "seem to have no feeling of shame." He was especially critical of unwed mothers, since "the girls who have given birth to illegitimate offspring have in the main refused to part with them, and seem to feel no compunction about the censure of society."[60] Among middle- and working-class families, intense shame at illegitimate offspring reflected the "proper" moral sensibilities. Unwed mothers in working- and middle-class families in this period often gave birth in maternity homes and relinquished children for adoption to avoid the stigma of being a "fallen woman."[61] According to Douglas, maintaining the shame of unwed pregnancy was an essential component of regulating women's sexuality and an aspect of moral citizenship.

Douglas's final chapter spelled out his formula to address the problem of the subnormal family. He posited a new role for the state assisted by the churches: rehabilitation. Families deemed by officials to be subnormal would be compelled to embrace the values of the majority society through law, education, and moral reform. He argued, "Since the state has the problem of legislating in the best interests of society, and since we have seen that the subnormal family is an ever increasing menace physically, mentally and morally, to say nothing of a constantly rising expense, it is surely the duty of the state to meet this problem."[62] Douglas proposed the improvement of marriage laws, articulated a policy of segregation for those deemed "subnormal," and proposed the sterilization of the unfit while providing increased knowledge of birth control.

Douglas was interested primarily in social segregation: relocating the "subnormal" class where the physical, mental, and moral effects listed would no longer contaminate the normal community. He claimed, "There can be little doubt that this group exercise an influence that is detrimental and which could be best removed by segregating them."[63] Men who were able to work but lacked initiative should be placed on state farms or colonies where competent supervisors could make decisions for them. Similarly, Douglas recommended, "With proper supervision the women could become better housewives and better managers of family finance." In addition, separate schools with specialized curriculums should be developed that would isolate students from contaminating other children, while teaching them useful skills.[64]

This treatise on the potential for the state to rehabilitate the "subnormal" contains substantial interest in moral and gender rehabilitation. Unlike earlier periods, when the state looked to churches and private charities to effect the work of moral regeneration, Douglas envisioned, then enacted, a colony regime directed by social welfare experts to assimilate Métis peoples. In interviews in the late forties he still utilized terms like *subnormal* to describe impoverished, under-educated groups of Saskatchewan residents. It was hoped that Métis subjectivities – that is the living standards, family structure, hygiene practices, kinship patterns, and educational and economic aspirations – would be refashioned to facilitate absorption into the surrounding settler communities by embracing the moral standards of Euro-Canadians.[65] Utilizing the early colony schemes and rehabilitation policies, the state attempted to bring about the moral regulation of Métis families in reproduction and proper gender roles.[66] According to Mariana Valverde, "Moral regulation was an important aspect to ruling, helping to constitute class, gender, sexual and race relations by interpreting both social action and individual identity as fundamentally ethical."[67] Tommy Douglas, as

progressive reformer, embraced the opportunity to employ his rehabilitation strategy once he became premier and was supported by rural
municipalities who sought government solutions to their economic burdens. This approach overlooked such complexities as the long-standing
issues of land loss, race, and the complicity of the surrounding white
communities in the economic marginalization of Métis families.

The CCF began relocating Métis road allowance families as early as
1947.[68] Green Lake, the previous Patterson government experiment,
became the destination of several relocated Métis families from communities around the province.[69] Henry Pelletier was married and
working at the time of the relocation and recalled the promise of forty
acres, assistance in setting up farms, and relief to live on until they were
able to clear the land. Henry recalled that as the family and community
waited for the train to arrive, they looked back to see their homes on
fire.[70]

Other Métis experienced having homes burnt and the disappoint-
ment when they arrived at the new community. Métis leaders Jim
Sinclair and Jim Durocher saw relocations as a way to rid white communities of the embarrassing reminder of their intolerance:

> Again to help us, but really to clear the land of our people. Try to
> shift us where no one was and they had the old Green Lake project,
> of which they shipped our people in trains, not in trains, in boxcars
> in 1947. I think in '46 and '47. They moved all our little belongings
> into the boxcars. I remember that as a boy and one of the things that
> really bothered me and it still bothers me today, our people lived in
> tar paper shacks, you know and very little shelter, and as these peo-
> ple left their community with all their stuff piled on their wagons
> and chairs and the little bit they had, the houses were purposely
> set on fire as they were leaving, as if to say it to them, these people
> "Don't ever come back here again." And that was done at Crescent
> Lake, that was done in Lestock, and it was done in other communi-
> ties. And as I, as I met with other half-breeds a few years later they
> had the same experiences. So again, it was, you know, people speak
> about the Holocaust for the Jews. Well, it was much the same for
> us in terms of trying to drive us from one place to another. And
> it was difficult for us, and it wasn't very long 'till most of those
> people just made their way back to Regina. And then we set up a

tent city, then we start moving into the nuisance grounds around Regina where all the half-breeds lived, and then we had tent cities, and then people would come in there with their cars and trucks at night and run over people's tents, you know, drive people out.[71]

Jim Sinclair felt the reason the government moved the Métis was that they were a political embarrassment: "I don't think it was the farmers so much. I think it was just the embarrassment to the government of Saskatchewan at that time and of course their philosophy of hoping to find us a better life, which never really was the issue. It was to get rid of us and put us in the North. Whether we survived or not, they didn't care."[72] They attempted to hide the shame of Métis poverty and marginalization by relocation to the north. "Just hide us wherever they could and hide their shame for the way they were treating the half-breeds and to keep our rights, sort of under the rug and to hope that we would never organize. And I think the worse they treated us the more we became aware of what was happening, and the more we became aware of what had to be done to move ourselves into a position to be part of Canada."[73] The relocation and rehabilitation of Métis road allowance communities after 1947 was one facet of the early CCF Métis policy.

Oral histories collected by the Gabriel Dumont Institute from Métis elders provide a narrative of the interconnection between relocation policies and the Green Lake children's shelter. Green Lake resident Peter Bishop was a child during the 1940s. He recalled the Green Lake shelter and the arrivals from the Métis resettlement program:

They had a couple of shelters there for mostly Métis kids from southern Saskatchewan. They were shipped there and they were looked after by the government. They had set up those houses. In fact there's one building that's still standing up there. That's the old Alec Bishop Childcare Centre. That's one of the shelters. And they had shipped a bunch of Métis, I think it was the late 1940s early '50s from all over southern Saskatchewan. Yeah. These are the road allowance people that Nora's talking about. Glen Mary and Duck Lake? Glen Mary, yes. And Kinistino. Baljennie – all those places. That's where these people came from. Okay? They arrived in the spring and they stored most of the furniture in the church. It was

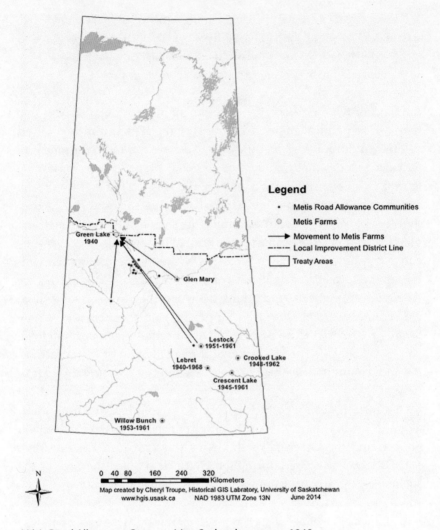

Métis Road Allowance Communities, Saskatchewan, ca. 1940

an only church by where we lived. My Dad gave them permission.
And they lived in tents because right away, soon as they moved to
Green Lake, they had to walk to the bush to cut logs so they could
build their own homes for the winter, before the winter set in. And
it was the local people that helped them, because they didn't know
how. My dad was one of them. And what was sad, particularly
sad about the children that came with them, they'd never gone
to school. They weren't allowed. See a lot of the road allowance

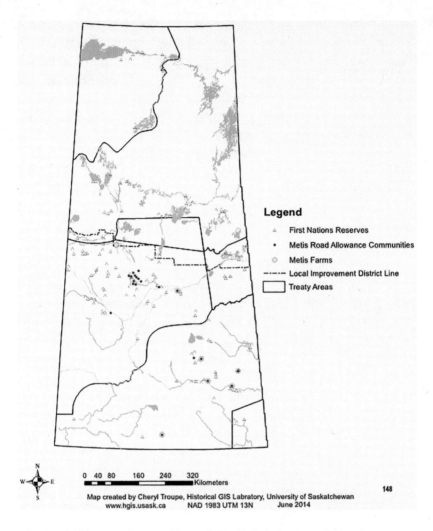

Legend

⚲ First Nations Reserves

• Metis Road Allowance Communities

⊙ Metis Farms

–·–·– Local Improvement District Line

☐ Treaty Areas

N
W—✦—E
S

0 40 80   160   240   320
▬▬▬▬▬▬▬▬▬ Kilometers

148

Map created by Cheryl Troupe, Historical GIS Labratory, University of Saskatchewan
www.hgis.usask.ca   NAD 1983 UTM 13N   June 2014

Métis Road Allowance Communities and First Nations Reserves, Saskatchewan, ca. 1940

people lived close to Indian reserves. The Indians wouldn't allow them in their schools, so they never went to school.[74]

Another former resident of the Lestock road allowance, Isadore Pelletier, a Métis elder who experienced relocation as a child, shared his memories of being moved from Lestock to Green Lake. He and his family lived on a road allowance community called the Chicago line, ten miles from Lestock. The men worked for farmers during summer months. They picked roots, helped with threshing, and chopped bush. Isadore recalled, "My dad would always make enough for 10 bags of flour. We'd be all right. Make it through the winter, we'd hunt deer and trap mink and muskrats, eat turnips and potatoes from the garden. My job was to start the fire, then go out to feed and water the horses."[75] The seasonal wage labour that was supplemented with hunting and trapping provided the family with an adequate living.

During the relocation, the family arrived in Meadow Lake, then Green Lake, where Isadore recalled the family received a cool welcome. The new arrivals placed additional strain on dwindling resources and job opportunities in Green Lake. Isadore felt, "They [Green Lake residents] resented us. Children had problems in the school. And it seemed even there, it was 'just like we always were.'"[76] Gradually the relocated Métis began to leave, since it appeared that there was not enough to make a living there. He remembered feeling bad for his community: "We made it back but all the way back, we were harassed."[77] It was the recommendation of a local Métis leader in Lebret, L—— who was working for the CCF government that led the local Métis to embrace the relocation to Green Lake as a new opportunity for future prosperity. He recalled the reasons the community were given: "We were living in squalor, children not going to school. Those were some of the reasons they gave." Upon returning to Lestock, the family found that there was nothing left and went to Regina. Isadore remembered fondly, "It was such a tight community. We had self-government. That was what we had, and it was good."[78]

Premier Douglas, who certainly intellectually and politically supported if not initiated the relocation and segregation of the Métis, faced criticism for the outcome of the relocations from opposition MLAs. Defensive of the government's Métis policy, Douglas replied to the opposition criticism from Vic DeShaye, Liberal MLA for the Melville riding:

> For some time the DSW has been working on a program for re-establishing the Métis on a self-supporting basis and has been doing so in cooperation with the several municipalities where they are located. However, in view of your comments in the legislature on Thurs March 2, I would take it that you are opposed to moving these people from the road allowances and re-establishing them in

areas where they can become self-supporting citizens. It is difficult for me to see how you can oppose that action of the government in moving these people when you are speaking in the legislature then write to me privately to ask what we are going to go about moving them. It is about time you made up your mind whether you are anxious to have these people rehabilitated or whether you are merely concerned with making political capital out of the situation.

I don't think that municipalities will take very kindly to the fact that the first time any constructive steps were taken to re-establish the Métis you did everything possible to have this action by the government misrepresented and misunderstood. I shall make it my business at my earliest opportunity to acquaint the municipalities in question with the stand which you have taken in the legislature as opposed to the concern which your letter shows for the difficult position in which the municipalities find themselves in connection with the Métis problem.[79]

In response, DeShaye reiterated the point that the relocation policy challenged the CCF image of a humane and just political alternative in its treatment of the Métis people. He replied, "If you will read the transcript of my speech you will see that what I criticized was not the movement of the Métis to Green Lake, but the failure to provide an adequate program and accommodation for them at Green Lake. The delegation that saw me said that they had to move away from Green Lake because they and their families had only tents to live in, and no accommodation was being made available for them for winter. Then when some returned to find their homes burnt they became a greater responsibility than before."[80]

The attempt to craft a Métis policy based on relocation and rehabilitation left the Métis further impoverished and at the mercy of municipalities. The financial commitment required to adequately re-establish and rehabilitate Métis at the Green Lake Métis colony was never in place, and Douglas's vision of the relocations and rehabilitation merely removed road allowance families and cast them adrift in the province.[81] In addition to Green Lake, the CCF government operated experimental farm colonies at Lebret and Willow Bunch, and smaller colonies at Crescent Lake, Baljennie, Crooked Lake, Duck Lake, and Glen Mary (see map and appendix).[82]

The implementation and outcomes of the relocation and rehabilitation policies at Green Lake and elsewhere received mixed reviews. In 1953 D.F. Symington, a Saskatchewan conservation officer, amateur ethnographer, and author, extoled the benefits of the CCF policy of relocation and rehabilitation. His "Métis Rehabilitation" in *Canadian Geographer* offered readers visual contrasts between the old and the new policies. He emphasized that rehabilitation held great promise for the Métis, whom he termed "a group that can be considered the west's forgotten minority."[83] Like others, he believed that the 850 Métis in Green Lake were in the midst of an economic and social revolution from extremely primitive to modern living. Until the government intervened, the Métis had "been gypsy-like, untrained and unwilling to work, despised by and despising the prosperous white man."[84] He stated, "Rehabilitation must take into consideration the traits and peculiarities of the Métis as a cultural group and as individuals, such as the Métis tendency to stress the value of personal enjoyment on a day to day basis, material possessions to be valued as they add to the enjoyment, discarded as they become a burden."[85] The goal of rehabilitation was to raise the standard of living in community. "In other words he had to make them wish to work."[86] Unlike the white settlers, who needed to work in order to eat, the Indigenous people "have never needed to work in order to exist, and had no such incentive."[87] Eliminating the seasonal cycles of living off the land ensured that by necessity the Métis would embrace subsistence agriculture, wage labour, or both.

According to this early publication, the relocated Métis from the southern road allowance communities brought a twofold benefit to the Green Lake community: they brought "new blood into the Green Lake settlement, where for two centuries the dozen major families had been intermarrying,"[88] and the relocated Métis had depended on social aid, living in shacks on road allowances, and by contrast in Green Lake, they had been given lumber by the government. For those who remained to build, "There are now none without board floors and roofs, and the unutterable filth of a decade ago has been replaced by something approaching cleanliness."[89] The writer failed to mention the large percentage of families who chose to leave rather than remain in Green Lake. The rehabilitation envisaged through farming plots would bring the Métis what had eluded them as seasonal trappers and hunters: a notion of private property and elimination of mobility. Symington claimed that, in "tying themselves to plots of land, they are beginning to look on their plots as their own."[90] Finally, rehabilitation included the education of Métis children. The next phase in the rehabilitation of the Métis would focus on Métis women in order to inculcate proper notions of morality by rehabilitating Métis views of illegitimacy. Symington observed, "Most of them remain amoral, and illegitimacy occasions no stigma."[91] Like the "subnormals" of Douglas's master's thesis, according to Symington the Métis lacked the sentiment of shame attached to unwed motherhood.

In response to fallout from the failed CCF Métis policy, a new partnership was struck. In 1955 the Local Improvement District, the government branch responsible for the administration of the Green Lake Settlement, and the Department of Social Welfare and Rehabilitation began to work together to solve the "Métis problem" in Green Lake. Together, government bureaucrats began to develop a new direction in Métis policy, bringing the expertise of social workers and social welfare professionals into Métis policies in a new fashion. Like elsewhere in Canada, a "welfare economy" was beginning to emerge, as the expansion of settlement and fishing and game restrictions reduced subsistence hunting and gathering, and growing industrial activities gave preference to white male labourers over Indigenous.[92] Despite officials' belief that their involvement would be temporary, the welfare state expanded exponentially after 1950, as did Indigenous poverty.[93]

4

The Green Lake Children's Shelter Experiment: From Institutionalization to Integration in Saskatchewan

The brief headline "Shelter Opened for Métis" in the *Regina Leader Post* on 29 September 1949 detailed the official opening of the Green Lake Children's Shelter for orphaned and neglected Métis children. The provincial CCF government built the first non-denominational children's institution in Saskatchewan specifically for the Métis, which housed up to fifty children and employed fourteen staff members in 1947. The article captured the words of Minister of Social Welfare and Rehabilitation John Sturdy, who spoke of the long-term goals for the children. In "dealing with the rehabilitation of the Métis, they should have pride in their ancestry. It is hoped all these children will eventually be placed in foster homes, or after reaching the age of 16 they will be able to take their place in society."[1] The Green Lake Children's Shelter closed amid a small scandal in 1951, four years after its opening. It stands as the earliest rehabilitation experiment applied to Indigenous children in the province. The Green Lake Children's Shelter utilized the application of CCF secular therapeutic assimilation strategy and was the first expression of Saskatchewan's Indigenous transracial adoption policy.

Rehabilitation was one side of a two-sided coin. On the flip side was relocation. Coinciding with the opening of the children's shelter was another experiment undertaken with members of the provincial Métis population. The article entitled "Experiment with Métis: Punnichy Settlers Did Not Stay Long – Children's Home Opened"[2] detailed the relocation of southern Métis people to the northern community of

Green Lake. Saskatchewan readers were given a brief history, complete with pictures of recently constructed buildings, and introduced to the Department of Social Welfare and Rehabilitation's Métis strategy. The contact zone was depicted as a liminal space requiring proper guidance in order to emerge fully modernized and integrated into the provincial society and economy. The author stated, "Green Lake now hangs precariously – in socio-economic balance – between a fur trade past and a frontier agricultural potential."[3] However, readers were assured that despite the regressive tendencies, indications pointed to a bright future for both the Métis and the north with reassuring images of progress under government supervision. Happy children in front of the newly built children's shelter stood smiling in one picture, and another had the principal proudly standing in front of the recently constructed schoolhouse. Another picture depicted the recently built church, and another a large and impressive government building. The three agents of modernization – the church, government, and school – would provide the necessary direction to ensure Métis children's future would be among white society. The photos also provide an eerie representation of Douglas's agents of intervention to correct the sociological problems of the subnormal family.[4] Under the photo of the smiling children in front of the shelter, the caption read, "Happy little girls, with children's Home in Background. Homeless Métis children have a community home financed by the government, until they become adopted into family homes."[5] The adoptive homes in question were with white families who the government hoped would play a role in their future.

Green Lake was the destination the government chose to relocate twenty-one Métis families from the Punnichy area and, eventually, several other Métis communities across the province.[6] According to the article, "The families had been squatting on road allowances without economic facilities or much hope for the future. They were given 40 acres at Green Lake of bush land with much of it cultivatable, with the option of 40 more acres. Whatever the reason, of the 21 families, 6 remain." The missing Métis did not seem to dampen enthusiasm for the project. When asked where the majority of the families had gone, the deputy minister of social welfare and rehabilitation, J.S. White, replied, "Where have the other 15 families gone? We don't know, though some of them did head back for Punnichy."[7] It was hoped that those settlers who did remain would stay and prove themselves in the

ST. PASCAL school at Green Lake, with Principal John Poitras in foreground. Three nuns assist the principal with 165 pupils in grades 1 to 9. Completed October, 1947, and built largely from spruce lumber produced in the Green Lake vicinity, the school building is wired for electric light generated in a diesel plant supplying the inner settlement.

BY JIM WRIGHT

GREEN LAKE settlement, a hundred air-miles north-west of Prince Albert, is 35 miles north-east of Meadow Lake.

The settlement by the eastern shore of long and narrow Green Lake (marked on large-scale maps), is like many another northern outpost. It is both old and new. A hundred years older than many prairie agricultural villages, Green Lake was a Hudson's Bay Company fur-trading post after absorption of the North West Company.

Today's Green Lake is new, both buildings and ideas. The Roman Catholic Church, which entered the area in the wake of the Hudson's Bay Company, abandoned its original log church building on the old site, now occupies a frame building on the

MÉTIS

Continued on Page 6, Column 4

Parishioners leaving the new Roman Catholic Church after Sunday afternoon service.

Announce Change In Train Arrivals

A general shakeup in Canadian National Railway schedules in and out of Saskatoon was announced this morning by E. G. Wickerson, district passenger agent. Effective Sunday there will be a number of changes in the arrival and departure times of trains at Saskatoon.

The westbound service from Montreal and other points in eastern Canada will arrive in Saskatoon at 10.10 o'clock every evening and leave for the west at 10.40 o'clock. The returning train from the west will arrive

Saskatchewan government administration building
—Saskatoon Star Phoenix

"Experiment with Métis," Saskatoon *Star Phoenix*, 1949

semi-agricultural settlement schemes. The messages printed in Saskatchewan were intended to be positive. The CCF government demonstrated that it was addressing concerns that had been raised about the condition of the Métis by the public and municipalities.

THE SOCIAL WORK PROFESSION AND THE RATIONALIZED LOGICS OF INDIGENOUS CHILD REMOVAL IN SASKATCHEWAN

Addressing the Regional Conference on Social Welfare in June 1946, Tommy Douglas articulated his vision for Saskatchewan in charting a new course for government-administered welfare services: "In terms of technological progress we will measure our success by what society does for the under privileged, the subnormal, for the widow, for the aged and the unwanted child, and recognize her responsibility for the weak in society. Canada will, in this way, take her place among the great nations of the World."[8] Through rehabilitating families to take their proper place in the modernizing province, the CCF envisioned social work professionals providing expert therapeutic services, case by case, for the "subnormals" and others deemed in need of assistance. The recently reorganized Department of Social Welfare would be the vanguard of social welfare and child welfare practice as the state moved in to ensure families carried out their responsibilities toward younger members, and offered therapeutic support for mothers without male breadwinners. The gendered nature of child welfare legislation has been identified by feminist historians to penalize mothers and fathers who were unable or unwilling to provide for offspring.[9] As Veronica Strong-Boag has argued, "The rights of those who were judged to be inadequate family men were to be limited by the male-led government that would better protect the nations' human resources."[10] Métis men, who had been provided the opportunity to be rehabilitated into the proper role of breadwinner and agriculturalist, were deemed to have failed by 1961. Reports of illegitimacy and common-law relationships among the Métis required the interventions of social workers who had become the nation's leading experts on the "problem of the unwed mother,"[11] while offering solutions to the dilemma of Indigenous integration. Métis children entered the child welfare system via three facets of child welfare legislation: apprehension due to neglect, identification through unmarried parents legislation, and legal adoption.[12]

Social workers came to play a critical role in assisting newcomers to adjust to the norms and laws of Canadian citizenship. As trusted "gatekeepers," social workers employed strategies to ensure that immigrant families and individuals integrate as modern democratic citizens for the health of the nation itself.[13] Mildred Battel, Saskatchewan's first professionally trained social worker, was part of the team engaged in modernizing the Department of Social Welfare, formerly the Department of Reconstruction, Labour and Public Welfare.[14] The development of Saskatchewan's child welfare legislation and administration had taken place gradually during the early twentieth century. Provincial responsibility for child welfare and social aid had been based on the division of powers at Confederation in the British North America Act, with "all matters generally of a merely local or private nature" given to the provinces.[15] At the time, caring for children was the responsibility of families, the churches, and voluntary societies; by the twentieth century reform efforts in public education, health, and welfare increasingly saw the state playing a larger role. Child protection legislation in Saskatchewan had been closely based on similar legislation first passed in Ontario under J.J. Kelso, entitled "An Act for the Prevention of Cruelty to and Better Protection of Children, 1893."[16] The defining aspect of child welfare legislation was the transfer of guardianship by the court from biological parents to an agency. Assisted by J.J. Kelso, Saskatchewan passed the Child Protection Act in 1908, after which a number of Children's Aid Societies arose in cities and towns across Saskatchewan. The Bureau of Child Protection formed in 1911 to administer the legislation and provide services for children in areas not covered by Children's Aid Societies.[17]

In the early years of the child welfare branch, the underlying premise, that "children must be protected," was based on the courts' determination of the "best interests of the child." The primary method of protection was through removing children from the care of parents into the care of the state, utilizing community resources such as foster homes, adoption, and institutions.[18] The Bureau of Child Protection, which operated from 1911 to 1944, had been the government agency responsible for implementing the legislation, and Children's Aid Societies made up of volunteers were tasked with the administration of

Mildred Battel, child welfare director, 1952–65 (R-A11592-1, SAB)

Children at Green Lake Orphanage, top, and the orphanage building, bottom (images above and on subsequent pages courtesy Lawrence Arnault, Gabriel Dumont Institute Archives)

Theresa Aubichon, Lillian Cook, Stella Aubichon, and unknown

protecting neglected or orphaned (primarily non-Indigenous) children. Not until the 1930s was there mention of case work and social work approaches, as well as the terms *unmarried mother* and *putative father*. The first social worker in the Bureau of Child Welfare was hired in 1943.[19] 1940 was the first year that the Métis problem was cited in the annual reports of the Department of Social Welfare revealing the prior exclusion of Métis families and children from social work services, while also separating Métis out as racialized and in need of specialized therapeutic interventions.[20]

In 1944 the Department of Social Welfare took over responsibility for the Child Welfare Branch and replaced the former Department of Reconstruction, Labour and Public Welfare under Minister O. Valleau.[21] One of the first projects of the newly reorganized department was planning for a children's shelter at the Métis settlement at Green Lake "to give proper care and training to upwards of 50 children who are either illegitimate or orphaned" as well as "a long-range plan for the rehabilitation of the

Roy (Kennedy) Eva, unknown, and Morin "Roy" Flavie

Métis population in the province."[22] There were plans for expansion of child welfare, and field staff in child welfare were encouraged to take courses in social work; it was hoped that the department would have a complement of fully trained social workers in the near future.[23]

The Green Lake Children's Shelter was a short-lived experiment in providing residential care for Métis children in a remote location using southern white employees. The shelter provided specifically for "Métis children who are wards of department, and from Northern parts of the province, neglected and illegitimate."[24] As the early social welfare professionals in Saskatchewan stated, often "neglected" Métis children were not so much in need of protection from neglectful parents as from poverty. Of prime concern was re-education:

> In certain areas of the province, neglect among this group is very serious – neglect arising from inadequate school facilities and improper housing. When it has become necessary to apprehend the children the problem of proper placement is difficult due to prejudice and the difficulty that the children have in adjusting themselves to a new environment. In cooperation with the Department of Municipal Affairs a survey was made of children in the Green Lake Area and as a result of this survey plans were instituted to build a shelter in which an attempt will be made to specifically train these children.[25]

While at the shelter, the children had access to medical and nursing care and attended a nearby school operated by the Department of Education. The non-denominational shelter opened 5 February 1947 and cared for twenty-five children up to sixteen years old. Non-Indigenous child welfare experts from the southern portion of the province staffed the shelter. Alice Dales, a child welfare consultant and social worker in the province reflected that "the decision was based on the assumption that it would be easier for the children if they were left in the surroundings familiar to them; because of their ethnic origin it was thought it would be difficult for them to move out to integrate with the 'white' outside world." [26] The social worker rationalized that Métis children required an institutional setting in Green Lake, rather than direct placement into foster homes, because moving children from their surroundings would have been too abrupt. Once at the home "most of them slept in beds for the first time and enjoyed foods and clothes unknown to the world they had formerly lived in. It was surprising how quickly these children were able to adapt themselves to the standards of their white cousins and how much pride and pleasure they took out of the finer things of life." Part of the government rationale was that Métis children needed to be trained in Euro-Canadian hygienic standards prior to being fit for adoption into white, middle-class family homes.

In the article documenting the rise and fall of this experiment, Saskatchewan adoption worker Alice Dales documented the shift from institutionalization to integration of Indigenous children. Likewise, she revealed her own and the government's racial and class-based ideology that informed their approach to the Métis children. The children were characterized as parentless and in need of rescue. She inaccurately claimed, "These children were from broken homes, orphans, children of unmarried parents, and children of unknown origin,"[27] rather than admitting that they were far from parentless children, and had possibly been abducted from poor Métis families and incarcerated for this social experiment. What had earlier been characterized as improper housing and lack of access to school facilities in the annual report was recast disingenuously to reinforce tropes of Indigenous inferiority and disordered family relations.[28] When explaining the rationale for closing the home, Dales blamed the community of Green Lake itself. She claimed that Green Lake suffered from "regressive tendencies" and was thus unsuitable for a true rehabilitation project.[29] She felt that "the standard of living is low, and because of the lack of opportunity and education the Métis appear shiftless and lacking in initiative."[30] Despite the commonly accepted child welfare practice that considered the best place for children was in the natural family setting, the Métis children, because of their race, were categorized as an exceptional case requiring an exceptional response. Forty to forty-five children, aged one to sixteen, had originally been part of the experiment.

Soon after the opening of the Green Lake shelter, difficulties arose. Documenting the radical new approach to integration and caring for Indigenous children, Dales's article detailed the process by which children were institutionalized then deinstitutionalized in Saskatchewan. Private correspondence also hints at another reason for the demise of the Green Lake Shelter.[31] Personnel issues and racial tensions between the local Métis and the white staff hired to look after the shelter created political problems for the CCF. Local Métis people resented its presence in their midst and questioned the purpose and quality of care the children received there. They felt the shelter was poorly run, and all positions within the shelter, with the exception of the lowest paid, were staffed by outsiders (white, southern government employees). An official sent north to investigate the charges conceded "the dismissal of the Métis janitor and the employment of the non-Métis person has apparently caused some resentment among the Métis people in this area."[32] Regardless of the precise reason to close the short-lived shelter, the rehabilitation of the Métis children was deemed a success. In this case, "success" meant that the children were deemed suitable to then proceed to white foster homes far from the scrutiny of the local community who could advocate on their behalf.

According to Dales, who reflected the ideology of the CCF government, the official reason for closing the shelter stemmed from a newly developing integrationist, colour-blind philosophy that Indigenous children were no different from Euro-Canadian children. Dales wrote that the government and social welfare professionals questioned the institutional approach, wondering if it were "adequately meeting the needs of the children it was set up to serve and that anyhow an institution was not what we wanted for these particular children, *whom we had grown to realize* were not different from other children."[33] A new methodology of caring for Indigenous children was taking shape as special staff meetings were held in various locations as the drive to find foster homes began.[34] Social workers sought to engage the public by seeking out church leaders through writing letters and personal visits in order to inform the wider Saskatchewan community of changes underway that required the increased inclusion of foster and adoptive families. Dales commented on the importance of home visits to white communities to inform them about their new role in integrating Métis children: "These visits were enlightening. We learned from them how uninformed communities can be about programs, and how frequently we forget to bring them [the community] along with us. The interest and concern for children aroused by these trips was encouraging, and proved that an enlightened community can make a valuable contribution to our work if given a chance."[35] The local white community was enlisted to assist with rehabilitating the individual Métis children, since the institutional setting had proven unworkable, perhaps expensive, and in a Métis setting that worked against the government's goals of integration. The Department of Social Welfare and Rehabilitation deemed the shelter unsuitable to the goals of full integration because of the location at Green Lake with the large concentration of Métis families and conflicting interests of the community and the government concerning Métis children.

Not all the local people saw the merits of the experiment. Social work professionals needed to re-educate the local Catholic sisters about the revolutionary new integration plans. Dales recalled, "During these trips we discussed the virtues of foster homes as compared with institutional care in general terms, without revealing too much of our future plans."[36] At first the nuns who taught the children were sceptical about foster homes because they had developed close relationships with the children and were protective of them. However, after being fully "educated" with the new theories on child rearing, the sisters gave social workers their blessing, even to the point of suggesting people who might have been interested in the program.[37]

After securing the support of the white community authorities, the task of revising a century of racial orthodoxy and engaging the public began. Dales initially met with resistance when educating the white public about its role in integration and assimilation: "The biggest obstacle encountered was the reluctance of communities and individuals to accept Métis children. We encouraged people to think about these children as children. And not as classes or colours, and helped to see that their wants and needs were the same as those of children the world over. Where it was possible to get this interpretation across, the great majority of people were able to accept the Métis child."[38]

The ultimate goal of the project was full integration into non-Indigenous middle-class society; therefore school boards, teachers, merchants, and municipal and public officials were interviewed and acquainted with their plans. The shelter closed in June 1951. Two years later, the children had been moved to various communities in the province.[39] From this experiment, Alice Dales concluded, "We learned from this experience that you do not plan impetuously for children, and our premise that a community would not accept a minority group such as the Métis was false. We also learned that in meeting the needs of these children institutional care was not the answer. We found out too what it means to have well informed communities and the importance of having them keep pace with our program."[40]

Closing the children's shelter did not immediately stimulate changes to the overall child welfare policies in the province but provided evidence that white families were willing to incorporate Métis children if provided with the proper preparation and compensation. After the Green Lake Shelter experiment demonstrated that white families were willing to foster Indigenous children, emphasis was placed on seeking homes for Métis children and providing services to Métis women.

The legislation guiding and defining family and state obligations toward children expanded in the 1946 Child Welfare Act. Modern notions of gender and childhood held by Anglo-Canadian middle-class reformers in the primarily rural, immigrant settler, agricultural province were reflected in the amendments.[41] According to former child welfare director Mildred Battel, underlying the Child Welfare Act of 1946 was "the assumption that children have rights, and the rights of parents can be limited or removed if children could be harmed by the actions of the parents."[42] The Act was to ensure that the child who is or is likely to become neglected, within the meaning of the Act, was protected. The Act broadened the scope of the child welfare program and authorized that "any officer of the department, local superintendent, constable or other peace officer may without warrant apprehend and take to a place of safety any child who is within one or more of the following descriptions, and may make entry without warrant into any premises for the purposes of such apprehension."[43]

The criteria for determining if a child was neglected were based primarily on the ability of the father as head of household to ensure that the mother and child's material, physical, and moral needs were met. While Métis and Indian children were not targeted specifically, many would fall under these categories following the removal policies, relocation, and social dislocation in urban centres and road allowance communities. The following criteria for neglect would be most relevant for Métis children living in impoverished circumstances and applied to any child

a: who is found begging or receiving alms in a street, building or place of public resort, or loitering in a public place after 10 o'clock in the evening;…

c: whose home, by reason of neglect, cruelty, or depravity on the part of his parent or parents, guardian, or other person in whose charge he may be, is an unfit and improper place for him;…

i: who is abandoned or deserted by his parents or only living parent, or who is deserted by one parent and whose other parent is unfit or unwilling to maintain him;

j: who is a child born out of wedlock whose mother is either unwilling or unfit to maintain him;…

o: who is subject to such blindness, deafness, feeblemindedness or physical disability as is likely having due regard to the

circumstances of his parents or family, to make him a charge
upon the public, or who is exposed to infection from tuberculosis or from any venereal disease by reason of proper precau-
tions not being taken or who is suffering from such lack of
medical or surgical care as is likely to interfere with his normal
development.[44]

The judge who found the child to be neglected had the option to return the child with supervision to its parents, order the child to be committed temporarily to the care of the department, or order a permanent
committal.[45] When the child was committed, the minister required information about its age, religious affiliation, racial origin, and nation-
ality. Once the child was committed as a ward to the department, the
minister became the legal guardian, until he or she reached twenty-one
years of age.

Prevalent attitudes towards the Métis in 1944 had led to the continued relocation and isolation of Métis peoples, and thus the initial
child-caring solution for Métis children was the short-lived Green Lake
shelter experiment. However, the Child Welfare Branch had been gradually reducing the use of institutions for white children by increasing
payments to foster families to make substitute caring more appealing.
According to historians of child welfare, Rooke and Schnell, this move
from institutionalization to foster homes reflected a newly developing
"rhetoric of family life [that] meant the best institution had to be inferior to all respectable working class families because families, unlike
[institutions], could provide for the psychological development as well
as the occupational training of children."[46] The move toward fostering
is based in part on the belief in the transformative power of respectable family life to properly socialize children as future citizens. Policies
that paid householders to receive such children as family members and
not as unpaid labour attempted to narrow the class gap between children and households, and limited numbers of children in individual
foster homes to ensure individual attention.[47] Child welfare practice
stressed the positive aspects of the "criteria of childhood."[48] If children were separated from unsavoury families and moral contamination, in exchange they received placement in respectable homes where
they could develop an association with positive lower-class life. This
method promised a preventative approach to social disorder through

inculcation of the habits of decency, industry, and regularity in stable families.[49] Foster families, paid by the state, ensured that the citizens did not question the criteria of disadvantaged Métis families and lent their assistance to socializing Métis children.

Unmarried Parents legislation had been on the books in Saskatchewan since 1930 and provided limited financial assistance to unmarried mothers or guardians, as a protective measure for children. After 1944 increased input from social workers who were ensuring that adoption followed the legitimate procedures led to revisions in the Child Welfare Act of 1946. Although the title sounded gender neutral, Unmarried Parents Assistance was designed specifically for unmarried white mothers who were reported to the director of child welfare by hospital staff after giving birth. Women were then provided the guidance of social workers in planning for their future.[50] In 1945 the program was transferred to Social Aid Branch, then in 1946 back to Child Welfare Branch, so that services such as adoption, already offered to unmarried parents by the Child Welfare Branch, could be combined to "ensure case work services to these recipients."[51] The early administration of Unmarried Parents assistance reflected social attitudes toward unmarried mothers and children. No Métis received assistance, mothers with "illegitimate" children received less assistance than those whose children were "legitimate," and no mother received assistance until the putative father had been contacted.[52] The objective of this program was to identify potential neglect cases, expand the realm of practice for professional social workers, bring putative fathers within the therapeutic circle, and prevent the feared "black market adoptions."[53]

The revised Unmarried Mother's Legislation (UML) passed in 1946 has been deemed "a revolutionary move" in an era when having a child out of wedlock was scandalous.[54] Some critics argued that the legislation condoned unwed motherhood.[55] In part the UML provided financial assistance to unmarried mothers and assisted women to obtain the financial support of putative fathers. The act read, "A single woman may apply to the director for advice and protection in matters connected with her child or the birth of her child and the director may take such action as may seem to him advisable in the interests of such single woman and child."[56] While financial assistance was available, in many of the cases children were simply surrendered for adoption.[57] If mothers opted to retain children, they were required to apply to the

Social Welfare Board for financial assistance. The legislation stated that the board was responsible to "determine whether or not such mother has made reasonable effort to provide a suitable home for the child, has assumed the duties and responsibilities of motherhood and has made a reasonable effort to obtain support from the father pursuant to the provisions of this act ... if in its opinion the application is meritorious the board may authorize the payment of a monthly allowance to the mother of such child, on the recommendation of the director, the allowance may be cancelled without notice."[58]

The board had the authority to judge the mother's ability to parent, and if she was found acceptable, would offer financial support. On the other hand, if found lacking, she would likely have to relinquish her child for state care, where the child would be either placed in foster care or placed for adoption.

The revisions also made it mandatory, rather than voluntary, for hospitals and maternity homes to report births to unwed mothers. This action brought all unwed mothers under the gaze of the state. The legislation simultaneously offered assistance and technologies of helping that would provide unwed mothers, often deemed "neurotic girls," the ability to resolve their hidden psychological tensions and relinquish babies for adoption to proper families.[59] As Mildred Battel recalled, "An unmarried mother was told of the services which were available. If she wished to give up her child, this problem was worked through with her. Their difficulties were many – sometimes it was concern about the father and her feelings in this area; sometimes her family; and frequently a complete lack of financial resources."[60] Within two weeks of the date a single woman entered an institution for pregnancy, the institution was required to fill out a form with the date of the birth and send it to the director. The legislation stated, "Any person violating subsection (1) shall be guilty of an offense and liable on summary conviction, to a fine of not less than $10 and not more than $100."[61] Hospitals, maternity homes, and midwives were required to inform Child Welfare Branch or face violating the new law. Each woman was required to submit to the technologies of helping offered by social work professionals to ensure their parenting plans met with the branch approval or face removal of children.

Prior to the late 1950s, Métis mothers were excluded from receiving Unmarried Mother's allowances. Neither did Métis mothers and children obtain state-based adoption services available to white infants and mothers.[62] Several possibilities may explain why. In part it had been feared that Métis women would "reproduce carelessly" and look to the state for assistance, since it was believed that there was not a cultural stigma attached to unwed motherhood.[63] Perhaps homes could not be found for Métis infants, or it was simply a matter of discrimination.[64] Nevertheless, after the success in placing Métis children from the shelter, the argument that white families would not accept Métis children could no longer be sustained. When attempting to determine how best to address the tensions involved in bringing Métis women into the definition of unwed mothers, Mildred Battel asked of this new approach, "How can there be provision for overall assistance without it being interpreted and publicized as a right?"[65] If Métis mothers did not internalize a sense of shame at having an unplanned pregnancy and did not identify as an "unwed mother," it was unlikely that they would respond to the interventions of social workers as the helping pseudo-mother. This aspect of "case work" planning and therapeutic intervention was highly racialized and culturally relative.[66] While some may have accessed adoption services voluntarily, Métis mothers now came under the intense scrutiny of social workers armed with legislation to assess their abilities as parents and to judge the validity of their "plan."

The Department of Welfare officially abandoned the Métis colony scheme in 1961, suspended support to Métis colonies, and encouraged the Métis to leave rural Saskatchewan and take up residence in the towns and cities.[67] In reflecting on the outcome of the colony schemes, Director of Welfare Talbot stated,

> The lack of resources in these communities has made it almost impossible to provide for the Métis people living there and we have directed our efforts toward diminishing the Métis population in these communities. We have encouraged and helped those who are able to do so to take work in urban centres and our vocational training program has trained and placed 39 Métis youngsters in permanent employment. Our problem at present involved those Métis between 17 and 30 years of age who have very low academic education coupled with some indifference to vocational training and employment.[68]

These men faced a bleak future and would have few economic prospects when entering the cities and competing with white men for jobs.

Child welfare statistics clashed with the positive assessment of Welfare Director Talbot, who wrote, "There has been a reduction in numbers of families in most depressed areas as a result of these activities, and discussion with city welfare officials does not disclose any special problems with those who have moved to urban centres and been employed."[69] The Child Welfare Branch became the primary department tasked with the policy of Indian and Métis integration in the years after 1961. Growing numbers of Métis and First Nations people came to the attention of child welfare authorities as Métis moved from colonies and road allowances to cities.[70] Social welfare workers observed the changing demographics: "It appears that more services are being provided to Indian unmarried mothers than in former years. More services as they move off reserve."[71] In the 1959 annual report of the Department of Social Welfare and Rehabilitation, the first mention was made of the province's Indian and Métis population becoming problematic, or over-represented. However, the department was optimistic in its new role of integrating children: "A serious attempt is being made to equip all children to become as useful citizens as possible."[72]

While official messaging spoke to colour-blind and uniform services for Indian and Métis children, the annual report for the Child Welfare Branch in 1960–1 was the first year in which wards of the department were differentiated on the basis of race. Of the 1,482 children in foster homes, 580 were Métis or Indian. Since Roman Catholic adoption and foster homes were in short supply, and many families were reluctant to accept Indian or Métis children, the department made concentrated efforts to find white adoption and foster homes for Indigenous children. It was believed that even for Indian and Métis children, if the child whose parents were no longer the guardians was legally free, the best plan was adoption.[73] Newspaper, radio, and television were used to entice white families in Saskatchewan to become foster and adoptive parents.[74] Not surprisingly, the increase in children entering the child welfare system was attributed to the greater number of Indian and Métis families moving to cities.[75]

A new problem was beginning to take shape on the horizon, threatening to derail the hopes of social workers that initially proposed to solve the Indian and Métis problem through integration into welfare services. Since white families were the essential ingredient in socializing Indigenous infants and small children, their unwillingness proved a serious liability. In 1963, at the annual meeting of the federal Canadian Welfare Council, provincial directors of child welfare discussed the adoption problems they experienced, and the need to expand the public's notion of "adoptability."[76] Social welfare professionals were constructing the "problem of the overrepresentation of Indigenous children," mystifying the loss of land, homelessness, poverty and severed kinship ties that post-war policies engendered.[77] At the national meeting, directors from the western provinces with large Indian and Métis populations spoke of the many children of mixed race who were being supported by provincial governments in foster homes. The directors sought to work together to "solve what is a national problem of finding homes for Indian, Métis and Negroes, and other children who are difficult to adopt because of physical handicaps."[78] Mildred Battel's problem was the hundreds of Métis and Indian children for whom she was responsible. She lamented, "It's always much easier to find homes for fair-haired, blue-eyed babies … it's the mixed-race children that represent the hard, unadoptable group." Education could solve this dilemma. She felt that "the answer must be found in a reflection of public opinion." Mr MacFarlane, welfare director for Alberta, noted that 1,300 Métis children were in foster homes in his province and endorsed advertising these children to find them homes. He termed the advertising an "expensive but efficient means to dispel old wives tales about adoption."[79]

Racial attitudes in Saskatchewan proved intractable and contributed to obstructing the idealized solution for permanent wards. According to Mildred Battel, Indian families rarely came forward to adopt children. However, as the following chapter will illustrate, Indian parents were indeed interested in adopting Indian children, but the legal and policy barriers prevented the adoption of Indigenous children into First Nations' family homes. Home studies, poverty, legal distinctions between children and parents, the need for marriage licences, forms, and medical exams all made social worker–sanctioned adoption unattainable or unappealing to Indian and Métis families. In 1965 twenty Indian children were adopted into white homes, but that was but a small fraction of potential adoptees, since one-third of children in permanent care were of Native ancestry.[80]

Increasing numbers of Indian and Métis children apprehended meant that children were placed in foster care with no possibility of permanent family connection, whether adoptive or biological. In 1965 the number of children apprehended from white parents began to decrease while Indian and Métis apprehensions increased. A total of 131 more children than the previous year were apprehended, and all from Indian and Métis parents. In addition, Indian and Métis mothers began to relinquish infants for adoption, whether voluntarily or because they were coerced by social workers armed with Unmarried Mothers legislation.[81] Rather than seeking an alternative to the apprehension of Indigenous children from poor families or those who lived in substandard housing in urban areas, the government pursued the transracial adoption solution with greater intensity. In discussing the problem in the local newspaper, Battel explained, "Not only is it essential that homes be found for Métis and Indian children, but the acceptance and attitude of the general public must change. It is hoped that the adoption of a non-white child will become just another adoption rather than a special placement."[82] Battel and other directors responsible for child welfare proposed this as the best solution to the emerging problem of over-representation of Indigenous children in the system. The key, she believed, was to craft a message that would transform adoption from what had previously been a mirror to the biological nuclear family, into a liberal experiment in race relations and integration.[83]

The CCF government under Premier Tommy Douglas initially developed a Métis policy founded on the program of rehabilitation articulated in his 1933 master's thesis, "The Problems of the Subnormal Family." This was premised on relocating, segregating, and rehabilitating entire communities of Métis in colonies, with the eventual goal of integration. Métis people came under the jurisdiction of the provincial CCF government, which had committed to applying reformist strategies aimed at the Indigenous family through the Department of Social Welfare and Rehabilitation, rather than addressing land loss and racial intolerance. The failure of the Métis rehabilitation experiment of segregation and rehabilitation was replaced with integration of children into the child welfare system. The case of the Green Lake Children's Home represents a bridge between the past policy of segregation and relocation through institutionalization, and the later policy of integration into Euro-Canadian foster and adoptive families. Also the Green Lake experiment is the earliest example of a government-directed transracial adoption program. This published example set the stage for how future

Indigenous children could be integrated into the larger provincial system. The experts viewed the Métis people, as both Indigenous peoples and provincial citizens, as best suited to integration.

While the CCF government had plans to solve the "Métis problem" when first elected, the "problem" tested the limits of expert knowledge. Furthermore, it highlighted the persistence of settler colonial mentalities in the drive to eliminate Indigenous land rights and self-determination. This early Métis relocation and rehabilitation experiment informed the government's approach to providing services to the Indian people after 1951. By viewing the needs of Indian and Métis people through the lens of welfare and rehabilitation, assimilation took the guise of benign and de-racialized technologies of helping. Likewise, Indigenous people also sought to negotiate the best option for their children amid the era of government neglect and racial marginalization. They engaged the government to address their political and economic grievances rather than accept paternalistic welfare services. The activist CCF provincial government sought to utilize a range of child welfare and adoption legislation to rehabilitate single mothers and Métis children, whereas the federal Indian Act sought the sexual reorganization of the Indian family and reduction of expenses. Adoption of Indian and Métis children slowly gained traction as a viable method for integration in the repertoire of child welfare caring options. The Métis were the first recruits in the early CCF years but they would not be the last.

5

Post-War Liberal Citizenship and the Colonization of Indigenous Kinship

Rational-secular social scientific solutions to the "Indian problem" proposed interventions to adjust the perceived problematic subjectivity of "the Indian." As Hugh Shewell has pointed out, social scientists in anthropology, sociology, and psychology turned increasing attention to the studying the acculturation, or lack thereof, of Indigenous peoples.[1] Anthropologists increasingly shifted attention from salvage ethnographies to cultural anthropology and community studies to determine various levels of conservatism and acculturation, and the processes by which individuals and groups retained or discarded Indigenous traditions.[2] As racial theories of difference fell out of favour, support for alternative approaches to Indigenous assimilation and integration gained traction following the publication of Dr Moore's malnutrition study in 1948 in the *Canadian Medical Association Journal*. After conducting research on Indian people during the Second World War, he found that what had been formerly understood as racial characteristics, such as "shiftlessness" and "indolence," could be the result of chronic fatigue stemming from malnutrition.[3] This shift away from racial explanations stimulated further study in the search for an alternate explanation for Indian people's lack of interest in assimilation.

In the 1940s attention turned to the earliest socialization of Indigenous children in their families as the possible origin of psychological difference of tribal peoples. Dr Bartlett, a physician from Favourable Lake, Ontario, in a letter to the Indian Affairs Branch, suggested early socialization might provide an alternative explanation for Indigenous people's lack of interest in assimilation, different from the findings of the malnutrition survey. Bartlett echoed missionaries from an earlier era who saw lax parenting as the sources of Indigenous resistance to Euro-Canadian assimilation attempts.[4] Bartlett contrasted the absence of corporal discipline of children to an unstated, but assumed, strict disciplinary regime of white parents and concluded that this was the origin of what Bartlett and presumably others perceived to be a lack of responsibility. He claimed that, as adults, Indigenous peoples retained these

> childhood patterns, and I suggest that they have persisted into adulthood because at no period in his life was he taught to disregard them and adopt adult thinking and discipline.
>
> In support of this we have the observation that Indians who have been brought up in a better environment, e.g.: a good school under a good teacher, who tried to do more than teach reading and writing, usually show more initiative, and usually have more sense of responsibility towards other people than do Indians raised entirely in native ways.[5]

Perhaps there is no apparent connection to Dr Bartlett's prescriptive letter and the subsequent Indigenous child removal policies that began in earnest in the 1960s, but it nonetheless suggests a long-held belief of the detrimental effect of the Indigenous family on children, and more importantly, on Indigenous assimilation.

Taking this approach to the next logical step, Marcel Rioux, a cultural anthropologist at the National Museum in Ottawa, studied social customs of the Iroquois at the Six Nations Reserve near Brantford. For his research on family life and social development, he composed an extensive and invasive questionnaire on child-rearing practices. Anthropologists with new academic interest in the intimate lives of Indian families had no misgivings about asking highly personal questions, such as "Question 14. Does the couple continue to have intercourse?" listed under the heading "Prenatal Period," and "Question 47. Is there much attention shown to the baby?" followed by "Question 48. How is he nursed? Breast or bottle fed?"[6] While the results of these questions remain unknown, it reveals greater intrusion into the lives of Indigenous peoples, thought to be powerless subjects trapped in government-controlled laboratories, in the paternalistic search for the elusive answer to the problem of assimilation.

The subjects of this particular study, the Mohawk of Brantford, strenuously objected to having researchers pry into their intimate lives. Mrs Farmer, a representative of the Local Council of Women in Brantford, wrote a letter of protest to Ross Macdonald, Speaker of the House of Commons, stating their displeasure. In a rare and candid response, the government stated that this study would help to uncover and eradicate "sources of maladjustments." A full investigation of "intimate" behaviour was necessary in order to arrive at a "full understanding" of a given society. In a conclusion that must have given the Mohawk women even further cause for concern, the government suggested that the study had been modelled after a Peabody Museum Study of the Navaho, and that as a result of this study, the Navaho "will in the near future be completely integrated into the active life of the county with their complete consent and satisfaction."[7] In short, the government felt that researchers needed to pry into areas of family life deemed private by Indigenous people. This biopolitical intrusion into the intimate family setting to secure Indigenous integration reflected a newly emerging settler-colonial logic that linked social scientific knowledge of the Indigenous family life to state efforts of elimination.

Several factors led to a revision of Indian legislation in the immediate post-war period. The Special Joint Committee of the Senate and the House of Commons to Consider and Examine the Indian Act (SJCSHC) sat from 1946 to 1948. For the first time since Confederation, Indigenous leaders from across Canada were invited to present their views on the policies of the department and conditions on reserves.[8] The joint committee considered a wide range of areas, including provisions for Indian status, band membership, schooling, taxation, land rights, treaties, and governance on reserves, including band membership and provision of child welfare services. In part, the hearings came in recognition of Indigenous demands for increased self-determination and legal recognition. Decades of Indigenous political organizing for improved recognition of Indigenous rights and unprecedented service in the armed forces during the Second World War created a politicized pan-Indian awareness of the infringement of Indigenous, treaty, and human rights.

Likewise, non-Indigenous Canadians had become acutely aware and discomfited by the injustices of the Indian Act system.

The other impetus for reform came from the government belief that the changes would lead Indigenous peoples to embrace modern industrial society and provide the necessary preparation for the voluntary adoption of future Canadian citizenship. From the outset, the objective was elimination of the Indian people, or, as Duncan Campbell Scott put it bluntly in 1920, "to continue until there is not a single Indian in Canada that has not been absorbed into the body politic, and there is no Indian question, and no Indian Department."[9] A modernized policy of "integration" enabled Indian people to retain aspects of their culture, while the Indian Act provided the legislative framework to assist Indigenous peoples to embrace the liberal political and social values presumably held by mainstream non-Native Canadians. As historian John Leslie has pointed out, the immediate post-war period is one of historical importance to the study of Canadian Indian policy, as it provides a historical bridge between the earlier protectionist era and the new integrationist era.[10]

The joint submission of the Canadian Welfare Council (CWC) and the Canadian Association of Social Workers (CASW) to the committee identified the critical role that could be played by social work professionals with their expertise in working with immigrants and families in crisis. The CWC and CASW mapped out a new role for social welfare experts and the helping services of professional social scientists in solving the Indian problem. The submission stated, "In our judgment, the only defensible goal for a national program must be the full assimilation of Indians into Canadian life, which involves not only their admission to full citizenship, but the right and opportunity for them to *participate freely* with other citizens in all community affairs."[11] The definition of *integration* and *assimilation* for these social welfare experts meant that Indians would no longer be relegated to receiving second-rate services from voluntary organizations and Indian agents. Instead, they would be joining the rest of Canada as fellow citizens in embracing the therapeutic ministrations of professionals, whether they be social workers, doctors, or educators.

In documenting the vast discrepancy between white and Indian communities in social indicators like tuberculosis, infant mortality, educational levels, and housing, the CWC and CASW attributed them to the state of dependence Indian people had been forced to endure as a result of their protected status. They supported full citizenship rights for Indian people since they had demonstrated their willingness to participate in the two world wars.[12] While offering commentary on aspects of Indian policy such as social conditions, education and health, and acknowledging the interrelationship between all three of these areas, social work professionals believed that social issues were most pressing and the area where the CASW and CWC could offer support. The problems identified as stemming from a lack of properly administered services included prostitution, venereal disease and unwed pregnancy, juvenile delinquency, the prevalence of Indigenous adoption, and the legal barriers the Indian Act erected between Indian mothers and their children with non-Indian fathers. The brief concluded, "Owing to the fact that the wards of the Dominion Government are not eligible for benefits under provincial legislation, Indian children who are neglected lack the protection afforded under social legislation available to children in white communities."[13]

Social workers sought to bring enlightened adoption practice to Indian children to provide them with what was believed to be the protection of years of accumulated professional expertise. Likewise, the submission pointed out the injustice of separating women and children from Indian families (through status legislation) as fundamentally problematic and abnormal.

The submission argued for the coordination of federal and provincial relations and the development social services on reserves. Critical of the outdated residential school system that perpetuated the breakdown of families, professional social workers attempted to modernize Indian policy to bring new knowledge and methodologies of family services to bear in Indian communities. Like orphanages, which had been abandoned in white society, it was felt that residential schools could not socialize children properly for the modern Canadian nation state. The joint submission recognized "that no institution is an adequate substitute for normal family life. We believe that foster home service should be developed within the Indian setting."[14] "Normal family life" – the idealized family life with a two-parent nuclear family – was profoundly racialized and gendered and did not reflect the realities or aspirations of Indigenous peoples. It was widely recognized that the schools were responsible for more than educating children and were used largely for orphaned and neglected children. The submission further recommended ending residential schools and bringing Indigenous peoples under the purview of provincial welfare agencies.[15] According to Children's Aid Societies and the Department of Child Welfare, Indian children could obtain "proper nurture" (Euro-Canadian) in a family-based setting like other neglected and dependent future citizens.

Based on the recommendation of the CWC and CASW and others, the revised Indian Act recommitted policy for the eventual integration of Indian people. However, Indian people would now play a role in helping themselves advance. The revised Indian Act brought Indian people across Canada under the scope of the provincial laws, via section 88, paving the way for provinces to provide educational, health, and welfare services.[16] With this, the newly understood "Indian problem" was no longer viewed through racial theories of physiological difference or social evolution. In the post-war period, psychological explanations for difference arose. An Indian Affairs circular asked,

> What is this so-called "Indian problem"? In essence it is this: The Indian is too often considered an outsider in our society. His reserve is palisaded with psychological barriers which have prevented close social and economic contact between Indian and non-Indian. It is the policy of the government to help the Indian, caught in an age of transition, to adapt himself to a larger and more complex society, to be able to earn a living within that society if he wishes to do so. But there are many factors which inhibit the Indian in his adaptation to a mid-twentieth century technological world. Most are but dimly understood.[17]

Indian Affairs effectively recast the barriers faced by Indian people, from external barriers such as the legislation preventing Indians from leaving the reserve or from non-Indians coming onto the reserve, into a collective psychological inferiority complex. The role of social welfare experts would be to help break down the internal "psychological barriers" and to bring to light the "dimly understood" factors that prevented Indian people from embracing the allegedly superior modern world.

The Indian Act, 1951, in addition to allowing provincial laws to be applicable on reserves, also expanded the enfranchisement section and altered the section on Indian status. Indian women who married out and their children were further disadvantaged. However, women obtained the right to vote in band elections for the first time. Section 11, devoted to stipulating who could claim Indian status in Canada for the purpose of the Indian Act, placed much greater emphasis on the male line of descent and the legitimacy of children. Because of the ambiguity around the Frances T—— case cited in chapter 2, the section detailing children's status clarified that adopted children could not claim Indian status.[18] The 1869 Indian Act amplified gender discrimination to determine who could claim Indian status and political rights. However, the 1951 revisions further stipulated that women who "married out" were now automatically deprived of Indian status and band rights from the date of their marriage. Children were also enfranchised along with their mother and no longer entitled to live on a reserve, and property that women may have owned was sold by the superintendent, and they were given the proceeds.[19] Previously, women who married a non-Indian had ceased to be Indian but were able to retain their treaty annuities and community membership. Likewise, illegitimate children were placed in a precarious position, unable to claim Indian status from their mothers.

Child welfare experts quickly understood the implications of these changes when reviewing the proposed legislative changes. In March 1951 Reg Davis, executive director of the Canadian Welfare Council, pointed out, "While Indians now must conform to all laws of general application from time to time in force in any province, he should also have the rights of any provincial citizen regarding will, maintenance of children etc."[20] The key difference between federal legislation and provincial child welfare legislation lay in the legal relationship between mothers and illegitimate children:

> The same point arises in regard to illegitimate children (s.11 9e). An unmarried mother is the legal guardian of her child, and yet this act would have the effect of depriving the child of that guardianship if his father is not an Indian, and preventing the child from being brought up on the reserve by his mother. This guardianship is recognized in regard to inheritance (s.48) (13) but it is much more important that the child should have the care of his mother than any money she may leave. The mother should be allowed to give that care on the reserve, if that seems desirable to her.[21]

The director also had noticed that there had been no clear policy regarding the extension of social welfare services on reserves. Davis replied that there were reports from provincial child welfare workers of the practice of removing illegitimate children from mothers by officials employed by Indian Affairs. In addition, adoption of these children who lacked Indian status could not take place since the legislation stipulated that only legitimate children were accorded Indian status. He further elaborated on his original letter:

> We have been informed by child welfare workers that there is often real difficulty in arranging for a child whose mother is Indian and whose father is white to be brought up by his mother on reserve. There seems to be a tendency *on the part of officials to think that it is preferable for him to be removed from his mother...*, The proposed Bill makes it socially difficult for the mother to act as a guardian of the child, although legally she has that right. The child, who is technically not an Indian would be on the reserve only on sufferance and not by right.[22]

As Davis could see, the legal and social limbo of Indian children of unwed mothers made it impossible for them to be adopted into Indian families, and they were unlikely to be adopted into white families as a result of the racial attitudes toward Indigenous people in Canada. This passage also implies that children of unwed mothers were routinely removed by "officials." The legislation consequently further marginalized Indigenous mothers and children.[23]

Also, while enabling the extension of provincial law on reserves, the bill failed to secure a role for Indigenous communities to participate in developing culturally relevant services – which Davis pointed out should be the goal of any progressive change in the law: "We should also like to see welfare services combined with health as among the items for which bands may take some responsibility.... We assume that Indians like other people learn to take responsibility by having it given to them, and if the financial assistance were accompanied by education, individual counselling, as it is available in some of the provinces, we predict that the Indians would need less and less supervision in such matters."[24]

The revised Indian Act was passed on 17 May 1951 without the suggested changes.

Without clear direction on child welfare and with no resolution of the impact of gendered discrimination, social welfare developed slowly and unevenly. As Jessa Chupik-Hall has concluded, child welfare services to Indian people evolved into a "patchwork" of residential schools as child welfare institutions, foster homes on reserves, community development, and removal of women and children.[25] In English-speaking Canada, the movement away from institutional methods of providing for the indigent and abandoned children – or in the case of Indigenous populations, residential schooling – came about as a result of new methodologies and ideologies of children and family life. Social workers sought to wrest adoption away from Children's Aid Societies, Indian agents, doctors, and lawyers through offering a rigorous scientific approach over sentimental, customary, or dangerous "black-market" adoptions. In the case of Canadian First Nations, Indigenous adoption, where families were involved in choosing the adoptive kin, and bands had the authority to either approve or deny adoptions based on cultural and material considerations, no longer took place once provincial adoption laws became applicable on reserves.[26] Unintentionally, Indigenous adoption and child caring practices were colonized in the effort to provide equal services and uniformity.

THE 1951 INDIAN ACT REVISIONS AND THE RISE OF "JURISDICTIONAL DISPUTES"

The 1951 revisions to the Indian Act, through the inclusion of Indian people under provincial legislation, provided the opportunity for the provincial Department of Social Welfare and Rehabilitation to simultaneously address the perceived Indian and Métis problems. While the Métis did not come under federal jurisdiction, Indian people's separate legal status added additional complexity to an already highly complex undertaking. The revisions to the Indian Act brought Indian people under provincial child welfare laws for protection, adoption, and juvenile delinquent legislation; however, it was unclear how this would proceed. The CCF, via the Department of Social Welfare and Rehabilitation (DSWR), viewed the Indian and Métis "problem" as stemming from a similar origin: a lack of integration into provincial health, educational, and social standards. Recalling the interprovincial meeting of the

ministers of welfare from the western provinces, Minister John Sturdy
saw the Métis problem as an overall Indigenous problem. He explained,

> Many Métis follow the cultural and economic pattern of the In-
> dians, and that of the Métis problem and that of the Indian is re-
> lated, together with the effect each group had on the other made
> it imperative that the living standards and cultural level of these
> minority groups as a whole should be brought up to a more accept-
> able level. It is an accepted fact that these groups fall short of the
> economic and cultural level of the white population and accord-
> ingly the groups had a higher incidence of illiteracy, destitution,
> illegitimacy, and other social problems.[27]

The conference recommended approaching Métis and Indian rehabilitation together, with assistance from the federal government. "An overall
welfare approach to the Dominion would be better if the broad aspects for
health and welfare on Dominion-Provincial relations could be arranged,
rather than on an individual approach for a Métis problem only. Métis
problem alone, or Indian and Métis problem? It appeared that the opinion of the meeting was both."[28] The problems of Métis and Indian people
in the province were constructed as primarily social maladjustment to
the familial model of the nuclear family, and the inability to integrate
into the modernizing economy and society in the west. Consequently, the
solution was seen as needing a coordinated welfare response.

Correspondence between the federal and provincial governments on
the future direction in provision of welfare services took place shortly
after the new Indian Act took effect. Minster of the Department of Social
Welfare and Rehabilitation (DSWR) John Sturdy met with Federal Minister Paul Martin (Sr) of Health and Welfare and Minister of Citizenship and Immigration Walter Harris in April 1952, to discuss Indian
and Métis issues. Minister Sturdy pointed out that Indigenous cultural
and living standards were below those of the rest of the provincial population. Isolation of reserves and jurisdictional disputes prevented the
provincial government from providing welfare services for Indian peoples, and he sought federal assistance in a combined approach to the
Métis and Indian problems in the province.[29] While the province was
eager to come to an agreement with the federal government, it quickly
found resistance to its approach from federal circles. In areas where

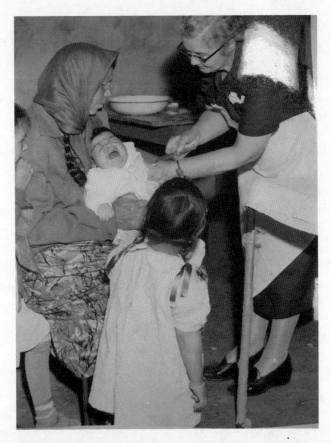

Above and opposite, provincial public health nurses visiting Moosomin Reserve, 1958 (used with permission of the Provincial Archives of Saskatchewan)

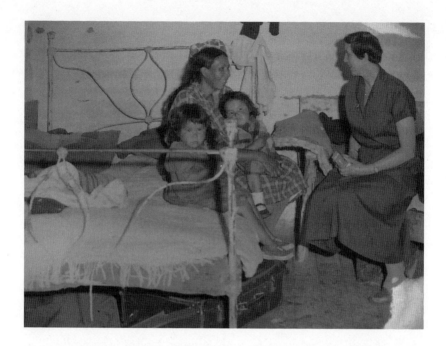

social workers could best apply their expertise, such as providing professional adoption services and rehabilitation for unwed mothers, provincial legislation and techniques conflicted with the Indian Act. In addition, the federal government refused to supply the necessary financial commitment to implementing a full-scale welfare response or take on responsibility for the Métis.

Following the meeting, Sturdy wrote to the minister outlining the most pressing issues for the provincial government concerning child welfare, especially in adoption services, protection of children, and services to unmarried mothers. The province's social welfare policies and procedures clashed with Indian Affairs' logic of elimination. He explained how the experiences of social workers in Saskatchewan removing non-Indian children from reserves presented "a very difficult situation because these children have been accustomed to the ways of the reserve and the Indians and they do not readily adjust, therefore to other standards."[30] White foster and adoptive homes would not accept the children removed from reserves, and children of Indian unmarried mothers, who had been relinquished for adoption, could not be placed with reserve Indian families as the result of status provisions. Mothers who chose to remain on reserves with children had to be able to prove that the father of the child was a status Indian. Sturdy pointed out, "She is legally Indian, the child is not, and thus not legally entitled to live with the mother. In order for the child to live with the mother on reserves, it had to be determined whether the father was Indian."[31]

There was also confusion about whether adopted children obtained the same status as their adoptive parents. The province required clarification regarding section 2 (b), in which a legally adopted child could be registered in an Indian band, which was seen to contradict section 12, which stated that persons of less than one-quarter Indian blood were not entitled to be registered. As a result of the new wording, social workers were hesitant to enter into adoption contracts with Indian parents if the child was illegitimate and the father possibly non-Indian. The author stated, "Our experience has been that the Indian Affairs Branch takes steps to remove the child before the legal adoption may be completed." The unclear legal status of the illegitimate Indian children then presented problems and questions about whether children could be adopted by Indian relatives. Even if adoption was secured, sometimes it was later discovered that the child did not have Indian status. Sturdy recalled times when recommendations for adoption had been made by a local Indian agent to approve an adoption, after which it was overruled by a higher authority.[32] The entire premise of legal adoption as providing a forever family for children and securing legal and cultural kinship was undermined by the patriarchal definition of Indian status.

The province asked for a conference to establish the new direction and begin planning "to give Indians the opportunity to reach adequate living standards." Sturdy suggested that the governments jointly commence research and planning in economics, health education, and welfare, and also include Métis peoples who were often intermarried with First Nations, with input from a committee of church, federal, provincial, and municipal representatives. The federal government opposed his suggestion. Writing in reply, W.E. Harris, Minister of Citizenship and Immigration, the federal department responsible for the Indian Affairs Branch, abruptly dismissed the concerns of the province for formulating a policy for the extension of provincial services on reserves for Indian people.[33] Whereas the province was looking to the federal government for financial assistance for the extension of programs and services to Indian people, the federal government felt that it was "undesirable for the Indian Affairs Branch to duplicate existing provincial services set up to deal with child welfare in areas contiguous to Indian reserves, and we shall be pleased to facilitate the extension of these services to include Indians on reserves in respect to child welfare generally in accordance with provincial law."[34] The lack of financial commitment to extending services or planning for coordination left the extension in a state later described as "unsatisfactory to appalling."[35]

While the IAB did not offer to assist with financing Indian welfare services, it did lend its assistance through hiring a social worker for consultation. In an apparent demonstration of modernization and harmonization with the provincial social welfare approach, the Indian Affairs Branch indicated that it had hired a fully qualified social worker with headquarters in Regina, who "will be pleased to co-operate in every way in matters concerning social welfare."[36] However, the single social worker for the entire province was a token gesture at best, and the lack of desire for a clearly outlined plan revealed the federal government's desire to offload its financial responsibilities to the provinces and disinterest in resolving legal inconsistencies.

Harris went further, disregarding Sturdy's examples of child removal, and maintained that the new Indian Act made provincial laws apply on reserves, regardless of the different legal regime or impact on women and children. In the matters of child welfare, Harris felt that the new clause in the Indian Act clarified previous ambiguities in federal-provincial responsibilities. Section 88 of the Indian Act – Legal Rights stipulated that all Indians were subject to provincial laws. According to Harris, this section covered the position of Indian children regarding provincial laws governing adoptions, neglect, and delinquency. Generally, in the absence of any provision in these respects under the Indian Act, provincial law applied equally to legally Indian children resident on or off reserves. It followed, therefore, that the adoption of Indian children by Indians or non-Indians, whether resident on or off a reserve, must be in accordance with provincial law. Similarly, provincial laws that governed the protection of children, child neglect, and delinquency applied to all Indian children in Saskatchewan. Harris maintained that rather than muddying the waters, the new act clarified the definition of an Indian and provided for the appointment of a registrar to deal with status and membership problems. If child welfare

officials had questions regarding Indian status, the province was coun-
selled to direct all inquiries toward the registrar.

Harris explained the IAB position on legal adoption for Sturdy. Adoption did not bestow a change in status for either Indians or non-Indians,
thereby simplifying adoptions for Indian children by non-Indian people and reducing the incidence of adoption of non-Indian children by
Indian parents or relatives. The now explicit policy of the government
on adoption was that adoption of children did not affect Indian legal
status. Section 2(B) of the Indian Act clarified a legally adopted *Indian*
child and therefore did not apply to any children who were not legally
Indian. For example, if a non-Indian child were to be adopted by Indian
parents, it would not affect status; the child would remain a non-Indian.
If an Indian child were adopted, the child would retain Indian status.

In recognizing the difficulty in finding satisfactory adoption placements for Indian children, the Branch provided its version of a sliding scale of preferred adoption and foster homes for Indian children,
revealing clearly its goal of fewer First Nations people on reserves. It
was the responsibility of the Indian Affairs Branch social worker to
compile a list of potential adoptive and foster homes classified according to the needs of Indian children. It read:

1) Enfranchised Indian families resident off reserves who would
   be prepared to accept children of Indian status.
2) Indian families who have not been enfranchised off reserve
   and who would be prepared to accept children of Indian
   status.
3) Suitable Indian families on the various reserves prepared to
   accept Indian children for either adoption or foster home care.
   Children placed in such homes on reserves would, of course,
   have to be of Indian status.
4) Foster homes other than Indian who would be prepared to
   accept children of Indian status but who by accident of birth
   have non-Indian physical characteristics.[37]

Not only did this list reflect the branch's racial outlook in stark terms,
it was also completely unrealistic in expecting off-reserve enfranchised
families to provide the majority of homes for Indian children. The enfranchisement rates had been dismally low, with few families choosing

to sever their Indian connections. The homes of enfranchised Indian families and off-reserve families were the top placement choices for Indian children, followed by on-reserve families, only after which non-Indian homes were sought. In addition, the branch embraced aspects of the provincial extension of services to Indian people on and off reserve without agreeing to any aspect of financial responsibility. In particular, it refused to contemplate addressing the issues of Indian and Métis people simultaneously since they had no legal obligation to the Métis.

Following the disappointing and unhelpful branch clarification of Indian policy, representatives of the Indian Affairs Branch and the Department of Social Welfare and Rehabilitation (DSWR) met on 23–4 October 1952 in Regina to further discuss the difficulties encountered by department staff surrounding federal policy of absorbing Indians into the mainstream.[38] The Indian Affairs Branch representatives included Colonel H.M. Jones, superintendent of Welfare Services; J.P.B. Ostrander, regional supervisor; and the IAB social worker. For the province of Saskatchewan, Miss V.M. Parr, Director Child Welfare; Mr. A.V. Shivon, Director of Rehabilitation; Miss M.E. Battel, Assistant Director of Child Welfare; and Mr. J.S. White, Deputy Minister represented the DSWR. IAB officials informed provincial social welfare representatives that the goal of Indian policy was that Indian people "should contribute to the economy of Canada, and while accepting the obligations of citizenship, should also benefit from Social Welfare programs provided for the rest of the population."[39] This pronouncement of the new relationship with provincial officials would have met a warm reception in Saskatchewan since the CCF government shared the desire to have Indian people integrated through social welfare and education.

The legal and historical barriers to a smooth transition from federal to provincial control of Indian integration were not easily overcome. The central place of adoption in the provincial social welfare strategy for Indian children is indicated by its location as the first item on the agenda for the interdepartmental meeting. Since adoptions were under provincial jurisdiction and no longer undertaken through the federal IAB Indian agents or band councils, as they had been prior to the 1951 revisions, the province needed to determine how to plan for Indian children placed for adoption. Provincial social workers were faced with the illogic that enabled Indian parents to adopt a non-Indian child, but adoption did not enable the child to assume the same status as the parents. Therefore, a non-Indian child legally adopted by Indian parents would not be registered with the band and not permitted to reside with the family on the reserve.[40] The central tenet of "modern adoption" was that the adopted child would, in every aspect, assume the same rights and privileges as the naturally born child. Thus, adoption among Indian people became a method of ensuring the gradual elimination of Indian status, and not the reverse. The conclusion was that "no adoption application would be proceeded with or considered until it was cleared by the Branch."[41] While the social welfare principle that "the best interests of the child" applied to the vast majority of children, for Indian children, financial considerations outweighed the social, moral, and ethical considerations. The policy stipulated that "a child who is adjudged a non-Indian should be removed from the reserve because of trespass."[42] In the case of Indian children, policy matters of adoption and child welfare boiled down to the principle "in the best interests of the Indian Affairs Branch."

At the meeting, federal and provincial officials also established when and for whom the DSWR provided services. In keeping with the newly developing policy of reducing reserve populations and encouraging urbanization, the federal officials proposed an arrangement whereby Indians who had left reserves would become the responsibility of the provincial welfare department after a one-year residence in a municipality. Welfare director for the IAB, Colonel Jones, stated, "This is in line with the Federal government's policy of making it possible for Indians to leave the reserves and become part of the economic stream of Canada."[43] Through the meeting it was mentioned that municipalities would not necessarily embrace the added financial responsibility for providing health and welfare needs. In addition, it appeared that the IAB was instituting a heavy-handed approach to residents of Indian reserves who had lost status, in all likelihood women and children. Officials said, "A very difficult problem may be encountered due to protests lodged by Indians concerning the status of certain persons presently living on Indian reserves. As a result of these protests some of these persons may be found to be non-Indians and therefore trespassers, for who provision may have to be made for residence and livelihood outside the boundaries of the reserve. These families, unless having made capital improvements, would have nothing to take with them and are likely to become public charges once they are removed from the reserves."[44]

While not stated explicitly, these individuals could be women and children who lost status through marriage but had returned to the reserve, Metis families who had married into First Nations communities, and other non-status folks who were related to First Nations families. The kinship bonds that connected these families were fractured through this heavy-handed legislation, and their removal proved especially devastating in these years following. Through the meeting, it was resolved that after one year the province would assume financial responsibility for Indians living off reserve, and the IAB would continue to provide support until that point.

Provincial officials in the DSWR remained troubled by the newly developing policy of the IAB, particularly the impact it would have on the numbers of children who would be separated from their mothers, and unresolved adoption issues. Not surprisingly, Saskatchewan's social welfare technocrats observed, "There appears to be considerable differences in the philosophy and intent between the provincial and federal legislation, creating as a result many of our residual problems."[45] The Indian problem, as understood by the province, stemmed partially from the boundaries established through legal Indian status, but they believed the cultural differences could be addressed through government rehabilitation policies. "Integration" seemed both the method and the logical solution to the Indian problem. As the DSWR had ascertained with the Métis population within its boundaries, Indian people needed adjustment to the modern economic and social reality. Boundaries formerly erected needed dismantling, since "the cultural, economic, and social pattern of this group was obviously a factor in their present circumstance with little opportunity to integrate themselves as ordinary citizens or the ability to accept responsibilities of citizenship."[46] Recognizing the national scope of their issue, the CCF agreed to approach the federal government with the plan to hold a federal-provincial conference on Indians and their future status as citizens. Rather than adopting a province-by-province approach, as the federal government appeared to want, Saskatchewan sought a national conversation with all the provinces to clarify their future roles in Indian integration.

The origin of "jurisdictional disputes" in child welfare arose from conflicting objectives expressed through law and policy. Following the departmental discussion, DSWR Deputy Minister J.S. White penned a

letter to Colonel Jones to express provincial dismay at the "opposite
views of our respective offices."[47] The province, in order to establish a
partnership with the IAB to integrate Indian people socially and economically into the Saskatchewan economy, felt hampered by the legal
barriers erected through IAB, whose only intention was to eliminate
Indian status. The newest agents enlisted to bring about Indian assimilation, social welfare experts, brought their professional expertise to the
project, soon to discover it was not necessarily welcomed. The sheer
insanity of the IAB policy toward unwed Indian mothers, their children, and adoption complications particularly vexed social welfare
experts in Saskatchewan. White reiterated his dismay at the Indian status provisions in legislation outlined in earlier correspondence: "The
foregoing clearly sets out the legal situation but disregards entirely the
social implications of a non-Indian child being adopted by Indian parents and not being allowed to live with them on reserve. Similarly, your
position that a child born out of wedlock takes its status from its father
is contrary to provincial practice, policy and legislation."[48] In its desire
to alleviate the social distance between Indian people and the rest of
the provincial population, the province hoped to look at the social factors contributing to the Indian problem, whereas the government of
Canada viewed only the legal aspects. Deputy Minister White again
requested that a committee be formed to organize the terms of reference for a federal-provincial conference in the hopes of developing a
comprehensive analysis of the Indian population in the province and
the country as a whole. Deputy Minister White stated, "The idea was
to compile information on all people of Indian ancestry in the province
in order to formulate a systematic and planned attack on Native problems."[49] CCF's love of social engineering and planning was resisted by
IAB, which refused to consider Métis and non-status issues together
with Indian issues. A conference was contemplated again in 1957, when
Conservative Prime Minister John Diefenbaker from Saskatchewan
took office, but it did not occur. First Nations people in Saskatchewan
were left with a confusing and conflicted system.[50] Ontario became the
only province in Canada to sign an agreement with the IAB to extend
all child protective services on reserves in 1965.[51]

The Indian Affairs Branch hired its first social worker in 1949. Previously, the IAB superintendents in each province had been responsible
for the welfare needs of status Indian people. The social work manual
laid out the purpose and policy to be followed by Indian Affairs social

workers, careful to first inform them that there were some essential differences between Indian Affairs social work and typical case work in a provincial welfare department. To begin with, "the role of the social worker is similar to that of a rural case worker in the Provincial social welfare departments in that she carries a general case load and does not specialize in any case category of social welfare."[52] The branch social workers would offer advice to agents on how to deal with specific problems, reporting and recommending action on certain welfare conditions. Social workers were also encouraged to supervise and establish Homemakers clubs on reserves, stimulate group activities, and develop leadership on the reserves.[53] Realistically, "the geographic location of Indian reserves and the scattered Indian population make it financially impractical to staff the Branch with a sufficient number of social workers to allow for this type of concentrated case work, and consequently it is necessary for the social workers to operate as part of a team."[54] Areas where it was suggested that social workers might offer assistance were in aspects of child welfare such as neglect, desertion, adoption, and foster home placement, as well as immorality and illegitimacy.

In the area of child welfare, the IAB informed workers that all provincial child protection legislation was applicable on reserves, and apprehensions might be authorized by courts for neglect. In the event of a child's apprehension, a transfer of guardianship was needed to make the child a ward of the provincial director of child welfare. In this respect, social workers were encouraged to help provincial agencies locate acceptable Indian foster or adoption homes for children when needed. In the case of foster home placements, the Indian Affairs Branch took financial responsibility for Indian children taken into non-ward care by a child welfare agency but warned social workers that such action should be limited as far as possible to emergency and short-term placements, primarily in urban areas.[55] Workers were encouraged to explore the possibility and availability of placements with relatives prior to and for the duration of alternative foster home care. Relatives should be assisted financially with the child's maintenance only if their circumstances were such that without assistance they would be unable to care for the child.[56] The manual stated, "In promoting the foster care programme the social worker should stress the idea of 'service' rather than financial remuneration for work done."[57]

Regarding adoption, social workers learned that that legal adoption fell under the scope of provincial legislation and included Indians within the adoption programs. Their role was to help provincial social workers by selecting suitable Indian homes. There again, IAB logic differed from child welfare practice, since the selection of appropriate adoptive parents was based on the need to assimilate and integrate Indians. The manual stated, "The success of any child welfare programme is largely dependent on the number and variety of permanent and temporary homes for placement and the need for Indian homes is increasing in proportion to the advancing civilization, the importance of finding homes is an important part of the social workers job."[58] Homes selected using the sliding scale of legal and geographical considerations mentioned above primarily reflected the goals of legal and social elimination, rather than the best interests of the child, family, and community.

The investigation of Indian status of illegitimate children also fell under the purview of social work responsibility. The manual stipulated that prior to band registration, an investigation was required for all illegitimate births, and sworn statements of paternity needed to be obtained from both parents, if possible, in order to be submitted to the registrar for status ruling. Until a definite ruling had been made on the status of the illegitimate child of an Indian woman, the IAB was willing to accept any financial responsibility. However, should the child be ruled non-Indian, it was then determined that the responsible government was required to reimburse IAB to the extent of the financial outlay on behalf of the child.[59]

After hiring social worker Monica Meade for the Saskatchewan Region, Jones explained the rationale of the IAB. As a social work professional, Meade might have been alarmed at the callous attitude toward women and children in branch policies. He cautioned her that "in the field of child welfare, the Indian Affairs Branch is not always in accordance with the philosophy with which you will be familiar as a result of your expertise in the CAS. Two points: the status of illegitimate children, and adoption and foster home placements. Both of which can be quite frustrating to a social worker unless you have an appreciation for the reason for the stand taken by the IAB."[60] First, the letter contrasted the approach of the provinces on the status of illegitimate children:

> Provincial legislation for protection of unmarried mothers and illegitimate children affords the mother all legal rights to her illegitimate child and traces all the child's legal rights through the mother.

The rights of the putative father are limited to financing the support of the child and the mother's medical costs during pregnancy. An example of the inherited legal rights of the illegitimate child is that of residence, the child's being traced through the mother, not the putative father. The determination of status in the case of the illegitimate Indian children runs contrary to this accepted child welfare philosophy. In theory no person is entitled to be registered a member of an Indian band with full Indian status unless both natural parents are Indian within the meaning of the Indian Act. In cases where one parent only has Indian status the child is considered "a breed" [*crossed out and replaced with "non-Indian"*] and not entitled to Indian status. This regulation was created to assure the progressive assimilation of people of only part Indian racial origins in to the non-Indian, or white community and thereby check the regressive trend of the assimilation of such people into the more backward Indian communities. In theory this regulation is sound. It protects the purity of the race (which is the desire of many Indians themselves, particularly in certain areas) it protects the Indian bands financially restricting shareholders in Indian monetary and land rights to the full blooded Indian for whom it was intended and who, in fact are the only legal heirs. And it prevents the development of a race of people who in them would become less Indian than "white" in racial origins, yet would be laying claim to rights and privilege designed for the civilization of a backwards group of people.[61]

Under the guise of protecting the "purity of the race," women and children bore the brunt of the IAB's gendered definitions of Indian status, and provincial welfare departments and their foster and adoptive programs provided a handy, although unwilling, source of support for children being removed.[62] White women who married Indian men assumed Indian status, and their children were deemed Indian despite their technically mixed-racial status. The letter continued,

Unfortunately this regulation frequently results in the unnatural situation of an Indian mother having a non-Indian child who is neither entitled to the same rights and privileges as the mother, nor permitted permanent residence on the reserve, but is in trespass and must eventually be prepared to go out on his own and settle elsewhere. Consequently, unwanted children with Indian appearance but non-Indian status present a difficult problem in placement. By reason of their appearance they would be more accepted in an Indian than non-Indian home, but as non-Indians they cannot be placed on reserves. Consequently, they frequently become the problem foster home cases well known to the CAS. The procedure for establishing the status of an illegitimate child is outlined in a department letter that will be on file in your office.[63]

The letter clearly states that women did not have a right to their children, since children could be removed from their care if found to be non-Indian. Women had the option to leave reserves with children, have them taken from them, or voluntarily relinquish them to social workers. Either way, race and gender converged so that women and children faced a greater likelihood of removal and relocation.

In addition, Miss Meade was informed that in adoption and foster home placements, contrary to professional experience and accepted practice, unmarried Indian women were not generally encouraged to relinquish their illegitimate children for adoption. Jones explained the reason was not that the IAB was unsympathetic to the child welfare philosophy that a child's future is more secure if raised in a home with two parents, but "simply the facts and figures of supply and demand."[64] Unlike in white communities, where there was an excess of potential adopting parents over and above children for adoption, the contrary was true in Indian communities, where it was felt that the demand for children was low, since "most Indian families have as many or more children as they can cope with, but the potential supply of adoptable children is extremely high owing to the prevalence of illegitimacy." Consequently, unless Miss Meade felt that the unwanted child would be neglected if left with its mother, or a family was known to exist who wanted such a child for adoption, a mother had to plan to keep her baby.[65]

Social workers, psychologists, and the state promoted a new role for families in the post–Second World War period. As Mona Gleason has argued, the idealized nuclear family envisioned by experts was no longer bound by outside forces such as the church, law, and economic necessity, but existed primarily to meet the psychological and emotional needs of the members. She quotes from a popular Canadian psychologist, Dr Samuel Laycock, who explained the shifting function of the modern family and the increased demand on parents. He explained this as a "shift in function" from a collaborative productive purpose, "making things," to the "insistent and urgent" building of personality.[66] Experts on family life concluded that in the normal family, not merely in the ideal family, the primary function would be the giving and receiving of love.[67] Gendered discourses supported the so-called traditional roles of men and women, with women instructed to be good wives and mothers who remained in the home, and men to be gentle leaders.[68] The exacting middle-class standards of psychologists and social workers made it profoundly difficult for groups such as immigrants and Native families living in poverty to live up to such ideals.[69] Those who were unable to conform to the race-based, class-based expectation could expect scrutiny of social workers and other helping professionals in assisting with their role. With the rise of psychology, early environmental exposure and experiences determined personality more so than heredity. As Gleason has concluded of the beliefs in the power of the family in the post-war period, "Strong cooperative industrious families meant a strong, cooperative industrious country."[70]

The entrenched belief that the solution to the Indian problem lay in removing children from the influence of their parents and reconfiguring kinship relations became reinvigorated with the specialized language of the expert. With introduction of the new Indian Act in 1951, two important developments have had long-lasting effects on the way Indigenous women and children relate to the state. First, the intensification of involuntary enfranchisement policies aimed at Indian women and children eliminated the ability of Indian people to adopt children who had lost status and raise them on a reserve. This development placed women and children in precarious social and economic situations.[71] While Indigenous adoption had been utilized for generations to care for children in need of security, the legal apparatus of the Indian Act had ensured that only those legally designated as Indians could be adopted. Second, the introduction of section 88, which enabled provincial laws to be applied to Indian people and on Indian reserves, brought federal patrilineal Indian status provisions into conflict with provincial laws enabling the rights of the illegitimate child to flow from the mother. The continued ambiguity and confusion have led to

"jurisdictional issues," which in turn have led directly to the dismal
state of child welfare in Canada. In addition, as social workers took
over the role of mediating adoptions, professional methodologies utilizing home studies, ensuring legal marriages and medical certificates,
replaced Indigenous criteria. After 1951 integration through transracial
adoption and fostering became the vanguard of the new criteria for
citizenship.

6

Child Welfare as System and Lived Experience

Consider a part Indian child if you are thinking of enlarging your family. The problems are very small and rewards are very great.[1]
— Adopt Indian and Métis advertisement, 1967

Termed the "Sixties Scoop," the removal and subsequent adoption or fostering of Indigenous children in non-Indigenous homes came as a consequence of the increasing child welfare intervention into First Nations Métis families and communities. Métis people in Saskatchewan were targeted for social welfare experimentation in the late 1940s and 1950s under the CCF government of Tommy Douglas in the Green Lake Children's Shelter, which was later used as a template for Indigenous child removal across Canada. By the 1960s what had been a localized experiment became province-wide. Former president of the Métis Nation–Saskatchewan and former foster child Robert Doucette experienced the child removal policies of the 1960s as a four-month-old infant. He recalled,

> When they were taking me away in the car, my *mushom* [Cree/ Métis word for grandfather] was swearing in four languages and throwing rocks at the car. And all through his life he would ask his daughters and his relations to find his little man, he just wanted to see him once. And it was the priest that took me, the priest told

social services my mother wasn't fit, she was too young. She was sixteen or seventeen, and they came and they took me, for no good reason. Because you know all about extended families in Aboriginal communities, it's not just one person. But that didn't happen in the sixties. They took all of us, well they took a lot of us. I was four months old when they took me. I was told I arrived in Duck Lake, I just had a diaper, some blanket and a bottle, I was just a big kid, a chubby little kid. Not much else.[2]

He is one of thousands of Indigenous children who shared the experience of growing up away from their relations, without any knowledge of who they were or where they came from. Robert said,

And that's not to say that non-Aboriginal homes are not loving homes, or don't teach really good values to kids. When you see what has happened to a lot of people what has happened because of residential schools and foster home, I think you can come to the conclusion that there has to be a better way of dealing with kids in the foster care system. There has to be.

Like why didn't they, when my grandfather came asking for me, why didn't they tell him where I was? What were they afraid of for God's sake? My cousin was living next door to me on Third Street in East Flat [Prince Albert], the next house!

Why? Why? Why is there such resistance to having those kinship ties? And telling people, "You know what, Robert, you're a foster kid and here's where you're from." I think, even if you tell the kid it's not a very good place, they'll understand. Maybe not the younger kids. I think adults don't give kids enough credit for capacity to understand…

What's wrong with telling me that "Robert, you're the eighth generation of the McKay clan from Buffalo Narrows. Here's who your relations are." I'd understand on the maybe woman's side or the man's side that they don't want anyone to know. I understand that. I still think it's important for families and individuals to know, to have the guaranteed right to know, where you're from and when you want your file, there's no bureaucracy no … and no legislations that says you can't have that.[3]

Doucette grew up in the northern Prairie city of Prince Albert, formerly known as "The Gateway to the North," fostered by the Doucettes. They were a respected, working-class French Catholic family who treated their foster children kindly. Nevertheless, Robert and his Métis family's experiences having him removed as an infant and raised without any connection to his community or kin reflected the aggressive policies of integration that First Nations and Métis people encountered.

As increasing numbers of Indigenous children – First Nations, Métis, and non-status – entered the care of the Ministry of Social Welfare in the 1960s, policymakers and politicians faced a financial and human resource burden. The "over-representation" of Indigenous children in this period was a reflection of a complex mixture of paternalistic professionalism of social welfare experts, provincial child welfare legislation that unfairly targeted Indigenous families, jurisdictional disputes between federal and provincial governments, gendered discrimination in the Indian Act, poverty and discrimination, residential school impacts, and Indigenous dispossession. In 1969 Indian and Métis people made up a small proportion the overall provincial population (7.5 per cent) in child welfare, while 41.9 per cent of all children in foster homes were Indian or Métis.[4] The lack of child welfare services on reserves meant that the provincial workers only apprehended children in cases of the most serious neglect if a child's life was in danger. However, adoption was available both on and off reserves. Social workers recognized that Indigenous children who were apprehended and remained wards permanently would likely never return home to their original families or communities. Rather than have them facing a life in foster home limbo, social work professionals in Saskatchewan such as Alice Dales, Mildred Battel, then Frank Dornstauder saw the solution in securing white adoptive homes, professionally selected, screened, and most importantly, "normal," to provide proper socialization for these kids.

The extension of provincial law onto reserves after Indian Act revisions in 1951 proceeded in unevenly and haphazardly, compounded by the conflicting objectives of the various levels of government. Indigenous peoples in Saskatchewan, subject to the contradictory legal regimes and hampered by racial and economic marginalization, continued to find methods to pursue ways of caring for needy children.

Whether by activating kinship networks, leaving reserves in search of better opportunities, or relinquishing children for adoption in spite of the resistance of IAB officials, Indigenous women negotiated opportunities despite the very many challenges they faced. The CCF government in Saskatchewan attempted to bring Indian women and children into the orbit of social workers and child protection legislation.

In 1959 child welfare, protection, and unmarried parents services were extended to all Indian families living off reserves, even if they did not meet the residency requirements.[5] In 1960 Saskatchewan had 107 Indian children in foster homes. The Indian Affairs Branch (IAB) explained the reason for the increase of over a hundred children since 1957 as "the result of increased services which child welfare agencies now provide Indian families."[6] It would appear that by increased services, the IAB meant apprehensions of children from families. In 1961 a new cost-sharing agreement was reached in Saskatchewan for children taken into care by the provincial Department of Social Welfare and Rehabilitation (DSWR). The branch accepted responsibility for children who were apprehended on reserve, while the province provided the funding for children who had been removed outside the reserve.[7] Between 1960 and 1967 Indian and Métis children increasingly left the care of their mothers, becoming permanent wards in a provincial child welfare system ill equipped to provide homes for Indigenous children. The DSWR lamented the lack of willing white families to take Indian and Métis children: "Not only is it essential that homes be found for the Métis and Indian children, but the acceptance and attitude of the general public must change. It is hoped that the adoption of the non-white child will become just another adoption rather than a special placement."[8] In the fifteen years between 1952 and 1967, transracial adoption of Indian children became a logical solution that appeared to resolve the complex web of problems termed "child welfare" stemming from gendered elimination legislation, racialized poverty, jurisdictional issues, and the urbanization of Indigenous people.

The following sampling of cases demonstrates that, despite the policy and legislation governments passed to rehabilitate and integrate Indian and Métis people, some families used adoption to retain family connections, seek relief from child-caring responsibilities, or respond to opportunities for state-based support for caring work.[9] Tensions between how Indigenous adoption would develop existed in a tenuous three-way competition between Indian Affairs officials in Ottawa and local IAB officials, provincial social workers, and Indian families. As a consequence, adoption and child welfare have remained contested. IAB attempted to exercise control over family-making by manipulating Indian status legislation, the provincial DSWR through adoption legislation and policy protocols, and Indigenous women and families through Indigenous adoption practices. Modern adoption practised by Saskatchewan's adoption experts reflected the emerging North American model that promised predictable and safe kinship design, legality, and state-sanctioning, while reinforcing the patriarchal nuclear family model. Describing their approach, Mildred Battel stated, "Each child has to be medically examined and his background investigated and evaluated and personal qualities estimated before a home could be selected for him. Each home in turn had to be as thoroughly studied and evaluated as the child had been in order to ensure that the best possible home was selected for the child. A great deal of time and effort must be given by the social worker to the intricate process of the adjustment of the child and adopting parents."[10]

Thus, as provincial law became activated on Indian reserves, social workers enforced adherence to professional adoption protocols in each case, evaluating the merits of private adoptions according to the standard procedures.

An early case of on-reserve Indigenous adoption took place before revisions to the Indian Act took effect in 1946 after an Indian husband returned home from serving in the military to find his wife had given birth to a baby girl. The Indian agent arranged for another family on the reserve to adopt the baby.[11] The agent wrote to his superiors, "We have an illegitimate child case which requires adoption in order to settle domestic difficulties between H.W. and her husband who returned from overseas a little while ago."[12] The mother in this case likely did not desire the child relinquished for adoption, but experienced pressure from the Indian agent and her returned husband. This example highlights the role of Indian agents arranging for private adoption on reserves prior to 1951.

Following 1951 Indian women could relinquish children to provincial child welfare agencies if their situation became untenable. One example of a mother who relinquished the care of her two children demonstrates federal and provincial cooperation to make arrangements for the care of Indian children. In a letter from Mildred Battel to Miss Meade, the IAB social worker, on 10 February 1956, they discussed a mother who requested her two treaty Indian children from southeastern Saskatchewan be placed for adoption. The DSWR looked to Miss Meade to obtain the assistance of the IAB to contact the families of the mother and father, as well as find adoptive parents following the policy established by the IAB.[13]

Another adoption case file from 1954 illustrates women's pursuit of adoption for their children. After giving birth, one unmarried mother insisted on adopting her baby out against the wishes of the department officials involved. Rejecting the construction that private adoptions were exclusively for middle-class, white women and girls, Mary (not her real name) left her Saskatchewan reserve to go to Winnipeg to have her child and receive adoptive services, much to the displeasure of the Indian agent and other bureaucrats in Saskatchewan. They wrote, "Mary refuses to go to [omitted] Manitoba to her father and also refuses to go to her reserve in SK. She wishes the boy adopted. As it now appears to be an Indian baby we feel it would be best to adopt it legally with a good Indian family on a SK reserve. The better types of families want legal papers.... We have no precedent for adopting a Treaty Indian from one province to another."[14]

The bureaucrats discussing the actions of the young First Nations mother seemed particularly concerned that she chose to relinquish her parental rights completely, attempting to find ways to have her maintain ties to her child:

> It would not be possible for us to have the baby adopted by Indians on a Saskatchewan Reserve, and moreover we are opposed to the fact of taking illegitimate babies from Indian girls and having them adopted, as we feel that the girls should be made to take responsibility for the matter. If the girl in question knows of a family on her reserve who would be willing to take the child, then we would make any necessary investigations, but we feel that she has responsibility to the child she has brought into the world, and that she be the one to find someone to take care of the child.[15]

In this case, it was advantageous for the IAB to encourage the maintenance of kinship relations between the child and his relations, rather than support the young woman's choice of adoption. It served no financial or assimilatory purpose, since the department would be responsible for the maintenance; however, it did serve an ideological purpose. The young girl had transgressed a number of expected behaviours from becoming an unwed mother to exercising her ability to determine where her child would be cared for, without the paternalistic involvement of the department or the Indigenous involvement of kin. She was constructed by department officials as a newly emerging "Indian girl problem":

> The trend lately has been for Indian girls to have babies, then to disclaim all responsibility for them. In many cases they name a non-Indian putative father, a man whose whereabouts are unknown. By doing this they think the Province will take responsibility for the child then the girl herself will be free to follow her previous pattern of life. We, together with the provincial welfare authorities, are trying to do everything possible to fight this trend, for we feel that it is in the interest of the girls in question, to the Indians as a whole, for us to not take responsibility for the care of illegitimate children, except in extreme cases where it is not possible for the girl to get a home for her child, or that the child is suffering in any way from neglect.[16]

After discovering the child's father belonged to an Indian band in Saskatchewan, the officials wrote the Children's Aid Society in Manitoba, asking for a social worker to speak with the girl "in order to see if there is any possibility of having the child placed with relatives, or if the mother is willing to take some responsibility in the matter."[17] Unfortunately for the officials, the mother of the baby signed her consent forms for adoption while she had been in Winnipeg, releasing the child for adoption. On a positive note, the officials acknowledged that the baby was healthy and attractive.[18] Despite misgivings, officials managed to locate a young couple on reserve who wanted to permanently adopt the baby in 1954.[19]

While department officials spent much time and effort to retrieve the baby who had been relinquished in Winnipeg, children of enfranchised Indian mothers were refused such consideration. One case in Saskatchewan illustrates the ambiguous place of orphaned children whose

involuntarily enfranchised mother passed away. Despite a resolution
passed by the Indian band council accepting the children as members,
the superintendent responded to the band council's decision presented
by the Indian agent: "In reply I am returning the signed Resolution to
you and as I am fully aware of the stand the department will take in
this matter, that is they will be against the admission of these children
because their mother married an outsider and the children are not considered as Indian under the interpretation of the Indian Act, I am not
submitting this to Ottawa."[20] In spite of the resistance of the federal
department, the children's grandparents approached the Department
of Social Welfare on 17 October 1955 to explore the possibility of adopting four of the five children, ranging in age from eight to fifteen. Three
had been living with their maternal grandparents on the reserve, and
two with relatives also on reserve. The mother of the children died in
1941, at the home of her parents. Following her death, their father had
remarried and was no longer involved in raising his children. According to the social worker involved in the case, "The children are receiving good care in the respective homes and the younger ones at least
would have no recollection of any other home. It would be desirable
to give them security of adoption if it is possible." The Indian agent,
who was interviewed by the worker, stated he would be willing to recommend this adoption. The reply, however, was consistent with the
department's position that stipulated paternal responsibility and patriarchal lines of descent: "For your information I should point out that,
generally speaking, I am not much in favour of the adoption by Indians
of non-treaty children, as we run into many different kinds of difficulty
with regard to education medical cost, etc., and in this particular case,
it would appear to me that our department is expected to be saddled
with the responsibility of three children while their father is alive and
apparently able to re-marry and support a second family."[21]

The Indian agent acknowledged the children's relationship with
their community and kin, but department policy was clear that no
white people (their terminology) were to be admitted to the band membership. The Indian agent was chastised for his role in advocating the
adoption of the children: "You are, surely, aware that it is the policy of
this branch to not admit any person of white status to Indian membership and as adoption would not change the status of the children they
could not be admitted to membership and should not be permitted to

reside on reserve."[22] Fortunately, despite the intended policy to remove the children and relocate them to their father, they remained on the reserve among their kin.

In another case, a potential adoptive father wrote to his Indian agent to ask how he might legally adopt the baby who had been left with his family at two years old. He needed to locate the mother and obtain her permission to have the baby registered as part of the adoptive parent's band. When the Indian agency wrote to the Department of Social Welfare in Saskatchewan on 23 February 1956, they needed much more information.[23] Several steps had to be followed prior to obtaining a legal adoption. The social workers needed to determine if the band would accept the child, they needed to obtain consents signed by the mother, and before the finalization of the adoption, a home study needed to be undertaken: "It is necessary that we have a social history of the child in question, and also that we obtain signed consents to Adoption from the Mother of the child."[24] While the lengthy process required by the DSWR made legal adoption complicated, this example and others have indicated that First Nations peoples actively pursued adoption under provincial statues to establish family for their kin.

During the early 1960s a young unmarried mother sought out adoption, writing a letter to the superintendent of the Southern Saskatchewan Indian Agency. She had been attending school in a small Saskatchewan city and became pregnant. She wrote, "I would really appreciate if you could make arrangements to have my baby adopted out because I don't feel I could support it or give it the care that it needs. As I was told you're the one I'm supposed to see about it. I was trying to get somebody to keep her but I could not get anyone. As I want to work, I have a job until winter."[25] The young woman's lack of kin relations, or inability for kin to assist, prevented her from finding anyone to care for her child. Unfortunately, due to her position as a Treaty Indian, she was not able to obtain services that other mothers might have had. The provincial Department of Social Services, the agency responsible for adoptions in Saskatchewan, did not provide Indigenous unmarried mothers the same support as white mothers.

The Department of Social Welfare explained, "The essence of our discussion with her is that in so far as Treaty Indians on reserves are concerned, we will only become involved with Juveniles and Private Adoptions. The exceptions to this are emergency protection situations.

In the latter instances, requests for services must be channelled through your social workers or regional supervisor who in turn will contact Miss Battel."[26] The department was only willing to remove neglected children, or help with private adoptions if there was already someone wanting to adopt. At this point, the DSWR was not providing adoption to Indian children on reserve for lack of willing white families to adopt Indian children.

While these adoptions indicate some mothers relinquished children voluntarily, the vast majority of children came into the care of social services through protection legislation.[27] When children were apprehended, most did not end up adopted, but rather entered the foster care system permanently.[28] In 1980 Philip Hepworth acknowledged that the available data did not account for why Indigenous children were coming into care.[29] It is still difficult to determine with complete accuracy because Saskatchewan's provincial privacy legislation protects case files from researcher scrutiny. Though it was not acknowledged at the time, communities were reeling from three generations of children removed to attend residential schools, who returned to communities as young adults with unresolved grief and trauma. Only in recent years have the intergenerational effects of residential schools and the historic trauma of Indigenous peoples been recognized as affecting parenting skills.[30] Many stories of the impact on individuals, families, and communities from survivor testimonies have come to light through the hearings of the Truth and Reconciliation Commission.[31] Several of the cases observed through the federal IAB files indicate families experienced extremely high levels of substance abuse, poor housing, spousal violence, illness, accidental death, suicide, and child abandonment.

Parents, despite their poverty and difficulties in providing a safe environment for their children, attempted to raise children. One case file in the RG10 files graphically illustrates the multiple layers of trauma facing Indian families in the late 1960s. On a northern Saskatchewan reserve, impoverished families experiencing difficulties with substance misuse and interpersonal violence sought the care of child welfare authorities. A mother with three small children died as a result of head injuries sustained by spousal violence. The children's father also had a severe drinking problem. His second wife also had a severe drinking problem, and their two children had been apprehended shortly after birth due to "failure to thrive."[32] The social worker looking after the case described the family home as a one-room 12' x 12' log shack consisting of one bed, a small table, two chairs, one small cupboard, a washstand, a wood heater, and a wood box. At the request of their grandmother, the two younger children from the father's first marriage were placed in a foster home in Regina shortly after the mother's death. Once there, the children's Métis foster mother hoped to be able to adopt the two children. However, the children's father still wanted to retain contact with his children. He wrote to the department requesting that his children be moved close to him so that he might be able to visit them more regularly: "Dear Sir, I am writing concerning my Children B. and K. I would like to have them back on the reserve or near this area where I can have easy access to visit them when I want to. Regina is such a long way to go and very expensive. I hope to get a house on the reserve where I can look after them. Thank you for your concern."[33] The children were eventually placed with a foster family on their reserve. Grandparents had provided child-caring in Plains First Nations, but family-based care networks were increasingly strained by poverty, addictions, and high mortality rates.[34] Grandparents, overwhelmed by caring for children, often sought the assistance of IAB for foster homes.

In some cases, parents who initially requested the assistance of child welfare professionals lost control once their children entered the system. One mother, perhaps unaware that adoption entailed a complete severance of parental ties, sought to regain access to her child once she had become better equipped to care for her child. She wrote, "Dear Sir, I am writing to you about my child [name and birthdate omitted]. I would like to have him back, and I will look after him with my mother's help. I am writing to you to help me get him back. Thank-you, [name omitted]."[35] The Indian agent referred the mother to the provincial Department of Welfare, and it is unknown whether she was ever able to have her children returned. Another mother who had been unable to care for her children as the result of substance abuse, poverty, and homelessness still wrote multiple letters over several years to department officials, attempting to regain custody of her apprehended children. The widowed mother initially sought assistance with caring for her one-year-old child following her husband's suicide on 1 February 1966. The reason given on her placement sheet was homelessness.[36]

In March 1966 she began writing to officials, looking to retrieve her daughter:

> I sure would like to know what you are going to do with my little
> B. I sure like to have her back soon I sure miss her. I hope you guys
> won't take her away from me. Maybe you are trying to give my
> little girl away. Hope not. This time I won't want the welfare take
> her away. I took that baby in the [omitted] hospital that she was
> sick and not for my drinking. Why don't they take [omitted] kid?
> That kid always goes to the hospital and she left her kids for a week
> or more. I know all about her instead of me they are lots of people
> from the reserve that's …
>
> And I want my B back. That's my kid. I had the kid for myself
> and not for anybody. No not for the welfare either. So this I want to
> know. What are you going to do? I am staying here at F.S.'s place.
> [Unclear] So please let me know real soon. From Mrs C.M.[37]

This mother's incomprehension at the lack of information and refusal to return her children is evident. She gave birth to another baby in August 1968, who was apprehended that November at the hospital, in response to severe neglect. That child was placed in a foster home, where a social worker reported in 1970, "She seemed happy there and was quite attached to Mrs F. There seemed to be a good and close relationship between the child and the foster parents."[38] The foster parents made inquiries to the Bureau of Indian Affairs social worker about adopting the little girl and were told about how to proceed.

This mother continued to pursue the return of her daughters. In 1973, after receiving another letter from the mother looking to have her children returned, social workers investigated the possibility of having the children returned. They reported, after visiting both the mother's home and the foster home,

> 13 March 1973: This home is modern, clean and comfortable. V
>   looks healthy contented and well cared for. Mrs F concerned
>   that V not be moved to a different home.
> 28 March 1973: Saw natural parents. Their home is overcrowded,
>   poorly maintained and in general disorder. Evidences of a
>   drinking problem. One other girl in foster home, evidence of
>   neglect of the rest of their children.

Recommendation: This is an excellent home and no attempt
should be made to change the situation at present.

The case file description used by the social worker to contrast the two homes is overdetermined with class and race based value-judgments. The term "neglect" used by the social worker, together with the terms "overcrowded" and "general disorder" signalled this mother's inability to provide an appropriate home to raise her children and ensured that she could never have her children returned.[39] Both children remained in foster homes despite the protests of their mother. Social workers felt the children were well provided for in homes that met their white, middle-class standards. Adoption was pursued by the foster parents of the girls, and since this information is covered by privacy legislation, it is not known whether it was concluded; however since both cases end in 1973, they may have been adopted at this time.

Pregnancies of young Indigenous girls who attended residential schools also emerged in the files. It is not clear beyond this brief note in the Indian Affairs files what the circumstances of the pregnancy may have been. However, the Truth and Reconciliation Commission Final Report has identified that former students from Saskatchewan account for the highest number of claims in the Independent Assessment Claims for cases of physical and sexual abuse, at 24 per cent.[40] Certainly Indigenous children were vulnerable to sexual abuse from school staff and other students, and pregnancies resulting from abuse were not unheard of.[41] In this case, a young First Nations girl, in grade nine at an unnamed residential school gave birth to a baby while at home for the Christmas holidays. She had given the child up for adoption to another family on the reserve. Her Indian agent wrote, "Irene [not her real name] is 15 years old. I have a return ticket to school on Monday. The principal of the school is not being advised by us of the reasons for her absence. May the adoption be approved at an early date, as the arrangements made seem to be the most satisfactory to us. The [family] are a responsible couple but like all Indians here are on relief. To get the child clothed, I have issued an emergency clothing order and also relief order to foster parents."[42]

The placement and adoption was referred to the Department of Social Welfare for its oversight. Because the province had certain legal procedures to follow, the adoption could not be completed immediately. "We will certainly visit the W——'s with regard to their wish to adopt this child, once you have obtained with them their marriage certificate, and once they have completed the attached medical examinations. We realize with the weather so severe they may not be able to complete the medicals soon. However we will be waiting to hear from you when they are completed."[43] The file does not indicate the outcome of this case.

Many factors must be taken into account when looking at the emergence of transracial adoption and the over-representation of Indigenous children. Settler colonial conditions in Saskatchewan rendered families vulnerable, without adequate access to resources for health, education, and healing, while racism acted as an ideological justification for marginalizing Indigenous peoples. Social workers increasingly targeted Indigenous families for child removal, as the case of Robert Doucette illustrates. Likewise, when families suffered from substance misuse related to trauma, poverty from lack of education, employment, and marginalization, without support, difficulties arose in providing for children. In some circumstances, mothers, grandmothers, and even children looked to the foster care system for assistance to cope with the difficult situations in the 1950s, 1960s, and 1970s on reserves and in cities in Saskatchewan. However, the system was not equipped or inclined to support Indigenous families in caring for children. One informant recalled his difficult childhood growing up with parents who had attended residential school. At age ten he left the reserve with his younger siblings to seek out foster care. His parents regularly left the children without food or warmth in the winter as they suffered from substance misuse. He remembered that he had hoped that the foster home system could provide him and his siblings with the necessities that his parents were unable to. His experience in a foster home did not turn out as he expected. Unprepared for life in in a non-Indigenous community and in a non-Indigenous home, he quickly asked to return home.[44] These examples demonstrate the difficulties in making generalizations about Indigenous adoptions.[45]

Over the course of the 1960s, the extension of provincial adoption laws onto reserves with the application of Section 88 of the Indian Act contributed to a dramatic increase in transracial adoptions of Indian children out of Indian communities. This development necessitated a clarification in registration of adopted Indian children. Since adoption did not change status, Indian children adopted by non-Indians remained on band membership lists. Children's names were placed under their birth parents' with an entry that explained that the child had been legally adopted out of the band in a remarks column.[46] In each case, a copy of the adoption order or other official document was attached to the membership list, giving the full details of the adoption and the child's new name. Adoptive parents' name did not appear on the membership return because information was always treated as confidential. Each child adopted out was entitled to share in all cash distributions made to the other band members.[47] The registrar in Ottawa required all the official documents in its attempt to establish procedures that would enable it to meet legal obligations to register persons in accordance with the Indian Act and provide maximum protection of confidential information.[48]

Keeping track of the increasing numbers of transracial adoptions of Indian children required a process to ensure the IAB retained a record of children no longer on band lists but still eligible for band funds, treaty money, and entitlements. The privacy legislation around adoption made this extremely difficult. Since provincial legislation prohibited the Child Welfare Branch from releasing information on adoptions, IAB officials had to look to Indian parents for copies of adoption orders as confirmation of the adopted child's eligibility for band registration. Policy directives going out to local superintendents requested that they report all adoptions: "It is requested that you report to Regional office on a confidential basis any information coming to your attention which indicates that a legal adoption involving Indians may have been granted. Regional office may request you ... advise Indian parents that copies of their adoption order are needed if their child is to be included on band membership lists."[49] Children leaving bands and communities may not have been recorded on lists if their information was not gathered from parents. Some may not have been informed by foster and adoptive parents that they were entitled to band funds and treaty entitlements when they came of age.

For both federal and provincial agencies, adoption of Indigenous children with or without status provided a solution to the jurisdictional ambiguity between the Saskatchewan provincial and federal governments over responsibility for Indigenous residents, once the legal status of Indigenous adoptees was clarified. Adopted children retained their Indian status, although it was up to the adoptive parents to decide if they wanted to reveal it to their children. Based on the 1951 Indian

Act status provisions and Indian affairs long-standing policy, children adopted by Indian people did not receive status through the adoption.[50] The Indian Affairs Branch created the position of registrar, who maintained a list of all children, adopted on the confidential "A" band list. The registrar also tracked treaty money and band shares, which were maintained in a special savings account.[51] Under the 1951 Indian Act, section 48 (16), legally adopted children were included in the definition of children eligible to inherit property of the intestate. After an amendment in 1956, children adopted through customary adoption could also inherit property of the intestate.[52]

Adoption as practised by the Department of Social Welfare in Saskatchewan varied, depending on the race and location of the people involved. The case studies reveal a complex interplay between the roles of the Indian Affairs Branch and the provincial Department of Social Welfare. Research of adoption and apprehension files revealed multiple variations of child placement pursued, making generalizations impossible. These cases indicate that the entry of provincial social workers onto Saskatchewan reserves in the 1950s, 1960s, and 1970s challenged the boundaries of their professional knowledge. Social workers privileged the privatized nuclear-family model situated within the privatized space of the middle-class home. That model reached its high-water mark in the 1960s and 1970s. As Philippe Aries has observed, "The concept of the family, the concept of class, and perhaps elsewhere the concept of race, appear as manifestations of the same intolerance of variety, the same insistence on uniformity."[53] Engineering adoptive kinship to mirror the North American idealized version of the "normal" nuclear family is most evident in the critical importance attached to the home, and the home study prior to the finalization of any professionally arranged adoption.[54] The meaning and role of the family had been given enormous responsibility for determining the social behaviours of children – in particular, these nuclear families who were engaged in remaking Indigenous citizens into Canadians.

Social workers preferred permanent, legal adoption to what they considered insecure, temporary placements or other family arrangements that left children without permanent belonging, whereas caring for kin in some Indigenous societies could include a variety of arrangements, some of which could be permanent.[55] For North Americans, adoption sought to replicate the nuclear family and provide assurances of permanency, primarily for the adoptive parents. According to Ellen Herman, "It was almost as safe, natural, and real as biological kinship. It might approximate normality through intelligent design."[56] With the increasing numbers of Indigenous children coming into provincial departments, remaking Indian and Métis children into acceptable family members became the new frontier in integration policy.

ADOPTING A SOLUTION TO THE INDIAN PROBLEM

In both Canada and the United States, transracial adoption of Indian children into white homes increased from the post-war period onward. In the United States, transracial adoption of Native American infants into white homes was stimulated in large part through the Indian Adoption Project (IAP) that ran from 1958 to 1967. The special adoption program, operated by the Child Welfare League of America (CWLA), with the financial assistance of the federal Bureau of Indian Affairs (BIA), sought to provide adoption placements for the Indian children who, according to Project Director Arnold Lyslo, were "'the forgotten child,' left unloved and uncared for on the reservation without a home or parents of his own."[57] The IAP began as a demonstration project to encourage white families to adopt Native American children by establishing an interstate adoption exchange between state and county welfare agencies and two eastern adoption agencies, the Louise Wise Services of New York City and the Children's Bureau of Delaware. The project initially targeted the western states of Arizona, Montana, Nevada, North Dakota, South Dakota, and Wyoming in response to their large American Indian populations. It focused on Indian children of one-quarter or more degree of Indian blood, who were considered to be "adoptable," emotionally and physically.[58] The exchange program, removing Indian children from reservations and regions to faraway families in urban areas, was felt to be necessary recognition that the prejudice against minority children was always strongest closest to their home communities.[59]

The establishment of the IAP came about during the height of American "termination" policies in Indian Affairs. The cold war era fears of communism sparked a rethinking of the previous reforms undertaken during the 1930s by Commissioner Collier. Termed the Indian "new

Deal," the Bureau of Indian affairs had reversed its decades long policies of assimilation and provided support for Indian self-determination during the 1930s.[60] After the Second World War, under Dillon S.
Myer, formerly the director of the War Relocation Authority responsible for the removal and internment of Japanese-Americans, the policy
of assimilation was restored. Ominously designated "termination," the
newest program renewed efforts to have Indian people leave reserves,
phase out the Bureau of Indian Affairs, and have states provide all services to everyone as regular Americans.[61] As had been previously done
in Canada with the 1951 revisions to the Indian Act, the U.S. Congress
passed Public Law (PL) 280 in 1953, giving states jurisdiction over
civil and criminal matters on reserves, including family law.[62] The BIA
also introduced a "relocation" program to stimulate the movement of
Indian from reserves into large urban areas. On what was known as
the second "trail of tears," Myers and the BIA relocated Indian people
from segregated reserves into urban areas as another facet of the integration program that would see tribal people meld into just another
minority in U.S. society. The goal of termination policies was to eliminate the barriers to accessing education and jobs, and eventually see
Indian people cease to be a separate legal and cultural entity within
American society.[63]

The Indian Adopt Project drew upon child-removal logic that had
made boarding schools the solution to Indian education, despite the
poor outcomes for children over the decades.[64] The entrenched belief
among the white public and policy-makers that the Indian family constituted a threat to the well-being of Indian children enabled white
women reformers in the United States who used their privileged race
and social position to act as teachers and moral reformers, softening
the masculine operation of Indian Affairs. As Margaret Jacobs writes
of the early twentieth-century progressives, "White women reformers
often claimed that they could transform indigenous homes and thereby
solve the so-called Indian or Aboriginal problem simply by teaching
removed girls middle-class domestic skills."[65] Through removing children from parents and homes where tribal knowledge, kinship relationships, and collective memories were shared, new subjectivities and
sensibilities could be cultivated that would align Indian children with
surrounding settler communities. In the shift from the public maternalism of first-wave feminist reformers through federal boarding schools,

to individualized private mothering in private homes, transracial adoption sought to inculcate the same social and cultural sensibilities with new methodologies that would enable white middle-class women to continue to provide a solution to the problem of Indian poverty.

Thus the Indian Adoption Project came at a time when American Indian policy shifted intensely towards terminating Indian tribal affiliations through urbanization and integration, and American culture strongly embraced privatized solutions to all manner of complex and troubling problems.[66] Extending modern adoption to Indian children, the most intimate form of integration, required selling its possibilities to tribal councils and Indian mothers. Thus, prior to its establishment, Lyslo first canvassed several Indian reservations and four national organizations to gauge Indian attitudes toward adoption of children into non-Indian families and explain to them the need for the project. While some groups, such as the Shoshone, Navajo, Winnebago, and some of the Sioux, had occasionally allowed off-reserve adoption, the Apache and Mojave strongly asserted their desire to have children remain within their own communities.[67] Lyslo was confident that once the superiority of such an approach had been demonstrated, with faith and goodwill, "those tribes now opposed to the adoption of Indian children by white families will acquiesce."[68] Although Lyslo had taken the time to consult with Indian leaders, their concerns were not taken seriously, nor was their desire to support tribal adoption considered.

The other prerequisite before transracial adoption could to reach its full potential was to fashion single Indian mothers into the unwed mothers of social case work, and children, as illegitimate children. Social workers needed to re-evaluate their approach to reservation women and children. This meant that Indian mothers would have to accept the casework services of social workers that pathologized Indian marriages and families, and sceptical social workers would have to envision Indian children as in need of adoption. While the BIA had employed social workers on Indian reservations, few had thought Indian mothers and children could benefit from adoption services, since few families considered Indian children as potential family members. Stella Hostbjor, a social worker with the BIA in the Sisseton Indian agency, published her experiences alongside Lyslo's first account of the IAP in 1961 in *Child Welfare*. Culturally and socially, Indian unmarried mothers presented a series of issues that added complexity for social workers attempting to offer typical unmarried mothers services as they would for an unwed white mother.

> The transition from the old kinship system to a nuclear family has meant less control over family relationships and a great increase in family breakdown. There are many stable marriages which may be legal or so-called "Indian custom." However, there are also many casual and temporary relationships which do not offer satisfaction or security to the couple involved or the children born to them. The members of this group do differentiate between a legal marriage, a true Indian custom marriage, and a temporary relationship, and are critical of the last. However their disapproval is not consistent enough or strong enough to be much of an influence. Since the state does not recognize the common law marriages all children born as a result of those temporary relationships or Indian custom are considered illegitimate.[69]

While the unmarried Indian mother was certainly influenced by her culture, and the social position she occupied as a result of her race and poverty, Hostbjor nonetheless felt that "we see her needs as being basically the same as those of other unmarried mothers, but her personality, experiences and cultural patterns, do create differences."[70] One primary difference between the white and the Indian unwed mother was the cultural perception of illegitimacy. Rather than a profound family crisis, as in white middle-class families, Indian families and communities were "very permissive and accepting.[71] There was little evidence of families rejecting children born out of wedlock. Unlike in white families, children were fully accepted, and "we never hear a disparaging tone or term used in speaking of the child, and we seldom hear anyone speak of him with pity because he is a fatherless child."[72] Motherhood without marriage was not seen to be a handicap for either the mother or the child.

The positive gloss placed on profoundly complex cultural and social issues continued unabated in Child Welfare League publications. Agencies responded to the opportunities presented to assist Indian children since, as May J. Davis, the supervisor from the Children's Bureau of Delaware wrote, "All Americans feel a certain sense of guilt about our treatment of the Indian and so we were glad of the chance to do something

concrete to offset out nebulous sense of shame."[73] White families interested in adoption were assured that the children placed with them had
been faced with a life of degrading poverty with little hope for future
happiness. Davis, after a tour of two reservations, offered her perspective on the advantages of adoption for these children:

> Since most children placed for adoption were born out of wedlock,
> perhaps it is also true that my knowledge is gathered from families
> with a degree of social pathology. Within these limits I have formed
> a few rather clear impressions of the Indian on the reservation. I
> have the sense that for many Indians living on a reservation, there
> is a dead-end quality and humdrumness to their existence which
> transcends any ability or wish to accomplish or achieve. The sopo-
> rific quality of life on a reservation must have some bearing on the
> fact that, among the families of our children, heavy drinking seems
> to be the rule rather than the exception.[74]

The IAP successfully aligned the interests of middle-class families,
state social service-providers, and the federal government through professional adoption technologies undermining tribal governments and
family ties, and negating the possibility to identify actual economic and
social needs of Indian people.

While the CWLA, through the IAP, stressed the importance of high
social work standards and application of proper legal adoption channels in transracial adoptions, these standards were not applied in many
instances of Indian transracial adoptions. Evidence emerged that Indian
mothers and children had become profoundly vulnerable to the heavy-
handed tactics of social workers. Similarly to the situation in Canada,
the passage of the 1953 law making reservations subject to state civil
and criminal law brought a dramatic increase in Indian children into
the cases of child welfare agencies. By 1968 one tribe had all its children
living in home care.[75] Poverty, racial and gendered characterizations of
Indian unfitness, and the intergenerational effects of colonial trauma
rendered Indian families and children vulnerable to the social welfare
interventions to rescue children from the dire futures workers believed
awaited Indian children if left on reservations.

By 1967, 395 Native American children in twenty-six states and
one territory, by fifty agencies throughout the United States had been

adopted through the IAP. The majority of children came from South Dakota (104) and Arizona (112), with the rest fairly evenly split among the other fourteen states.[76] By the end of the project, Lyslo proudly stated, "One can no longer say that the Indian child is the 'forgotten child,' as was indicated when the Project began in 1958."[77] Stimulation of adoptions brought about by favourable national media representations encouraged 5,000 prospective parents to enquire about adopting an Indian child. Positive "sentiment for our first Americans" in Eastern U.S. communities, according to Lyslo, brought about by the adoption exchange, "caused social agencies in the child's home states to take a 'new look' at the Indian child's adoptability with the result that many more Indian children are being placed for adoption in their own state."[78] The appeal of the Indian adopted child had reached such a level in South Dakota that the BIA social worker stated, "Here in South Dakota these activities have expanded to such an extent that we really no longer consider the Indian infant a hard-to-place child."[79]

By 1967 the success, according to American policy-makers and adoption advocates, of the IAP was clear. It had not only stimulated transracial adoptions of Indian children in faraway regions, it also led to interest in Indian adoption in local states and communities. From 1967 onward, the CWLA developed a transnational exchange. The Adoption Resource Network of America (ARENA) included not only Native American children but also Black, mixed-race, and family groups, and connected children to adoptive families in both Canada the United States. Using the same logic as the IAP, social work professionals believed that greater geographical distance between children and racially intolerant communities would "help overcome the uneven availability of homeless children and suitable adoptive families that now exist throughout the country."[80] Professionals working in transracial and transnational adoptions in the United States and Canada believed that the creation of an international exchange was a necessity for children handicapped by race, family situation, or physical and mental disability. For Indian and Métis children from Canada, it was hoped ARENA would "by-pass the regional prejudices that prevent many homeless children from being adopted."[81]

The creation of the Adopt Indian and Métis program in April 1967 in Saskatchewan shared many of the same goals of the Indian Adoption Project. Adopt Indian and Métis sought to secure the permanency of adoption for Indian and Métis children relinquished or removed from reserves and reduce pressure on foster homes by enlisting "normal" Saskatchewan families to adopt Indian and Métis children. The impetus behind the development of a public relations campaign to reconfigure Indigenous children as potential family members was the increasing numbers of Indigenous children being taken into care by the Department of Social Services, for neglect or relinquishment by biological family members.[82] Indigenous integration through the provincial child welfare system was failing to live up to its promise, hampered by the unwillingness of the non-Indigenous public to assume its role as potential foster parents or adopters. Selling the idea that the public could provide a solution to the "racial problem" paradoxically relied on denying the relevance of race of Indian children and reassuring non-Indigenous potential parents that the children were in every way the same as non-Indigenous children.

The Adopt Indian and Métis program brought the needs of Indigenous children to the attention of the viewing public in Saskatchewan, erasing their ties to their Indigenous heritage, and offering the public the opportunity to imagine themselves as parents forging a new colourblind society. The social construction of childhood as a central responsibility of the state and middle-class population first became widespread in the early nineteenth century with the child rescue movement in Britain. The Adopt Indian and Métis program shared a common language and goal with the nineteenth-century child rescue movement in the creation of specific kinds of subjects and bodies to be fundamental in the making of the body politic.[83] The "child as future citizen" was the core tenet of child rescue discourse. In the nineteenth century, children were transformed from private parental property to future citizens, and hence the responsibility of the nation.[84]

Through the use of books, periodicals, melodrama, and children's literature, the public became aware of its responsibility to assist in rearing poor children and youth. Like the Adopt Indian and Métis ads, often parents were absent from the stories. The primary objective of the publications was first to identify the problem to the public, then attract the financial support of the public for the orphan rescue institutions. As Shurlee Swain points out, "The neglected child, however romanticized, had to be made real if they were going to attract financial support."[85] From its beginnings, child rescue discourse lacked any call for social

Ross Thatcher and Métis children at Green Lake, 1966 (R-B7227 SAB)

justice or a roadmap for eliminating the causes of poverty and neglect of children. Like the Adopt Indian and Métis ads, early child rescue literature erased children from their families and histories. According to Swain, "Through the publications, children were constituted as victims, not of an unjust society but of the failing of their parents or other caregivers, often articulated in the old evangelical discourses of morality and sin."[86] The images and discourses of victimized children moved working- and middle-class families to support children's homes and eventually transracial adoption programs such as Adopt Indian and Métis.

With the election of Liberal leader Ross Thatcher in 1964, the CCF twenty-year rule came to an end. Declaring the province "open for business," Thatcher gave high priority to resolving "the Indian problem."[87] The expression of this Euro-Canadian intellectual construction has shifted, depending on time and place, but in mid-1960s Saskatchewan the "Indian problem" signified the extreme poverty and growing welfare dependence of Indian and Métis people. In April 1965 the Liberal government created the Indian and Métis Branch in the Department of Natural Resources, the only one of its kind in Canada. The branch was intended to "accelerate the process by which these people become an integral part of Canadian society." The primary purpose of the department was to find employment for Indian and Métis people.[88] In 1967, 89.1 per cent of residents living on reserves in southern Saskatchewan derived their income from welfare, compared with a 4.5 per cent rate for the non-Indian population of the same area.[89] Thatcher differed from the previous CCF social democratic government he had replaced; he believed in an individualist strategy, helping individual Indians and Métis take their place in the work world through individual job placements.

In crafting Indian and Métis policies, Thatcher was deliberately indifferent to the legal and cultural differences between Indian and Métis people. Not surprisingly, both Indian and Métis political organizations objected to the direction he took. Thatcher's emphasis on individual job placements came out of his right-of-centre political philosophy, his opposition to welfare programs, and his desire to see measurable results. According to historian Jim Pitsula, "His vision of the future was that Indians would be economically integrated and culturally assimilated into the dominant society."[90] Thus he shared a common outlook with the federal IAB in bypassing problematic legal and cultural issues and ensuring that individuals assumed their economic and social responsibilities.

From the perspective of the newly elected government, the state of child welfare services for Indian and Métis children appeared troubling and destined to escalate. In a confidential planning document, the Department of Social Welfare outlined the trajectory of child welfare responsibilities if the province continued its course of providing services to Indian and Métis children without the assistance of the federal government or working-class and middle-class Saskatchewan families. While Indian and Métis people made up a small percentage of the overall provincial population (7.5 per cent) in child welfare, 41.9 per cent of all children in 1969 in foster homes were Indian or Métis, and "additionally, an increasing number of Indian unmarried mothers avail themselves of provincial adoption services and leave their children."[91] Lack

of child welfare services on reserves meant that the province apprehended children only in cases of the most serious neglect if a child's
life was in danger, and the only other service available was adoption
on and off reserves. In most cases, unmarried mothers were told to
return to their reserves.[92] Planners suggested the need to negotiate for
immediate extensions of provincial child care services to reserves or
to call for changes to child welfare legislation so that IAB staff could
legally take action in neglect cases. The piloting of the Adopt Indian
and Métis program in 1967 called for little financial investment and did
not require extensive negotiation between federal and provincial counterparts or a radically new approach to resolving underlying economic
and social factors contributing to increasing numbers of Indigenous
children coming into provincial care. In keeping with the individualist ethos of the Thatcher government, individual children adopted by
individual families provided an important method by which to reduce
the financial responsibility of the government and provide the nurturing and permanence that was idealized by social work professionals as
in the "best interest of the child."

The first step in creating the Adopt Indian and Métis project was sur-
veying the Indian and Métis children who were permanent wards. In
April 1966 adoption consultant Alice Dales, who had been responsible
for the Green Lake experiment, conducted a region-by-region survey.
She reviewed 373 files to determine which Indian and Métis children
were legally free for adoption.[93] The stated purpose of the project was
to determine if a special approach to the problem of Indian and Métis
over-representation would increase adoptions, so fewer children would
remain in foster homes. Through the creation of a specialized advertising campaign and immediate follow-up by a unit of workers, Frank
Dornstauder, the project architect, hoped the program would encourage white families to adopt Indian children. This plan fundamentally
altered the understanding of racial boundaries that the federal government had assiduously erected over the past century in western Canada
through its Indian and Métis policies of segregation.

Dornstauder claimed to be inspired by the Montreal Open Door Society, which he was familiarized with while studying for his master's
degree in social work at McGill. The society had been created in 1959
by three families to assist adoption professionals who sought to raise
the prominence of interracial adoption of part-Black children through

education and support.[94] Dornstauder acknowledged that Saskatchewan differed profoundly from Montreal – first, that racial attitudes in Saskatchewan toward Indian and Métis were "more negative than in Montreal," and second, that the vast rural landscape required an approach that was different from Montreal's. The project was limited initially to a small geographical area, and after measuring the results, the study would allow administrators to see if the ad campaign could be effective throughout Saskatchewan. Not only would children benefit from the permanency of an adoptive family, there were also pragmatic reasons to explore adoption. As Dornstauder mused, "If it is successful, it will also be a major saving in maintenance costs for children."[95]

The federal Ministry of Health and Welfare approved the Adopt Indian and Métis pilot budget for 1967–8, providing funds to run the program for two years. Dornstauder hoped that by demonstrating the universal appeal of children and targeting one specific geographical area with "consistent, continuous, specific publicity," people would ultimately see the appeal of including Indigenous children as "family."[96] His hope was that "AIM will try to provide the spark and the initiative so that people will investigate the possibility."[97] The southeastern portion of the province targeted by the AIM campaign coincidentally also had the highest concentration of Indian reserves, and although not mentioned by officials, the greatest Indigenous poverty. It consistently ranked last in the Hawthorn Report's survey of socio-economic conditions across Canada. The per capita income of residents in 1966 was $55 per year, significantly less than the highest paid reserve, Skidegate in British Columbia, at $1252. James Smith Band, one of Saskatchewan's richest agricultural areas, had an average per capita income of $126. The survey also noted that all households were receiving welfare; at Piapot that number was 86.5 per cent.[98]

Television was an ideal medium to spread the message through the rural province to a diverse swath of the viewing population. In the televised advertisements for the Adopt Indian and Métis project, playful and innocent First Nations and Métis children appeared detached from their history, communities, and indigeneity. By doing so, the advertising company that created the ads enabled white families to imagine the children as family members and perceive themselves as providing a solution to the poverty and marginalization of Indigenous peoples.[99] Ads for the Adopt Indian and Métis project depicted Indigenous children as "normal" everyday children that communicated the colour-blind nature of the project. One thirty-three-second Adopt Indian and Métis commercial showed white parents, and the occasional Indigenous parent, providing care to First Nations and Métis youngsters. Children appeared playing catch, going fishing, practising piano, drinking milk, going to school, being comforted when upset, and being tucked into bed by loving parents. Indigenous children, all between the ages of five and ten, engaged in very typical actions that any Canadian child might. In one scene, a young boy about aged ten appeared to be a fishing companion to a single older man. These children, not infants, represented Indigenous transracial adoption as an opportunity for citizens, moved by the ads, to adopt. The commercial, until then accompanied only by a song, instructed viewers that they could "give a new life to a child in your home. Contact AIM."[100]

Advertisements ran in the small local community papers as well as in the Regina *Leader Post*. Newspaper articles provided responses to legal questions that adoptive parents might have about adoption of status Indian children. For example, the article with the title "Homes Sought for 160 Indian and Métis Children: Adopted Children Retain Status" ran 22 July 1967.[101] In it Dornstauder outlined how adoptions of Indians would work, explaining, "Until an adopted Indian child reaches the age of 21, laws pertaining to Indians pertain to him. If adopted by non-Indians, he is removed from the natural parents' band number and registered in a special index for that band. If adopted by Indians, he is registered under their band number."[102] According to Dornstauder, adoptive parents were told by the agency arranging the adoption whether the child was Indian or Métis but were not given the name of the band or band number. It was up to the parents whether they informed their child of his or her Indian status. At that time, the greatest numbers of children available for adoption were Catholic Métis children. The article explained how the children came to be wards of the state – first through illegitimacy, and second through neglect.[103]

With the completion of the pilot project in late 1969, the department gained new understanding of the power of the media to influence Euro-Canadian Saskatchewan families' perception of Indigenous children. From the Adopt Indian and Métis project, families took at face value ads' messages that Indian children were not different from any other child. To quote the government, "Advertising does pay." It was proven that the definition of the adoptable child went beyond the "blue ribbon baby," or the white infant in perfect health. Likewise, the streamlined process utilized by Adopt Indian and Métis expanded to all other areas of adoption. In 1970 the Department of Social Welfare introduced the AIM program, broadening the focus to all children who needed plans.[104] The AIM program supposedly no longer represented racial designation of Adopt Indian and Métis, and Indian and Métis children became homogenized under the label "hard to place children," with the promise that adoption "gives the less-than-perfect children the hope of a home and family."[105] The new approach sought to overcome the traditional barriers to adoption that included hereditary risks, health, education, welfare problems, age, sex, race, and membership in a family group. No longer would children be labelled "hard to place," but rather defined by their greater level of service needs, and the focus shifted from special children to special services.[106] Adoption made financial sense, and it was seen as preferable to multiple foster home placements in the lives of children. In the new policy manual, the author rationalized the expansion of the Adopt Indian and Métis program: "One child placed for adoption represents a savings of $1,000 per year minimum. Over a twenty-year period or the duration of wardship it represents a savings of $20,000. If this program placed 10 children for adoption that normally would not be placed, the program would pay for itself. The Adopt Indian Métis program as it is presently constituted places an average of 70 children per year."[107] The Adopt Indian and Métis program provided a complete solution for children and the government, so it would seem.

The imagery of the commercials and messages provided by newspaper articles had a two-fold impact on Saskatchewan residents. On one hand, it stimulated interest in transracial adoption, as planned. During the first year in operation, 16 children were placed through the Adopt Indian and Métis project, and by 1970 the number had risen to 50. However, 137 Indian and Métis adoptions had taken place throughout Saskatchewan outside of the specialized project. Between April 1967, the year AIM's pilot began, and 19 January 1970, 160 Indigenous children were placed in adoptive homes. With the expansion of the program and office in Saskatoon, adoptive placements of First Nations and Métis children increased. By 1970 there was a balance between children available for adoption and willing homes (see tables 6.4 and 6.5).

Table 6.1. Indian Adoptions in Canada, 1963–75

Year	Adoptions by Indians	%	Adoptions by non-Indians	%	Number of adoptions	Status Indian population
1963			94		168	204,677
1964–5	44	32.1	93	67.9	137	
1965–6	43	25.9	123	74.1	166	
1966–7	87	48.3	93	51.7	180	
1967–8	54	35.5	98	64.5	152	
1968–9	57	22.9	201	77.1	258	
1969–70	70	31.1	155	68.9	225	
1970–1	36	15.0	205	85.0	241	244,113
1971–2	53	15.8	282	84.2	335	
1972–3	41	12.7	281	87.3	322	
1973–4	75	20.0	300	80.0	375	
1974–5	101	27.8	262	72.2	363	

Source: Figures from annual reports of the Department of Citizenship and Immigration 1963–74; Hepworth, *Foster Care and Adoption in Canada.*

Table 6.2. 10 Years of Provincial Services to Status Indians in Canada

Year	No. children in care	No. adoptions	Expenses ($000s)
1970	5,395	241	10,042
1971	5,531	335	10,458
1972	4,467	322	11,494
1973	4,422	375	12,351
1974	5,270	363	14,091
1975	5,390	406	16,076
1976	5,952	581	19,806
1977	5,336	441	20,992
1978	5,659	519	24,773
1979–80	5,426	568	25,626

Source: Canada, *Annual Report of the Department of Indian and Northern Affairs Canada, 1980–1981,* "Child Welfare Services, 21," https://www.bac-lac.gc.ca/eng/discover/aboriginal-heritage/first-nations/indian-affairs-annual-reports/Pages/item.aspx?IdNumber=38290.

Officials judged AIM a success in raising awareness of the need for homes by non-Indigenous people, yet recognized that only 5 per cent of homes were Indian or Métis and consistently lamented that they did not recruit more Indigenous peoples. While these

Table 6.3. Statistics on Admission of Children into Care, Saskatchewan, 1973–4

	Apprehension	Relinquished	% apprehensions
Indian children	519	33	94.0
Métis children	557	46	92.4
Non-Indigenous children	712	297	70.5

Table 6.4. AIM Adoption Placements (under 10 years), 1967–70

Year	Girls adopted	Boys adopted	Total
1966–7			16
1967–8	27	19	46
1968–9	36	28	64
1969–70	33	17	50

Table 6.5. Provincial Adoption Placements, Saskatchewan

Year	All adoptions	Indian Métis adoptions	Indigenous adoption as % of total
1966–7	501	50	10.0
1967–8	556	96	17.2
1968–9	636	137	21.6

Sources: The numbers in tables 6.3, 6.4, and 6.5 are taken from G. Joice, chief, Special Services, to regional directors and adoption supervisors, re: Committee on Adoption Criteria Discussion Paper, 3 June 1974, file I-49, Coll. R-935, Adopt Indian and Métis program, Saskatchewan Department of Social Services, SAB.

numbers represent a large increase, in reality, of those coming into care, only 3.5–4.5 per cent of children were adopted, with the rest remaining in foster care, only rarely returning home.[108] Given that the primary reason Indigenous children came into care was poor housing, it was unlikely they would ever return home, for lack of family resources.

Métis children, like Robert Doucette, who were apprehended or relinquished during this period were prevented from having contact with their families and their communities, or having any knowledge of their cultural background. The rich heritage of Métis histories, kinship ties, and land-based identities were either invisible to white experts or deemed insignificant in light of the benefits children would derive from gaining an economically secure nuclear family. Neither Robert nor his grandfather accepted the logic of child welfare or the efforts to erase the kinship connection. Robert reconnected with his family and Métis identity, but the loss of his early years was still a source of pain and disconnection:

> My grandfather was one of the founders of Buffalo Narrows, was a justice of the peace for twenty years, had a huge library in the middle of the northern Saskatchewan bush. In the forties and fifties he represented people in court. I didn't know that growing up. As a matter of fact, doing research, I come across pictures of him every now and then, and I usually shed a tear when I see pictures of him. One day I was in the archives, and I found a picture of him with a caption that that reads, "Happy Métis grandfather with his 13 grandchildren." Except one. I started bawling, and the archives came there, and asked, "Are you OK?" I said, "Yeah! It's kind of a sad crying and happy crying, because I finally got to see who my grandfather was. A picture of him." And there were all my uncles and aunties, just little kids. And you so know when you find pictures like that it's kind of sad because I never met the guy.[109]

In the period between 1952 and 1973, the province of Saskatchewan began to integrate Indian and Métis families into emerging child welfare programs. Provincially delivered child welfare services were tasked with socializing families and children to voluntarily accept the roles and responsibilities of citizenship by adjusting personal outlooks and attitudes to embrace Euro-Canadian gender roles, educational aspirations, and employment patterns. It was believed that this outcome could best be achieved through professionally managed transracial adoptions. Realistically, these services never achieved the outcomes promised. Child welfare for Indigenous children operated primarily as child removals in extreme cases of neglect, with increasing numbers of transracial adoptions. Federal and provincial law came into conflict over women's reproductive choices, with women often losing their children to the provincial welfare department. Gendered and racialized laws intersected, severing familial and tribal ties for involuntarily enfranchised women and children, as social workers became responsible for enforcing the logic of elimination on behalf of the federal government. The extension of provincial child welfare legislation to Indian people meant primarily that Indian parents came under a legal regime that criminalized their many perceived deficits. For both Indian and Métis people in Saskatchewan, the long history of military, economic, and social suppression was ignored, leaving traumatized families to struggle to maintain their integrity and raise their children. For some, adoption and fostering offered the opportunity to stabilize personal situations that included abuse, violence, homelessness, abandonment, and poverty.

The system rarely looked sympathetically upon struggling Indian and Métis families and compared them unfavourably with more stable state-selected families. The Adopt Indian and Métis project shared many characteristics with early nineteenth-century child rescue movements in Britain and North America. The imagery of the vulnerable child in need of rescue through permanent adoption homes appealed to many families in Saskatchewan who had a genuine interest in providing loving homes to children who needed them. The commercials and radio and newspaper ads constructed children as "normal, healthy, and mostly happy children except for the fact they did not have parents and distinguishable from other children only by the fact they were of Indian or part-Indian ancestry."[110] In reality, many of the children did have parents, and their ethnicity as Indian or part Indian mattered a great deal more than the advertising indicated. As was increasingly apparent, the department acknowledged that many Indian and Métis children in care "were found to have a medical, mental, genetic or social problems other than that associated with age or racial origin."[111] The troubling pasts of the children were not erased with a change in birth certificate and removal from their birth homes. Social welfare experts hoped that adoptive parents could "disassociate the handicap from their child's racial identity and assist the child and community in differentiating between the racial identity and the handicap."[112] The promise of Euro-Canadian methods of child welfare service, and adoption in particular, proved elusive and demanded increasing investment and perhaps a change in focus. The Métis Society and the SNWM rejected the tropes used in the commercials and demanded a say in the creation of policies for Indian and Métis children. Claims made by newspapers and commercials whitewashing the experiences of poverty, racism, and neglect of Indian and Métis people demanded a response.

The programs and policies administered by the Department of Social Services operated under the paternalistic Euro-Canadian belief that the child welfare bureaucracy and family courts alone could interpret the "best interests of the [Indigenous] child." As Indigenous families struggled to meet the needs of children, and Métis people organized to stem the increasing removal of children from homes and communities, provincial social workers and bureaucrats remained unwilling to divert from the path that was becoming increasingly entrenched.

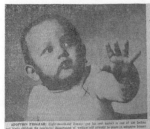

Adoption program planned

Homes wanted for 150 Indian and Metis children

Race not principal issue in Indian, Metis adoptions

Homes sought for 160 Indian and Metis children

Adopted children retain status

Early newspaper ads and posters for Adopt Indian and Métis (from Department of Social Services Collection, file I-49, Coll. R-935, Adopt Indian and Métis program, 1967–73, Saskatchewan Department of Social Welfare, SAB)

Indian couples eligible to adopt children

By NANCY GELBER
Staff Reporter

Why Indian couples seem uninterested in adopting children of Indian heritage is a puzzlement to A.I.M. Ba Adopt Indian-Metis Centre.

The reason makes Frank Dornstauder, director of the welfare department's centre, shrug.

"I'm not sure I know the answer yet," he said, simply as he listed possibilities.

Perhaps they feel the centre sets such high standards that applicants wouldn't be accepted. Or they may believe the white welfare workers would consider them strange for wanting to adopt, he if it was the white man's prerogative.

"This is only a guess, but the couple is logical. What if they feel once the children have been salvaged from an unhappy situation in the reserve, we therefore wouldn't want to give any of our children back to a reserve couple," he reasoned.

A.I.M. wants Indian couples as full participants in its program. Mr. Dornstauder registered several items during the interview that if was their right to take advantage of the service an bureau offers.

"It's important these Indian couples don't feel we're stamping to do them a favor. We want them to take a full part. This is one ground for our experiment. As far as I know the department has never made a concerted effort to put into the reserves babies," Mr. Dornstauder said.

While A.I.M. is putting a certain amount of emphasis on Indian couples, it doesn't want the image to be that of a true apple.

"We're definitely not spending an Indian children must be adopted by Indian families but we will recruit Indian couples who wish to adopt our children as we have many white couples who have expressed interest as that," he explained.

A.I.M. feels only a decent suitable home for its children. One worry is that the image of good, white couple only is beginning to prevail.

There, however, Mr. Dornstauder said. The matters sought are to be found in such Indian and white homes. Housing, general relationship standards and economic security are definitely not determining factors in placement, he pointed out.

What is important is the centre see marriage stability, family ties and adjustment of children in the community.

This is where our decision standard takes over. We think of security as being $15,000 a year brought home by the head winner. But this may not be a good family too as. It's because of half could be coming apart from the seams," he said matter-of-factly.

Unfortunately Mr. Dornstauder thinks the reserve babies have to be the answer in the Fatherland. So increasingly few Ixr children are reserve. Workers will go to 10 reserve one hour band relation.

If these discoveries are positive, numerous such reserves on socialites and child will follow along if is every record A.I.M. may be going where we are based, to serve A.I.M. will set them back anywhere. Any serum work at he part of the workers will be a result of an attitude step.

"We certainly have much to learn. We hope the Indian people with give us their ideas on adoption. We don't have to agree with each other at all, but we'll be certainly the problem to around a year," he said.

Besides Mr. Dornstauder, there are four A.I.M. workers, Miss Genevieve Snyder, Miss Shirley Hope, Jerry Jacobs and Miss Hazel Satterwas.

Young Indian children
suffer plight of the orphaned

By GERRY SENIUK
Staff Reporter

Somewhere in Saskatoon two Indian children, David, 8, and Delores, 6, are being cared for by welfare officials trying to show them that the life they felt was shattered in July, still held hope, brightness and a chance for happiness.

Their story may not be scandalous or shocking, but it is an example, even if extreme, of the plight of an orphaned child.

If their story is unique, which welfare officials say is not necessarily so, the loneliness and fear they must have felt is not an unknown feeling among foster children everywhere.

Almost three years ago, welfare officials took them off a

Then, this spring, welfare officials found an Indian couple, living in a two room bungalow on a reserve, willing to adopt David and Delores. The officials investigated them and, on discovering that the couple were reliable and steadily employed, concluded they would make excellent parents.

They gave their findings to Mrs. Ulricht and she and her husband agreed to allow the children to visit for a five-day period with the couple to see if they liked it.

After their return, they impressed different people differently.

The welfare worker thought they did like it and recommended that adoption plans proceed.

"They didn't like it," said Mrs. Ulricht. "They told me that when they returned. Delores told me she told the worker that."

"They had no milk while they were there. They were poorly fed, getting porridge for breakfast and supper. The whole family slept in one room and they had no privacy."

On July 25, two welfare men came to take them away.

"They were frightened," said Mrs. Ulricht. "As soon as they saw the car they locked the front door."

When the welfare workers

ated this home and were satisfied. There was nothing like neglect. But Mrs. Ulricht had this feeling about reserves," he said.

It now appears quite certain that the children will not be sent to the young couple because of this attitude the children now have.

Mrs. Ulricht said she had no aversion to the children living on the reserve as long as it's a good home.

"However, the picture the social worker painted of the place was nothing like the story the children brought back with them . . . It's cruel to drag them off the reserve, give them a better life for three years and then send them back to the same thing. It's taking a step backward," she said.

Adoption sought
for Indian children

PRINCE ALBERT — A. W. Sihvon, deputy provincial minister welfare, said the department will seek an adoption home for two Indian children presently located in Saskatoon.

It was department policy to place children in adoption homes as soon as possible and foster parents were made aware of this from the beginning, Mr. Sihvon said.

"The Ulricht's gave the chidlren excellent care, but took exception to the choice of adopting home and the initial choice will not be considered further," he said.

Mr. Sihvon's comment was in reply to an inquiry regarding an incident at the Ulricht farm when David, 8 and Delores, 6 were placed for adoption with an Indian family on a reserve. At this time, Mrs. Ulricht expressed disapproval and concern, he said.

"The children are entitled to a permanent home and we must make every effort to give them this security," Mr. Sihvon said.

Families of their own

There is something tenderly appealing in the bedtime prayers of every child. Yet not every child is fortunate enough to be able to kneel beside his own bed and confidently recite, "God bless Mummy and Daddy". For many of the wards of the Saskatchewan department of welfare the question of a permanent home and the loving care prospective parents must be young enough to insure the protection and security of home life until the child reaches adulthood. Attitude of mind is given prior importance in granting custody. There must be no hint of condescension or sense of "rescuing" the child. Inevitably, of course, this attitude could only breed frustration or a sense

Adoption of natives doubles

Adoptions of Indian and Metis children have more than doubled in the past year. Welfare Minister C. P. MacDonald said Thursday.

The Adopt Indian Metis (AIM) program, a pilot project operating in the southeastern part of the province, was launched one year ago. And, in that area, adoptions tripled to 45 from 16 the previous year.

Over the province as a whole, the number of children of native descent who have been adopted has doubled, to 100 from 50.

Mr. MacDonald said the special adoption project was put into operation because, for the past five years, the number of children in the care of his department increased by approximately 180 a year.

AIM results said splendid

The Saskatchewan government's program to encourage adoptions of Indian and Metis children has produced some splendid results. Welfare Minister MacDonald said Thursday.

The Adopt Indian Metis (AIM) program, a pilot project operating in the southeastern part of the province, was launched one year ago.

The number of adoptions of Indian and Metis children in the project has tripled since AIM was started, Mr. MacDonald said.

Over the province as a whole, the number of children of native descent who have been adopted has doubled.

In the project area, which includes the Regina, Moose Jaw, Weyburn and Qu'Appelle welfare department regions, 45 Indian and Metis children have been adopted since AIM was launched. In the previous year, there were 16 adoptions of native children in the same area. Over the province, the number has gone up from 50 to 100 in the same period.

Mr. MacDonald said the success of the AIM project can be attributed not only to the attitude and response of the adoptive parents but the attitude of the community as a whole.

AIM seeks to find homes for Indian, Metis children

By KEN POLE

REGINA (CP) — The six-year-old girl became tearful and refused to eat when the young couple told her they were all going to the courthouse to sign her adoption papentage, who are wards of the provincial welfare department.

Concentrated in the southwest part of Saskatchewan, AIM is the first program with Indian children as its target.

old, or the parents might have abandoned them."

These children would be hard to place, even if they were white-skinned. Some came from unwed mothers, but these created the least

50 during the previous year. In the project area, consisting of the Regina, Moose Jaw, Weyburn and Qu'Appelle welfare regions, the total rose to 45 from 16.

The $120,000 project is being

ARTHUR

Arthur is a 2½ year old boy' with a nice wide smile. He has large, round, dark-brown eyes and dark-brown hair. Although shy at meeting new people, he plays boisterously with children he knows. He likes toys, especially his plastic skidoo. He also likes being told stories, being cuddled and sung to. Arthur is used to a big family and lots of activity. For further information on the adoption of Arthur, contact:

Aim Centre

2340 Albert Street
REGINA, Saskatchewan
S4P 2V7
Phone: 523-6681

Room 210, 1030 Idylwyld Dr. N.
SASKATOON, Saskatchewan
S7L 4J7
Phone: 653-2056

GWEN

Gwen is a beautiful little girl with a deceptively sad looking appearance, now 2¾ years old. While she is wary of strangers she does like lots of love and cuddling. She is independent and can readily amuse herself. Gwen works off lots of energy riding her tricycle. She gets along well with playmates.

While Gwen enjoys general good health, her left foot is affected by cerebral palsy which causes her to walk with a slight limp and to wear a leg brace below the knee. This condition will not deteriorate. When she is 4 years old she will have a "tendon transfer" operation which will strengthen her foot. She will then continue to wear the brace until she is about 13 years of age at which time she will have a second operation to perform bone surgery on her heel. After that, it is expected that she will be able to go brace free.

Parents wishing to discuss the adoption of Gwen may contact:

Aim Centre

2340 Albert Street
REGINA, Saskatchewan
S4P 2V7
Phone: 523-6681

Room 210, 1030 Idylwyld Dr. N.
SASKATOON, Saskatchewan
S7L 4J7
Phone: 653-2056

New adoption program now underway for Indian, Metis children

By Ken Pole
Canadian Press staff writer
REGINA — The six-year-

short history of the Adopt Indian and Metis (AIM) program, set up by the Sas-

were the best range for us," he said. "These kids were already a community responsi-

were white-skinned. Some came from unwed mothers, but these created the least problems.

Indian and Metis children since the start of AIM, compared with 50 during the

gave us 50 or 60 one-minute spot ads without any fee." A problem has been the

have been placed with Indian and Metis families. "Perhaps they felt the centre set such a high stand-

wouldn't be accepted," Mr. Dornstauder said.

One of his social workers, Genevieve Singiton, said AIM is not interested in the

---

Program Aims At Finding Homes For Mixed And Indian Children

SASKATOON (CP) — Louise is a dark-eyed, bright 3½-year-old who, although her mind can't comprehend it yet, is engaged in a desperate battle which will shape her future.

The fight is for security, something she hasn't found in three different homes and something which her fourth-parents hope to give her.

Louise's fight is different from that of most adopted children because her new family is white and she is Metis—part Indian and part white.

taking her and I expect everyone to like her.

"We haven't met any discrimination yet — but perhaps it's discrimination of a form when people say 'Aren't you the good Samaritan'"

Louise was abandoned at two years of age and lived in two foster homes. When taken into the care of the province she spoke only Cree.

Mrs Vickers said most people who go to AIM already have families, either natural or adopted or a mixture.

Few childless couples adopted Indian or Metis chil-

legal rights to the child are transferred to the new parents.

Before AIM was established the number of Indian and Metis children awaiting adoption had been increasing at about 100 a year.

In October, 1969, there were 305 Indian and Metis children under provincial care and by last month 186.

Mrs Vickers says that AIM is at least keeping ahead of the increase and that the program has boosted the number of adoptions of all types in Saskatchewan.

AIM—Adopt Indian-Metis—giving children white parents

By JIM POLING

SASKATOON — (CP) — Louise is a dark-eyed, bright 3½-year-old who, although her mind can't comprehend it yet,

is engaged in a desperate battle which will shape her future.

The fight is for security, something she hasn't found in three different homes

something which her fourth — and probably permanent — parents hope to give her.

Louise's fight is different from that of most adopted children because her new

family is white and she is Metis — part Indian and part white.

She represents a challenge not only to her new parents, but to a branch of the Saskatchewan department of

31, 1969, a total of 140 were placed in permanent homes. Sixty of them were placed by AIM's Regina office and its Saskatoon branch and the rest by the welfare department which handles Indian and

aware that it does to some people."

Louise's new parents, who have two boys, aged 9 and 10, and a girl 8, were drawn to AIM by its publicity campaign and a long-standing interest in

of thought went to AIM because they felt they could help the problem of Indian and Metis children by adopting one.

"At first I thought that when I took her shopping with

the family and the child can adjust. At the end of that time the child may be returned — though not many are — or the legal rights to the child are transferred to the new parents.

SAFE!
IN YOUR HANDS

Your hands could hold the future of a Metis child. Without parents, without a home free from prejudice and full of love, these children of Indian Heritage face an uncertain future. If you have such a home and would like to adopt as your own a Metis boy or girl, then you can become part of AIM.

Consider a part Indian child if you are thinking of enlarging your family. The problems are very small and the rewards are very great.

Children should be treated with the respect which is due to their innocence of the world.
—H. P. Liddon

ADOPT INDIAN METIS Centre /AIM

2340 ALBERT ST., REGINA, SASKATCHEWAN TELEPHONE 523-6681

DEPARTMENT OF WELFARE

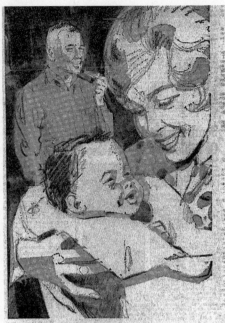

OUT OF
NOWHERE,
INTO HERE...

Once this child's life and future was uncertain, lonely. He faced the problems of a Metis child growing up without parents to guide him. Now he lives in a home full of love, free from prejudice. If yours is a childless home, or if you want to complete your family, there is a little Metis boy or girl longing for you. You can become part of AIM and give your lives new meaning.

Prospective adopting parents can rest assured that children offered for adoption are carefully evaluated, to ensure, as far as is humanly possible, that they are in every way normal.
—Dr. K. C. Grovett
Director of Child Health

I have often thought what a melancholy world this would be without children.
—Samuel Coleridge-Taylor

ADOPT INDIAN METIS Centre /AIM

2340 ALBERT ST., REGINA, SASKATCHEWAN TELEPHONE 523-6681

DEPARTMENT OF WELFARE
A FEDERAL-PROVINCIAL PROJECT DIRECTOR: FRANK DORNSTAUDER

HERE'S SOMETHING...
YOU CAN'T BUY

Who can put a price on happiness? There are wards, of Indian heritage, who have no hope of knowing the joy and happiness that comes with being part of a family. Give a child a little love and you'll receive a great deal in return. You can do it by adopting one of these forgotten children, and becoming part of AIM.

COMMENTS OF PARENT:

It is now more than nine years since Mark, our son, joined our family. He has always been as much a part of it as our natural children.

All who would win joy, must share it; happiness was born a twin.
—Lord Byron

PT INDIAN METIS *Centre* / **AIM**

BERT ST., REGINA, SASK CHEWAN • TELEPHONE 522-6681

GEE!
WHAT A GRIP

You can do no greater thing than to give your hand and heart to a little child, a child that will give your life new meaning. If yours is a childless home, if you want to complete your family, or share your family's happiness with another, then there is a little boy or girl of Indian Heritage waiting for you. You can become part of AIM and give your own lives new meaning.

COMMENTS OF PARENT:

Four children, two of Indian heritage, mean frequent surprises and endless joy. We are proud of each child, and grateful for each one.

Children have more need of models than of critics.
—Joseph Joubert

ADOPT INDIAN METIS *Centre* / **AIM**

2340 ALBERT ST., REGINA, SASKATCHEWAN • TELEPHONE 523-6681

DEPARTMENT OF WELFARE

A FEDERAL-PROVINCIAL PROJECT · DIRECTOR FRANK DORNSTAUDER

THE FIRST STEP
...YOURS

Seems like only yesterday they took their first steps. We took ours too, adopting a sister for Tom. Rosemary was such a happy little Metis baby. She's made our family complete, and now she has a chance for a wonderful future. We're proud of both our children. When you become part of AIM, you'll know the joy that comes when you give a child of Indian Heritage a future.

By offering a child a home filled with warmth and affection, you will create the everlasting love of a child, the pride of a teenager and the humble appreciation of an adult.

Comment by:
Mr. Howard Brachman
Director,
Child Guidance Clinic

The dew of our destiny, wander where we will, lies at the foot of the cradle.
—Jean Paul Richter

ADOPT INDIAN METIS Centre / AIM
2340 ALBERT ST., REGINA, SASKATCHEWAN   TELEPHONE 523-6681

DEPARTMENT OF WELFARE
A FEDERAL-PROVINCIAL PROJECT   DIRECTOR: FRANK DORNSTAUDER

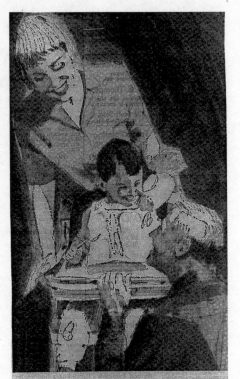

GIVE A CHILD
HAPPINESS

Have you the desire to give a child love and happiness? Why not consider a child of Indian heritage. There is a little Metis boy or girl waiting to fill your home with the magic only a child can create. Give a child a little love and you'll receive a great deal in return. If there is room in your heart, you can become part of AIM.

The color of a child's skin, his creed or his handicap does not take away the God-given right to a home and family of his own — children deprived of this right cannot speak for themselves. We, on their behalf, challenge you to take up their plea.
—Alice Dales, Former Adoption Consultant.

He who gives a child a home builds palaces in Kingdom Come!
—John Masefield, "Everlasting Mercy"

ADOPT INDIAN METIS Centre / AIM
2340 ALBERT ST., REGINA, SASKATCHEWAN • TELEPHONE 523-6681

QUESTIONS PEOPLE ASK
AND THE ANSWERS

Q. May we adopt more than one child?
A. You certainly may.

Q. How long does it take to adopt a child?
A. This depends very much on readiness of the adopting couple. Hopefully, we can prepare applicants for placement of children within four months.

Q. May we state our preference for a boy or a girl?
A. Yes, but when you specify selection, our choice is limited and it will likely take longer to place than if you are prepared to accept a child of either sex or any age.

Q. When the adoption is finalized is the child legally ours?
A. Yes, he is just as much yours as if he had been born to you.

Q. May we adopt a child even if we have children of our own?
A. Yes. Provided that an adoption will not jeopardize your existing family.

Q. If I am a working mother, may my husband and I still adopt a child?
A. The fact that a mother is working does not in itself constitute a barrier to adoption.

Q. Is there an income requirement?
A. No, we only require that the head of the home can adequately support his family.

Q. Is there any cost involved?
A. No, the Department of Welfare makes no charge whatever.

PUBLISHED BY AUTHORITY OF THE
MINISTER OF WELFARE

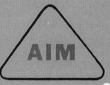

ADOPT INDIAN METIS
Centre

2340 ALBERT STREET
REGINA, SASKATCHEWAN
TELEPHONE 523-6681

FRANK A. DORNSTAUDER, DIRECTOR, AIM CENTRE
DEPARTMENT OF WELFARE

AIM in Saskatchewan is a Joint Federal-Provincial Program

ADOPT INDIAN METIS

is a special concentrated effort under the Child Welfare Branch, Department of Welfare, to place children of Indian heritage in adoption homes. These children range in age from infancy to six years of age or more.

WHY ADOPT A CHILD?

Because you both love children and have not had any of your own, or, having your own you would like another boy or girl to round out your family.

WHAT DO WE NEED TO ADOPT A CHILD?

You should:
... have a well adjusted marriage and ... be very sure you both want a child or more children
... have a steady income
... own or rent a home or apartment where there is room for a child
... be of an age that the child could have been born to you.

These and other particulars about adopting a child are in the Department of Welfare pamphlet "Adopting a Child" which is available on request.

WHY ADOPT AN INDIAN OR METIS CHILD?

They need the love and security of parents and a home just as much as any child. They also bring joy and happiness to your home since they are as capable of giving love as receiving it.

WHAT MORE DOES IT TAKE TO ADOPT AN INDIAN OR METIS CHILD?

You need to be the kind of people who can fully accept a child into your home and heart and to assist him to appreciate the fact of his dual heritage. You should both be sufficiently mature to be able to help him with the particular problems he may encounter as he grows to adolescence and maturity.

You must be prepared to help the child handle and overcome any prejudice he may encounter as an adopted child or as a child of Indian heritage. He may be faced with this problem within your family, circle of friends or neighborhood. You may be Protestant, Catholic or Jewish, but there is a somewhat greater need for Catholic homes.

Children to be placed come from any part of Saskatchewan but the campaign to find homes is being concentrated in the south-eastern part of the province. The area includes the four South-eastern Welfare Regions; namely, Qu'Appelle, Regina, Moose Jaw and Weyburn.

The reasons for concentrating in an area such as this are:
... because of the greater population
... to permit an all-out effort
... to enable the special staff to meet with interested parents as soon as possible after they have expressed their interest.

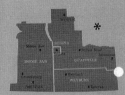

Interested persons in other parts of the province should contact the nearest

**Regional Office,
Department of Welfare.**

Your inquiry will be welcome and your application will be handled the same as other adoptions.

7

Saskatchewan's Indigenous Resurgence and the Restoration of Indigenous Kinship and Caring

These ads are racist propaganda against the Métis and Indian people.
— Howard Adams, 1971[1]

In response to Adopt Indian and Métis advertising, the Métis Foster Home Committee led by Howard Adams and Métis activists Phyllis Trochie, Nora Thibodeau, and Vicki Racette researched the creation of a Métis-controlled foster home program. In their letter to the Department of Social Welfare, the committee stated, "In this plan we are proposing a system of foster home care of our Métis children to be placed in Métis foster homes or in group foster homes under the control and management of Métis people."[2] The group had eleven reasons that the government-run system was detrimental to children, parents, and the Métis community. The objections centred on the lack of acceptance by white foster parents who raised the children and the larger white society in which the children were being raised. The final point stated, "We are opposed to a foster home scheme as a relocation or integration program."[3] The society proposed a transfer of the government-run child-caring institution, Kilburn Hall in Saskatoon, to Métis control through a board of Métis parents. They claimed that past experiences with the welfare department had proven that the government was unable to treat Métis people as equal and full citizens. Any new programs or policies without the input and consent of Indigenous peoples would continue to be administered in a repressive and discriminatory way.[4] While the discourse of equal treatment and colour blindness permeated the department's official pronouncements, Métis and Indian people drew upon their own collective experiences of discrimination to formulate their position on child welfare.

During the 1970s Métis and non-status people in Saskatchewan organized to resist the child welfare system. The provincial Métis Society submitted two proposals to provide an Indigenous alternative to caring for Métis children, while organizations formed in Regina and Saskatoon to develop local, community-based responses. In these actions and proposals the Métis identified the complex and historic issues that drove child neglect and removal in Saskatchewan and drew upon historic Métis collectivity support families and children in need. Recognizing the economic and social issues leading to child removal, Métis leadership offered culturally relevant solutions and attempted to mitigate the harms of child apprehension and family breakdown. The foster home proposals were part of the Métis larger self-determination and decolonization movement that recognized the centrality of family to the Métis community.

The Métis Society organized in the early 1930s as the "Halfbreeds of Saskatchewan" to fight for Métis land rights, changing their name to the Saskatchewan Métis Society in 1937 with the creation of a new constitution. The society went through a period of inactivity until the mid-1960s.[5] The Métis Association of Saskatchewan, based in Prince Albert, organized in 1964 to represent northern Métis interests, while the Métis Society of Saskatchewan organized in 1965 in Regina to represent southern Métis interests. The two organizations combined in 1967 as the Saskatchewan Métis Society under the leadership of Joe Amyotte.[6] In April 1969 Howard Adams replaced Amyotte as president. Influenced by the

Howard Adams (used with permission from the Gabriel Dumont Institute)

Black nationalist and decolonization movement while undertaking his PhD at Berkeley in the late 1960s, Adams called on the Métis to decolonize and avoid government funding of any sort, echoing the earlier perspective of northern Métis leader Malcolm Norris.[7] The media viewed Adams as a militant and revolutionary, stoking white public fear of violence similar to the U.S. race riots taking place.[8]

Adams was one of the first Métis intellectuals to write about imperialism, white supremacy, and colonization in Canada. Originally from St Louis, Saskatchewan, Adams sought the decolonization of Indigenous peoples in Saskatchewan after his experience of the civil rights movement while doing his PhD at Berkeley during the 1960s. Adams returned to Saskatchewan in 1966, seeking economic, social, and cultural autonomy for Métis people in Saskatchewan. During his presidency, the Métis Society began publishing *New Breed* magazine, the voice of the growing Métis nationalist movement in Canada. In 1975 he published *Prison of Grass*, asserting that Indigenous peoples and people of colour lived in a white racist society, and that racism is the product of economics.[9] Indigenous peoples experienced the white supremacy of government, churches, schools, and courts, and in the larger nationalist culture. The "white ideal" was evident everywhere: in the books and movies, and on TV. Through day-to-day experiences of racialization and culturally replicated ideas of inferiority, Indian and Métis were taught to be inferior and seek acceptance in white society. In what Jim Pitsula has called "the rebirth of Métis nationalism," Adams rejected integration and argued for a separate and decolonized Métis political existence.[10]

The Métis Society specifically targeted the Adopt Indian and Métis advertising that perpetuated white supremacy and Indigenous degradation. They argued, "These ads are racist propaganda against the Métis and Indian people."[11] The ads implied that Métis parents were unable to look after their children, and they degraded Indigenous children as inferior and unwanted, since "they are displayed as surplus and unwanted children." To the Métis community, the entire premise of the ad campaign was objectionable because "it portrays our people and nation as being weak because we are portrayed as begging white people to take our children." Métis people in Saskatchewan felt the ads used their children "to degrade and humiliate our people by playing on our children's pathetic appearance to have white people care for and support our children." The society claimed that AIM created the public impression that

Métis children were "so unwanted and ugly that the government has to make great efforts to find some kind of home for them." Further, it suggested that the children were so desperate for homes they would accept any white family who were sympathetic enough. Métis people said the ads were merely the reinvention of a paternalistic racism, reinforcing the negative stereotypes about Indian peoples. Finally, they promoted the idea that Métis parents did not want or love their children.[12] They also demanded an end interprovincial and transnational adoption of Métis children into white homes in other provinces or the United States. Seeking control over child welfare was only one component in an overall "revival of Métis nationalism."[13] Métis people began to speak up and challenge the images governments generated for public consumption. Or, as Maria Campbell states of this period, "They started talking back."[14]

In response to the letter received from the Métis Society, officials at the Department of Welfare called a meeting with Howard Adams and the Métis Foster Home Committee in Saskatoon. There the government minimized the concerns of the Métis people: "There seemed to be a good deal of confusion in the minds of the Métis people with regard to our Department's requirements for foster parents. This was clarified very quickly and we indicated that we would be only too pleased to have their assistance in locating Métis foster homes."[15] Officials acknowledged that the strongest point of view presented by Adams was resistance to the images of children used in the Adopt Indian and Métis ads. They considered altering the name, Adopt Indian and Métis, to AIM, to appease the activists and dropping the reference to race, and giving the program a much broader focus. Officials admitted that the resistance engendered by the ads had seriously hampered their ability to work: "The situation is this: our Adopt Indian and Métis Centres in Regina and Saskatoon have been almost immobilized because we have not been able to recruit prospective adopting parents through the media because of the objections raised by the Métis Association."[16] This event marked the beginning of pollination between this group and the Native Women's Association.

Adopt Indian and Métis publicity ended 1 December 1972 as the result of objections raised by the Métis Society and a commitment to change the focus to include all children. As a result there was a notable drop in inquiries.[17] The "change in focus" entailed a name change, from Adopt Indian and Métis to Aim Centre, as well as a silencing on the racial nature of the majority of children the program served. The government responded to "concerns by some native groups ... voiced because to these groups the program was seen as a negative reflection on native people."[18] However, internally, officials acknowledged that the majority of children were still of Indigenous origin, but also claimed they had additional "characteristics in addition to being a minority race that were inhibiting placement." These characteristics included membership in family group, medical problems, physical handicaps, mental handicaps, slow development, age beyond infancy, and other factors that would give a more realistic picture of children's needs.

While the racial focus of Adopt Indian and Métis was submerged, the centre took on a new role in the facilitation of out-of-province adoptions. Both in receiving inquiries and sending the profiles of difficult-to-adopt children to other agencies, a new international adoption paradigm was taking shape in the early 1970s. The government memo about the change in name also explained the new direction in adoption policy: "With increasing number of referrals coming from other provinces it has become desirable to channel these inquiries and responses through one source and Aim Centre, Regina is currently providing this co-ordinating service as well as referral through ARENA."[19] In 1971 the Adopt Indian and Métis began publishing a bulletin featuring pictures and write-ups on children available for adoption, distributing to provincial adoption authorities across country. Since then, the government began receiving home studies from Ontario, Montreal, Alberta, and Nova Scotia. That year, three infants were placed, one in Quebec, two in Ontario. The new role of the AIM centre was to facilitate transnational adoptions, in the first year placing three family groups of three children in Minnesota, New Jersey, and Colorado. One nine-year-old boy was placed in Colorado, and one four-year-old in Wyoming.[20]

Despite Indigenous objections, the government decided to increase advertising in 1972–3 and placed a heavy emphasis on its new name and the "change in focus." On 16 March 1972 a memo sent to all staff indicated, "This is to confirm that effective immediately the Adopt Indian Métis program will be known simply as Aim.... In addition I wish to confirm that the Aim program will no longer pertain solely to Native children."[21] Social workers argued that Indigenous children's race was merely one factor in a constellation that affected planning and placement possibilities. The Aim Centre merely applied the same principles in adoption service – direct and indirect marketing, specialized and streamlined

Nora Thibodeau Cummings (used with permission from the Gabriel Dumont Institute)

processes – while denying that the intention was to gain support for the adoption of Native children. The department recognized that Native organizations were increasingly opposed to singling out Indian or Métis children for publicity. However, they rationalized that "while our change in focus will not change the facts of the situation and those facts being that a disproportionate percentage of new permanent wards each year are of Indian and Métis origin, it may be possible to meet some of the concerns of the Native people while at the same time reflecting more accurately the needs of the children."[22] While the Aim Centre claimed to be racially neutral, Indigenous people in Saskatchewan found little to differentiate it from Adopt Indian and Métis: it lacked input from Indigenous people and it continued to rely on the same logic that contributed to the breakdown of families and oppression of Indigenous peoples.

The Saskatchewan Native Women's Movement (SNWM) came into existence on 6 December 1971, bringing together Indian and Métis women from across the province to politicize gender and race, and was open to any women of Native ancestry or married to a Native man. The movement advanced the interest of all Native women, whether status, non-status, or Métis. Together, they promoted their common interests through collective action, engaged in research to promote interest in Native women, lobbied government, co-operated with other organizations, and supported the treaty rights of Indian women and the civil and human rights of all Native women in the province.[23] Their slogan was "The unity of all women of Native ancestry."[24]

Nora Thibodeau (now Cummings) had first-hand experience of the "technologies of helping" provided by Saskatchewan social workers in this era. When interviewed about her life and the time she spent as president of the SNWM, she spoke of her own experiences and those of her sisters and aunts, who were continually under the surveillance of social workers and Catholic nuns. She recalled being a single Métis woman in the city with children and expecting another:

> When I had my children, and I had my four children and I was pregnant with my fifth…. They decided that because my first husband and I separated, and they tried to take my children. "We will give you the oldest boy, and we will take the younger boy and the babies." I said, "You will take nothing." My exact words: "If you think I'm a bitch dog you got another thing coming. 'Cause you are not taking my babies." And I remember he had his feet up and I took his feet, and I said, "Send a social worker to my house, I will hammer her. You are not taking my babies." And they didn't take my babies. 'Cause I stood up for me. And I know how they did it. It was Sister Obrien's way of doing things. I had a half-sister who moved away to Edmonton and they tried to take her baby. And these things happened in the city and they happened on the reserve and they happened in our community.
>
> They would walk into homes in the north. And my husband is from Buffalo Narrows. They just walked in and took the baby. And that's how they'd do things. My aunt, when she was pregnant with her child. It was Bethany home at that time. That's where mothers would go and that's where they would take their babies. And

there's lots of untold stories that went on in our city, and I can speak of our city. I was more fortunate because I had my mom, my grandmother, my aunties. I was more fortunate. Other Métis didn't have that support, and fell into that system, and lost their children.[25]

An outspoken advocate for Métis women, Métis families, and communities, Thibodeau played an important role in shaping the SNWM. The provincial organization was in Saskatoon and played a coordinating function, hosting the annual meeting, conducting board meetings, developing special projects, and publishing the monthly newsletter, *Iskwew*. The first provincial meeting was held in October 1972 in Regina and focused primarily on women's leadership training. Women from Saskatoon, Buffalo Narrows, La Ronge, Prince Albert, Battleford, Yorkton, Cumberland House, Meadow Lake, Uranium City, and other outlying areas participated. The main function was based on four points: first, to organize at the local level and create unity among all Native people; second, to create social awareness among all Native women to better themselves through community action; third, to help develop programs and to support programs at the community level, such as recreation, day care, old age homes, halfway houses, equal employment, child welfare, foster homes, and education; and finally, to carry out research into Native women's rights. Unlike other male-run organizations, SNWM organized both treaty and non-treaty women. While they acknowledged that previous organizations had failed, the women hoped to succeed through a better understanding of the historical and political background, along with knowledge of the changes within the Native family unit.

The SNWM looked at areas that male organizations neglected, such as day-care centres in Indigenous communities, on reserves, and in residential neighbourhoods, as well as assistance for mothers who were working, training, or ill. The women sought to establish a halfway home for Indigenous women leaving jail, along with other programs for cultural and economic regeneration of Indian and Métis women. Above all, they hoped to provide needed services from a Native perspective. Their two-year budget amounted to $287,200.[26] The organization suffered from unstable funding, since it was viewed by funding agencies as replicating services provided by other Indigenous groups, such as the Métis Society and FSI. It was unable to obtain funding from

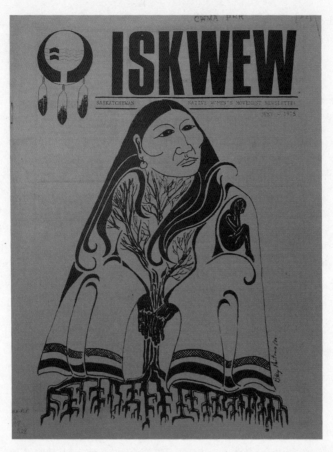

Iskwew monthly newsletter (File E.98 S28 ISKWEW - SASK Native Women's Movement Newsletter - Regina, Sask. Canadian Women's Movement Archives [CWMA], University of Ottawa)

Indian Affairs because its membership was open to non-status and Métis women.[27]

Indigenous women's knowledge and experiences informed their decisions on which areas to focus their political and organizing energies. Two themes figured large on the agenda of the SNMW: women's ability to birth and rear their children and building up the Native family unit. In one meeting, women raised concerns about involuntary sterilizations of Native women in Saskatchewan and suggested speaking to the College of Physicians and Surgeons about the issue. They recognized that they needed to combat what they saw as genocide through forced sterilization and birth control.[28] At the same meeting, they discussed their plans to speak out about Aim and work toward its eventual abolition by getting to the root of the social problems that caused Aim to be established. In their analysis of the community child-care needs, the Native women challenged the expectation that grand-parents could carry the burden alone of caring for their grandchildren. Extended families had always cared for needy children, but the women realized that people no longer wanted to keep their grandchildren and nieces without financial support because it was increasingly difficult to afford to support additional children. The women believed that working together would enable both men and women to find creative solutions that were culturally and socially relevant to Indian and Métis people.

In an interview with Nora Cummings about the SNWM and the Aim program, she proudly stated, "The Aim ads – we changed it!" She became interested in the Aim after encountering a mother whose children had been advertised by the department for adoption.

> I was involved. I was president of Native Women in 1973, and I went to pick up this lady; she was one of my girls I used to work with. I would take her to meetings. That was what we do, we'd work with the women. Her name was Lillian. I went to pick her up; she had this paper and she was crying and she held it. "Look at this: these are my children." And I look at it and I asked, "What do you mean these are your children? Are you drinking? What do you mean they're your children?" I turned my car off. And she cried and she told me her story. Her husband died. And she had a break-down. She had these seven children. So she had a breakdown, and they walked in and took these kids. And they would never give them back to her. And they said they were adopted out; all these year she thought they were adopted out.[29]

The children were being advertised for adoption and in fact had not been placed for adoption as she had been told. Nora said,

> I came back to my little office, I got on the phone and I phoned the women, and we got together with Minister Taylor. Alex Taylor was the Minister of Social Services.... We always made sure that we

got involved. We had a meeting at the friendship centre off Second
Avenue. We had over 200 people show up at that time the program
changed from AIM: Adopt Indian Métis. We didn't stop there. We
did researching more and more, legal aid was just starting then.
Judge Barry Singer. So we ended up getting transferred from the
Battleford court. It was sad. It was. We got Minister Taylor to work
with us. And we found all her children. And she got all her children
back. But then she needed a lot of support, so we needed to do
that. Last year, at the reconciliation [Truth and Reconciliation Commission meetings] I was one of the elders here at the Prairieland
Exhibition, they had a teepee and they had a circle and I was one
of the speakers. As I was sitting there someone grabbed me and
hugged me and said I was her saviour. And I said, "It can't be."
And she said, "It is." And she hugged and hugged and cried and
cried. And she told everybody, "This is my saviour: she got my
children back." And we changed that name [Aim] and she's got
grandchildren and great-grandchildren. We are always proud of
that. We helped this one lady. And from then things started changing. We were able then to go into the system and build on that. We
had women's groups all across Saskatchewan, women's centres.
People had an opportunity to work with them.[30]

From late winter to early summer of 1973, the SNWM was engaged
in an ongoing campaign to challenge the legitimacy of the Aim program. On 28 February 1973 the Saskatchewan Native Women's Movement circulated petitions through the *New Breed* magazine, asking
for support to end Aim in Saskatchewan and replace it with a Native
Family Foster Home Program. They objected to the ads and the lack
of voice in crafting policies for Indigenous children. The SNWM also
submitted a brief to the Saskatchewan Human Rights Commission,
seeking their support in challenging the policies that excluded Métis
and First Nations families from fostering and adopting through the
program. Evidence also suggests that the Saskatchewan Native Wom-
en's Movement enlisted the assistance of the American Indian Movement. Department officials at the Aim Centre received a call from an
individual claiming to represent the American Indian Movement. The
memo stated,

In the telephone call he indicated that he was opposed to sending Native children for adoption out of the country, that the American Indian Movement was going to file an injunction against [ARENA] and they were prepared to file an injunction against Aim as well. No further details were available on these particular points, but the man indicated that he would be back in Regina in about a month's time if the director of Aim wished to learn more about the matter. He indicated to the worker who took the call that he was serving Aim with notice of their intention. He indicated that they were backing the Saskatchewan Native Women's Movement.[31]

The combined frontal assault on the Aim program forced the Department of Social Services to sit up and take notice. The SNWM effectively immobilized the Aim advertising campaign. By today's standards, the department's response was tentative and superficial, but realistically it was the first concession to an Indigenous group on input into child welfare policies. In a letter between directors discussing the escalating attacks, Aim Centre Director Gerald Joice stated, "Though the letter [from SNWM] obviously contains misinformation, such fallacies are irrelevant over the long run and we should be addressing ourselves to what seems to be a growing opposition to have the Aim program terminated."[32] He proposed two alternatives for the department: first, they could continue to run the program despite opposition and it would die for political reasons, or they could seize the moment to negotiate through the Saskatchewan Human Rights Commission to change the Aim program in exchange for support of the Native groups developing resources for the children. He suggested the department opt for the second. The Aim director felt that "if it could be possible to work co-operatively with the SNWM groups then a great deal more could be accomplished."[33] He suggested they discuss the SNWM's objections and make concessions. First, they would be willing to drop the name "Aim." Second, they were prepared to drop advertising of children aged six years or older, and finally, the department was willing to set up a publicity campaign directed specifically at developing Native homes though not to the exclusion of other homes. In return for these concessions, they asked that the Native Women's Movement approve the program and support the department's work whenever possible.[34]

The new focus on finding Native families acknowledged prior exclusion of Indian and Métis families because of racial and material considerations. Joice made a recommendation:

> Basic to a concerted effort to locate homes among Native people is
> the establishment of a policy with regard to eligibility requirements.
> For instance it is a fact that Native families by comparison have less
> to offer materially in terms of educational opportunities, financial
> security and housing. In order to recruit successfully and develop
> resources in the Native community, it will be necessary to accept a
> good number of the Native homes who may be financially depen-
> dent on welfare, have only one parent and may be poorly housed
> compared with homes that might be available within the major-
> ity society where there are two parents, much better income and
> educational opportunities and generally better housing conditions.
> Unless the department is fully prepared to accept the different stan-
> dards that will be found in the Native community, there is little or
> no point in initiating a recruitment campaign for that community.[35]

The preference for middle-class adoption homes, the goal since the
beginning of the Adopt Indian and Métis program, had again hit a
snag. While white middle-class families were now more than willing
to embrace Indian and Métis children as kin, Indigenous people voiced
their rejection of this violation of their own kinship systems. The heavy-
handed attempt to exclude Indian and Métis people from participating
in the program had been challenged when SNWM and the Métis Society utilized their political and social power to indigenize the policies at
the Department of Welfare.

In the fall of 1973 the director of the Aim Centre, now known as
Resources for the Adoption of Children (REACH), sent out a memo
informing employees of the changes. The new attempt to include
Indigenous families as foster and adoptive applicants, rather than as
clients, working alongside Indigenous organizations and advertising
in Indigenous publications, had never been previously considered. The
new objective was to make the adoptive needs of Native wards known
amongst parents and potential parents in the community through publicity in Native newspapers. The primarily non-Indigenous employees
needed departmental preparation. The circular stated, "The department

New Breed, February 1973 (The Virtual Museum of Métis History and Culture, http://www.metismuseum.ca/media/document.php/04207.1973%20(02)%20February.pdf)

must be prepared to receive inquiries and process home studies from the Native community on a priority basis. The department must adopt the position that Native wards if at all possible should be placed in suitable homes of Native ancestries. This position requires that the Department give priority to Native inquiries in view of the large number of unplaced and unplanned for Native wards."[36]

Not only was the tentative step uncomfortable for the department; for the Métis editor of *New Breed* magazine, advertising Indigenous children for adoption pushed the boundaries of what Métis people felt were proper family-making techniques. In response, co-editor Linda Finlayson grudgingly agreed to publish ads that had been cleared through the Native Women's Movement of Saskatchewan:[37] "We object very seriously to the advertisement of Native children for adoption

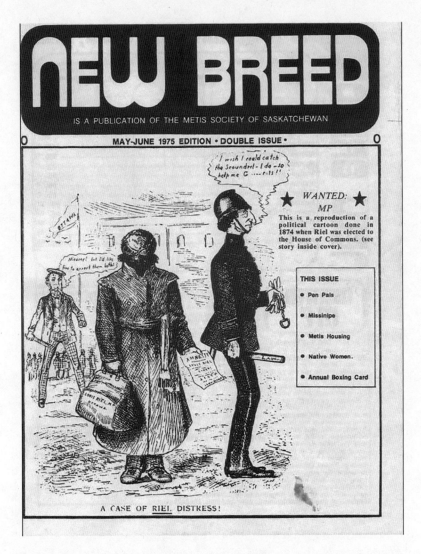

New Breed, May/June 1975 (The Virtual Museum of Métis History and Culture, http://www.metismuseum.ca/media/document.php/05114.1975%20(04)%20 May%20June.pdf)

through the mass media as the indication is present that our children are being advertised as pets, however as much as our staff object to white families adopting Native children, we have no objection to making your program known to Native people in order that more Native adoption homes can be located and utilized."[38] The tension between the ideology of Indigenous pride and the reality of child welfare needs

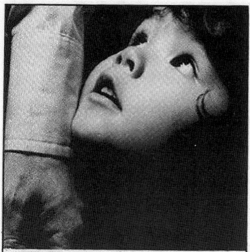

REACH

REACH is a program designed to meet the special needs of some very special children.

These children may have emotional problems, learning problems or physical handicaps.

Many are brothers and sisters who should be placed together in family groups.

And there are children of native ancestry. There is a special need for native families who want to adopt a child.

What these children need is a permanent home, with parents who can reach and accept them.

In order to find the right homes for these children we have people in every Department of Social Services office in the province and in the Department of Northern Saskatchewan.

If you'd be interested in considering the adoption of a special needs child, please get in touch.

You can write us at 2240 Albert Street, Regina. Or call 523-6681. If you live outside Regina you can call us toll free. Our toll free number in Saskatchewan is 1 or 112-800-667-3678. Or you can contact your nearest regional office, Department of Social Services and ask for a REACH worker.
IT COULD MAKE ALL THE DIFFERENCE IN THE WORLD.

RESOURCES FOR ADOPTION OF CHILDREN

DEPARTMENT OF SOCIAL SERVICES, 2240 ALBERT STREET, REGINA

Page 18, New Breed

REACH advertisements and posters.
Left: advertisement published in *New Breed* magazine, May/June 1975.
Following pages: Provincial Archives of Saskatchewan, Poster Collection, VII.157 ("It doesn't take much to make a child happy…") and VII.156 ("Children are Waiting"), REACH programme, Departments of Social Services and Northern Saskatchewan, ca. 1975–76.

made running the ads an act of compromise between the government and Métis Society. This tension was apparent in the *New Breed* magazine where the REACH ads ran alongside an article on genocide, news from Indigenous communities in North America, and the report from the Committee on Indian Rights for Indian Women.[39]

Victory for the SNWM in the battle over the representation of Native children in mass media gained the organization a foothold in negotiating with the department. The REACH advertisements portrayed Native

"Children are waiting..."

"We might be able to introduce you to someone you've been waiting for..."

REACH
RESOURCES FOR ADOPTION OF CHILDREN

A PROGRAM JOINTLY SPONSORED BY THE DEPARTMENT OF SOCIAL SERVICES AND THE DEPARTMENT OF NORTHERN SASKATCHEWAN

families adopting Native children and attempted to represent First Nations and Métis families in a realistic manner that could generate the desired response, that of Native families "reaching" out to adopt a ward of the province. This first step, alongside the creation of day-care centres, women's centres, publications, and community building was an important aspect of the history of transracial adoption in Saskatchewan. The national alarm over the "disproportionate number of Native children in the child welfare system" was not sounded until the early 1980s.

Saskatchewan's Native women saw this materializing, in their own lives and the lives of their family members since the inception of the Adopt Indian and Métis project in 1967, and organized to challenge it.

In addition to fighting back against oppressive adoption policies, the SNWM developed an extensive plan to open a Native-run foster home in 1973. Arguing that all should have a right to their cultural identity and heritage, they asserted that white middle-class homes "do not afford them the opportunity to grow in the understanding of the beauty of their heritage and the wisdom of their forefathers."[40] Children raised by white parents were caught between two cultures and ended up suffering from emotional and social problems. "In addition to being unable to function successfully in white society, these children are left without the ability to re-establish themselves in their rightful place in Native society."[41] They incorporated Native Homes for Native Children–Saskatoon Society to deal with placement of Native children in foster and adoptive homes. Through the collective efforts of the Natives Homes Society and Department of Social Services, the women envisioned jointly encouraging participation of Indigenous families in foster and adoption programs. The society would not take over control of child caring but would complement the services of the department, assessing needs of Native children, and recommending the most appropriate Native family to social workers. The women also proposed an Indigenous-operated receiving home for Native children, directed and administered by Indigenous people as interim accommodations for children pending placement. In the receiving home, Indigenous staff would assess children and provide counselling for children to assist in adjusting to moving from their family home.

The Native Society consisted of a board of directors, with fifteen people chosen from the community, some with membership in the SNWM and others in related professional fields. Overseen by a director, secretary accountant, staff of ten, and three field workers, the society was envisioned as community-based to provide culturally relevant services. Field workers with community awareness would encourage Native families to participate in the program. In developing the homes, the SNWM identified a need in the community and organized to provide a viable alternative to the government-run system that proved itself unsuitable for Indigenous families. The women recognized the importance of providing Indigenous services for children who were involuntarily caught in unfortunate situations. The first director, Myrna

McCulloch, began to search for a suitable home shortly after formation. The society received a $4,000 starter grant, with funding to come from the provincial government. "We have found that the children going that route come out a really mixed-up bunch of individuals."[42]

The SNWM also requested a greater role in recruiting Indigenous families as foster parents and a role in the operation of Social Services, calling for the hiring of Indigenous workers: "To date, over a dozen homes have been recruited, seven homes have been approved and three or four are in use. Their tenure for a three month period has been extended a month. The work of these individuals is improving as is their appreciation of the broader problems of placing native children. This is a benefit to the education of both our staff and the native community."[43] With the women's success, the department proposed further meetings to determine appropriate involvement of Native organizations in its operation.

The collective effort of the SNWM on Indigenous involvement in child welfare led social welfare bureaucrats to seriously consider reforming their policies for the first time. Management agreed that they would have to "come to grips" with the "radical" question of Native staff. On 8 January 1975 in a meeting between Frank Dornstauder, Gerald Jacob, and SNMW representatives Rose Boyer and Vickie Wilson, they were advised that the provincial Métis Society had submitted a separate child-caring proposal, but this was seen to be problematic since they were unable to speak about Indian Children.[44] SNWM said they were perfect candidates. REACH Director Gerald Jacob relayed to his boss, "I indicated in this meeting that there must be some budget approved in the coming fiscal year for hiring Native persons for adoption recruitment placements and that I would be discussing their request to become involved in a recruitment program." Following the meeting with the Department of Social Services, the SNWM held a meeting 24 January 1975 at the Regina Friendship Centre regarding adoption and invited representatives from the Department to be present to answer questions from the grassroots members about adoption and about REACH.[45]

At the Annual SNWM Conference in 1974, the connections between child removal, self-determination, and the human rights of Indigenous peoples was made explicit. The diverse groups of Indigenous women, First Nations, Métis, and non-status from all across the province with

all levels of education made a strong stand for the rights of Indigenous peoples. The women who attended made recommendations for
improving the lives of Indigenous peoples in Saskatchewan, in particular, the lives of children. Their recommendation for child-care services
for Native children in Saskatchewan called on the province to end the
removal of children, a violation of the human rights of Indigenous
peoples:

> Whereas: the Provincial Department of Social Services Practises
> cultural genocide by purposely placing Native children in White
> Homes.
>
> Whereas: Native children suffer cultural shock when placed in
> an alien white environment and experience further cultural shock
> when they return to the families in the case of foster care.
>
> Whereas: Aim Centre is contravening no section of the Saskatche-
> wan Bill of Rights and is therefore legally practicing cultural Genocide.
>
> Whereas: The children affected by this bureaucracy have no
> right to prosecute.
>
> We recommend:
>
> 1) That the principle of the right to self-determination be included
>   in the amendments to the Saskatchewan Bill of Rights ...
> 4) That a concerted effort be made by the Provincial Government
>   to recognize and act on a basic principle of Human Rights
>   stated in the United Nations International Covenant on the
>   Economic, Social and Cultural Rights Article 1 Section 1. "All
>   peoples have the right of self-determination by Virtue of that
>   right to freely determine their political status, and freely pur-
>   sue their economic, social and cultural development."[46]

Indigenous women in Saskatchewan argued that the child welfare
system violated their human rights and was a form of genocide. Indigenous child welfare did not become a national issue until scholars began
to tabulate the numbers of children across Canada in the care of social
service agencies.[47] Combining the statistics from provincial agencies
with those kept by the Indian Affairs Branch, a startling trend began to
emerge. From 1973 to 1980, the numbers of Indigenous children coming
into care escalated until, in Saskatchewan, Métis and Indian children

hovered around 63 per cent of all child welfare cases.[48] Indian Affairs kept careful track of the numbers of Indian children adopted, whether into white homes or Indian homes. Transracial adoption of Indigenous children took place in 91 per cent of cases in 1977, but went down to 80 per cent in 1981.[49] Social scientist Patrick Johnston termed this process the "Sixties Scoop," referring to the decade in which Indigenous children became the majority population of the child welfare system in British Columbia. The following chapter will address the way in which First Nations leadership in Saskatchewan responded to this information, drawing on cross-border affiliations and activating transnational Indigenous networks of activists who had worked to curb similar trends in the United States.

8

Confronting Cultural Genocide
in the 1980s

The increase in adoption has been viewed by Indian people as a form
of assimilation and genocide, however the courts have attempted to
negate them by ruling that an Indian child does not lose his-her status
upon adoption. This however has not been acceptable to Indian people.
                                                    — Ovide Mercredi, 1981[1]

On 14 September 1983 Gordon Dirks, Minister of Social Services in
Saskatchewan, addressed the Peyakowak Committee in Regina: "I am
today establishing a Ministerial Advisory Council consisting of experienced community individuals and experts in the area of child and family services. I shall be directing this council to hold public meetings and
receive public opinion, and to review legislative and policy themes."[2]
Dirks was responding to calls from many segments of the community
for a public inquiry into the death of a toddler in a Saskatchewan foster home and an examination of the general state of Indigenous child
welfare in Saskatchewan. During the previous year, the Peyakowak
Committee had been raising awareness about the high proportion of
Native children in the care of Social Services. In addition, it had vocally
questioned the quality of care provided by the Department of Social
Services. The advisory council was an act of compromise between the
Saskatchewan government and the Peyakowak Committee, who had
called for a provincial inquiry along the lines of the inquiry that had

taken place in Manitoba.[3] During the meetings held in Saskatchewan's three major cities, the council highlighted the views of many within the Indigenous community who were dissatisfied with the state of child welfare and adoption in the province. During the first part of the 1980s, a growing chorus of Canadian First Nations and Métis leaders and activists began to resist the logic of the child welfare system, joined by supportive members of the white academic community.[4]

Following the failure of the 1969 Liberal White Paper, attitudes toward Canada's First People underwent a significant transformation. By 1980 tangible gains – legally and socially – were visible. The movement toward Indigenous self-government was strengthened in large measure by the protections afforded Indigenous rights in the Constitution Act, 1982, and a broadened definition of Indigenous peoples to include "Indian, Métis and Inuit."[5] This in turn led Indigenous leaders to consider the role of child-rearing in articulating and defining "existing Aboriginal rights." As had been the case in the United States with the passage of the Indian Child Welfare Act, 1978, child placement decisions and the strengthening of the Indian family were fundamental areas Native American tribes sought to reclaim in the larger movement for political and social self-determination. From 1980 to 1984 the common sense business of transracial adoption and apprehension that had continued in Saskatchewan despite the Native Women's Movement's resistance and the Métis Society's challenge came under attack, bolstered by the success of Indian people south of the border and the positive climate for human rights activism in Canada.

International, national, and local factors shaped the articulation of child welfare issues that became prominent in the public discussions surrounding Saskatchewan's review of the Family Services Act. Native American activists and their supporters in the United States had recently scored a legal victory for Indian families that sent vibrations across the continent. Indian legal scholars in Canada immediately seized the possibilities afforded by the recently drafted national legislation in the United States entitled the Indian Child Welfare Act (1978) or ICWA, which gave tribal courts jurisdiction over the placement of Indian children. ICWA legislation provided Canadian scholars and First Nations with a framework for articulating a position on child welfare jurisdiction as part of the larger goal of self-government. The second force shaping the discussion in Saskatchewan was the national movement for self-government among Indigenous people in Canada and the subsequent inclusion of section 35 in the Constitution Act, 1982, recognizing and affirming Aboriginal rights. Simultaneously, there was growing awareness of Indian and Métis children removed from parents through provincial child welfare legislation. The inclusion of Indigenous peoples and Indigenous rights in the Constitution of Canada created an "uneasy and undefined relationship with the colonizing state."[6] Crafting a unified national strategy on child welfare was one area where Indian and Métis rights activists asserted their pre-existing rights. Last was the development of the Peyakowak.[7] In Saskatchewan this diverse activist organization brought together Indigenous and non-Indigenous community members organized to challenge the power and legitimacy of the Department of Social Services. The discourse in Saskatchewan around transracial adoption reflected the intersection of local, national, and international knowledges shaped by the settler colonial historical context of Indigenous child removal policies.

Absent from discussion of child welfare and transracial adoption was any recognition of the gendered constraints experienced by Indigenous women or the impact of gendered policies affecting the Indigenous family. Adoption occupied a marginal space in the public hearings but was a primary concern for Indigenous leaders who sought control over Indian child welfare. Through looking at the published hearings from the ICWA, the printed report of the advisory council for the Family Services Act (1973), and the Indian Control of Indian Child Welfare document produced by the Federation of Saskatchewan Indian Nations (FSIN), transracial adoption came under fire, as Indian leaders demanded the right to define Indigenous kinship, adoption, and citizenship as an aspect of self-government.

Two publications drew the plight of Indigenous children to the attention of the academic and activist communities in Canada, providing irrefutable evidence for what Indigenous peoples had been claiming for decades. First, H. Philip Hepworth published *Foster Care and Adoption in Canada* in 1980, devoting a chapter to the anomalous situation facing Indian children in Canada, who were simultaneously underserved by child welfare services, yet over-represented in foster and adoption homes.[8] Shortly thereafter, Patrick Johnston published *Native Children and the Child Welfare System*, scrutinizing Indian child welfare, province by province, and examining factors that contributed to the

dismal record of providing welfare to children since 1951. Saskatchewan had the dubious distinction of the highest percentage of children
in the care of social services and the Department of Northern Development. Between 1976 and 1981, Native children ranged between 62.8 and
63.8 per cent of all children in the care of social services in the province.[9]
Transracial adoption was given a prominent place in Johnston's analysis because it was so problematic. For example in Saskatchewan in 1977,
91 per cent of Indian children were adopted by non-Indian families; by
1981 that figure had dropped to 80.5 per cent. But the percentages do
not tell the whole story. The total number of children adopted in 1977
was seventy-eight; in 1980 it was eighty-three. In 1977 the number of
status children in care was 573, and by 1980 it had risen to 789. As a
percentage of the total status Indian population, in 1977, 14 per cent of
Indian children in care were adopted, and in 1980 it was 11 per cent.
As a percentage of the total outcome for Indian children who entered
into the care of the Department of Social Services, Indian children often
remained in foster care, but when adopted, primarily went into the
homes of Euro-Canadians.

In Saskatchewan the struggle taking shape over control of Indian
child welfare emerged in a political climate that was more receptive to
the political activism of Indian people than ever before. The passage of
the Indian Child Welfare Act (1978) in the United States, a major victory of Native American families, influenced how Indian and Métis
leaders, as well as non-Indian scholars and activists, approached the
political, cultural, and legal understanding of over-representation of
Indigenous children in Saskatchewan's child welfare system. The legislative approach to resolving the issues of child welfare, while an essential component for restoring Indigenous people's rightful role in caring
for their children, submerged other potentially liberating approaches
offered by Indigenous women at this time. Undertaking a comparative history of this period offers one the opportunity to interrogate cir-
cuits of knowledge production, governing practices, and connections
in the political rationalities that supported racial distinctions as well as
worked to eliminate them.[10]

The Association on American Indian Affairs (AAIA) originated in
1922 as the Eastern Association on Indian Affairs to support the New
Mexico Pueblo Indians. Made up of Euro-American members from
New York, they lobbied in support of issues related to the well-being

of tribes throughout the United States. William Byler was president of the AAIA from 1962 to 1980, the period in which the child welfare crisis came to light. As one member of the AAIA, Mr Ortiz, expressed it in 1973, "The Association had set as its major and immediate goal the comprehensive implementation of Indian self-determination in all its aspects.... American Indian people today are at a crossroads in their destiny; the Association stands ready to help insure that Indian people themselves ultimately determine that future."[11]

In response to an Indian family from South Dakota who had their children illegally removed, the AAIA began to collect evidence to determine the extent of child removal practices in the United States.[12] Through a national survey utilizing the numbers provided by the BIA, the AAIA demonstrated that many Indian children were growing up in white foster and adoptive homes, or in faraway boarding schools. The AAIA became a driving force behind the politicization of transracial adoption and Indian child welfare in the United States in the 1970s. When inquiring further into this incident at Devil's Lake Reservation in South Dakota, they discovered that one fourth of all this reservation's children were living elsewhere. The tribal council strongly resisted the removal of children and invited the AAIA to assist in fighting this trend.

In addition, the AAIA was asked to conduct a statistical survey for the American Indian Policy Review Commission taking place in the United States in 1968 to determine the number of Indian children living out of their homes across the nation. Their report provided a state-by-state breakdown of the rates of children who had been apprehended and placed by social service agencies in non-Indian homes. The AAIA found that children were being removed from their families at rates far beyond their proportion of the population in many states across the continental United States and Alaska, where as many as 25–35 per cent of children had been removed.[13] This removal included boarding schools, foster homes, adoptive homes, and other child-care institutions.[14] The statistics were merely a cold and quantifiable launching for the tragic human story that was unfolding. Published by the AAIA in their *Indian Family Defense*, Native American people and experts began exploring the meaning and significance of those numbers.

To bring national attention to the Indian child welfare crisis, the Association on American Indian Affairs mobilized a wide range of supportive cross-disciplinary friends and published their findings in *Indian*

Family Defense. Most critically, the organizing of the AAIA caught the attention of legislative aide Sherwin Broadhead, who had attended a child welfare strategy meeting sponsored by the association in January 1974.[15] Senator James Abourezk (D-SD), chair of the Senate Subcommittee on Indian Affairs, invited the AAIA and Native American peoples to attend its meetings in Washington, DC, in April to provide testimony about the Indian child welfare crisis. Once there, Native American peoples had the opportunity share their experiences of suffering at the hands of the system(s) to the public record.

At the subcommittee hearings, Indian women told of the forceful removal of their children without reasonable grounds. One witness stated, "On many reservations the most feared person in the community is the welfare worker."[16] Another stated that when they saw the welfare worker, "the children ran into the rooms and hid under the bed."[17] Stories recounted by Native American peoples from across the United States highlighted the aggressively coercive actions of police and social workers. These remarks echoed similar stories of children being removed from communities to be placed in residential schools in other settler-colonial nations.[18] One example from a former residential school survivor testified to the impact of removal and the commensurate powerlessness experienced by family members. She recalled, "The mothers and grandmothers cried and wept, as mine did, in helplessness and heartache. There was nothing, absolutely nothing they could do as women, to reverse the decision of the 'Department.'"[19] Indian people interpreted the action of police, social workers, and government officials as a continuation of the policies of assimilation pursued through the residential school system. As one submission to the Senate Select Committee stated, "In the past, it seems as though the public and private welfare agencies have operated on the premise that Indian children would have greatly benefited from the experience of growing up non-Indian. This premise has resulted in the abusive practices of removal of Indian children from their families, and has contributed to what many Indians and non-Indians have called 'cultural genocide' of Indian people and Tribes."[20] The AAIA believed Indian children were removed from communities and families at a shockingly high rate in response to the unrealistic judgments of white middle-class social workers, lack of attention to due process, and the state of poverty caused by colonization.[21]

Biases against Indian families, combined with the concept of the pathologically unfit Indian mother, shaped responses to child neglect and Indigenous forms of child care. One research project reported by the AAIA gives an example that Indian people were denied preventative services on the basis of race. A study comparing white families and families of Indian ancestry who approached social agencies in Minnesota between 1956 and 1971 for aid for deteriorating family situations such as unemployment, strife, alcoholism, or spousal death or separation revealed that Indian families routinely had their children removed as a solution.[22] A more appropriate response might have been counselling services, homemaking services, or financial assistance, such as white families received. Indian families ended up fragmented and dispersed.

Negative perceptions of Indigenous women and Indigenous gender relations have historically justified the coercive actions of the professionals working on behalf of the state, whether doctors or social workers.[23] Powerful pronouncements by middle-class medical professionals characterized Indigenous women as detrimental to the health and mortality of their children.[24] The Native American women who testified in front of the Senate Subcommittee recounted the coercive and incoherent actions of social workers. In one example, Cheryl Spider DeCoteau, a twenty-three-year-old member of the Sisseton-Wahpeton Sioux Tribe, had to defend the right to parent her children after they had been removed because she had left them with her mother. After the birth of her second child, welfare workers hounded her until they finally obtained her child for adoption.[25] Other examples contained in the AAIA publication involve women being subjected to involuntary sterilizations in addition to surveillance from welfare workers.[26] At the Lac de Flambeau Reservation, there were two examples reported of women being sterilized in exchange for not having their children removed, then having them removed anyway.[27] Sterilization and child removal policies operated as parallel strategies to reduce Indian populations. The right to Indigenous motherhood and the right to define what Indigenous motherhood entailed emerge from the history of state intervention into families through resistance narratives of women who organized to challenge social workers' construction of the unfit Indian mother.[28]

In highlighting these women's experiences at the hands of social workers, one cannot conclude that Indigenous women in some cases chose to relinquish children. As Devon A. Mihesuah points out, "There was and is no such thing as a monolithic, essential Indian woman."[29] However, Indigenous groups emphasized the rights of Indian tribes to determine the best interests of children in these negotiations. During the hearings, the issue of women's desire for privacy was brought to the attention of the committee by Mr Butler, representing the BIA. He opposed the legislation creating placement standards as invasion of the privacy of unwed mothers who sought to have their children adopted without the knowledge of their community.[30] Likewise, the issue of privacy concerned the representative from ARENA, the organization most responsible for arranging the adoption of Indian children in this period, asserting, "Our organization stands for the concept that every child has the right to a permanent nurturing family of his own."[31] She voiced concern that children could become caught up in a lifetime of temporary care. She argued that "experience and research shows us that transracial adoptive placements can produce stable adults with a sense of ethnic identity."[32] She also feared that the drafted legislation would invade the rights of parents to choose care for their children. Despite the concerns of the bureau and ARENA representatives, the Indian Child Welfare Act (1978) placed the jurisdiction for adoptions under tribal courts. Tribal courts were empowered to weigh the questions of permanency and privacy against the needs of families and children.

The AAIA drafted a bill entitled the Indian Child Welfare Act (1976) to address five perceived issues at the root of the removal of Indian children from their homes and communities: first, parents did not understand the nature of the court proceedings; second, there was no legal representation or awareness of rights; third, there was no knowledge and respect for Native customs; fourth, there were no reasonable grounds to remove children; and finally, tribal governments were not consulted about the proceedings.[33] The resultant Indian Child Welfare Act, passed in 1978, acknowledged the "special relationship between the United States and the Indian tribes and their members and the Federal responsibility to Indian peoples" based on article I, section 8, clause 3 of the United States Constitution, as well as other statutes, treaties, and dealings, which indicated that the government had a relationship of protection for Indian tribes.[34] In recognition of the "alarmingly high percentage of Indian families that are broken up by the removal, often unwanted, of their children," ICWA set minimum federal standards for the removal of Indian children and placement in foster and adoptive homes.[35] Title I, section 101 (a) gave Indian tribes exclusive jurisdiction over child custody proceedings involving Indian children through the tribal court system; likewise it established restrictions on agencies prior to removal. In voluntary placements or termination of parental rights, consent had to be received in writing from tribal authorities, and preference was given to placing children with extended family members or in tribal foster homes, Indian homes, or institutions approved by the Indian tribes. Likewise, the Act called for direct funding to tribes for provision of services to preserve families and placement of children on reservations.[36] The passing of ICWA signalled a transformative moment in supporting self-determination and restoring tribal kinship forms to American Indian communities.

The Act dramatically recognized the federal-tribal relationship and provided a tool for tribal governments to begin to apply their own community standards in providing child and family services to their members. Tribal sovereignty of American Indians in law has been based both in Canada and the United States on the Royal Proclamation of 1763 and the ruling of Justice Marshall on appeal that Indian nations were considered distinct, political communities retaining some of their original natural rights.[37] These two elements set the stage for future federal-state-Indian relations such as the ICWA. In the court case Cherokee Nation vs Georgia (1831) 30 U.S. (5 Pet.) 1 (U.S.S. c), the place of the Cherokee and thus all Native inhabitants in the federal state was resolved as "domestic dependent nations," in a trustee relationship with the federal government, acknowledging that Indigenous peoples retained residual sovereignty.[38] At the time of the passing of the ICWA, the state of tribal courts varied from community to community. They were started under the provisions of the Indian Reorganization Act of 1934 under John Collier, commissioner of the Bureau of Indian Affairs from 1933 to 1945, as part of the reforms of Indian policy intended to restore lost land and tribal sovereignty from past abuses.[39]

First Nations in Canada did not immediately seize upon the importance of the ICWA as a dramatic recognition of tribal sovereignty in child welfare. Indian and Métis groups who had experienced very similar child welfare policies sought several different methods to secure control over child welfare and stem the removal of children. Indeed, there were many similarities in Indian policy between Canada and the

United States, primarily as a result of the shared foundation in British law, the negotiation of treaties, creation of reserves, wardship, and assimilation through education and institutionalized paternalism.[40] One significant divergence between Canada and the United States is the role the Canadian Indian Act has played in determining who obtains and retains Indian status. While U.S. Indian status is derived from a combination of blood quantum and tribal membership rules, in Canada it flows from the patrilineal descent.[41] Legislation in the United States did not attempt to define who qualified as Indian and relied primarily on the courts to decide, case by case. Women who married white men but continued living on their reservations with their husbands and children remained tribe members, with courts often recognizing the mother-right rule, or rights of tribes to define their own membership.[42] The presence of mixed-bloods on reservations has been a common aspect of tribal communal life in the United States, whereas in Canada the notion of racial blood quantum has been complicated by the legal and gendered regime for Indian status.[43]

Gendered experiences of colonization have led male and female leaders to approach self-determination through different avenues in Canada.[44] Colonization of Indigenous peoples brought about a loss of men's and women's political and economic power, and in addition, transformed those that had been egalitarian societies into economies where males controlled production of products of exchange and maintained political control. One area of Indigenous women's organizing from 1970 onward focused on restoring the status and community membership of Indian women, from whom it had been involuntarily stripped.[45] Utilizing the courts to restore their lost connection to rights and treaty benefits negotiated by their ancestors, Canadian Indian women rejected the assaults on Indigenous kinship systems and their ability to pass on cultural and tribal inheritances to their children that removal entailed. The right to define membership in accordance with Indigenous definitions of belonging, be it through marriage or adoption, was seen as a matter of self-determination.[46] Jeannette Corbiere-Lavell, an Ojibway woman from the Wikwemikong First Nation, was one of the first Indigenous women to challenge the sex discrimination in the Indian Act. After marriage to David Lavell in April 1970, she received a letter that she was no longer a member of her community, under the Indian Act, section 12(1)(b). She argued that her loss of status upon marriage violated her equality before the law, guaranteed by section 1 (b) of the Canadian Bill of Rights.[47] While certainly this loss of status posed an individual hardship to her and her future children through the loss of community support, inequality loomed over the lives of all Indian women in Canada, in part, hampering their abilities to provide for their children. Lavell recalled that knowing that her children would not benefit from the connections developed growing up in their community strengthened her resolve to pursue her case. Although she lost in the county court, she appealed the decision to the Federal Court of Appeal, which ruled in her favour; however, under pressure from the federal government and several federally funded Native organizations, it was appealed to the Supreme Court of Canada, where she lost by one vote.[48] Indigenous women such as Lavell and the members of the Native Women's Association of Canada recognized that underlying racist legislation posed a threat to their well-being and the well-being of their children and adopted a feminist approach to ending patriarchy as a road to resolving child welfare issues.[49]

An example from Anishinaabe-kwe (Anishinaabe woman/female) ideology of motherhood and mothering illustrates how kinship systems support women and children. Mothering and motherhood are seen as a complex web of relations that provide support and solidarity among women.[50] Each woman has a responsibility to foster and nurture the next generation and allows others to assist in that process, such as aunties and grandmothers. Motherhood does not refer only to biological motherhood, but is expressed also through the teaching and nurturing of the next generation. Women often assisted in raising the children of their sisters and daughters, on occasion adopting kin to raise. Women removed from communities and on the outside of these relations and networks likely found themselves negotiating the services provided by provincial agencies and all the difficulty that would present. As Jo-Anne Fiske has observed through her time spent with Indigenous women in British Columbia, federal policies responsible for Indigenous women intersect with provincial policies that regulate women who live on the social and economic margins.[51]

Indigenous kinship relations, used to supplement meagre incomes and provide assistance, were targeted as a fundamental stumbling block to full integration into the Canadian economy.[52] The authors of the Hawthorn report identified Indigenous social relations, which they termed "kin obligations," as a significant detriment to the economic position of the individual Indian worker. They stated, "The burdens of aid to kin and friends seem to underlie a multitude of problems in addition to those of employment and income alone. In some cases alcoholism is induced by the feelings of helplessness and resignation – nothing to work for or see ahead – as well as a means of blunting the interpersonal conflicts and tensions that arise from overcrowding and friction with kin and others."[53] Rather than a source of support and strength, white social scientists and social workers viewed the extended family system as sources of retrogression and impediments to integration. The gradual weaning of Indigenous people from kinship obligations, and replacing the supports provided by family with the rationalized and regularized services provided by the state in the form of social welfare, education, child-rearing advice, day care, and public health services were idealized as the solution to poverty and separation that contributed to the marginalized place of Canada's First Nations.

Rather than support, Indian and Métis people in Canada ended up with children removed and placed in underfunded and poorly run provincial child welfare systems. Child removal policies provided an opportunity to discipline non-conforming women, shape family relations to approximate those of the two-parent nuclear family, and socialize Indian children into normative working-class roles. Following the ill-conceived federal attempt to resolve Indigenous poverty and marginalization by drafting the White Paper, and the subsequent fallout and politicization, the shifting cultural and political landscape of the late 1970s and early 1980s in Canada little resembled the postwar era of integration.[54] The most significant transformation occurred with the relationship between Indigenous peoples and the government of Canada. Mirroring the move toward self-determination that occurred in the United States in the mid-1970s, First Nations, Métis, and Indigenous women's organizations mobilized around land claims, self-government, and equal rights. The 1982 repatriation of the British North America Act of 1867 (Constitution Act, 1867) and adoption of the Charter of Rights and Freedoms revitalized federal and democratic engagement in constitutional politics. Prior to the passing of the Constitution in 1982, the only reference to Indigenous peoples in the BNA Act was section 91(24), giving the federal government sole jurisdiction over "Indians, and lands reserved for the Indians." The recognition and affirmation of Aboriginal and treaty rights in the Constitution 1982 came from the strong position of the National Indian Brotherhood, later known as the Assembly of First Nations, and the Native Women's Association of Canada. As a result of intense lobbying of Indigenous rights groups, the drafters of the Constitution inserted the clause, "The existing Aboriginal and treaty rights of the Indigenous peoples of Canada are hereby recognized and affirmed." Likewise, Aboriginal people were defined to include "Indian, Métis and Inuit." It then became necessary to determine what these rights were.[55] According to political scientist Joyce Green, "Citizens would henceforth have rights guarantees under the Charter, including protection from race and sex discrimination and recognition of Aboriginal and treaty rights."[56] Indigenous women's groups played an important role in obtaining inclusion of sex equality rights in the Charter, and inclusion of unsurrendered Indigenous and treaty rights in the Constitution.[57] However, male Indigenous and non-Indigenous politicians did not always welcome women's views. For example, mainstream Indigenous governments and bands resisted the passage of Bill C-31 enabling women who lost their status under the discriminatory Indian Act to regain it.[58] Thus there remained tension between male and female Indigenous organizations over how their newly granted rights would unfold, and how newly revitalized Indian and Métis nations would define their citizenship.[59]

In Saskatchewan the Federation of Saskatchewan Indian Nations (FSIN), representing treaty and status Indians in Saskatchewan, the Indian Federated College, and the Canadian Indian Lawyers Association looked south to the United States for inspiration on how to frame their position on Indian child welfare since Hepworth's statistics had revealed the troubling trends of over-representation. The first group to consider the Indian Child Welfare Act of 1978 as a model for Canadian legislation was the Indigenous Lawyers Association sponsored by the Saskatchewan Indian Federated College. At a workshop on Indian Child Rights held in Regina in March 1981, lawyers representing jurisdictions from across Canada listened to presentations by experts on the problem of Indigenous child welfare and attempted to draft a solution.[60] Clem Chartier, consultant for the Indian Law Program at the Saskatchewan Indian Federated College and president of the Canadian Indian Lawyers Association, had invited AAIA Executive Director Steven Unger to attend the convention. Chartier requested that Unger attend to discuss the role of the AAIA in advancing the rights of Indian children and families in the United States.[61] Nancy Tuthil, the assistant director of the American Indian Law Center, had also been invited to explain the ICWA to those gathered. The ground-breaking recognition of the rights of the collective tribal entities to dictate not only the futures of Indian children, but the definition of Indian families through the passage of ICWA in the United States enabled Canadian Indian leaders and lawyers to consider pressing for a national law similar to that of the United States, removing jurisdiction from the provinces for Indigenous children and placing it with Indian peoples.

In addition to legislative revisions like that of ICWA under consideration by Indian leaders and lawyers, the conference also heard from Chief Wayne Christian. His band in British Columbia implemented an alternative approach to stop child removal through the legal framework of the Indian Act. In 1980 the 300-member Spallumcheen Band near Enderby passed a band by-law taking full responsibility for child custody based on their inherent right to self-determination and the right to care for their children.[62] Responding to the removal of 150 children over a thirty-year period, Chief Christian took advantage of section 81 of the Indian Act that enabled Indian bands to pass by-laws.[63] Taking the individual initiative to reverse the trend toward removal, harm, and family breakdown, the new child welfare by-law echoed much of the 1978 ICWA legislation. Emphasizing the importance of children to the long-term survival of the people, and the devastating and community-wide impact of removal, the by-law gave the band "exclusive jurisdiction over any child custody proceeding involving an Indian child, notwithstanding the residence of the child."[64] In addition, it stipulated a preferential scale of placements for band councils when considering with whom to place Indian children, after the child's wishes had been considered and every effort had been made to restore the original family. Family resources were considered to be the preferred option, followed by on-reserve band members, off-reserve band members, then Indians on or off reserve. Finally, "only as a last resort shall the child be placed in the home of a non-Indian living off the reserve."[65] While the federal government initially rejected the band's by-law, it was allowed when presented the second time. While child welfare was recognized as a provincial jurisdiction, the band sought an agreement with the BC authorities that recognized their jurisdiction over children and developed a plan to provide the necessary resources to develop a program of support.[66] Elsewhere bands had begun to delve into securing agreements to keep children on reserves.[67]

In light of the changing climate around self-government, child welfare and transracial adoption became issues for political leaders seeking areas where Indian and Métis people could potentially obtain control. At the convention Ovide Mercredi, who became chief of the Assembly of First Nations in 1991, and Clem Chartier, future chair of the Métis National Council in 1983, drafted a formal statement on the importance of Indian child welfare to the future of Indian self-government. They stated that from the White Paper onward, Indian people had been asserting their nationhood and expressing their right to self-determination. One common thread was the right to ensure the safety and security of children in order to secure the future of Indian nations.[68] On evidence of the increase in transracial adoptions from 1964–5 to 1976–7, Mercredi and Chartier explained, "The increase in adoption has been viewed by Indian people as a form of assimilation and genocide, however the courts have attempted to negate them by ruling that an Indian child does not lose his-her status upon adoption. This however has not been acceptable to Indian people."[69] This problem, articulated by Indian lawyers, stemmed from the lack of federal legislation providing direction on child welfare. Further, the legal experts asserted that any future changes to child welfare legislation or provision must take place with the consultation of Indian people: "Any negotiations between the federal and provincial government without the prior consultation and participation of Indian associations are viewed with a great deal of suspicion and resentment."[70] Provincial responsibility for child welfare was rejected by First Nations people. The current child welfare crisis was attributed to the deep poverty of Indigenous people who had been denied a share of the vast resources of Canada.

In response to emerging interest among Indigenous leadership, the Native Law Centre at the University of Saskatchewan provided direction on responsibility for the provision of child welfare for First Nations. Kent McNeil looked at the legal issues in delivery of services, with emphasis on the jurisdictional question.[71] McNeil considered the feasibility of implementing legislation similar to the Indian Child Welfare Act in Canada. Like in the United States, federal jurisdiction over

Indians in Canada enabled the government to recognize band councils' jurisdiction. "By passing the ICWA, the United States Congress accepted responsibility for Indian child welfare matters and used its legislative power to transfer jurisdiction in this area back to the tribal level. Under section 91(24) the BNA Act, Parliament has the authority to enact similar legislation in Canada, if it so chooses. Lack of a tribal court system in Canada would need tribunals, or could be filled by band councils."[72] The poor state of Indian child welfare in Canada had been due to the jurisdictional disputes between the provinces and the federal government. The provinces were reluctant partners in the provision of services for two reasons: their belief that Indians in Canada were solely a federal responsibility, and Prairie Indian people refused to accept provincial control based on the treaty relationships they had with the Crown. McNeil envisioned two possible ways Indian governments could pursue control over child welfare. The first was to pressure the federal government to enact legislation similar to that of the American ICWA. The second was for bands to enact by-laws like the Spallumcheen band in BC (1980), which required that the federal government amend the Indian Act to give band councils power to make by-laws in that area.[73]

Unlike the United States, Canada did not develop a nationwide, grassroots, cross-cultural child welfare movement to challenge the status quo. Without the widespread support for a national paradigm shift in Indian child welfare, there was little hope for major change. In February 1982 Saskatchewan began an internal policy review of child welfare policy, with an eye to revising the legislation. The Family Services Act, passed in 1973, reflected the thinking of the time and had been based on an uncertain relationship regarding services to treaty Indian people.[74] Winds of change were blowing in the form of the Charter of Rights and Freedoms and Indigenous self-determination, and the province was mindful of its failure to address concerns that Indigenous people raised in the past decade. Looking to Manitoba as a possible template for future action, the Department of Social Services circulated a memo containing recent events in its provincial neighbour. On 23 February 1982 the Manitoba and federal governments and the Four Nations Confederacy signed an agreement to develop and deliver on-reserve child welfare services. The agreement provided a full range of child welfare services to all Indian communities who opted in. Funding for the programs came directly from the federal government to agents delivering services.[75]

Shortly thereafter, the Department of Indian Affairs and Northern Development, formerly Indian Affairs, released a policy statement. It simply indicated that the provinces would continue to provide services to all treaty people but provided a framework to begin negotiation of the tripartite agreements between provinces, First Nations, and the federal government.[76] It reiterated that provincial child welfare services should be extended to all reserve communities and families on Crown lands, and that they would fund child welfare services to residents of Indian communities. In contrast to the ICWA, Indian Affairs made clear that provincial and territorial governments had legal responsibility to provide child care and protection.[77] DIAND's role was financial and not developmental. In response, the Saskatchewan government issued a revised Family Services Policy Statement to continue to provide all services to off-reserve First Nations people, with the federal government providing payment. On reserves, the Department of Social Services would step in only for extreme cases of neglect or if there was a request to remove a child by the Department of Indian Affairs. This policy applied when a child's safety was at stake, in the absence of a federal policy, or upon refusal of the federal government to respond to a child protection situation on the reserve.[78] The lack of presence on reserve, other than to remove children in cases of abuse or neglect, certainly would not have endeared workers to residents. Likewise, apprehensions and adoption appear to be the only services to which on-reserve people had access.

Child removal, in the form of apprehension and adoption, remained the only services available for Indian children and families residing on reserves, while off-reserve families technically had access to the whole range of preventative services. The unresolved jurisdictional disputes that arose as a result of section 88 of the Indian Act were exacerbated as the federal government refused to legislate an alternative national child welfare framework, or provide national policy directives to develop Indigenous child welfare services on reserve. This unsatisfactory arrangement left the provincial government reluctantly providing second-rate services to on-reserve children, and Indigenous peoples and children in particular in limbo. With the emergence of the Peyakowak Committee, the politicization of child welfare in Saskatchewan took a new turn. Formed as a steering committee for the Taking Control Project at the University of Regina's Faculty of Social Work, Peyakowak was a diverse community-action committee. Led by social work professor Harvey Stalwick, Peyakowak played a community-activist role, seeking out new solutions for Indigenous child welfare in Saskatchewan. The Taking Control group received financial support from the federal government to revise social work education in Canada. It eventually became a three-year project with the working title "Indian and Native Social Work Education in Canada: A Study and Demonstration of Strategies for Change." The group shortened their name to "Taking Control," centred on the concept of Indigenous self-government.[79] Using the participatory action model, they defined their role as supporting the advancement of social justice, stating, "Research is a means of understanding conditions, being in dialogue and becoming involved in change."[80]

In 1983 the Peyakowak Committee set out to "learn from elders, communicate with others, share with those who still suffer, re-establish evaluation of the Family Services Act, stop apprehensions where alternative exist, create cross-cultural awareness with non-Natives and do it ourselves."[81] A conference in 1983 brought together members in the Regina Indigenous community involved in the child welfare system, to identify important issues, then take them to the provincial Department of Social Services. It is clear from the list of resolutions that the Taking Control Group shared the perspective of the FSIN, that child welfare and transracial adoption were tied to the expression of self-government in ways that echoed the ICWA in the United States. For example "Resolution: Indian children are being placed or adopted in non-Native foster homes without the consent of their natural parents or Indian governments (Chief and Councils)."[82] Resolution D also echoed the provisions of the ICWA of 1978 in calling for control by band governments.[83] The Taking Control Conference identified the need for more Native adoptive and foster homes, which the Métis Society and the Native Women's Movement had been advocating for many years. From the 1970s onward, the Métis Society and the Native Women's Movement worked alongside the department while developing community resources to reform the system. In the 1980s, First Nations and Métis leadership, along with sympathetic academics, saw "taking control" of child welfare as the solution to the over-representation of Indian and Métis children in white foster homes. The membership of the Peyakowak Committee had academics from the University of Regina and activists engaged in social movements like the right to Indian self-government sweeping the country.

Peyakowak lobbied the provincial government to launch an inquiry into the child welfare system in Saskatchewan to raise the profile of Indian child welfare. With the change in government in May 1982, from the NDP under Allan Blakeney to the Progressive Conservatives under Grant Devine, conditions were ripe to revise past NDP legislation. On 27 May 1983, following the death of toddler Christopher Aisaican in a foster home, Lavina Bitternose, secretary of the Peyakowak Committee, wrote to the Minister of Social Services Patricia Smith. The group charged that Native children in the system received poor care and were more likely to be made permanent wards or adopted rather than being returned to their families. Peyakowak raised several questions: "Who advocates on behalf of the child? What protection for child's rights, for family's rights? We have a charter of rights and freedoms, yet there is no visible protection for children in the system – in the care and custody of the department. The department has sole authority for the care of the children – and it is a system that has a severe lack of resources for protection of the child."[84] In Saskatchewan there were no mechanisms to ensure that once children were removed from their families and communities, they were protected. For example, the government did not have a system to monitor foster homes. One area that needed attention, the committee believed, was the legislation that provided direction for the Department of Social Services, the Family Services Act (1973). In particular, they highlighted the lack of sections that dealt with prevention, as well as a lack of cultural resources for Native children in foster care. Likewise, there had been cutbacks in funding, insufficient support for families, not enough social workers, and general lack of support for vulnerable families and children.

Minister Smith rejected the need for an inquiry, claiming the department had completed an internal review and a prepared discussion paper. In truth, the discussion paper never came together. In her official statement, she replied, "I do not believe an inquiry would be an efficient or appropriate means of resolving these issues."[85] Rather than an inquiry, the department suggested a consultation and requested that Peyakowak take part.[86] While the government remained resistant to an inquiry, a number of allies called for and supported the demand for an inquiry. For example, from the Conference of Mennonites in Canada, Henry Bartel, chair of the Native Support Committee, wrote to the department advocating an inquiry.[87] Patrick Johnston, who had just published his critically important contribution to the discussion, *Native Children and the Child Welfare System*, knew the need for it better than anyone. In supporting an inquiry, he stated, "In my opinion, the problems inherent in the delivery of child welfare services are most acute in Saskatchewan and barriers to constructive change most complex."[88] Certainly the support of these well-respected individuals gave credibility to the idea of a public review. The department recognized that change was necessary, stating, "Our efforts in this area need to be stepped up. Native participation in decisions of this kind is absolutely essential."[89] But the inquiry did not materialize.

Shortly thereafter, Gordon Dirks replaced Smith as Minister of Social Services and initiated a revision of the Family Services Act. Prior to the public review, an internal discussion paper identified areas of concern with the Child and Family Services legislation as it stood in 1983.[90] The primary concern was legislative emphasis on the removal of children in need of protection. Too often children were removed from families and placed in group homes or foster homes until the child was returned home or adopted. Also there was failure to include families in planning or community groups in the provision of services. Too much power was concentrated in the hands of the department. The role of the courts was problematic, since it created an adversarial atmosphere and again contributed to apprehension. Native groups also criticized the trauma faced by Indigenous children entering into care in large numbers. Finally, the internal discussion paper suggested that legislation needed to broaden the definition of parent to include unmarried father, grandparent, relative, or friend, or Indian band.[91]

In addition to updating the legislation, the government also began an internal conversation about Indigenous customary adoption.[92] In response to the moratorium on adoptions in Saskatchewan proposed by the FSIN, Peyakowak, and other Indigenous organizations, a paper on custom adoption by law student Linda Lock was circulated to caucus. "Custom Adoption and Its Implications on the Breakdown of the Indian Culture," submitted on 15 April 1983 for a Native law course at the University of Saskatchewan, proposed custom adoption as a "viable alternative to the somewhat arbitrary selection of foster and adoption homes being forced on Indian children by government officials."[93] The paper strongly condemned the unsatisfactory situation in Indian child welfare in jurisdictions across Canada, pointing to efforts underway to restore Indigenous decision-making and give customary adoptions the force of law in Canadian courts. Specifically, Lock looked at the customary adoption approach in the North, the American Indian Child Welfare Act, and other systems emerging to turn the tide of Indigenous child removal.[94] Lock illustrated clearly that Canada was enacting cultural genocide through its child welfare policies, through "the forcible transfer of children of the Indian group to another group."[95] The paper made an extremely strong case for governments to get out of the dirty business of Indigenous cultural genocide through child welfare apprehensions and adoptions.

On 14 September 1983 Gordon Dirks, Minister of Social Services, presented an address to the Peyakowak Committee outlining the proposed direction of the government. He commended the group for their role in bringing these issues to the attention of the public and the government.[96] The next step was to gather public input into the changing direction on child and family services, as well as perhaps uncovering other areas of concern for groups in the community. In his address, Dirks officially established the ministerial advisory council on child protection. The council held public meetings in Regina, Saskatoon, and Prince Albert. Chaired by child psychiatrist Peter Matthews, president of the Saskatoon Society for the Protection of Children, the committee had five members of the Indigenous community, including Ivy Seales from Regina Native Women.[97] Questions were distributed for direction in areas that included adoption. For the adoption of children, Matthews was curious about adoption of children by step-parents, privately arranged adoptions, adoption of adults, and de facto adoptions where a child had been in the care of a particular family but was not legally a member of that family.[98] Over the next several months, public meetings were held across urban Saskatchewan. First Nations governments had the opportunity to provide input, and in doing so they developed a political position on Indian child welfare that supported their larger claims to self-government.

Saskatchewan residents, few of whom likely had experience with the Department of Social Services, discovered that services provided with their tax dollars were less than satisfactory. Three themes emerged from the three days of meetings held in Saskatoon: lack of services for prevention through family support systems, abusive by department employees in pushing parents aside, and harm to Native children by uniform application of the law. In addition, First Nations sought to take control of child welfare services.[99] When questioned on how to balance needs for prevention with protection, Minister Dirks replied, "It's not an either/or situation." Clearly Dirks found it complicated to determine "who defines what is a family in need of services, who is responsible to give those services, what role does the family have in saying no." He also indicated that the final legislation would need to satisfy general public concerns, and not just one group.[100]

In the Regina meetings, Indigenous representatives articulated the need to utilize the extended family for foster placements to prevent children from having their relationship to their communities severed. Chief Standing Ready, from White Buffalo First Nation, stated that children had been removed without proper input from Indian people. He felt that when children were adopted into white homes, they did know not who they were. He believed that what was needed was more Indian foster homes. At the same time he recognized that a major problem for Indian people was lack of housing. Leona Blondeau, a representative from the Saskatchewan Native Women's Association, argued that apprehensions should be only a last resort. Indigenous families in Saskatchewan needed support and education to retain children and strengthen families. She felt that the goal for some social workers was for Native children's ultimate adoption and integration into white society.[101]

The council heard that First Nations peoples accused the Social Services Department of causing cultural and social genocide in its treatment of Indigenous children. Claudia Agecoutay, of Cowessess Reserve, outlined the need for Native control, provisions for Indian families, notification of band or community leaders about adoption or fostering even in the case of children living in the cities, finding Indian foster and adoptive homes, and placing children with members of extended families. The council also heard from Nancy Ayers, a Saskatoon lawyer, about the impact of jurisdictional disputes between federal and provincial governments, suggesting that the province could delegate responsibility to bands and enter tripartite agreements like Manitoba.

Provincial law should be amended so bands could administer their own programs and child services.[102]

The provincial government anticipated that the FSIN position on child welfare would be related to the ultimate goal of Indian self-government and saw Indigenous resistance as adversarial, rather than intrinsic to Indigenous survival. Saskatchewan First Nations sought a federally funded Indian child welfare system under the control of First Nations bands without the involvement of the provincial government. In the report drafted for the hearings, *Indian Control of Indian Child Welfare*, the FSIN focused solely on securing control over child welfare.[103] The introduction read, "The principal reason for the high numbers of Indian children in the care of the present child welfare system is the lack of control Indian people have over the lives of Indian families and children. Without this control, Indian people cannot ensure the continuity and stability of the culture from generation to generation."[104] They rejected provincial provision of services and used their recent constitutional position to argue for control of child welfare services: "The Indian people of Saskatchewan, through their bands, districts, regional and national organizations have strongly supported the entrenchment of Indigenous rights and treaty rights, and the recognition of Indian self-government in the constitution. The struggle to entrench those rights led to an intense period of national and international lobbying during the recent deliberations concerning the patriation of the Canadian constitution."[105]

To show their determination to obtain control and see an end to transracial adoption, the FSIN passed a resolution at the First Annual Legislative Assembly insisting there be a one-year moratorium on Indian adoptions, while urging the province to support Indian control over Indian child welfare. The minister of social services offered no comment.[106]

Following the submission of the FSIN position paper and the rather hasty round of hearings in October and November 1983, the council prepared its final report for the Department of Social Services and the Saskatchewan people. It soundly rejected the FSIN demand for Indian control of Indian child welfare. In the final report, Indian control was viewed in economic rather than political terms, pointing to the lack of financial and human resources of Indian bands. The council resolved that it was impossible at that point for Native communities to offer protection for their children. The council recommended limiting Indigenous transracial adoption outside Saskatchewan, except to family members. It endorsed financially supported adoptions as an alternative to regular adoption for Indigenous people, as well as handicapped children. The council also called for increased cooperation with Native communities across Saskatchewan through the Department of Social Services. On the basis of input from the Peyakowak Committee on adoption, which was strongly opposed to cross-cultural adoption, the council recommended that private adoptions, as arranged by Native communities from time immemorial, begin to receive the force of law. It suggested a gradual move in the direction of Native control, using the model of tripartite agreements in Manitoba and elsewhere. The council was hesitant to relinquish complete control to First Nations and Métis groups, since "because of the requirement for skills and expertise in the area, the department must continue to be involved until satisfied with the quality of service that can be delivered."[107] Overall, the council warned against using children as pawns in the political process. Finally, the council rejected the FSIN recommendation that there be a moratorium on interracial adoption like Manitoba and the United States. The council argued that the only alternative to adoption would be to make children permanent wards, and the better solution would be to find Native homes for the children. The council was hopeful that a supportive relationship between the newly forming Indian child welfare organizations and the departments would develop.[108]

Saskatchewan's review of the Family Services Act (1973) in the second half of 1983 was part of a countrywide movement to address problems that beset provincial governments when providing child welfare services to Indigenous peoples and to bring legislation in line with the cultural and legal changes that had taken place over the past decade.[109] The Saskatchewan public review process offered an explanation and presented recommendations to address the high proportion of Indigenous children in care and the lack of preventative care for families. These explanations didn't satisfy Indigenous leaders or activists who had sought full control and recognition of their rights to determine the future of their children. It also provided a public forum to air grievances and raise awareness about these issues in the greater community. In the decade since the Métis Society and the Native Women's Movement first challenged the child removal logic of the Department of Social Services,

Indigenous peoples in North America had grown increasingly vocal in protesting government policies that led to the breakdown of the Indian family, for education or protection. Beginning with decolonization in Canada and the United States, control of the provision of child and family services to Indigenous children occupied a central position in discussions of self-determination. Ending transracial adoption symbolized ending the unequal and unilateral policies of integration after the Second World War.

While Indigenous women took part in the council and were heard at community meetings, no meaningful analysis of women's experiences or analysis of gender emerged. The silence around Indigenous motherhood, the breakdown of the Indigenous family, and the impact of residential schools left a legacy that prevented governments from addressing the increasing rates of Indigenous children entering the child welfare system.

The conservative perspective of the council was unable to reconcile the connection between retaining children in communities and the future health of Indigenous cultures. The advisory nature of the council also limited its impact, and the two-month duration and three-city tour limited the scope. By contrast, Judge Kimelman's inquiry in Manitoba ran from May 1982 until February 1983, travelling from Brandon to Churchill, visiting reserves in the north and south. In Saskatchewan there were no significant changes in child welfare until 1989, when the Child and Family Services Act was revised. In 1991 the first tripartite agreement was signed. Rather than acquiring tangible gains, the council's value was that it provided a forum for groups to enter a public dialogue about the strengths and weaknesses of Saskatchewan's child welfare system. Transracial adoption, while statistically minor in Saskatchewan, was symbolically significant in the struggle over child welfare for Indigenous groups. Indigenous peoples in Canada in the early 1980s sought means to regain control over family relationships severed through policies, ignorance, and good intentions, and to restore Indigenous kinship systems as a foundation of self-determination.

In recent years the Lac La Ronge First Nation in northern Saskatchewan has reversed the trend in increasing apprehensions. Their child and family services organization, the Lac La Ronge Indian Child and Family Services Agency (LLR-ICFSA) is disrupting child removal. As one of the few nationally accredited child-caring agencies in Canada, they have reduced their children in out of home care by 30 per cent in the first year of accreditation, in 2019.[110] Operating under the provincial legislation, the Saskatchewan Child and Family Services Act (1989), the agency has focused on keeping children in the community, and as Denali Youngwolfe has demonstrated, "to mitigate harm caused by generations of child removals the LLR-ICFSA ... will not make children permanent wards."[111] While providing services to families to prevent removals, the band is reclaiming Indigenous kinship systems and disrupting the settler-colonial logic of child removal.

Conclusion: Intimate Indigenization

Indigenous transracial adoption, promoted and publicized through the Adopt Indian and Métis Project, dismantled Indigenous kinship systems in pursuit of Indigenous elimination. Transracial adoption integrated Indigenous children into the Euro-Canadian nuclear family to be socialized for proper Canadian citizenship. Technologies of helping applied by professional social workers armed with provincial child welfare legislation applied unilaterally to all Indigenous peoples reflected the secular evolution in the bleeding heart of settler colonialism. Indigenous suffering from almost a century of colonial dispossession, residential schooling, poverty, trauma, and dislocation from loss of land was recast as a child welfare matter, leading to interventions and the crisis of over-representation in child welfare systems across Canada. Specifically, for First Nations women and children, conflicts between provincial and federal laws created a state of limbo, where the provincial Department of Social Welfare and Rehabilitation and social welfare workers became a substitute for ensuring the care of enfranchised women and children. For Métis peoples, failed relocation and rehabilitation schemes were replaced by individualized responses to child neglect and lack of housing. The over-representation of Indigenous children in the 1960s and 1970s emerged from post-war Indian policies and gendered and racialized laws meant to enforce a singular version of the formation of the nuclear family on Indigenous peoples. Child removal and integration into Euro-Canadian (and in some cases

Euro-American) adoptive homes were but another mechanism in the continuum of the colonization of Indigenous kinship.

A new direction for Indian Affairs in Canada took shape after the Second World War, symbolized by the transfer of the Indian Affairs Branch from the Ministry of Mines and Resources (1936–50) to the Ministry of Citizenship and Immigration (1950–65). With the new focus on citizenship came a revision in the legal regime that directed bureaucrats in administering the policies that dominated the lives of Indian people in Canada. The Indian Act, an evolving body of laws respecting Indian people in Canada, underwent further revision in 1951 to remove the most egregious aspects while placing greater emphasis on the preparation of Indian people to accept the voluntary nature of democratic citizenship.[1] A new terminology reflecting voluntary citizenship replaced the more coercive terminology as Indian assimilation shifted to Indian integration.[2] The alteration of tribal kinship systems and gender relations to mirror that of Euro-Canadian heterosexual nuclear families, as in previous times, was an essential aspect of preparation for Canadian citizenship.[3] After 1951 colonization of Indigenous kinship by policing genealogies and removing women who married non-Indian men, as well as the application of provincial laws on reserves, meant that Canadian citizenship became gendered and racialized more than ever before.[4] The gendered and racialized laws activated unique forms of disadvantage for Indian women and children. On one hand, the Indian Act was a disincentive to legal marriage and destabilized families. It also enhanced gendered form of compulsory enfranchisement that originated in the Gradual Enfranchisement Act of 1857 when women were enfranchised along with their husbands.[5] While feminist scholars recognized that this provision has contributed to the historic and current gender tensions among First Nations men and women, there are also implications for child welfare. The tenuous nature of this arrangement, the sole dependency of enfranchised women on their male provider, becomes evident through research into transracial adoption and child welfare history.[6]

The outcome of gender tensions, combined with new theories in child socialization and the rise of therapeutic government, legitimized child removal and transracial adoption as a "common sense" solution to colonization. This complex history of the child welfare system, with its colour-blind experiment in Indigenous transracial adoption, took shape immediately after the Second World War, when Canada embarked on a modern nation-building project. Childhood socialization was one area where the origins of Indian difference was thought to be located.[7] Early childhood socialization took on greater significance once the pseudo-science of racial theory had been dismantled. Knowledge gained of the intimate through "scientific inquiry" by experts in psychology, ethnology, or anthropology could be wielded to effect integration with "complete consent and satisfaction."

During the review of Indian Act legislation in 1946–8, social welfare experts represented by the Canadian Association of Social Workers and Canadian Welfare Council, positioned themselves as ideally suited to assist the Department of Indian Affairs with integration of Indian people into Canadian social and economic life. Their expertise in adjusting personalities and individuals to the new social realities, working with unwed mothers, juvenile delinquents, and putative fathers in white society, could be applied to Indian people. The submission acknowledged crises facing Indian people, such as poor housing and the high rates of tuberculosis and infant mortality.[8] On malnutrition, the submission pointed to the 1945 medical survey, which concluded that malnutrition, rather than racial characteristics, likely contributed to "Indian malaise"; the characteristics historically termed "shiftlessness," "indolence," and "improvidence and inertia," "so long regarded as hereditary traits in the Indian race, may at the root be really manifestations of malnutrition. Further it is probable that the Indian's greatest susceptibility to many diseases, paramount among which is tuberculosis, may be attributable among other causes to their high degree of malnutrition arising from lack of proper foods."[9]

The elusive causes of Indian poor heath, starvation, and poor housing were the consequence of federal Indian policies.[10] However, these were brushed aside by social welfare experts to shift to their primary concern. Directly following the references to ill health and malnutrition was the concern about increasing rates of prostitution and juvenile delinquency, the practice of custom adoption, illegitimate Indian children being forced off reserve, and lack of provincial legislation on reserves. The recognition that such outcomes were due to failed government policies was erased. Instead, attention was directed to the social pathologies and individual maladaptation that social work professionals felt could be alleviated with their specialized knowledge.

Social welfare professionals strongly positioned themselves to participate in partnership with Indian Affairs by aligning themselves with the goal of Indian assimilation. They stated, "In our judgment, the only defensible goal for a national program must be the full assimilation of Indians into Canadian life, which involves not only their admission to full citizenship, but also the right and opportunity for them to participate freely with other citizens in all community affairs."[11] As members of a profession seeking legitimacy, which had gained respect from work with immigrant and urban populations during the Depression, they found that Indian Affairs appeared to provide a virtually unlimited field for their specialized services. Social workers recalibrated the Indian problem as one of personal, social, and economic adjustment, offering the tools of their trade, such as adoption and apprehensions, to enact integration. Like past attempts at assimilation, "success" proved elusive.

Saskatchewan was an early pioneer in utilizing social welfare expertise to solve the manifestations of settler colonialism that have been referred to as the "Indian problem."[12] Under the direction of Tommy Douglas, Métis rehabilitation was orchestrated through the provincial Department of Social Welfare and Rehabilitation. Marginalization, poor health, extreme poverty, lack of education, and poor housing characterized Métis experience through the 1930s and 1940s. Unlike the First Nations people, Métis did not fall under the Indian Act legislation and as such were provincial citizens. However, they remained outsiders to provincial Euro-Canadian social and economic life. Like First Nations people, Métis suffered from the Euro-Canadian belief that they stood outside modernity as relics of a bygone era.[13] After the defeat of Louis Riel in 1885, Métis people recreated small communities on road allowances.[14] The CCF government experiment in the rehabilitation of the "subnormal" Métis initially took shape in relocating families to colonies to be trained as subsistence farmers and housewives. Métis children were to be educated in schools run by the Department of Social Welfare and Rehabilitation. When the government officially abandoned the relocation and brief colony scheme in 1961, rehabilitation attention shifted to prioritizing children and unmarried mothers. From 1961 onward, social workers were on the front lines where they could best enact the rehabilitation of Métis women and children through child welfare legislation.

The colonization of Indigenous kinship after the Second World War departed from earlier attempts through education of children in residential schools and domestication of women in the home and shifted to integration into the child welfare system and surveillance by social workers through provincial child welfare laws surrounding "neglect."[15] Indigenous children removed from families and communities increasingly became wards of Saskatchewan's Social Welfare Department. Social workers proposed establishing kin relations with non-Indigenous parents through "modern adoption" as a potential solution. The Adopt Indian and Métis program enticed Euro-Canadian families in Saskatchewan to consider adopting either a First Nations or Métis child through an extensive television, radio, and slide-show advertising campaign. After the successful pilot in the southeastern portion of the province, the Adopt Indian and Métis program was extended to include the rest of Saskatchewan.

State-directed Indigenous transracial adoption represented a radical rethinking of racial boundaries that had been erected between Indigenous and non-Indigenous peoples on the prairies. Transracial adoption was the most intimate form of integration that Canadian policymakers had attempted. It erased children's history of indigeneity and severed ties to family and communities. Simultaneously, the problems of Indian and Métis families were individualized and pathologized. Social work professionals became a primary group in Canadian to manage the fallout from loss of land, sovereignty, poverty, residential school abuse, and gender tensions that followed from Indian Act legislation. Managed by professional social workers and bolstered by legal protections, transracial adoption promised "safety, naturalness, and authenticity."[16] The rational and professional methodology used by social workers – such as regulation, interpretation, standardization, and naturalization – promised to minimize the potential risk in creating families through transracial adoption. These softer "technologies of helping" appealed to post-war Euro-Canadian politicians and citizens. Adoption was promoted as a legal, safe, and morally neutral method to create families and manage Indigenous relations. Adoption services provided by Saskatchewan's Department of Social Services promised privacy for adoptive and birth parents. Closed records gave children new futures, as past histories were eliminated. New homes in chosen locations with chosen families gave individual Indian and Métis children opportunities to enjoy the advantages of working-class or middle-class status. However, the hegemony of "modern adoption" essentially abolished the practice of Indigenous adoption that had taken place for centuries without the assistance of social workers, under their Indigenous legal systems of government. With the extension of provincial adoption laws onto reserves, Indigenous adoption essentially became illegal, or at the least, an illegitimate form of family making.

In 1966–7 Indian and Métis transracial adoptions in Saskatchewan accounted for only 10 per cent of all adoptions, but by 1977 rose to 35 per cent.[17] According to social scientist Phillip Hepworth, social workers, not surprisingly, viewed adoptions as preferable to institutionalization. He, like many in this field, felt that infant adoption was the best solution to the problem of illegitimacy for unmarried, single, or poor mothers, and was a preventative measure for children likely to suffer from maternal deprivation or neglect. In Saskatchewan 50 per cent of all children committed into care were Indigenous, yet very few ended up in adoptive homes. Indigenous mothers tended to keep their children, only to have them apprehended when they were older and, therefore, given less opportunity for adoption placement. In 1980 Philip Hepworth noted, "As one of the major reasons of Indian and Métis children coming into care is poor housing, it is more than likely that more of them will stay in care rather than return home."[18] Hepworth shared the perspective of other social work professionals, who viewed adoption as in the "best interests of the child," because it provided the care of two parents and established a permanent, legal relationship. In addition, it was vastly cheaper than both fostering and institutional care.[19]

This point of view diverged from that of members of Saskatchewan's Native Women's Movement (SNWM), who were as concerned as Hepworth about the growing numbers of single girls and women giving birth. They proposed an Indigenous feminist approach to address the impact of colonization in the lives of First Nations and Métis women in Saskatchewan. For example, they provided education and support to teen mothers to support their children. Also the SNWM opened the first Native-run day-care centre in the downtown core of Regina in 1973. Their voices were an important alternative to experts who were constructing the "problem of Indian child welfare" in the 1980s.[20] When researchers are considering agency and choice, their work can be fraught with difficulties and may oversimplify a complex situation that is affected by the limitations of the sources consulted. There is evidence that Indigenous mothers sought out welfare services such as adoption to secure homes for children they felt would otherwise suffer deprivations. Adoption provided an important child-caring option from a limited range of options in a social and political climate that was hostile to Indigenous mothers and children. The historically specific and varied responses from First Nations and Métis women in mid- to late twentieth-century Saskatchewan point to the need to take into account changes in gender relations in Indigenous communities. By looking comparatively at transracial adoption in Canada and the United States, as well as the resistance it engendered, the research in this volume seeks to find the heart of colonial politics through the management of affective ties, and attempts to explain changing national identities that transracial adoption sought to create.

Reproductive justice for Indigenous women means being accorded the opportunity to parent children free from coercive policies, or secure child welfare services that do not presume Indigenous mothers are pathological. Archival evidence and published adoptee accounts demonstrate that in some cases Indigenous women opted to relinquish their children for adoption. It is important to acknowledge that some Indigenous women may have pursued this option, from among a small range of choices. The right to Aboriginal motherhood and to define Aboriginal motherhood and kinship are a key area where decolonization is taking place. White ideology of Aboriginal motherhood – as the pathological unfit mother – shaped responses to child neglect and Indigenous forms of child care.[21]

Exploring the history of transracial adoption brings into focus the malleable nature of racial difference, while illustrating simultaneously the persistence of settler-colonial logics that structure Indigenous child removal. It highlights how child welfare responses contributed to First Nations and Métis marginalization, albeit in new and virtually unrecognizable ways. Evidence presented here demonstrates that the policies and legislation developed by the Department of Indian Affairs, particularly on Indigenous gender relations, manifested with growing poverty, family breakdown, substance misuse, unplanned pregnancy, child neglect, and apprehension. The effects were mystified and submerged through programs such as Adopt Indian and Metis, REACH, and the Indian Adoption Project and later through demands by First Nations leaders for control over child welfare.[22] Indigenous people rejected the narrow scope for relations that the creation of adoptive kinship ties provided through the modern secretive adoption process. While adoption promised the permanency of loving families and legal protections for Indigenous children that the fostering system could not, Indigenous peoples, globally, have rejected this form of child welfare service. While transracial adoption has been rejected by the vast majority of Indigenous people, culturally relevant alternatives are slowly emerging in Saskatchewan.[23] Nevertheless, it is clear that there must be proper oversight to ensure the safety of vulnerable children who are placed in kinship care or through adoption, and La Ronge Child and Family Service Agency provides one promising template.[24]

During the 1980s, when Indian child welfare became politicized in Canada, Indigenous leaders and legal experts looked south to consider the relevance of the 1978 Indian Child Welfare Act for First Nations in Canada. Indian boarding schools and transracial adoption programs, such as the Indian Adoption Program and ARENA, were recognized in the United States at that time as to be a *national* phenomenon detrimental to the future of Native American tribes. This form of cultural genocide interrupted the transmission of language and culture, and prevented Native American children from claiming their identities as rights-bearing Indigenous peoples. ICWA (1978) challenged the logic of child removal in the United States. It established a legal framework to ensure the role of tribal governments in crafting locally relevant solutions while providing funding to preserve Indian families.[25] In Canada the federal government has remained the reluctant funder of on-reserve child and family service agencies and provided provincial governments with dollars to provide services to Indian families. No national equivalent in Canada provides direction, evaluation, or guidance to Indian child welfare.[26]

The first five "Calls to Action" for the Truth and Reconciliation Commission of Canada call on all levels of government to reduce the number of children removed from families and address the lethal legacy of residential schools.[27] While the first seeks to reduce the number of children in care with several suggestions for culturally based preventative social work, the second calls for all levels of government to conduct research into their programs and report annually on their progress. Reducing the numbers of children apprehended in the first place through culturally appropriate forms of preventative family support is a message that has been articulated for several decades by Indigenous peoples. The much more complex yet urgent task, to decolonize child welfare, appears to be on the horizon.

Epilogue: Coming Home

My journey of coming home includes restoring relationships that were put on pause when I was adopted, not only with my family members but also with a landscape that has been part of my family's collective memory for generations. My own experience living and raising my four children on these lands, the seventh generation to live in Flett's Springs, has informed my own sense of Métis historical consciousness.

Theorizing coming home is part of critically interrogating the ways in which colonization has disrupted relationships to land, family, and our Indigenous histories while envisioning and enacting decolonization and collective healing. Neal McLeod states, "To be home means to dwell in the landscape of the familiar, collective memories."[1] Being home is have access to land, to raise your own children, and have a collective sense of dignity. Part of being an adoptee is the sense of exile experienced, compounded with the sense of exile that many Métis people experience in their homelands.

BECOMING MÉTIS IN SASKATCHEWAN: FIDLER MALE KINSHIP PATTERNS OF SETTLEMENT

I am part of a Métis family that moved from Red River to Saskatchewan in the 1870s, then married into local Métis families. The English-speaking Fidler family descend from Hudson's Bay Company

Red River cart, Flett's Springs Presbyterian Church (author's collection)

mapmaker and surveyor Peter Fidler and Mary Mackagone.[2] As part of the Métis diaspora out of Red River, brothers James Edward, William, and Peter settled on river lots alongside their father on the North Branch of the Saskatchewan River in the English-speaking Métis community of Prince Albert at time when the English-speaking Métis in Saskatchewan were developing a sense of collective Métis Identity.[3] The family of Edward Fidler arrived in Prince Albert at time when land tenure in the Northwest Territories was becoming increasingly uncertain for the Métis. The large multigenerational Fidler family arrived in Prince Albert shortly after the community submitted petitions seeking recognition for their land tenure.[4] Petitions sent to the government in January 1878 indicate that English-speaking Métis residents sought recognition of their land tenure, as well as the right to the same provisions for Métis heads of families and children that had been secured in the Manitoba Act.[5]

My grandmother Marion, daughter of Alex Fidler and Flora Sayese, was one of the older children in her family and has shared many stories with me about her life and experiences. Like her father, she joined the war effort in the Second World War, ending up in Ottawa censoring incoming mail. She remains very proud of this time in her life. She raised four boys and worked in town as well. She was a very strong woman who has endured the tragic loss of her son, as well as the sudden death of her husband in an accident in 1986. In her later years, she began to undertake research on our ancestor, surveyor for the HBC Peter Fidler, an important figure that her father told stories of in her childhood.

The erasure of Métis identity and spaces, knowledge, and kinship ties has taken place most commonly through the federal government scrip policy and subsequent speculation, relocation policies under Tommy Douglas, but also through the pioneer narratives in the local history books in countless Saskatchewan communities. This historical erasure, at times done by families documenting their own histories, and silencing of the Métis peoples has implications for the embodied experience of the Métis in Saskatchewan and in the rest of Canada. Not only are we disappeared from the meaningful inclusion in settler history books, we are disappeared through transracial adoption, and in the case of my father, we are disappeared off the streets in Prairie cities across the west. As Sherene Razack has pointed out in her recent *Dying from Improvement*, which looks at Indigenous deaths in custody, the narrative of the dying/vanishing/disappearing race is as old as settler colonial society.[6] She states, "The road to settler success is lined with legal decisions and reports which declare what settlers hope to make true on the ground, namely that they have become the original citizens through their enterprising spirit."[7]

Historic relations, gender, and spatial distribution intersect to produce spaces where Indian and Métis bodies encounter the violence of settler-colonialism masked as the inevitability of alcohol and drug-fuelled self-destruction. Prince Albert, Saskatchewan, the Beautiful Gateway, is one such site. As Razack states, "The city belongs to rational men and women individuals who are owners of themselves. Fences, borders are enactments rather than permanent lines. Settlers lay constant siege to the city – inscribing their claims on the ground and on bodies in the language of rationality and order, thereby marking the

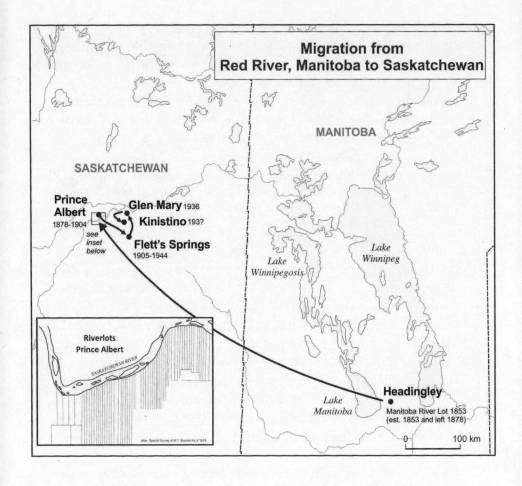

lines of force of the colonial project."[8] Like countless other family members before me, I seek to challenge the official narrative of my disappearance and that of my father and those before us whose presence and lands have been disappeared, but not through a naturalized and inevitable process.

When my father disappeared in Prince Albert in July 1980, he was twenty-nine years old. Each year his photo is displayed among those of other men and women in Saskatchewan who are missing. This re-enactment of his disappearance operates as a ritualistic reminder to the settler population of their legitimate claim to the lands formerly inhabited by my father's ancestors. In exploring the connection to colonial masculinity Rob Innes and Kim Anderson have asked, "Who

Saskatoon *Star Phoenix*, 25 April 2009

is walking with our brothers?"[9] And in many cases, fathers and sons?
It is also important to note that colonization has worked to dispossess
men in specifically gendered ways. While there had been several theories about his disappearance, none were conclusive, and so, just as I was
erased through adoption, he was erased through his disappearance.

When I first met my family in 1996, my younger cousin Brad Wiggins asked if I knew who Peter Fidler was when I told him I was attending university to major in history. At the time I was embarrassed that I had never heard of him, and I didn't know that I was related to him. My lack of knowledge of this critical piece of family pride highlighted my sense of loss and alienation from my own history and kinship connections, and as I came to understand western history, the erasure of a Métis history of place, and Métis historical consciousness. To me, coming home has been a journey to understand the power dynamics in rural Saskatchewan that has rendered some families pioneers in protection of their lands, and others vulnerable to removal and erasure. Coming home has also meant coming to understand kinship, insistence/resistance, and resilience in the face of the imperative to erase the Métis presence from the landscape. Coming home also means that someone is waiting for your return. Coming home is landed, embodied, and storied; it stiches together peoples separated by time and space.

Appendix: Road Allowance Communities in Saskatchewan

GOVERNMENT-OPERATED FARMS[1]

Green Lake
Lebret farm (1940–68) colony operated by the DSWR jointly with the
　　Catholic Church
Willowbunch farm (1953–61)

REHABILITATION PROJECTS OPERATED
BY THE DSWR

Lestock (1951–61)
Crescent Lake (1945–61)
Crooked Lake (1948–62)

ROAD ALLOWANCE COMMUNITIES RELOCATED
TO GREEN LAKE

Baljennie (1951 and 1952)
Glen May (1945/6?)
Punnichy (little Chicago road allowance community 1949)

ROAD ALLOWANCE COMMUNITIES SURVEYED BY CCF GOVERNMENT (1945, 1955)

Baljennie
Cana
Canwood
Hawkeye
Mount Nebo
North Prince Albert
Orkney
Park Valley
Pascal
Polwarth
Prince Albert
Qu'Appelle
Saltcoats
Sandy Lake
Victoire
Yorkton

Notes

Prologue

1 Deanna Reder, "Âcimisowin as theoretical practice; autobiography as Indigenous intellectual tradition in Canada" (PhD diss., UBC, 2007).

2 Margaret Kovach, *Indigenous Methodologies: Characteristics, Conversations, and Contexts* (Toronto: University of Toronto Press, 2009), 3–4.

3 A special thanks to my close friends and colleagues Dr Cheryl Troupe and Dr Tara Turner, who insisted that it was important to include my own story from the beginning.

4 Kim Anderson, *Life Stages and Native Women: Memory, Teachings, and Story Medicine*, Critical Studies in Native History 15 (Winnipeg: University of Manitoba Press, 2011), xix.

5 Ethelton Sunset Club, *Ethelton Pioneers* (Ethelton: Ethelton Sunset Club, 1976), 109, Land Title NE2 44 21A W2, isc.ca.

6 Family background history for Allyson Donna Lawrence, 9 November 1976, personal collection.

7 Gregory A. Scofield, *Thunder through My Veins: Memories of a Métis Childhood* (Toronto : HarperFlamingo Canada, 1999), 166–7.

8 Neal McLeod, *Cree Narrative Memory: From Treaties to Contemporary Times* (Saskatoon, SK: Purich Publications, 2007), 54–8.

Introduction

1 *Cree Dictionary*, s.v., "Kisiskâciwan," http://www.creedictionary.com /search/index.php?q=kisiskâciwan&scope=1&cwr=24969.

2 Harold Cardinal, *Treaty Elders of Saskatchewan: Our Dream Is That Our Peoples Will One Day Be Clearly Recognized as Nations* (Calgary, AB: University of Calgary Press, 2000), 10.

3 Bill Waiser, *A World We Have Lost: Saskatchewan before 1905* (Markham, ON: Fifth House Books, 2016), 57–9.

4 The starvation policies of Edgar Dewdney and John A. Macdonald, the 1885 Resistance, and subsequent subjugation of the Prairie Indigenous peoples mark out this territory as ground zero of Canadian colonialism. The literature on this subject is vast and continually emerging. See a select bibliography: Robert Alexander Innes, "Historians and Indigenous Genocide in Saskatchewan," Shekon Neechie: An Indigenous History Site, https://shekonneechie.ca/2018/06/21/historians-and-indigenous-genocide-in-saskatchewan/; Alexander Laban Hinton, Andrew Woolford, and Jeff Benvenuto, *Colonial Genocide in Indigenous North America* (Durham, NC: Duke University Press, 2014); J.R. Miller, ed., *Sweet Promises: A Reader on Indian-White Relations in Canada*, 4th ed. (Toronto: University of Toronto Press, 1991); Miller, *Skyscrapers Hide the Heavens: A History of Native-Newcomer Relations in Canada*, 4th ed. (Toronto: University of Toronto Press, 2017); Howard Adams, *Prison of Grass: Canada from a Native Point of View*, 2nd ed. (Markham, ON: Fifth House, 1989); Maureen Lux, *Medicine That Walks: Disease, Medicine, and Canadian Plains Native People, 1880–1940* (Toronto: University of Toronto Press, 2001); Sarah Carter, *Lost Harvests: Prairie Indian Reserve Farmers and Government Policy* (Montreal and Kingston: McGill-Queen's University Press, 1993); Katherine Pettipas, *Severing the Ties That Bind: Government Repression of Indigenous Religious Ceremonies on the Prairies* (Winnipeg: University of Manitoba Press, 1994); James Daschuk, *Clearing the Plains: Disease, Politics of Starvation, and the Loss of Aboriginal Life* (Regina, SK: University of Regina Press, 2013); Neal McLeod, *Cree Narrative Memory: From Treaties to Contemporary Times* (Saskatoon, SK: Purich Publishing, 2007); Blair Stonechild and Bill Waiser, *Loyal till Death: Indians and the Northwest Rebellion* (Markham, ON: Fifth House, 2010).

5 This research is aligned with a developing approach that critically interrogates place as a means of decolonizing settler colonial practices of domination. See Eve Tuck and Marcia McKenzie, *Place in Research: Theory, Methodology and Methods* (New York: Routledge, 2015).

6 Patrick Johnston, *Native Children and the Child Welfare System* (Toronto: James Lorimer, 1983), 23.

7 For the significance of child removal to the genocide of Indigenous peoples, see Robert Krieken, "Rethinking Cultural Genocide: Aboriginal Child Removal and Settler-Colonial State Formation," *Oceania* 75, no. 2 (2004): 125–51, https://doi.org/10.1002/j.1834-4461.2004.tb02873.x.

8 Joyce Green, ed., *Making Space for Indigenous Feminism* (Winnipeg, MB: Fernwood Publishing, 2007).

9 *Iskwew*, Saskatchewan Native Women's Movement Newsletter, May 1975.

10 L. Gilchrist, "Aboriginal Street Youth in Vancouver, Winnipeg and Montreal" (PhD diss. University of British Columbia, 1995).

11 From Maria Campbell and Sherry Farrell Racette, *Stories of the Road Allowance People* (Penticton: Theytus Books, 1995). Retold here with permission from Maria Campbell and GDI, 88–92.

12 From Maria Campbell and Sherry Farrell Racette, *Stories of the Road Allowance People*, 94.

13 From Maria Campbell and Sherry Farrell Racette, *Stories of the Road Allowance People*, 97.

14 From Maria Campbell and Sherry Farrell Racette, *Stories of the Road Allowance People*, 100.

15 V. Sinha and A. Kozlowski, "The Structure of Aboriginal Child Welfare in Canada," *International Indigenous Policy Journal* 4, no. 2 (2013): 1–21, http://ir.lib.uwo.ca/iipj/vol4/iss2/2, 3.

16 Sinha and Kozlowski, "Structure of Aboriginal Child Welfare in Canada."

17 Denali Youngwolfe, "Miyo-Ohpikāwasowin – Raising Our Children in a Good Way: Disrupting Indigenous Child Removal Systems through Kinship Care in Northern Saskatchewan," MA thesis, University of Saskatchewan, 2017, 19–39; Jennifer Clibbon, "First Nations Child Advocate Wins 1st Battle with Ottawa on Services," CBC News, 19 April 2012, http://www.cbc.ca/news/canada/first-nations-child-advocate-wins-1st-battle-with-ottawa-on-services-1.1149966.

18 Jorge Barrera, "Indigenous Child Welfare Rates Creating 'Humanitarian Crisis' in Canada, Says Federal Minister," CBC News, 2 November 2017, http://www.cbc.ca/news/indigenous/crisis-philpott-child-welfare-1.4385136.

19 Numbers taken from table 11, in Johnston, *Native Children and the Child Welfare System*, 37.

20 In Johnston's study, no province came close to the high proportion of children in their welfare systems. Ontario and Quebec had 8 per cent and 2 per cent, respectively; 27–53.

21 Child Welfare Review Panel Report, *For the Good of Our Children and Youth: A New Vision, a New Direction*, December 2010, 18, https://cwrp.ca/publications/saskatchewan-child-welfare-review-panel-report-good-our-children-and-youth.

22 Child Welfare Review Panel Report, *For the Good of Our Children and Youth*, 11. The Adopt Indian and Métis program was identified as an extension of the residential school assimilation policy. Coined by Johnston in *Native Children and the Child Welfare System*, the central tenet of the sixties scoop paradigm is that the government was responsible for removal of First Nations children without justification and placing them in non-Aboriginal homes. Although both Cheryl Marlene Swidrovich, "Positive Experiences of First Nations Children in Non-Aboriginal Foster or Adoptive Care: De-Constructing the 'Sixties Scoop'" (MA thesis, Native Studies, 2004), 138–42; and Raven Sinclair argue the "sixties scoop" is a problematic term – three

of her sixteen interviewees were apprehended – the majority were voluntarily relinquished. Raven Sinclair, "All My Relations – Native Transracial Adoption: A Critical Case Study of Cultural Identity" (PhD diss., University of Calgary, 2007), 254, the term *Sixties Scoop* has come to designate these policies.

23 *Ottawa Citizen*, "Proposed Adoption Exchange," 19 May 1963.
24 *Ottawa Citizen*, "Proposed Adoption Exchange," 19 May 1963.
25 *Ottawa Citizen*, "Proposed Adoption Exchange," 19 May 1963.
26 *Star Phoenix*, "Indian and Métis Children Pose Adoption Problems for Welfare," 30 June 1965.
27 A good look at other failed "solutions" can be found in Noel Dyck, *What Is the Indian "Problem"? Tutelage and Resistance in Canadian Indian Administration* (St John's, NL: Institute for Social and Economic Research, Memorial University of Newfoundland, 1991).
28 Other jurisdictions that reviewed their child welfare legislation at this time included Alberta (Bill 105), Ontario (Child and Family Services Act of Ontario, 1984), Manitoba (Manitoba Child and Welfare Services Act), and British Columbia (Minister's Advisory Council on Child Protection, 4).
29 McLeod, *Cree Narrative Memory*, 14–15.
30 James Sákéj Youngblood Henderson, *First Nations Jurisprudence and Aboriginal Rights: Defining the Just Society* (Saskatoon, SK: Native Law Centre, University of Saskatchewan, 2006), 110.
31 This topic is explored in depth by historian Laura Briggs, "Mother, Race, Child, Nation: The Visual Iconography of Rescue and the Politics of Transracial and Transnational Adoption," *Gender and History* 15, no. 2 (2003): 179–200.

1. The Bleeding Heart of Settler Colonialism

1 D.C. Fraser, "Sask. Government to Issue Apology for Sixties Scoop pm Jan. 5," *Regina Leader-Post*, 17 December 2018, https://leaderpost.com/news/saskatchewan/the-saskatchewan-government-will-issue-an-apology-for-the-sixties-scoop-on-jan-7.
2 CBC News, "Apology Coming but No Money for Sixties Scoop: Sask. Premier Brad Wall," 24 June 2015, https://www.cbc.ca/news/canada/saskatchewan/apology-coming-but-no-money-for-sixties-scoop-sask-premier-brad-wall-1.3126003.
3 Bryce Hoye, "Manitoba Premier Greg Selinger Apologizes for Sixties Scoop," CBC News, 17 June 2015, https://www.cbc.ca/news/canada/manitoba/manitoba-premier-greg-selinger-apologizes-for-sixties-scoop-1.3118049.
4 Alberta, "Sixties Scoop Apology," 28 May 2018, Alberta.ca/SixtiesScoopApology.
5 Nicole Huck, "Merchant Law Firm Launches Class-Action Lawsuit for '60s Scoop' Adoptees," CBC News, 9 February 2015, https://www.cbc.ca

/news/canada/saskatchewan/merchant-law-firm-launches-class-action-lawsuit-for-60s-scoop-adoptees-1.2949635.

6 Gloria Galloway, "Métis Left Out of '60's Scoop Settlement," *Globe and Mail*, 11 October 2017, https://beta.theglobeandmail.com/news/politics/Métis-say-they-should-not-have-been-left-out-of-sixties-scoop-compensation/article36536782/?ref=http://www.theglobeandmail.com&.

7 Miller, *Skyscrapers Hide the Heavens*, chap. 11.

8 J.R. Miller, *Shingwauk's Vision: A History of Native Residential Schools* (Toronto: University of Toronto Press, Scholarly Publishing Division, 1996).

9 Miller, *Shingwauk's Vision*, 40.

10 Miller, *Shingwauk's Vision*, 41.

11 Miller, *Shingwauk's Vision*, 114.

12 John Milloy, *A National Crime: The Canadian Government and the Residential School System, 1879–1986* (Winnipeg: University of Manitoba Press, 1996), 22.

13 Milloy, *National Crime*, 52.

14 Milloy, *National Crime*, 190.

15 Roger L. Nichols, *Indians in the United States and Canada: A Comparative History* (Lincoln: University of Nebraska Press, 1998), 129.

16 Nichols, *Indians in the United States and Canada*, 185.

17 Nichols, *Indians in the United States and Canada*, 185.

18 Nichols, *Indians in the United States and Canada*, 194.

19 Nichols, *Indians in the United States and Canada*, 214.

20 Nichols, *Indians in the United States and Canada*, 337.

21 David Wallace Adams, *Education for Extinction: American Indians and the Boarding School Experience, 1875–1928* (Lawrence: University of Kansas, 1995), 14.

22 Adams, *Education for Extinction*, 173.

23 Margaret D. Jacobs, *Settler Colonialism, Maternalism, and the Removal of Indigenous Children in the American West and Australia, 1880–1940* (Lincoln: University of Nebraska Press, 2009), 11.

24 Jacobs, *Settler Colonialism*, 371.

25 Jacobs, *Settler Colonialism*, 392.

26 Lux, *Medicine That Walks*.

27 Mary-Ellen Kelm, *Colonizing Bodies: Aboriginal Health and Healing in British Columbia, 1900–1950* (Vancouver: UBC Press, 1996), 103.

28 Donald L. Fixico, *Termination and Relocation: Federal Indian Policy, 1845–1960* (Albuquerque: University of New Mexico Press, 1986), 38.

29 Hugh Shewall, *"Enough to Keep Them Alive": Indian Welfare in Canada, 1873–1965* (Toronto: University of Toronto Press, 2004), 173.

30 Shewall, *"Enough to Keep Them Alive,"* 153–5.

31 Jessa Chupik-Hall, "'Good Families Do Not Just Happen': Indigenous People and Child Welfare Services in Canada, 1950–1965" (MA thesis, Trent University, 2001).

32 Chupik-Hall, "'Good Families Do Not Just Happen,'" 64.

33 Chupik-Hall, "'Good Families Do Not Just Happen,'" 66.

34 John Lutz, *Makuk: A New History of Aboriginal White Relations* (Vancouver: UBC Press, 2008), 287.

35 Lutz, *Makuk*, 47.

36 Lutz, *Makuk*, 238–9.

37 Lutz, *Makuk*, 273.

38 Helen Buckley, *From Wooden Ploughs to Welfare: Why Indian Policy Failed in the Prairie Provinces* (Montreal and Kingston: McGill-Queen's University Press, 1992), 70.

39 Buckley, *From Wooden Ploughs to Welfare* 72.

40 Between 1941 and 1959, the Aboriginal population in Saskatchewan doubled; Laurie Barron, *Walking in Indian Moccasins: The Native Policies of Tommy Douglas and the CCF* (Vancouver: UBC Press, 1997), 101.

41 Jim Pitsula, "The Saskatchewan CCF Government and Treaty Indians, 1944–64," *Canadian Historical Review* 71, no. 1 (1994): 21–52. He discusses the CCF liberal democratic philosophy regarding Indian policy in the province that sought to eliminate special status. Through providing Indian people with the provincial vote and amending liquor laws to allow Indians the right to drink alcohol, as well as transferring the responsibility for Indian people from the federal government to the province, the CCF believed they would remove the barriers that prevented Indian people from enjoying the same prosperity as the non-Aboriginal citizens in the province.

42 F. Laurie Barron, "The CCF and the Development of Métis Colonies in Southern Saskatchewan during the Premiership of TC Douglas," http://www3.brandonu.ca/cjns/10.2/barron.pdf, 30.

43 Barron, "CCF and the Development of Métis Colonies," 61.

44 See appendix 1 for a list of colonies and Road Allowance Communities in Saskatchewan. From Barron, "CCF and the Development of Métis Colonies."

45 Barron, "CCF and the Development of Métis Colonies," 261.

46 Barron, "CCF and the Development of Métis Colonies," 261.

47 Murray Dobbin, "Prairie Colonialism: The CCF in Northern Saskatchewan, 1944–1964," *Studies in Political Economy*, 16 (1985): 5.

48 David M. Quiring, *CCF Colonialism in Northern Saskatchewan: Battling Parish Priests, Bootleggers and Fur Sharks* (Vancouver: UBC Press, 2004), 190.

49 Dobbin, "Prairie Colonialism," 14.

50 Dobbin, "Prairie Colonialism," 16.

51 Dobbin, "Prairie Colonialism," 22.

52 Dobbin, "Prairie Colonialism," 29.

53 Dobbin, "Prairie Colonialism," 32.

54 Quiring, *CCF Colonialism*, 256.

55 Sarah Carter, *Capturing Women: The Manipulation of Cultural Imagery in Canada's Prairie West* (Montreal and Kingston: McGill-Queen's University Press, 1997), 185; Adele Perry, *On the Edge of Empire: Gender, Race, and the Making of British Columbia, 1849–1871* (Toronto: University of Toronto Press, 2001), 123.

56 *Métis*, the French term meaning "to mix" derived from the Latin *miscere*, has been adopted to describe all people of mixed European and First Nations ancestry descended from the fur trade. Previously, *Métis* was applied only to French-speaking mixed-ancestry peoples. D. Bruce Sealey and Antoine S. Lussier, *The Métis: Canada's Forgotten People* (Winnipeg: Pemmican Publications, 1975), 1–2; Jacqueline Peterson and Jennifer S.H. Brown, introduction to *The New Peoples: Being and Becoming Métis in North America* (Winnipeg: University of Manitoba Press, 1985), 4.

57 Emma LaRocque, "The Colonization of a Native Woman Scholar," in *Women of the First Nations: Power Wisdom, and Strength*, ed. Christine Miller and Patricia Chuchryk (Winnipeg: University of Manitoba Press, 1996).

58 Maria Campbell, *Halfbreed*. Canadian Lives, vol. 16 (Halifax, NS: Goodread Biographies, 1973).

59 For a discussion of the image of Aboriginal women in popular discourse, see Carter, *Capturing Women*, esp. chap 5, "In Sharp Relief: Representations of Aboriginal Women in the Colonial Imagination," 159.

60 Critical forms of feminist ethnohistory in Canada include Adele Perry, *On the Edge of Empire: Gender, Race, and the Making of British Columbia, 1849–1871*, Studies in Gender and History (Toronto: University of Toronto Press, 2001); Mary Ellen Kelm, *Colonizing Bodies: Aboriginal Health and Healing in British Columbia, 1900–1950* (Vancouver: UBC Press, 1999); and Mary Ellen Kelm and Lorna Townsend, eds, *In the Days of Our Grandmothers: A Reader in Aboriginal Women's History in Canada* (Toronto: University of Toronto Press, 2006); Myra Rutherdale and Katie Pickles, *Contact Zones: Aboriginal and Settler Women in Canada's Colonial Past* (Vancouver: UBC Press, 2005); Robin Brownlie, *A Fatherly Eye: Indian Agents, Government Power, and Aboriginal Resistance in Ontario, 1918–1939* (Don Mills, ON: Oxford University Press, 2003); Mary Jane Logan McCallum, *Indigenous Women, Work, and History, 1940–1980*, Critical Studies in Native History, 16 (Winnipeg: University of Manitoba Press, 2014).

61 Fiona Paisley, "Childhood and Race: Growing Up in the Empire," in *Gender and Empire*, ed. Philippa Levine, Oxford History of the British Empire Companion Series (Oxford : Oxford University Press, 2007), 240.

62 Philippa Levine, "Introduction," *Gender and Empire*, 2.

63 Sylvia Van Kirk, *Many Tender Ties: Women in Fur Trade Society 1670–1870* (Winnipeg, MB: Watson and Dwyer, 1996). A recent publication pays homage to the groundbreaking work of Van Kirk, assessing the significance of her scholarship to Aboriginal history, Western history, and women's history worldwide. See Robin Jarvis Brownlie and Valerie J. Korinek, eds, *Finding a Way to the Heart: Feminist Writings on Aboriginal and Women's History in Canada* (Winnipeg: University of Manitoba Press, 2012;) Sylvia Van Kirk, *Many Tender Ties: Women in Fur Trade Society 1670–1870* (Winnipeg, MB: Watson and Dwyer, 1996).

64 Ann Laura Stoler, "Tense and Tender Ties: The Politics of Comparison," in *Haunted by Empire: Geographies of Intimacy in North American History*, ed. Ann Laura Stole (Durham, NC: Duke University Press, 2006), 24.

65 Ann Laura Stoler, "Intimidations of Empire: Predicaments of the Tactile and Unseen," in *Haunted by Empire: Geographies of Intimacy in North American History*, ed. Ann Laura Stoler (Durham: NC: Duke University Press, 2006), 2.

66 "The second, formed somewhat later, focused on the species body, the body imbued with the mechanics of life and serving as the basis of the biological processes: propagation, births and mortality, the level of health, life expectancy and longevity, with all the conditions that can cause these to vary. Their supervision was effected through an entire series of interventions and *regulatory controls: a biopolitics of the population*. The disciplines of the body and the regulations of the population constituted the two poles around which the organization of power over life was deployed. The setting up, in the course of the classical age, of this great bipolar technology – anatomic and biological, individualizing and specifying, directed toward the performances of the body, with attention to the processes of life – characterized a power whose highest function was perhaps no longer to kill, but to invest life through and through." Michel Foucault, *The History of Sexuality* (New York: Vintage Books, 1980), 139–40.

67 Ann Laura Stoler, *Race and the Education of Desire: Foucault's History of Sexuality and the Colonial Order of Things* (Durham, NC: Duke University Press, 1995), 32–3.

68 Stoler, *Race and the Education of Desire*, 112.

69 Ann Laura Stoler, *Carnal Knowledge and Imperial Power: Race and the Intimate in Colonial Rule* (Berkeley: University of California Press, 2002), xii.

70 Linda Tuhiwai Smith, *Decolonizing Methodologies: Research and Indigenous Peoples* (London: Zed Books, 2013), 36.

71 I received approval from the University of Saskatchewan's Behavioural Research Ethics Board to conduct interviews with elders and families of origin. University of Saskatchewan Behavioural Ethics Board Approval 13 February 2012 BEH# 11-74.

72 Canadian Institute of Health Research, Natural Sciences, and Engineering Research Council of Canada and Social Sciences and Humanities Research Council of Canada, "Tri-Council Policy Statement: Ethical Conduct for Research Involving Humans," December 2010.

73 National Aboriginal Health Organization (NAHO), "Six Principles of Métis Health Research: Ethical Principles to Guide the Métis Centre in Its Work," accessed 1 May 2012, www.naho.ca/Métiscentre.

74 Privacy laws in Saskatchewan prohibit the disclosure of adoption records for research.

75 Donald J. Auger, "The Northern Ojibwe and Their Family Law" (PhD diss., York University, 2001). Andrea Smith and Rickie Solinger discuss how "choice" is complicated by class and race, limiting women's range of viable options, and penalizing them as poor "choice makers." Rickie Solinger, *Beggars and Choosers: How the Politics of Choice Shapes Adoption,*

Abortion and Welfare in the United States (New York: Hill and Wang, 2001), 35; and Andrea Smith, *Conquest: Sexual Violence and American Indian Genocide* (Cambridge, MA: South End, 2005), see chapter 4, "Better Dead Than Pregnant: The Colonization of Native Women's Reproductive Health."

76 *Final Report of the Truth and Reconciliation Commission of Canada*, Vol. 1, *Summary: Honouring the Truth, Reconciling for the Future* (Ottawa: Truth and Reconciliation Commission of Canada, 2015). A transnational historiography of child removal policies in settler colonial nations is emerging, in large part based on the work of Margaret Jacobs, *White Mother to a Dark Race: Settler Colonialism, Maternalism, and the Removal of Indigenous Children in the American West and Australia, 1880–1940* (Lincoln: University of Nebraska Press, 2009); and Jacobs, *A Generation Removed: The Fostering and Adoption of Indigenous Children in the Post-War World* (Lincoln: University of Nebraska Press, 2014). A special edition of *American Indian Quarterly* was devoted to the politics of child welfare in settler colonial nations: *American Indian Quarterly* 37, no. 1–2 (Winter/Spring 2013), which brought together feminist scholars from Australia, New Zealand, Canada, and the United States to reflect on the commonalities and differences between countries. A common finding was the prevalence of child removal as a means of assimilation in each location.

77 Patricia Monture, "'A Vicious Cycle': Child Welfare and First Nations," *Canadian Journal of Women and the Law* 3 (1989–90): 1–17.

78 Marlee Kline, "Complicating the Ideology of Motherhood: Child Welfare Law and First Nation Women," *Queen's Law Journal* 18 (1993): 306.

79 Marlee Kline, "Child Welfare Law, 'Best Interests of the Child' Ideology and First Nations," *Osgoode Hall Law Journal* 30, no. 2 (1992): 375–425.

80 Kline, "Child Welfare Law," 384.

81 Kline, "Child Welfare Law," 384.

82 Kline, "Child Welfare Law," 389.

83 Two powerful documentaries that follow the journey of former adoptees to reconnect with their birth families are National Film Board of Canada, *A Place in Between: The Story of an Adoption*, 2007; and Lost Heritage Productions, *Red Road: The Barry Hambly Story*, 2005.

84 S. Fournier and E. Crey, *Stolen from Our Embrace: The Abduction of First Nations Children and the Restoration of Aboriginal Communities* (Vancouver, BC: Douglas & McIntyre, 1997).

85 Tara Turner, "Re-Searching Métis Identity: My Métis Family Story" (PhD diss., University of Saskatchewan, 2010), looks at how the death of her grandparents led to her father and his siblings' distribution between foster care, residential schools, and, for the youngest siblings, into permanent adoptive homes. The reunion of all the siblings in later life and reflection on their Métis identity forms the bulk of the dissertation. Her family history reveals the contradictory role of adoption in offering the opportunity

for new beginnings, simultaneously severing past ties and kinship relations with families of origins and Aboriginal ancestry.

86 L. Nicholson, "Native People and the Child Welfare System: A Study of
Multigenerational Experience" (MSW, University of Toronto, 1996); S.
Nuttgens, "Life Stories of Aboriginal Adults Raised in Non-Aboriginal
Families" (PhD diss., University of Alberta, 2004); Cheryl Marlene
Swidrovich, "Positive Experiences of First Nations Children in Non-
Aboriginal Foster or Adoptive Care: Deconstructing the 'Sixties Scoop'"
(MA thesis, University of Saskatchewan, 2004); Raven Sinclair, "All My
Relations: Native Transracial Adoption: A Critical Case Study of Cultural
Identity" (PhD diss., University of Calgary, 2007).

87 Jeannine Carrière and Cathy Richardson, "From Longing to Belonging:
Attachment Theory, Connectedness and Aboriginal Children in Canada,"
in *Passion for Action in Child and Family Services: Voices from the Prairies*,
ed. Ivan Brown, Sharon Mckay, and Don Fuchs, 49–68 (Regina: Canadian
Plains Research Centre, 2009); Jeannine Carrière and Susan Strega, *"Walking This Path Together": Anti-Racist and Oppressive Practice in Child Welfare*
(Halifax: Fernwood Publishing, 2009); and Susan Scarth, "Aboriginal
Children: Maintaining Connections in adoption," in *Putting a Human Face
on Child Welfare: Voices from the Prairies*, ed. I. Brown, F. Chaze, D. Fuchs, J.
Lafrance, S. McKay, and S.T. Prokop, 203–21 (Prairie Child Welfare Consor-
tium and Centre for Excellence for Child Welfare, 2007).

88 Jeannine Carrière, "The Role of Connectedness and Health for First Nation
Adoptees" (PhD diss., University of Alberta, 2005).

89 Jacobs, *A Generation Removed* explores the Canadian experience as part o a
larger process of child removal in settler colonial nations.

90 Joyce Timpson., "Four Decades of Child Welfare Services to Native Indians
in Ontario: A Contemporary Attempt to Understand the Sixties Scoop in
Historical, Socioeconomic and Political Perspective" (PhD Dissertation,
Wilfrid Laurier University, 1993).

91 Ibid., xvi.

92 Ibid., 6.

93 Karen Andrea Balcom, *The Traffic in Babies: Cross-Border Adoption and Baby-
Selling between the United States and Canada, 1930–1972*, Studies in Gender
and History (Toronto: University of Toronto Press, 2011).

94 Karen Andrea Balcom, *The Traffic in Babies: Cross-Border Adoption and Baby-
Selling between the United States and Canada, 1930–1972*, Studies in Gender
and History (Toronto: University of Toronto Press, 2011).

95 See Veronica Strong-Boag, *Finding Families, Finding Ourselves: English
Canada Encounters Adoption from the Nineteenth Century to the 1990's* (Don
Mills, ON: Oxford University Press, 2006); and Strong-Boag, *Fostering
Nation: Canada Confronts Its History of Childhood Disadvantage*, Studies in
Childhood and Family in Canada (Waterloo, ON: Wilfrid Laurier Univer-
sity Press, 2011).

96 Karen Dubinsky, *Babies without Borders: Adoption and Migration across the Americas* (Toronto: University of Toronto Press, 2010) 5.
97 Dubinsky, *Babies without Borders*, 92.
98 For spatial organization of reserves as gendered and racialized space in Saskatchewan, see Pamela Margaret White, "Restructuring the Domestic Sphere: Prairie Indian Women on Reserves: Image, Ideology and State Policy" (PhD diss., McGill University, 1987); and Sherene Razack, "Gendered Racial Violence and Spatialized Justice: The Murder of Pamela George," in *Race, Space and the Law: Unmapping White Settler Society*, ed. Sherene Razack, 91–130 (Toronto: Between the Lines, 2002); and in British Columbia, Cole Harris, *Making Native Space: Colonialism, Resistance, and Reserves in British Columbia* (Vancouver: UBC Press, 2002). For a discussion of the relegation of Indian people to reserves after 1885 through the imposition of the pass system, see James Daschuk, *Clearing the Plains: Disease, Politics of Starvation, and the Loss of Aboriginal Life* (Regina, SK: University of Regina Press, 2013); for a discussion of the cultural perception of Indian peoples, see Sarah Carter, *Capturing Women: The Manipulation of Cultural Imagery in Canada's Prairie West* (Montreal and Kingston: McGill-Queen's University Press, 1997).
99 Keith D. Smith, *Liberalism, Surveillance and Resistance: Indigenous Communities in Western Canada, 1877–1927* (Edmonton, AB: Athabasca, 2009), 8.
100 For an analysis of American Indian policy and race, see Patrick Wolfe, *Traces of History: Elementary Structures of Race* (London: Verso Books, 2016).
101 Mark Cronlund Anderson and Carmen L. Robertson, *Seeing Red: A History of Natives in Canadian Newspapers* (Winnipeg: University of Manitoba Press, 2011).
102 Doug Owram, *Promise of Eden: The Canadian Expansionist Movement and the Idea of the West, 1856–1900*, repr. with new pref., Reprints in Canadian History (Toronto: University of Toronto Press, 1992), http://www.deslibris.ca/ID/417497.
103 Carter, *Capturing Women*, 161.
104 Ian McKay, "The Liberal Order Framework: A Prospectus for a Reconnaissance of Canadian History," *Canadian Historical Review* 81, no. 4 (2000): 624, https://doi.org/10.3138/chr.81.4.616.
105 McKay, "Liberal Order Framework," 624.
106 McKay, "Liberal Order Framework," 626.
107 McKay, "Liberal Order Framework," 628.
108 McKay, "Liberal Order Framework," 631.
109 While author and artist Gerald McMaster is speaking about the transformation of Indigenous children into colonial subjects, I think the same can be argued for the land. Gerald McMaster, "Colonial Alchemy: Reading the Boarding School Experience," in *Partial Recall*, ed. Lucy Lippard (New York: New York, 1992), 79.
110 Thomas Biolsi, "The Birth of the Reservation: Making the Modern Individual among the Lakota," *American Ethnologist* 22, no. 1 (February 1995): 28–53.

111 John Borrows, *Recovering Canada: The Resurgence of Indigenous Law* (Toronto: University of Toronto Press, 2002).

112 G.F.G. Stanley, *The Birth of Western Canada: A History of the Riel Rebellions* (Toronto: University of Toronto Press, 1992).

113 Patrick Wolfe, "Settler Colonialism and the Elimination of the Native," *Journal of Genocide Research* 8, no. 4 (December 2006): 388.

114 Wolfe, "Settler Colonialism," 388.

115 Lorenzo Veracini, "Introducing Settler Colonial Studies," *Settler Colonial Studies* 1 (2011): 7.

116 Scott Lauria Morgensen, "Theorizing Gender, Sexuality and Settler Colonialism: An Introduction in Settler Colonial Studies," *Settler Colonial Studies* 2, no. 2 (2012): 3.

117 Morgensen, "Theorizing Gender," 10.

118 Morgensen, "Theorizing Gender," 11.

119 Morgensen, "Theorizing Gender," 12.

120 Arthur J. Ray, J.R. Miller, and Frank Tough, *Bounty and Benevolence: A History of Saskatchewan Treaties*, DesLibris Books Collection (Montreal and Kingston: McGill-Queen's University Press, 2000), http://www.deslibris.ca/ID/400325; Cardinal, *Treaty Elders of Saskatchewan*; and Sharon Venne, "Understanding Treaty 6: An Indigenous Perspective," in *Aboriginal and Treaty Rights in Canada: Essays on Law, Equity and Respect for Difference*, ed. Michael Asch, 173–207 (Vancouver: UBC Press, 1997).

121 John L. Tobias, "Protection, Civilization, Assimilation: An Outline History of Canada's Indian Policy," in *As Long as the Sun Shines and Water Flows: A Reader in Canadian Native Studies*, ed. Ian A.L. Getty and Antoine S. Lussier (Vancouver: University of British Columbia Press, 1983), 44–5.

122 Kathleen Jamieson, *Indian Women and the Law in Canada: Citizens Minus* (Ottawa: Advisory Council on the Status of Women, 1978), 42.

123 Jamieson, *Indian Women and the Law*, 29–30.

124 Robin Jarvis Brownlie, "Intimate Surveillance: Indian Affairs, Colonization, and the Regulation of Aboriginal Women's Sexuality," in Pickles and Rutherdale, *Contact Zones*, 165, 169.

125 Indian Act in bound Statutes of Canada, chap. 18, vol. 1, 1876, 43–73.

126 Wolfe, *Traces of History*, 187.

127 Indian Act in bound Statutes of Canada, chap. 18, vol. 1, 1876, 43–73.

128 For the shifting legalities of interracial marriages, see Van Kirk, *Many Tender Ties*; Perry, *On the Edge of Empire*; Sarah Carter, *The Importance of Being Monogamous: Marriage and Nation Building in Western Canada to 1915*, West Unbound, Social and Cultural Studies (Edmonton: University of Alberta Press, 2008).

129 Julia V. Emberley, "The Bourgeois Family, Aboriginal Women, and Colonial Governance in Canada: A Study in Feminist Historical and Cultural Materialism," *Signs* (Autumn 2001): 63.

130 Nancy Cott, "Afterword," in *Haunted by Empire: Geographies of Intimacy in North American History*, ed. Ann Laura Stoler (Durham, NC: Duke University Press, 2006).

131 Mark Rifkin, *When Did Indians Become Straight: Kinship, the History of Sexuality and Native Sovereignty* (London: Oxford University Press, 2011), 7.

132 John Borrows, *Canada's Indigenous Constitution* (Toronto: University of Toronto Press, 2010), ProQuest ebrary, 28 October 2014, 138.

133 The impact of colonization on kinship in Saskatchewan is explored by Rob Innes, *Elder Brother and the Law of the People: Contemporary Kinship and Cowessess First Nation* (Winnipeg: University of Manitoba Press, 2013), 117–19.

134 Brenda Macdougall, *One of the Family: Métis Culture in Nineteenth-Century Northwestern Saskatchewan* (Vancouver: UBC Press, 2010), 3.

135 For a discussion of the child removal policies of the United States and Australia, see Jacobs, *White Mother to a Dark Race*.

136 J.R. Miller, *Shinguak's Vision: A History of Native Residential Schools* (Toronto: University of Toronto Press, 1996), 76.

137 Milloy, *National Crime*, 24.

138 Milloy, *National Crime*, 30–1.

139 There are several excellent newly published histories of adoption from many important angles. Two books document the experiences of the young mothers; see Ann Fessler, *The Girls Who Went Away: The Hidden History of Women Who Surrendered Children for Adoption in the Decades Before Roe vs Wade* (New York: Penguin Press, 2006), 8–9; and Merry Bloch Jones, *Birthmothers: Women Who Have Relinquished Babies for Adoption Tell Their Stories* (Chicago: Press Review, 1993), xiv.

140 I use the term "illegitimate" to reflect the terminology of the time, and not as a label for children of unmarried mothers.

141 Philip Hepworth, *Foster Care and Adoption in Canada* (Ottawa: Canadian Council on Social Development, 1980), 115.

142 Hepworth, 115, Table 38: All Native Children as % of In-Care Population, 51.5%.

143 Patrick Johnston, *Native Children and the Child Welfare System* (Ottawa: The Canadian Council on Social Development, 1983), 100.

144 Hepworth, 121.

145 Karen Dubinsky, *Babies without Borders: Adoption and Migration across the Americas* (Toronto: University of Toronto Press, 2010), 81.

146 Margaret Jacobs, "Remembering the Forgotten Child: The American Indian Child Welfare Crisis of the 1960s and 1970s," *American Indian Quarterly* 37, no. 1–2 (Winter/Spring 2013): 147.

147 Anderson, *Life Stages and Native Women*, 167.

148 Anderson, *Life Stages and Native Women*, 168.

149 Anderson, *Life Stages and Native Women*, 170.

2. Adoptive Kinship and Belonging

1 A portion of this chapter was published as Allyson Stevenson, "The Adoption of Frances T: Blood, Belonging, and Aboriginal Transracial Adoption in Twentieth-Century Canada," *Canadian Journal of History* 50, no. 3 (2015): 469–91.

2 I have omitted information such as names and locations that might identify any of the children and family members who appear in the archival record. This has been done to protect their privacy.

3 M. Christianson, general superintendent of Indian Agencies, to Indian Agent Bryant, February 1942, file 117/13–4, acc. 2000-0321-4, Pelly Indian Agency – Adoption, 1940–68, RG 10, Library and Archives Canada (LAC).

4 Department of Social Welfare, Province of Saskatchewan, to Indian Affairs Department, 19 August, 1949, file 117/13–4, acc. 2000-0321-4, Pelly Indian Agency – Adoption, 1940–68, RG 10, LAC.

5 J.P.B. Ostrander, regional supervisor of Indian Agencies, to Indian Agent B., Regina, 22 August 1949, file 117/13–4, acc. 2000-0321-4, Pelly Indian Agency – Adoption, 1940–68, RG 10, LAC.

6 Director MacKay to Indian Agent B, 3 October 1949, file 117/13–4, acc. 2000-0321-4, Pelly Indian Agency – Adoption, 1940–68, RG 10, LAC.

7 Macdougall, *One of the Family*, 3.

8 Damien Lee, "'Because Our Law Is Our Law': Considering Anishinaabe Citizenship Orders through Adoption Narratives at Fort William First Nation" (PhD diss., University of Manitoba, 2017), 156.

9 F. Laurie Barron, "Poundmaker," in *Encyclopedia of the Great Plains Indians*, 159–60.

10 Mary Rogers-Black, "Effects of Adoption on the Round Lake Study," in *Stranger to Relatives: The Adoption and Naming of Anthropologists in Native North America*, ed. Sergei Kan (Lincoln: University of Nebraska Press), 107.

11 Quoted in David G. Mandelbaum, *The Plains Cree: An Ethnographic, Historical and Comparative Study* (Regina, SK: Canadian Plains Research Centre, University of Regina, 1979), 127.

12 Mandelbaum, *Plains Cree*, 127. The point about adoption serving to mimic biological relationship is also made by Macdougall, *One of the Family*, 82.

13 Recent studies on Indigenous people have utilized kinship to explore the retention of community connections and persistence of Indigenous kinship practices, such as Innes, *Elder Brother and the Law of the People*; Macdougall, *One of the Family*; Bea Medicine, "American Indian Family: Cultural Change and Adaptive Strategies," *Journal of Ethic Studies* 8, no. 4 (Winter 1981): 13; Patricia Albers, "Autonomy and Dependency in the Lives of Dakota Women: A Study in Historical Change," *Review of Radical Political Economics* 17, no. 3 (1985): 109–34.

14 DeMallie, quoted in "Editor's Introduction," in Kan, *Stranger to Relatives*, 15.

15 For a discussion of the role of adoption in Native American societies, see Kan, *Stranger to Relatives*, 3–4. To see the role of adoption in North

American middle-class society, see David H. Kirk, *Shared Fate: A Theory and Method of Adoptive Relationships* (Port Angeles, WA: Ben-Simon Publications, 1984).

16 Kinistin chief, Peter Nippi, interview by author, 4 February 2011.

17 Macdougall, *One of the Family*, 8.

18 Macdougall, *One of the Family*, 3.

19 McLeod, *Cree Narrative Memory*, 14–15.

20 Macdougall, *One of the Family*, 81.

21 Macdougall, *One of the Family*, 82.

22 Macdougall, *One of the Family*, 23.

23 Carter, *Importance of Being Monogamous*.

24 Kim Anderson and Bonita Lawrence, eds, *Strong Women Stories: Native Vision and Community Survival Life Stages and Native Women: Memory Teachings, and Story Medicine* (Winnipeg: University of Manitoba Press, 2011), 122–3.

25 Anderson and Lawrence, *Strong Women Stories*, 124.

26 This was part of a broader trend in Canadian society, explored by Wendy Mitchinson, *Giving Birth in Canada, 1900–1950* (Toronto: University of Toronto Press, 2002).

27 Anderson, *Life Stages and Native Women*, 163.

28 Anderson, *Life Stages and Native Women*, 42.

29 Feminist scholars Sarah Carter, Jean Barman, and Joan Sangster have connected the significance of regulating women to pursuing Indian assimilation; Carter, *Importance of Being Monogamous*; Jean Barman, "Aboriginal Women on the Streets of Victoria: Rethinking Transgressive Sexuality during the Colonial Encounter," in Pickles and Rutherdale, *Contact Zones*, 205–27.

30 Joan Sangster, *Regulating Girls and Women: Sexuality, Family and the Law in Ontario, 1920–1960* (Don Mills, ON: Oxford University Press, 2001), 169.

31 Scholar Mary Eberts connects the patriarchal Indian Act provisions to the high rates of missing and murdered Indigenous women and girls in Canada. Mary Eberts, "Victoria's Secret: How to Make a Population of Prey," in *Indivisible: Indigenous Human Rights*, ed. Joyce Green (Halifax: Fernwood, 2014), 149.

32 Linda Stone, *Kinship and Gender: An Introduction*, 2nd ed. (Boulder, CO: Westview, 2000), 1–2.

33 Lee, "'Because Our Law Is Our Law.'"

34 David M. Schneider, *American Kinship: A Cultural Account* (Englewood, NJ: Prentice-Hall, 1968); see also Cindy L. Baldassi, "The Legal Status of Aboriginal Customary Adoption across Canada: Comparisons, Contrasts and Convergences," *University of British Columbia Law Review* 39 (2006): 63, https://ssrn.com/abstract=963046.

35 Stone, *Kinship and Gender*, 269.

36 See Strong-Boag, "Introduction," *Finding Families, Finding Ourselves*.

37 Julie Berebitsky, *Like Our Very Own: Adoption and the Changing Culture of Motherhood, 1851–1950* (Lawrence: University of Kansas Press, 2001), 22.

38 E. Wayne Carp, *Adoption in America: Historical Perspectives* (Ann Arbor: University of Michigan Press, 2002), 7.

39 Carp, *Adoption in America*, 6.

40 Ellen Herman, *Kinship by Design: A History of Adoption in the Modern United States* (Chicago: University of Chicago Press, 2008), 21.

41 An important look at the role of psychologists in the post-war period is Mona Gleason, *Normalizing the Ideal: Psychology, Schooling and the Family in Postwar Canada* (Toronto: University of Toronto Press, 1999).

42 Berebitsky, *Like Our Very Own*, 36.

43 Herman, *Kinship by Design*, 34.

44 Carp, *Adoption in America*, 8.

45 Carp, *Adoption in America*, 38.

46 Carp, *Adoption in America*, 10–11.

47 Herman, *Kinship by Design*, 50–1; Katerina Wegar, *Adoption, Identity and Kinship: The Debate over the Sealed Birth Records* (New Haven, CT: Yale University Press, 1997), 49–50.

48 Wegar, *Adoption, Identity and Kinship*, 26.

49 Berebitsky, *Like Our Very Own*, 129.

50 Herman, *Kinship by Design*, 7.

51 Section 30 of Saskatchewan's Adoption Law, The Adoption of Children Act, states, "A person who has been adopted in accordance with the provisions of this part, and his issue, shall not withstanding any law or statue to the contrary, have the same rights of succession to property from or through the adopting parent as though the person adopted had been born to such parent in lawful wedlock in the date of the order of adoption." Quoted in Mildred E. Battel, *Children Shall Be First: Child Welfare in Saskatchewan, 1944–1964* (Regina: Local History Program, 1980), 115.

52 Battel, *Children Shall Be First*, 115; also see Kerry O'halloran, *The Politics of Adoption: International Perspectives on Law, Policy & Practice*, vol. 41 (Dordrecht: Springer Netherlands, 2006); Elizabeth Bartholet, *Family Bonds: Adoption and the Politics of Parenting* (Boston: Houghton Mifflin, 1993), 48–9.

53 Saskatchewan passed its first adoption law in 1922. Before that, adoptions were considered de facto, in name only.

54 J.D. McLean to Walton Lean, Ottawa, 24 July 1913, file 430100, reel C-9670, LAC.

55 Auger, "Northern Ojibwe," 182.

56 George H. Race, Indian agent, to C.E. Hughes, 26 January 1918, file 508261, reel C-10205, Black Series, RG 10, LAC.

57 J.D. McLean, assistant deputy and secretary, to C.E. Hughes, Indian agent, Saddle Lake, 15 February 1918, file 508261, reel C-10205, RG 10, LAC.

58 Memo: Ottawa, 1 August 1918, Duck Lake, file 513362, reel C-10205, Black Series, RG 10, LAC.

59 J.D. McLean, assistant deputy and secretary, Department of Indian Affairs, to C.E. Schmidt, Indian agent, Duck Lake, file 513362, reel C-10205, Black Series, RG 10, LAC.

60 Lee, "'Because Our Law Is Our Law,'" looks at how legal definitions of adoption changed over time in the Indian Act.
61 Frances Gertrude T—— Mr and Mrs Joseph C—— of the Chipewyan Indian Band Whether the effect of adoption of child by Indian couple would confer full Indian status upon the child having regard to the definition of Indian in the Indian Act, 21 February 1939, file 9-139664, vol. 2581, pt 1, RG 13, LAC.
62 Lee, "'Because Our Law Is Our Law,'" chap. 5.
63 Lee, "'Because Our Law Is Our Law,'" chap. 5.
64 Memorandum for deputy minister of justice, 21 February 1939, file 9-139664, vol. 2581, pt 1, RG 13, LAC.
65 D.B. MacKenzie, solicitor, Attorney-General's Department, to C. Gariepy, re: Adoption of Frances Thompson, 27 March 1939, file 9-139664, vol. 2581, pt 1, 21 February 1939, RG 13, LAC.
66 MacKenzie to Gariepy, 27 March 1939.
67 Department of Mines and Resources, Indian Affairs Branch, to Edouard Gariepy, 22 April 1939, file 9-139664, vol. 2581, pt 1, 21 February 1939, RG 13, LAC.
68 Gariepy to deputy minister of justice, 10 May 1939, file 9-139664, vol. 2581, pt 1 , 21 February 1939, RG 13, LAC.
69 Gariepy to deputy minister of justice.
70 Gariepy to deputy minister of justice.
71 P.W. Head to C.E. Gariepy, 26 May 1939, file 9-139664, vol. 2581, pt 1, 21 February 1939, RG 13, LAC.
72 John Demos, *Unredeemed Captive: A Family Story from Early America* (New York: Alfred Knopf, 1994), 142.
73 Carter, *Capturing Women*, 157.
74 Deputy minister of justice to director of Indian affairs, re: Adoption of Frances G. T—— by Indians of the Chipewyan Band, Alberta, 19 July 1940, file 9-139664, vol. 2581, pt 1, 21 February 1939, RG 13, LAC.
75 Deputy minister of justice to director of Indian affairs.
76 Deputy minister of justice to director of Indian affairs.
77 Deputy minister of justice to director of Indian affairs.
78 Deputy minister of justice to director of Indian affairs.
79 Memorandum for deputy minister of justice, 29 July 1940, file 9-139664, vol. 2581, pt 1, 21 February 1939, RG 13, LAC.
80 Two further memoranda were sent to Deputy Minister of Justice Miall, further arguing against admitting Frances as an Indian, as defined by the Indian Act: 21 February 1939, file 9-139664, vol. 2581, pt 1, RG 13, LAC.
81 The shift can be seen by comparing the 1927 and 1951 versions of Indian Act. In 1927, "Indian" means (i) any male person of Indian blood reputed to belong to a particular band, (ii) any child of such person, (iii) any woman who is or was lawfully married to such a person (Indian Act, RS, c 81, s 1 d). In 1951, "child" included a legally adopted *Indian* child (Indian Act, c 29, s 1 b), italics mine.

82 Pamela Palmater, *Beyond Blood: Rethinking Indigenous Identity* (Saskatoon, SK: Purich Publishing, 2011). Especially see chap. 1, "Legislated Identity: Control, Division, and Assimilation."

3. Rehabilitating the "Subnormal [Métis] Family" in Saskatchewan

1 Report, 1954, file 522 Native Welfare Policy, coll. R-190.3, Department of Natural Resources, Saskatchewan Archives Board (SAB).
2 James C. Scott, *Seeing Like a State: How Certain Schemes to Improve the Human Condition Have Failed*, Yale Agrarian Studies (New Haven, CT: Yale University Press, 1998), 88–9.
3 The white settler-colonial hinterland objectives include ensuring all resources accrue to white settlers and private business, remaining Indigenous lands are transformed into private property, and Indigenous peoples cease to exist as distinct peoples.
4 Frits Pannekoek, "Métis Studies: The Development of a Field and New Directions," in *From Rupert's Land to Canada: Essays in Honour of John E. Foster*, ed. Theodore Binnema, Gerhard Ens, and R.C. McLeod (Edmonton: University of Alberta Press, 2001), 124. Pannekoek argues the need for greater research in this critical period of Métis history. There are a large number of scholarly works on the history of the Métis peoples and their role in the 1885 rebellion. Known as the "forgotten people," Métis historiography tends to focus on Métis history from contact to 1885, then re-emerges with the era of Métis nationalism in the later 1960s and early 1970s. For a good but now dated look at the historiographical preoccupations of earlier historians of the Métis, see J.R. Miller, "From Riel to the Métis," *Canadian Historical Review* 69, no. 1 (March 1988): 1–20.
5 Métis scrip is the government-issued land certificate for the descendants of European fur traders and Indian women who developed into the Métis people in western Canada. In recognition of the Indigenous rights to the land inherited from their Indigenous mothers, the government dealt with the Métis on an individual basis through offering men, women, and children a scrip certificate for cash or land. See Camilla Charity Augustus, "Métis Scrip," http://scaa.sk.ca/ourlegacy/essays/OurLegacy_Essays_07_Augustus.pdf.
6 A road allowance is land set aside by the Crown for future development of roads. Since they were not legally titled to any one individual, the Métis established homes without the need to purchase land. This land was not taxable by the municipalities for schools and services; hence the Métis children did not attend schools in the nearby communities or obtain health benefits that landowners would be eligible for. Many Métis have embraced the descriptor "road allowance people" to defy this characterization, and fondly recall the family connections and cultural autonomy that developed in those locations; Campbell, *Stories of the Road Allowance People*; and documentaries produced by the Gabriel Dumont Institute: *Road Allowance People: A Story about Community Persistence and Survival* and *The Story of the Crescent Lake Métis: Our Life on the Road Allowance*, 2002.

7 Erin Millions, "Ties Undone: A Gendered and Racial Analysis of the 1885 Northwest Rebellion in the Saskatchewan District" (MA thesis, University of Saskatchewan, 2004).

8 Marie Campbell, *Halfbreed* (Toronto: McClelland and Stewart, 1973); and Adams, *Prison of Grass*.

9 Antoinette Draftenza, secretary, Business Girls Club, to W.J. Patterson, premier of Saskatchewan, 15 March 1943, R-283 Legislative Assembly of Saskatchewan Session, 1943, box 177, file LXVI 15 Métis, SAB.

10 Draftenza to Patterson.

11 Draftenza to Patterson.

12 *Regina Leader Post*, "Claims of the Métis," 31 January 1939.

13 "Documents and Articles about Métis People," "Métis" Pamphlet Collection (Saskatchewan Legislative Library, 1972). See Manitoba Métis Federation Inc v Canada (AG), [2013]), which demonstrates how scrip was devalued in Manitoba.

14 The Métis Population Betterment Act established eight large settlements guaranteeing the Métis of Alberta a land base and some measure of self-determination. The Métis Population Betterment Act is the only Métis-specific legislation in Canada. Nicole O'Byrne, "'No Other Weapon Except Organization': The Métis Association of Alberta and the 1938 Metis Population Betterment Act," *Journal of the Canadian Historical Association / Revue de la Société historique du Canada* 24, no. 2 (2013): 311–52. https://doi .org/10.7202/1025081ar; Sprague, *Canada and the Métis, 1869–1885* (Waterloo, ON: Wilfrid Laurier University Press, 1988).

15 Barron, *Walking in Indian Moccasins*, 46.

16 Merle Massie, *Forest Prairie Edge: Place History in Saskatchewan* (Winnipeg: University of Manitoba Press, 2014), 14.

17 G. Matte, *Report on Green Lake Settlement*, 1941, file Métis Settlement at Green Lake, SHS 141, Métis Settlements, SAB.

18 G. Matte, *Report on Green Lake Settlement*.

19 CCF Party Convention, 19 July 1944:

> Whereas, we have many Indian Reserves in Saskatchewan, inhabited by the Métis people, these same people living without any schools and medical care, many of their children being diseased and blind, under present conditions none of the children in the reserve allowed to attend any of the adjoining schools, there being at this time 52 children of school age on the Little Bone Reserve who are now unable to attend any schools,
>
> Therefore Be It Resolved: That we request the Provincial Government to take the necessary steps to see that these Métis people be given proper treatment and care, so that they can associate with other people.
>
> Be it further resolved: That scholarships be granted to Métis people so that they can educate themselves adequately to take their place in the legislature and other places and represent their own people. Carried.

Barron, *Walking in Indian Moccasins*, 31.

20 *Leader Post*, "Métis Problem Discussed: Indians and Métis Figured in Deliberations of Delegates of SARM – Friday," 27 February 1948.

21 *Leader Post*, "Métis Problem Discussed."

22 Barron, *Walking in Indian Moccasins*, 42.

23 "The Conference of the Métis of Saskatchewan," proceedings 30 July 1946, file "Métis" Conference Proceedings, coll. R-E 139, SAB.

24 "Conference of the Métis of Saskatchewan."

25 "Conference of the Métis of Saskatchewan," 35.

26 "Conference of the Métis of Saskatchewan," 53.

27 "Conference of the Métis of Saskatchewan," 56.

28 Métis Conference, with Alberta and Manitoba, 13 July 1949, file 859 (44), 1 of 3, T.C. Douglas fonds, SAB.

29 Métis Conference.

30 Métis Conference.

31 Sherene Razack, *Dying from Improvement: Inquests and Inquiries into Indigenous Deaths in Custody* (Toronto: University of Toronto Press, 2015), 19, argues that common across settler-colonial spatial and temporal ranges is the "pernicious myth that ... Indigenous peoples possess a mysterious incapacity for modern life."

32 1954 report (author unknown), file 522, R-190.3, Department of Natural Resources, Native Welfare Policy, SAB.

33 1954 report.

34 J.W. Churchman, memo, Native Rehabilitation, 21 January 1957, file 522, R-190.3, Department of Natural Resources, Native Welfare Policy, SAB.

35 See Campbell, *Halfbreed*; and Adams, *Prison of Grass*.

36 Richard Allen, "The Social Gospel as the Religion of the Agrarian Revolt," in *Riel to Reform: A History of Protest in Western Canada Saskatoon*, ed. George Melnyk (Calgary: Fifth House Publishers, 1992), 139. This point was originally made by Ramsay Cook, *The Regenerators: Social Criticism in Late Victorian English Canada* (Toronto: University of Toronto Press, 1985); and moral purity is discussed by Mariana Valverde, *The Age of Light, Soap and Water: Moral Reform in English Canada, 1885–1925* (Toronto: McClelland and Stewart, 1991), 29.

37 This was finally resolved with the Supreme Court Daniels decision, 2014.

38 Joan Sangster has explored the impact of moral regulation on Native women and girls in Ontario and the incarceration of young women for sexual offences in *Regulating Girls and Women*, 15.

39 Laura Neilson Bonikowsky, *Canadian Encyclopedia*, s.v. "Tommy Douglas: 'Greatest Canadian'" last modified 13 October 2015; and Bonikowsky, "The Rise of the Co-operative Commonwealth Federation," 14 June 2013, https://www.thecanadianencyclopedia.ca/en/article/tommy-douglas-greatest-canadian-feature. A search of "Tommy Douglas" yielded 136 results in the University of Regina library.

40 A.W. Johnson, *Dream No Little Dreams: A Biography of the Douglas Government of Saskatchewan, 1944–1961* (Toronto: University of Toronto Press, 2004); and Thomas H. McLeod and Ian McLeod, *Tommy Douglas: The Road to Jerusalem* (Edmonton: Hurtig Publishers, 1987).

41 The dynamic leader of the CCF, Thomas Clement "Tommy" Douglas, was born in Scotland in 1904. His family immigrated to Winnipeg in 1911, where he witnessed the Winnipeg General Strike of 1919. He became involved in J.S. Woodsworth's Methodist All People's Church and Mission in North Winnipeg, which embraced the Social Gospel. He received his Baptist education at Brandon College and arrived in Weyburn in 1929 as pastor for Calvary Baptist Church at the beginning of the Depression. Douglas first got involved in politics through the United Famers of Saskatchewan and Independent Labour meetings at the beginning of 1932. He was elected to the House of Commons as a CCF member of Parliament in 1935, then left this position to become leader of the provincial CCF when it was elected in Saskatchewan in 1944 as government. He remained Saskatchewan's premier from 1944 to 1961. From Michael Shevall, "A Canadian Paradox: Tommy Douglas and Eugenics," *Canadian Journal of Neurological Sciences* 29 (2012): 36–7.

42 Shevall, "Canadian Paradox," 139.

43 Cook, *Regenerators*, 229.

44 Eugenics was a pseudo-scientific field that emerged in the late nineteenth and early twentieth centuries, combining the Darwinian principles of natural selection and a Mendelian understanding of genetics. It evolved as a proposed solution to the problems of urbanization, immigration, and social unrest, and the belief in the capacity of science to solve them. The focus was on improving the human condition through selective breeding to improve the species. The goal was removal of inferior stock from the gene pool, such as those who had mental illness, intellectual disabilities, or social diseases; Shevall, "Canadian Paradox," 25.

45 McLeod and McLeod, *Tommy Douglas*, 40.

46 McLeod and McLeod, *Tommy Douglas*, 40–1.

47 Alberta passed the Sexual Sterilization Act in 1928, and BC in 1933. The laws were based on the perceived threat to society by those who were mentally ill, and passing on defective traits to children; Shevall, "Canadian Paradox," 37.

48 Shevall, "Canadian Paradox," 38. In a recent publication on eugenics, medical historian Erica Dyck looks at Douglas's place in its history. Dyck situates Douglas's thinking on eugenics and degeneracy within a larger intellectual framework in the period before the Second World War: "Canadian mental hygiene reformers fit within a broader international movement of intellectuals and activists interested in testing eugenic theories of social degeneration, the heredity of delinquency and criminality, and the associations between 'mental abnormality' and 'illegitimacy, prostitution, and dependency.'" Erica Dyck, *Facing Eugenics: Reproduction, Sterilization, and the Politics of Choice* (Toronto: University of Toronto Press, 2013), 39.

49 T.C. Douglas, "The Problems of the Subnormal Family" (MA thesis, McMaster University, 1933), 1.

50 Anne McClintock, *Imperial Leather* (New York: Routledge, 1995), 108.

51 Douglas, "Problems of the Subnormal Family," 1.

52 The terminology used by eugenicists is appalling to the modern reader
and offensive to those so categorized. I use these terms in order to reflect
the thinking of the time. Whereas today, these terms are merely considered
empty of meaning, to those involved in the "science" of eugenics, these
terms denoted the intellectual level of the individual rather than a subjec-
tive judgment.

53 "Significance: effect on society. Case and effects study a group of indigents
who are entirely dependent upon charity for support. Focus on 12 immoral
or non-moral women. Charts have submitted 175 living descendants, 12
women had 95 children, 105 grandchildren. Of the 175 living, 34 graded
"normal" defined as able to move through school at a reasonable pace,
and find employment. Group intermarries. "The result is an ever increasing number of morons and imbeciles who continue to be a charge upon
society." Douglas, "Problems of the Subnormal Family," 6.

54 Douglas, "Problems of the Subnormal Family," 6.

55 Douglas, "Problems of the Subnormal Family," 6–7.

56 Douglas, "Problems of the Subnormal Family," 8.

57 Douglas, "Problems of the Subnormal Family," 9.

58 Douglas, "Problems of the Subnormal Family," 11.

59 Douglas, "Problems of the Subnormal Family," 15.

60 Douglas, "Problems of the Subnormal Family," 17.

61 Regina Kunzel, *Fallen Women, Problem Girls: Unmarried Mothers and the Professionalization of Social Work, 1890–1945* (New Haven, CT: Yale University
Press, 1993); and Ann Fessler, *The Girls Who Went Away: The Hidden History
of Women Who Surrendered Children for Adoption in the Decades before Roe v
Wade* (New York: Penguin, 2006); both discuss the role of shame in middle-
class white families whose daughters had unplanned pregnancies.

62 Douglas, "Problems of the Subnormal Family," 20.

63 Douglas, "Problems of the Subnormal Family," 24.

64 Douglas, "Problems of the Subnormal Family," 29.

65 Valverde, *Age of Light, Soap and Water*, 154.

66 Valverde explains this type of reform: "Moral reform, like moral regulation
generally, seeks to construct and organize both social relations and individual consciousness in such a way as to legitimize certain institutions and
discourses –particularly the patriarchal nuclear family, racist immigration
policies – through the point of view of morality." Valverde, *Age of Light,
Soap and Water*, 164.

67 Valverde, *Age of Light, Soap and Water*, 164.

68 For a list of the Métis colonies in Saskatchewan, see appendix 1 at the end
of the chapter.

69 For more information on the CCF colony scheme, see Laurie Barron,
*Walking in Indian Moccasins: The Native Policies of Tommy Douglas and
the CCF* (Vancouver: UBC Press, 1997); and Barron, "The CCF and the

Development of Métis Colonies in Southern Saskatchewan during the Premiership of TC Douglas," n.d., http://www3.brandonu.ca/library /cjns/10.2/barron.pdf.

70 Henry Pelletier, interview, 17 March 1978, Regina, SK, Gabriel Dumont Institute, Virtual Museum of Métis History and Culture, http://www .metismuseum.ca/resource.php/01139.

71 Jim Sinclair, Jim Durocher, and Ron Laliberte, Métis Political Activist Interviews, 17 April 2004, Gabriel Dumont Institute, Virtual Museum of Métis History and Culture, http://www.metismuseum.ca/resource.php/06095.

72 Sinclair, Durocher, and Laliberte interviews.

73 Sinclair, Durocher, and Laliberte interviews.

74 Nora Cummings, Peter Bishop, and Ron Laliberte interviews (11) re: Green Lake Children's Shelter, 2004, Gabriel Dumont Institute, Virtual Museum of Métis History and Culture, http://www.metismuseum.ca/media/ document.php/05912.C,%20B,%20and%20L%20(11).pdf.

75 Isadore Pelletier, interview, 23 November 2000 (04), Gabriel Dumont Institute, https://www.youtube.com/watch?v=6gZ2pJaGl6Y.

76 Pelletier, interview.

77 Pelletier, interview.

78 Pelletier, interview.

79 T.C. Douglas to Vic De Shaye, 7 March 1950, file XL. 859 a(44), 1 of 3, T.C. Douglas fonds, SAB.

80 Vic DeShaye to T.C. Douglas, 10 March 1950, file XL. 859 a(44), 1 of 3, T.C. Douglas fonds, SAB.

81 Ten years later, the city of Winnipeg removed the residents of Rooster town to make room for suburban expansion: "In the spring of 1959 the City of Winnipeg ordered the removal of fourteen families, mostly Métis, from land needed for the construction of a new high school in south Winnipeg. For at least a decade, the presence of Rooster Town, as the squatters' shantytown was known, had drawn complaints from residents of the new middle-class suburbs who objected to the proximity of families of mixed ancestry who seemed indolent, immoral, and irresponsible and whose children brought contagious diseases into the elementary school." David G. Burley, "Rooster Town: Winnipeg's Lost Métis Suburb, 1900–1960," *Urban History Review* 42 no. 1 (2013): 3.

82 Barron, "The CCF and the Development of Metis Colonies," 251–2.

83 D.F. Symington, "Métis Rehabilitation," *Canadian Geographical Journal* 46, no. 4 (April 1953): 128.

84 Symington, "Métis Rehabilitation," 130.

85 Symington, "Métis Rehabilitation," 131.

86 Symington, "Métis Rehabilitation," 131.

87 Symington, "Métis Rehabilitation," 134.

88 Symington, "Métis Rehabilitation," 134.

89 Symington, "Métis Rehabilitation," 137.

90 Symington, "Métis Rehabilitation," 137.
91 Symington, "Métis Rehabilitation," 139.
92 John Sutton Lutz, *Makuk: A New History of Indigenous-White Relations* (Vancouver: UBC Press, 2008), 286–8.
93 Tina Loo, "Africville and the Dynamics of State Power in Postwar Canada," *Acadiensis* 39, no. 2 (Summer/Autumn 2010): 23–47.

4. The Green Lake Children's Shelter Experiment: From Institutionalization to Integration in Saskatchewan

1 *Regina Leader Post*, "Shelter Opened for Métis," 28 September 1949.
2 Jim Wright, "Experiment with Métis," *Saskatoon Star Phoenix*, 21 September 1949.
3 Wright, "Experiment with Métis."
4 See chapter 4, "Suggested Remedies for the Subnormal Family," which outlines roles for the state, school, and church in rehabilitating the multi-problem subnormal family. Douglas, "Problems of the Subnormal Family."
5 Wright, "Experiment with Métis."
6 It is difficult to say with accuracy how many Métis families were transported, since the archival documents that would support this number contain information that violates provincial privacy legislation.
7 Wright, "Experiment with Métis."
8 Battel, *Children Shall Be First*, 16.
9 Kline, "Child Welfare Law"; Kline, "Complicating the Ideology of Motherhood"; Karen Swift, *Manufacturing "Bad" Mothers: A Critical Perspective on Child Neglect* (Toronto: University of Toronto Press, 1995).
10 Strong-Boag, *Fostering Nation*, 70–1. See also Andrea Smith, *Conquest: Sexual Violence and American Indian Genocide* (Cambridge, MA: South End, 2005).
11 Leontine R. Young, "The Unmarried Mother's Decision about Her Baby," 1947, file 300-30, vol. 300, MG 28 I 10, LAC. Young, an influential social worker and an expert on the unwed mother, said, "Speaking generally, we know that the unmarried mother is an unhappy and neurotic girl who seeks through the medium of an out-of-wedlock baby to find an answer to her own unconscious conflicts and needs." The role of the case worker was to enable to girls to recognize their own inability to plan for their children, and thus relinquish them to the worker for adoption.
12 Since I have not been able to view individual case files of children, these laws are discussed in general terms of how they probably would have contributed to apprehensions.
13 Franca Iacovetta, *Gatekeepers: Reshaping Immigrant Lives in Cold War Canada* (Toronto: Between the Lines, 2006), 50–1.
14 *Regina Leader Post*, "Social Work Leader Honoured," 14 March 1991.

15 Frank Dornstauder and David Macknak, "100 Years of Child Welfare Services in Saskatchewan: A Survey," http://sasw.in1touch.org/uploaded/web/CW/100-ChildWelfarePaper.pdf.

16 Andrew Jones and Leonard Rutman, *In the Children's Aid: J.J. Kelso and Child Welfare in Ontario* (Toronto: University of Toronto Press, 1981).

17 Battel, *Children Shall Be First*, 6–7. See also Therese Jennissen, *One Hundred Years of Social Work : A History of the Profession in English Canada, 1900–2000* (Waterloo, ON: Wilfrid Laurier University Press, 2011); Dornstauder and Macknak, "100 Years."

18 Battel, *Children Shall Be First*, 1.

19 Battel, *Children Shall Be First*, 9–10.

20 Battel, *Children Shall Be First*, 8.

21 Battel, *Children Shall Be First*, 15–16.

22 Department of Social Welfare and Rehabilitation, SW1.1 *Annual Report of the Department of Social Welfare of the Province of Saskatchewan, 1944–45*, SW.1 Annual Reports, 1944/5–1963–4, Saskatchewan Government Publications.

23 Department of Social Welfare and Rehabilitation, SW1.1 *Annual Report … 1944–45.*

24 Department of Social Welfare and Rehabilitation, SW1.1 *Annual Report … 1944–45.*

25 Department of Social Welfare and Rehabilitation, SW1.1 *Annual Report of the Department of Social Welfare of the Province of Saskatchewan, 1945–46*, SW.1 Annual Reports, 1944/5–1963–4, Saskatchewan Government Publications.

26 Alice Dales, "Closing a Children's Institution in Saskatchewan," *Canadian Welfare* 30, no. 6 (1954): 39.

27 Dales, "Closing a Children's Institution," 39.

28 The *Annual Report, 1944–45*, 39, gave the original justification for the children's incarceration in the Green Lake Children's Shelter as "neglect arising from inadequate school facilities and improper housing," rather than reinforcing negative stereotypes of Indigenous women and families as disorganized and morally reprobate, Dales, 39.

29 Dales, "Closing a Children's Institution," 39. See also Sherene Razack, *Dying from Improvement: Inquests and Inquiries into Indigenous Deaths in Custody* (Toronto: University of Toronto Press, 2015), for the settler colonial construction of Indigenous incongruity with modernity.

30 Dales, "Closing a Children's Institution."

31 G.H. Castleden to T.C. Douglas, 14 June 1950, file XVIII, 34 (19-1-5), Green Lake Children's Shelter, T.C. Douglas coll., R-33.2.

32 Castleden to Douglas, 14 June 1950.

33 Dales, "Closing a Children's Institution," 40.

34 Dales, "Closing a Children's Institution," 40.

35 Dales, "Closing a Children's Institution," 41.

36 Dales, "Closing a Children's Institution," 43.

37 Dales, "Closing a Children's Institution," 42.

38 Dales, "Closing a Children's Institution," 42.

39 Dales, "Closing a Children's Institution," 43.

40 Dales, "Closing a Children's Institution," 43.

41 To illustrate the mobility of rural populations, in 1951 30 per cent of the population in Saskatchewan lived in urban areas, and by 1971 the figure had risen to 53 per cent. For a thorough look at the changes to Saskatchewan's society and demographics, see Bill Waiser, *Saskatchewan: A New History* (Calgary, AB: Fifth House, 2005), 498.

42 Battel, *Children Shall Be First*, 49.

43 Battel, *Children Shall Be First*, 49.

44 1946, c 91, An Act Respecting the Welfare of Children, Part One, 4, 751.

45 1946, c 91, An Act Respecting the Welfare of Children, Part One, 11, A-c.

46 Patricia Rooke and R.L. Schnell, *Discarding the Asylum: From Child Rescue to the Welfare State in English-Canada (1800–1950)* (Lanham, MD: University Press of America, 1983), 396.

47 Rooke and Schnell, *Discarding the Asylum*, 396.

48 Rooke and Schnell, *Discarding the Asylum*, 396; the criteria of childhood held by middle-class reformers include notions of protection, segregation, and dependence; 11.

49 Rooke and Schnell, *Discarding the Asylum*, 397.

50 Battel, *Children Shall Be First*, 75.

51 Battel, *Children Shall Be First*, 79.

52 Battel, *Children Shall Be First*, 79.

53 Battel, *Children Shall Be First*, 76. Social workers in this period commonly employed the technique of stressing the dangers of the prevalence of "black market adoptions" to the public as one method of obtaining professional control over adoptions in Canada and the United States. The highly publicized case in Alberta in the traffic in babies across the Canada-U.S. border in 1947 was the focus of Charlotte Whitton's survey and a subsequent call for greater social work standards and national collaboration. For more on control of adoption, professionalization, and cross-border baby scandals, see Karen Balcom, *The Traffic in Babies: Cross-Border Adoptions and Baby Selling between the United States and Canada* (Toronto: University of Toronto Press, 2011).

54 Rickie Solinger, *Wake Up Little Susie: Single Pregnancy and Race before Roe v Wade* (New York: Routledge, 1992).

55 Battel, *Children Shall Be First*, 79.

56 1946, c 91, An Act Respecting the Welfare of Children, Part One, 115, 785.

57 SW1.1 *Annual Report of the Department of Social Welfare of the Province of Saskatchewan, 1945–46.*

58 1946, c 91, An Act Respecting the Welfare of Children, Part One, 115, 785.

59 Young, "Unmarried Mother's Decision about Her Baby."

60 Battel, *Children Shall Be First*, 76.

61 Battel, *Children Shall Be First*, 76.

62 L.E. Brierley, regional administrator, Green Lake Project, report, 12 August 1955, file XI-30, R-933, Department of Social Welfare and Rehabilitation; Mildred Battel makes this point also: Battel, *Children Shall Be First*, 142.

63 "The majority have more than one child out of wedlock and often several children are born in this status. There is comparatively little community rejection of the unmarried mother, and consequently very little guilt feeling or remorse is experienced by the unmarried mother. Local Improvement District services by way of financial assistance is often withheld and this seems to have been done to act as a deterrent, which, of course, is questionable." L.E. Brierley, regional administrator, Green Lake Project, report, 12 August 1955, file XI-30, R-933, Department of Social Welfare and Rehabilitation.

64 For an analysis of the differential treatment of unwed mothers in the United States on the basis of their race, see Solinger, *Wake Up Little Susie*.

65 Battel, *Children Shall Be First*, 142.

66 See Solinger for the difference race makes in the treatment of white unwed mothers, and Black unwed mothers in the United States.

67 R. Tabot, director of welfare, to J.S. White, deputy minister, 16 October 1961, Re: Provincial Programs in Northern Saskatchewan and Provincial Programs Related to Indians in Department of Social Welfare-Rehabilitation Branch, file III 23, Métis-General Correspondence, R-85-308 933, SAB.

68 Tabot to White, 16 October 1961.

69 Tabot to White, 16 October 1961.

70 Tabot to White, 16 October 1961.

71 SW1.1 *Annual Report of the Department of Social Welfare of the Province of Saskatchewan, 1959–60*; Minister A.M. Nicholson, Deputy J.S. White, M.E. Battel, director of child welfare, SAB.

72 SW1.1 *Annual Report 1959–60*.

73 SW1.1 *Annual Report of the Department of Social Welfare of the Province of Saskatchewan, 1960–61*.

74 *Annual Report, 1960–61*.

75 *Annual Report, 1960–61*; of the 2,476 children in care in 1960, 670 were Métis or Indian, or 27 per cent.

76 *Ottawa Citizen*, "Proposed Adoption Exchange," 19 May 1963.

77 The term "mystifying" is used here to indicate that the reasons children were coming into care stemmed from the colonization effects of racism, loss of land, and failed relocation policies, but were presented as individualized personal failings of Indigenous families in child welfare terminology: "illegitimacy" and "neglect."

78 *Ottawa Citizen*, "Proposed Adoption Exchange."

79 *Ottawa Citizen*, "Proposed Adoption Exchange."

80 *Star Phoenix*, "Indian and Métis Children Pose Adoption Problems for Welfare," 30 June 1965.

81 SW.1 *Annual Report, 1965–1966,* SAB; informants interviewed for this project have indicated that either they or their family members had children involuntarily removed from them at the hospital after giving birth.

82 SW.1 *Annual Report of the Department of Social Welfare of the Province of Saskatchewan, 1965–1966.*

83 Berebitsky, *Like Our Very Own,* 129, illustrates the changing understanding of adoption in North American culture.

5. Post-War Liberal Citizenship and the Colonization of Indigenous Kinship

1 Hugh Shewell, "'What Makes the Indian Tick?' The Influence of Social Sciences on Canada's Indian Policy, 1947–1964," *Histoire Sociale / Social History* 34, no. 67 (1 May 2001): 150, http://hssh.journals.yorku.ca/index.php/hssh/article/view/4542.

2 Andrew Nurse, "Tradition and Modernity: The Cultural Works of Marius Barbeau" (PhD diss., Queen's University, 1997), 520–5.

3 For further information on the nutritional studies conducted on Indigenous communities and in residential schools, see Ian Mosby, "Administering Colonial Science: Nutrition Research and Human Biomedical Experimentation in Aboriginal Communities and Residential Schools, 1942–1952," *Social History* 46, no. 91 (May 2013): 145–72.

4 Miller, *Shingwauk's Vision.*

5 Correspondence from Dr L.C. Bartlett to G. Swartman, superintendent of Sioux Lookout Agency, 10 September 1948, that he quotes in his correspondence to branch headquarters, file 1/1-15-1, vol. 8618, CR series, RG 10, LAC, quoted in Shewell, *"Enough to Keep Them Alive,"* 212.

6 Shewell, *"Enough to Keep them Alive,"* 214.

7 Questionnaire on Childhood among the Iroquois (excerpts), document 7.1, found in Shewell, *"Enough to Keep Them Alive,"* 213.

8 John F. Leslie, "Assimilation, Integration or Termination? The Development of Canadian Indian Policy, 1943–1963" (PhD diss., Carleton University, 1999), 9.

9 This famous line by Duncan Campbell Scott is taken from J.R. Miller, *Skyscrapers Hide the Heavens: A History of Indian-White Relations in Canada,* 4th ed. (Toronto: University of Toronto Press, 2017), 229.

10 Leslie, "Assimilation, Integration or Termination?," 4.

11 "Joint Submission by the Canadian Welfare Council and the Canadian Association of Social Workers to the Special Joint Committee of the Senate and the House of Commons Appointed to Examine and Consider the Indian Act," Ottawa, January 1947, Canadian Welfare Council, vol. 118, MG 28 I 10, LAC.

12 "Joint Submission," 3.

13 "Joint Submission," 6.

14 "Joint Submission," 9.

15 "Joint Submission," 12.

16 Indian Act (1951), s 88, read, "Subject to the terms of any treaty and any other Act of Parliament, all laws of general application from time to time in force in any province are applicable to and in respect of Indians in the province, except to the extent that such laws are inconsistent with this Act or any order, rule, regulation or by-law made thereunder, and except to the extent that such laws make provision for any matter for which provision is made by or under this Act."

17 Shewell, *"Enough to Keep Them Alive,"* 207.

18 Indian Act, RSC 1971, c I-6, s 11. Quoted in Jamieson, *Indian Women and the Law,* 7–8.

19 Jamieson, *Indian Women and the Law,* 63.

20 Reg Davis, executive director of Canadian Welfare Council, to Minister W.E. Harris, Department of Citizenship and Immigration, Comments on Bill No. 79 (revisions to the Indian Act), 27 March 1951, vol. 118, MG 28, I 10, Canadian Welfare Council, LAC.

21 Davis to Harris, 27 March 1951, 2.

22 Davis to Harris, 28 April 1951, vol. 118, MG 28, I 10, Canadian Welfare Council, LAC.

23 Brownlie also points out that the Indian Act status provisions likely worked against increasing marriages and conformity to middle-class norms, as women opted to enter common-law relationships with non-Indians rather than lose status by marriage; Brownlie, *Fatherly Eye,* 169–70.

24 Davis to Harris, 28 April 1951, vol. 118, MG 28, I 10, Canadian Welfare Council, LAC.

25 Chupik-Hall, "'Good Families Do Not Just Happen,'" 34.

26 For Indigenous perspectives on custom adoption, see Darin Keewatin, "An Indigenous Perspective on Custom Adoption" (MSW thesis, University of Manitoba, 2004); Jeannine Carrière, ed., *Aski Awasis/Children of the Earth: First Peoples Speaking on Adoption,* Fernwood Basics (Black Point, NS: Fernwood Publications, 2010).

27 Métis Conference, with Alberta and Manitoba, 13 July 1949.

28 Métis Conference.

29 John H. Sturdy, minister of social welfare and rehabilitation, to Walter Harris, minister of citizenship and immigration, 16 May 1952, file IV.7, R-935, Department of Social Services and Rehabilitation, SAB.

30 Sturdy to Harris, 16 May 1952.

31 Sturdy to Harris, 16 May 1952, 3.

32 Sturdy to Harris, 16 May 1952, 3–4.

33 Harris to Sturdy, 4 July 1952, file IV.7, R-935, Department of Social Services and Rehabilitation, SAB.

34 Harris to Sturdy, 4 July 1952.

35 H.B. Hawthorn, *A Survey of the Contemporary Indians of Canada: A Report on Economic, Political, Educational Needs and Policies*, 2 vols (Ottawa: Indian Affairs Branch, 1966–7), 327.
36 Sturdy to Harris, 16 May 1952.
37 Sturdy to Harris, 16 May 1952, 5.
38 Recording of Meetings between Representatives of the Indian Affairs Branch and the Department of Social Welfare and Rehabilitation, Regina, 23 and 24 October 1952, file IV.7, R-935, Saskatchewan Department of Social Services and Rehabilitation, SAB.
39 Meetings between Representatives, 23 and 24 October 1952.
40 Meetings between Representatives, 23 and 24 October 1952.
41 Meetings between Representatives, 23 and 24 October 1952.
42 Meetings between Representatives, 23 and 24 October 1952.
43 Meetings between Representatives, 23 and 24 October 1952.
44 Meetings between Representatives, 23 and 24 October 1952, 5.
45 "Indian Problem," file IV.7, R-935, Department of Social Services and Rehabilitation, SAB.
46 "Indian Problem."
47 J.S. White, deputy minister, to H.M. Jones, director Indian affairs branch, 6 November 1953, file IV.7, R-935, Department of Social Services and Rehabilitation, SAB.
48 White to Jones, 6 November 1953.
49 White to Jones, 6 November 1953.
50 Barron, *Walking in Indian Moccasins*, 121–2.
51 Indian Affairs Branch, *Annual Report*, year ending 1956.
52 *Reference Manual: Social Welfare*, 1, July 1953, file 1/23-21, pt 1, vol. 8463, RG 10, LAC.
53 Indian Affairs Branch, *Annual Report*, year ending 1954.
54 *Reference Manual: Social Welfare.*
55 *Reference Manual: Social Welfare.*
56 *Reference Manual: Social Welfare.*
57 *Reference Manual: Social Welfare.*
58 *Reference Manual: Social Welfare.*
59 *Reference Manual: Social Welfare.*
60 H.M. Jones, superintendent of welfare services, to Monica L. Meade, social worker, Indian Affairs Branch, 7 April 1953 (draft), file 1/23-32, pt 1, vol. 8463, RG 10, LAC.
61 Jones to Meade, 7 April 1953 (draft).
62 First Nations communities responded in a variety of ways to the imposition of Euro-Canadian legal definitions of Indian status. To gain an appreciation of this complexity one can read transcripts of the Special Joint Committee of the Senate and the House of Commons Appointed to Examine and Consider the Indian Act, especially appendix ES, Submission of the Union of Saskatchewan Indians in Canada, "Special Joint Committee Appointed to Examine and Consider the Indian Act,

Minutes of Proceedings and Evidence" (Ottawa: Printer of the King, 1946).

63 Jones to Meade, 7 April 1953 (draft).
64 Jones to Meade, 7 April 1953 (draft).
65 Jones to Meade, 7 April 1953 (draft).
66 Gleason, *Normalizing the Ideal*, 88.
67 Gleason, *Normalizing the Ideal*, 92.
68 Gleason, *Normalizing the Ideal*, 52–3.
69 Gleason, *Normalizing the Ideal*, 92.
70 Gleason, *Normalizing the Ideal*, 111.
71 Brownlie, "Fatherly Eye," 169.

6. Child Welfare as System and Lived Experience

1 Adopt Indian and Métis Project advertisement, file I-49, Department of Social Services Collection R-935, SAB.
2 Robert Doucette interview, 10 October 2012.
3 Doucette interview, 10 October 2012.
4 *Annual Report*, Department of Social Welfare, Government of Saskatchewan 1968–9, Government Publications, SAB.
5 Indian Affairs Branch, *Annual Report*, 1959.
6 Indian Affairs Branch, *Annual Report*, 1960.
7 Indian Affairs Branch, *Annual Report*, 1961.
8 Department of Welfare, *Annual Report*, 1965–6, Province of Saskatchewan, WE.1, Government Publications, SAB.
9 These cases come from the Indian Affairs Branch archives, RG10 collection. I was not able to view the actual adoption case files of the Department of Social Welfare due to strict privacy legislation around adoption files. These may have indeed provided a different view of adoption.
10 SW1.1 *Annual Report of the Department of Social Welfare of the Province of Saskatchewan*, 1948–9, SW.1 Annual Reports, 1944/5–1963–4, Department of Social Welfare and Rehabilitation, Saskatchewan Government Publications.
11 Indian Agent Bryant to Indian Affairs Branch, Ottawa, 11 February 1946, file 117/13-4, Pelly Indian Agency – Adoption, 1940–68, acc. 2000-0321-4, RG 10, LAC.
12 Bryant to Indian Affairs Branch, 11 February 1946.
13 Mildred Battel to Miss Meade, social worker, Department of Indian Affairs, Regina, 10 February 1956, file 117/13-4, Pelly Indian Agency – Adoption, 1940–68, acc. 2000-0321-4, RG 10, LAC.
14 Mr D., regional supervisor of Indian agencies, to J.A. Davies, superintendent, Indian Agency, Kamsack, SK, 3 September 1954, file 117/13-4, Pelly Indian Agency – Adoption, 1940–68, acc. 2000-0321-4, RG 10, LAC.
15 E.S. Jones to R.S. Davies, regional supervisor of Indian agencies, Winnipeg, 15 September 1954, file 117/13-4, Pelly Indian Agency – Adoption, 1940–68, acc. 2000-0321-4, RG 10, LAC.

16 Jones to Davies, 15 September 1954.
17 Jones to Davies, 21 September 1954.
18 Jones to Davies, 2 November 1954.
19 The "girl problem" arose as young women left the rural areas for cities at the early turn of the century. Constructed as a "problem" because young women demonstrated increasing independence, both sexual and financial, concerned onlookers attempted to find methods to clamp down on this new problem of urbanization and industrialization. See Carolyn Strange, *Toronto's Girl Problem: The Perils and Pleasures of the City, 1880–1930* (Toronto: University of Toronto Press, 1995).
20 M. Christianson, general superintendent of Indian agencies, to Indian Agent Bryant, February 1942, file 117/13-4, Pelly Indian Agency – Adoption, 1940–68, acc. 2000-0321-4, RG 10, LAC.
21 J.P.B. Ostrander, regional supervisor of Indian agencies, Regina, to Indian Agent B., 22 August 1949, file 117/13-4, Pelly Indian Agency – Adoption, 1940–68, acc. 2000-0321-4, RG 10, LAC.
22 Director MacKay to Indian Agent B., 3 October 1949, file 117/13-4, Pelly Indian Agency – Adoption, 1940–68, acc. 2000-0321-4, RG 10, LAC.
23 Letter to Department of Social Welfare, 23 February 1956, file 117/13-4, Pelly Indian Agency – Adoption, 1940–68, acc. 2000-0321-4, RG 10, LAC.
24 Response from Department of Social Welfare and Rehabilitation, 28 February 1956, file 117/13-4, Pelly Indian Agency – Adoption, 1940–68, acc. 2000-0321-4, RG 10, LAC.
25 Letter from Mildred K., 16 August 1962, file 117/13-4, Pelly Indian Agency – Adoption, 1940–68, acc. 2000-0321-4, RG 10, LAC.
26 Letter from Mildred K., 16 August 1962.
27 See table 5.3 of this chapter. For Indian children, 94 per cent came into care through apprehensions, and only 6 per cent voluntarily, in 1973.
28 H. Philip Hepworth, *Foster Care and Adoption in Canada* (Ottawa: Canadian Council on Social Development, 1980), 118–19; 3–4 per cent of status Indian children were adopted. The experience of multiple foster home placements and failed adoption attempts is described by Jacqueline Maurice, "De-spiriting Aboriginal Children: Aboriginal Children During the 1960s and 1970s Child Welfare Era" (PhD diss., University of Toronto, 2003).
29 Hepworth, *Foster Care and Adoption*, 121.
30 Amy Bombay, Kim Matheson, and Hymie Anison, "Intergenerational Trauma: Convergence of Multiple Processes among First Nations People in Canada," *International Journal of Indigenous Health* 5, no. 3 (2009): 6–47.
31 Final Report. Vol. 1, *Summary*.
32 Care of Children, Dates 1979–81, file 677/29-4, acc. E-1996–97/252, RG 10, LAC.
33 Care of Children, Dates 1979–81.
34 Albers, "Autonomy and Dependency in the Lives of Dakota Women," 126.
35 Miss B.M. to Indian Agent F.J. Dodsall, Whitewood, SK, 14 May 1968. Adoption General Dates: 1958–69, file 673/13-4, confidential, acc.

2000-0321-4, box 1, RG 10, Central Registry Files and General Operational Records of the South District, Saskatchewan Region, 1933-1997.

36 Care of Children, Dates 1979–81.

37 Care of Children, Dates 1979–81.

38 Care of Children, Dates 1979–81.

39 Swift, *Manufacturing "Bad" Mothers.*

40 *Canada's Residential Schools: The History, Part 2, 1939–2000. The Final Report of the Truth and Reconciliation Commission of Canada.* Vol. 1 (Montreal and Kingston: McGill-Queen's University Press, 2015), 499.

41 *Canada's Residential Schools,* 445–6.

42 Superintendent to regional supervisor, 9 January 1963, Adoption General Dates: 1958–69, file 673/13-4, confidential, acc. 2000-0321-4, RG 10, LAC.

43 A.L. Clements, supervisor, to J. Woodsworth, superintendent Crooked Lake Agency, Adoption General Dates: 1958–69, file 673/13-4, confidential, acc. 2000-0321-4, RG 10, LAC.

44 G.W., interview by author, 19 September 2012, Marguerite Riel Centre.

45 This point is also made by Dubinsky, *Babies without Borders,* 82–4.

46 Registrar to superintendent, Crooked Lake Agency, 4 March 1959, Adoption General Dates: 1958–69, file 673/13-4, acc. 2000-0321-4, RG 10, LAC.

47 Registrar to superintendent, 4 March 1959.

48 R.T. Smith to Dorothy Moore, 14 July 1961. Adoption General Dates: 1958–69, file 673/13-4, acc. 2000-0321-4, RG 10, LAC.

49 Regional supervisor, SK, to all Superintendent Indian Agencies, 14 July 1961, Adoption General Dates: 1958–69, file 673/13-4, acc. 2000-0321-4, RG 10, LAC.

50 W.E Harris to J.H. Sturdy, minister of social welfare and rehabilitation, Ottawa, 4 July 1952, file I-48, R-935, SAB.

51 Adoption General Dates: 1958–69, file 673/13-4, acc. 2000-0321-4, RG 10, LAC. See Larry Gilbert, *Entitlement to Indian Status and Membership Codes in Canada* (Scarborough, ON: Carswell, 1996). After the 1985 amendments to the Indian Act, legal adoptions now confer Indian status on non-Indian children adopted by Indians, 48–9.

52 The Indian Act, SC 1951, c 29, s 48, ss 16, in Sharon Helen Venne, *Indian Acts and Amendments, 1868–1975: An Indexed Collection* (Saskatoon: University of Saskatchewan, Native Law Centre, 1981).

53 Phillipe Ariès, *Centuries of Childhood: A Social History of Family Life,* trans. Robert Baldick (New York: Vintage Books, 1962), 415.

54 The modernization of the Euro-American nuclear family came about in part because "the rearrangement of the house and the reform of manners left more room for private life; and this was taken up by a family reduced to parents and children, a family from which servants, clients, and friends were excluded." Ariès, *Centuries of Childhood,* 415.

55 Auger, "Northern Ojibwe," 118.

56 Herman, *Kinship by Design,* 95.

57 Arnold Lyslo, "Adoptive Placement of American Indian Children with Non-Indian Families," part 1, "The Indian Adoption Project," *Child Welfare: Journal of the Child Welfare League of America* (May 1961): 4.

58 Lyslo, "Adoptive Placement," 5.

59 Karen Balcom, "The Logic of Exchange: The Child Welfare League of America, the Adoption Resource Exchange Movement, and the Indian Adoption Project, 1958–1967," *Adoption and Culture* 1, no. 1 (2007): 7.

60 Brian Dippie, *The Vanishing American: White Attitudes and U.S. Indian Policy* (Lawrence: University Press of Kansas, 1982), 336.

61 Fixico, *Termination and Relocation*.

62 Laura Briggs, *Somebody's Children: The Politics of Transracial and Transnational Adoption* (Durham, NC: Duke University Press, 2012), 71.

63 Dippie, *Vanishing American*, 342.

64 This point is made by Jacobs, "Remembering the Forgotten Child," 145. The Meriam Report, produced in 1928, found the children taught in bureau boarding schools "ill fed, overcrowded, unhealthy, poorly taught, unduly regimented, and still obliged to contribute too much labour to keep the institutions going." Christine Bolt, *American Indian Policy and Reform: Case Studies of the Campaign to Assimilate the American Indians* (London: Allen and Unwin, 1987), 234. While changes to the schools came about, they continued to operate well into the twentieth century.

65 Jacobs, *White Mother to a Dark Race*, 305–6.

66 The familial consensus, essentially a belief that the greatest expression of American freedom was through the ideal family of the breadwinner father and homemaker mother, in the post-war era, was meant to allay anxieties over nuclear proliferation and cold war militarism. From Elaine Tyler-May, *Homeward Bound: American Families in the Cold War Era* (New York: Basic Books, 1988), 27.

67 Lyslo, "Adoptive Placement," 5. Balcom also draws attention to Lyslo's paternalism in "Logic of Exchange," 18.

68 Lyslo, "Adoptive Placement," 5.

69 Stella Hostbjor, "Social Service to the Indian Unmarried Mother," *Child Welfare* (May 1961): 7.

70 Hostbjor, "Social Service to the Indian Unmarried Mother," 7.

71 Hostbjor, "Social Service to the Indian Unmarried Mother," 8.

72 Hostbjor, "Social Service to the Indian Unmarried Mother," 8.

73 May J. Davis, "Adoptive Placement of American Indian Children with Non-Indian Families: Part II," *Child Welfare* (June 1961): 12.

74 Davis, "Adoptive Placement of American Indian Children," 15.

75 Briggs, *Somebody's Children*, 72.

76 *Indian Adoption Project, 1958–67: Report of Its Accomplishments, Evaluation and Recommendations for Adoption Services to Indian Children,* Child Welfare League of America Archives SW0055, series 2.2, Indian Adoption Project, folder 4, Adoption – Report, box 17, Social Welfare History Archives, University of Minnesota.

77 *Indian Adoption Project, 1958–67.*

78 *Indian Adoption Project, 1958–67,* 6.

79 *Indian Adoption Project, 1958–67.*

80 Child Welfare League of America, "America's Social Frontier: A National Adoption Exchange?," *Current,* August 1966, 57.

81 Child Welfare League of America, "America's Social Frontier," 57.

82 The report on the Aim Program states, "For several years prior to that time, the number of Indian and Métis children coming into the care of the Department was increasing by approximately 100 per year." From the Adopt Indian and Métis, a joint federal-provincial pilot project, Saskatchewan Department memo, G. Joice, chief, Special Services, to regional directors and adoption supervisors, re: Committee on Adoption Criteria Discussion Paper, 3 June 1974, coll. R-935, Saskatchewan Department of Social Services, I-49 Adopt Indian and Métis program, SAB.

83 Stoler, *Carnal Knowledge and Imperial Power,* 9.

84 Shurlee Swain and Margot Hillel, *Child, Nation, Race and Empire: Child Rescue Discourse, England Canada and Australia, 1850–1915* (Manchester: Manchester University Press, 2010), 3.

85 Swain and Hillel, *Child, Nation, Race and Empire,* 40.

86 Swain and Hillel, *Child, Nation, Race and Empire,* 72.

87 *Encyclopedia of Saskatchewan,* s.v. "Thatcher, Wilbert Ross," https://esask.uregina.ca/entry/thatcher_wilbert_ross_1917-71.jsp.

88 Jim Pitsula, "The Thatcher Government in Saskatchewan and Treaty Indians, 1964–1971: The Quiet Revolution," *Saskatchewan History* 48, no. 1 (1996): 3.

89 M. Mickleborough, program consultant, to D. Cowley, director, Program Division, "Services to Indians," 8 August 1972 (draft), file I-80b, R-933, Department of Social Services, SAB.

90 Pitsula, "Thatcher Government in Saskatchewan," 7.

91 *Annual Report,* Department of Social Welfare Government of Saskatchewan 1968–9, Government Publications, SAB.

92 *Annual Report,* Department of Social Welfare Government of Saskatchewan 1968–9.

93 Department of National Health and Welfare, Welfare Grants Division, Application of Welfare Demonstration Grant, "Special Adoption Unit to Place Indian and Métis Children for Adoption, Province of Saskatchewan," file 49 (4.9), coll. R-935, Adopt Indian and Métis program, AIM, 1967–73, Saskatchewan Department of Social Welfare, SAB.

94 Mixed Racial Adoption: A Community Project (Open Door Society, 1967), file 49 (4.9), coll. R-935, Adopt Indian and Métis program, AIM, 1967–73, Saskatchewan Department of Social Welfare, SAB.

95 *Regina Welfare Council Newsletter* 5, no. 3 (April 1967), file 49 (4.9), coll. R-935, Adopt Indian and Métis program, AIM, 1967–73, Saskatchewan Department of Social Welfare, SAB.

96 *Regina Welfare Council Newsletter.*

97 Department of National Health and Welfare, Welfare Grants Division, Application of Welfare Demonstration Grant, "Special Adoption Unit to Place Indian and Métis Children for Adoption, Province of Saskatchewan."

98 Numbers taken from Hawthorn, Cairns, and Tremblay, *Survey of the Contemporary Indians of Canada*, 51, 120.

99 For a discussion of the historic use of images of Indigenous children in Canadian culture, see Allyson Stevenson, "Karen B. and Indigenous Girlhood on the Prairies: Disrupting the Images of Indigenous Children in Adoption Advertising in North America," in *Children's Voices from the Past: New Historical and Interdisciplinary Perspectives*, ed. Kristin Moruzi, Nell Musgrove, and Carla Pascoe Leahy, 159–90 (Cham: Palgrave Macmillan, 2019).

100 Struthers and Associates, file R227.12, Provincial Archives of Saskatchewan.

101 *Leader Post*, "Homes Sought for 160 Indian and Métis Children: Adopted Children Retain Status," 22 July 1967, file 49 (4.9), coll. R-935, Adopt Indian and Métis program, AIM, 1967–73, Saskatchewan Department of Social Welfare, SAB.

102 *Leader Post*, "Homes Sought."

103 *Leader Post*, "Homes Sought."

104 W.K. Morrissey, director of program division, to A.W. Sihvon, deputy minister, 4 January 1972, from draft AIM report originally known as KIN, file 49 (4.9), coll. R-935, Adopt Indian and Métis program, AIM, 1967–73, Saskatchewan Department of Social Welfare, SAB.

105 Morrissey to Sihvon, 4 January 1972.

106 Morrissey to Sihvon, 4 January 1972.

107 Morrissey to Sihvon, 4 January 1972.

108 Hepworth, *Foster Care and Adoption in Canada*, 119.

109 Robert Doucette interview, 10 October 2012.

110 "Some Guidelines: re: Adopt Indian Métis Change in Focus," file I-49, coll. R-935, Adopt Indian and Métis program, Saskatchewan Department of Social Services, SAB.

111 "Some Guidelines."

112 "Some Guidelines"

7. Saskatchewan's Indigenous Resurgence and the Restoration of Indigenous Kinship and Caring

1 "Métis Foster Home Plan: Saskatoon," December 1971, file 49 (4.9), coll. R-935, Adopt Indian and Métis program, AIM, 1967–73, Saskatchewan Department of Social Welfare, SAB.

2 "Métis Foster Home Plan."

3 "Métis Foster Home Plan."

4 "Métis Foster Home Plan."

5 Murray Dobbin interview with Thomas Major, 14 March 1978, http://ourspace.uregina.ca/bitstream/handle/10294/1414/IH-395%2c%20395A.pdf?sequence=1&isAllowed=y.

6 Jim Pitsula, "The Thatcher Government in Saskatchewan and the Revival of Métis Nationalism, 1964–1971," *Great Plains Quarterly* 17, no. 3 (Summer/Fall, 1997): 222.

7 Murray Dobbin, *The One-and-a-Half Men: The Story of Jim Brady and Malcolm Norris, Métis Patriots of the Twentieth Century* (Vancouver: New Star Books, 1981).

8 Pitsula, "Thatcher Government in Saskatchewan and the Revival of Métis Nationalism," 225.

9 Adams, *Prison of Grass*.

10 Adams, *Prison of Grass*; and Pitsula, "Thatcher Government in Saskatchewan and the Revival of Métis Nationalism," 233.

11 "Métis Foster Home Plan: Saskatoon," December 1971, file 49 (4.9), coll. R-935, Adopt Indian and Métis program, AIM, 1967–73, Saskatchewan Department of Social Welfare, SAB.

12 Métis Foster Home Plan, December 1971, file 49 (4.9), coll. R-935, Adopt Indian and Métis program, AIM, 1967–73, Saskatchewan Department of Social Welfare, SAB.

13 Pitsula, "Thatcher Government in Saskatchewan and the Revival of Métis Nationalism," 223.

14 Campbell, *Halfbreed*, 183.

15 A.W. Sivhon to J.S. Sinclair, 14 December 1971, Métis Foster Home Plan, file 49 (4.9), coll. R-935, Adopt Indian and Métis program, AIM, 1967–73, Saskatchewan Department of Social Welfare, SAB.

16 A.W. Sihvon to G.R. Snyder, 16 December 1971, Métis Foster Home Plan, file 49 (4.9), coll. R-935, Adopt Indian and Métis program, AIM, 1967–73, Saskatchewan Department of Social Welfare, SAB.

17 "Aim Centre Program, 1973–1974," file I-49, coll. R-935, Adopt Indian and Métis program, AIM, 1967–73, Saskatchewan Department of Social Services, SAB.

18 "Aim Centre Program, 1973–1974."

19 "Aim Centre Program, 1973–1974."

20 "Finding Cleo," podcast by Connie Walker in the Missing and Murdered Series on CBC Radio focused on Cleo, a young girl placed for adoption in the United States, and her family who searched for her, https://www.cbc.ca/radio/findingcleo/click-here-to-listen-to-missing-murdered-finding-cleo-1.4557887. "Aim Centre Program, 1973–1974," file I-49, coll. R-935, Adopt Indian and Métis program, AIM, 1967–73, Saskatchewan Department of Social Services, SAB.

21 G.E. Jacob to Aim staff, Regina and Saskatoon, department memo, "Re: Change in name and formate [sic] for Adopt Indian Métis," file I-49, coll.

R-935, Adopt Indian and Métis program, AIM, 1967–73, Saskatchewan Department of Social Services, SAB.

22 Jacob to Aim staff.

23 Province of Saskatchewan, The Societies Act Application for Incorporation, D-921 Human Resources Development Agency Records, file I.C. 19 b) Saskatchewan Native Women's Movement 1975–76, SAB.

24 Report to SNWM to The secretary of state in Ottawa, D-921 Human Resources Development Agency Records, file I.C. 19 b) Saskatchewan Native Women's Movement 1975–76, SAB.

25 Nora Cummings, interview by author, 4 May 2013. This point was made by some of the female Indigenous informants I spoke with. Informant E.B, interviewed at the Marguerite Riel Centre on 19 September 2012, recalled her sister's infant removed at the hospital in Wakaw, SK, after giving birth. The child was adopted and never heard from again. Informant J.P. interviewed on 16 October 2012, in Prince Albert, SK, was present the day her nephew was removed from his mother by a local priest in Buffalo Narrows, SK, the same incident that Nora was referring to. Informant R.J, interviewed on 20 October 2014, in Saskatoon, had her baby apprehended at a hospital in Winnipeg, MB, but refused to sign a consent for adoption. She regained custody of her son after she married the boy's father and established a home in the city. More research is needed to determine how many babies were removed at birth from mothers without proper informed consent.

26 Proposal for federal government for funding from 1972 to 1974, "The Saskatchewan Native Women's Movement," 25 August 1972, D-921 Human Resources Development Agency Records, file I.C. 19 b) Saskatchewan Native Women's Movement, 1975–76, SAB.

27 Helene Jasefowiz, social development officer, "Historical Perspective of the Saskatchewan Native Women's Movement," Department of the Secretary of State, Citizenship Development Branch, 15 March 1976, D-921 Human Resources Development Agency Records, file I.C. 19 b), Saskatchewan Native Women's Movement, 1975–76, SAB.

28 Minutes, Annual Board Meeting, 10 April 1973, D-921 Human Resources Development Agency Records, file I.C. 19 b), Saskatchewan Native Women's Movement, 1975–76, SAB.

29 The story of this family is the focus of the CBC podcast "Finding Cleo."

30 Nora Cummings, interview by author, 4 May 2013.

31 G. Joice, chief, Special Services (Children), to D.G. Cameron, director of social services, re: Saskatchewan Native Women's Movement vs AIM Centre, 6 June 1973, file I-49, coll. R-935, Adopt Indian and Métis program, Department of Social Services, SAB.

32 G.E. Jacob, director, AIM Centre, to G. Joice, Special Services, Children, re: Saskatchewan Native Women's Movement vs Aim Centre, 9 April 1973, file I-49, Adopt Indian and Métis program, coll. R-935, Department of Social Services, SAB.

33 Jacob to Joice, 9 April 1973.

34 Jacob to Joice, 9 April 1973.

35 Jacob to Joice, 9 April 1973.

36 Department Memo: Advertising Campaign: *New Breed* and the *Saskatch-ewan Indian*, 3 October 1973, G.E. Jacob, file 5.19, Native Media, 1973 Collection, coll. R-1721, Department of Social Services, SAB.

37 Métis Society of Saskatchewan, publisher of *New Breed Magazine*, to Gerald Jacob, AIM Centre, 15 November 1973, Native Media, 1973 Collection, coll. R-1721, Department of Social Services, SAB.

38 Métis Society to Jacob, 15 November 1973.

39 *New Breed Magazine*, May/June 1975.

40 "A Proposal to Establish a Native Home for Native Children in Saskatoon," submitted by Saskatchewan Native Women's Movement, 18 June 1973, file 5.114, coll. R-1721, Native Groups Department of Social Services, 1 April 1972–March 1977, SAB.

41 "Proposal to Establish a Native Home."

42 *Star Phoenix*, "Native Adoption Groups Looking for a Home," 25 October 1973, file 5.114, AIM Program, coll. R-1721, Department of Social Services, SAB.

43 Department Memo from Deputy Minister F.J. Bogdasavich to Minister Herman Rolfes re: Métis Society of Saskatchewan Foster and Adoptions Homes Proposal, 19 November 1975, re: Native Homes Project, file 11.65, Foster Homes: Native Homes Project, coll. R-935, Department of Social Welfare, SAB.

44 For a detailed analysis of the Métis child-caring proposals, see Allyson Stevenson, "Demanding the Right to Care for Métis Children In Saskatchewan: A History of the Métis Society Resisting Child Removal in the 1970's," in *Métis Rising*, vol. 3, ed. Yvonne Boyer and Larry Chartrand (Winnipeg: University of Manitoba Press), forthcoming.

45 G.E. Jacob, director REACH, to G. Joice, Special Services to Families and Youth, department memo re: Contracts with Saskatchewan Native Women, 3 February 1975, file 11.65, Foster Homes: Native Homes Project, coll. R-935, Department of Social Welfare Files, SAB.

46 Included in file 5.114, AIM Program, coll. R-1721, Department of Social Services, SAB.

47 Hepworth, *Foster Care and Adoption in Canada*, "Chapter 8: Native Children in Care," was followed by Johnston, *Native Children and the Child Welfare System*.

48 Johnston, table 12, 39.

49 Johnston, table 13, 40.

8. Confronting Cultural Genocide in the 1980s

1 Ovide Mercredi and Clem Chartier, "The Status of Child Welfare Services for the Indigenous Peoples of Canada: The Problem, the Law and the

Solution" (paper presented at the Indian Child Welfare Rights Conference, Regina, SK, 19 March 1981).

2 Minister's Advisory Council on Child Protection, Family Services Act Review, submitted to Gordon Dirks, February 1984, 3.

3 The Manitoba government initiated the Kimelman Inquiry, led by Judge Kimelman, to look into the high rates of transracial adoption of Indigenous children into the United States. The published findings, *No Quiet Place: Final Report to Honourable Muriel Smith Minister of Community Services*, Review Committee on Aboriginal Adoptions and Placements, 1985, identified the cultural bias throughout all levels of the child welfare system that worked to strip Indigenous people of their rights to survive as a people. From the *Report of the Aboriginal Justice Inquiry of Manitoba*, 1991, http://www.ajic.mb.ca/volume1/chapter14.html.

4 Portions of this chapter were published as Allyson Stevenson, "Vibrations across a Continent: The 1978 Indian Child Welfare Act and the Politicization of First Nations Leaders in Saskatchewan," *American Indian Quarterly* 37, no. 1 (2013): 218–36.

5 The clause in the Constitution Act, 1982, states, "The existing Aboriginal and treaty rights of the Aboriginal peoples of Canada are hereby recognized and affirmed." From Miller, *Skyscrapers Hide the Heavens*, 284.

6 Joyce Green, "Balancing Strategies: Aboriginal Women and Constitutional Rights in Canada," in Green, *Making Space for Indigenous Feminism*, 142; see also "Up the Creek: Fishing for a New Constitutional Order," *Canadian Journal of Political Science* 28, no. 4 (2005): 923–53.

7 The term *Peyakowak* is derived from the Cree term meaning "They are alone," referring to the children who are removed from their families and communities.

8 Hepworth, *Foster Care and Adoption in Canada*, "Chapter 8: Native Children in Care," 111–21.

9 Numbers taken from table 11, in Johnston, *Native Children and the Child Welfare System*, 37.

10 Stoler, "Tense and Tender Ties," 844.

11 "Summary Information, History of Association on American Indian Affairs," Association on American Indian Affairs Fonds, 1851–2010, Mudd Manuscript Library, Princeton University Library, https://findingaids.princeton.edu/names/133150993#related.

12 "Summary Information."

13 Briggs, *Somebody's Children*, 79.

14 One example: in South Dakota, 1 out of every 9.9 children were in adoptive or foster homes, as compared to 1 out of every 27.2 non-Indian children. *Indian Child Welfare Act of 1977. Hearing before the United States Select Committee on Indian Affairs, Ninety-Fifth Congress, First Session, on S-1214, to Establish Standards for the Placement of Indian Children in Foster or Adoptive*

Homes, to Prevent the Breakup of Indian Families, and for Other Purposes (Washington: United States Government Printing Office, 1977), 592.

15 Association on American Indian Affairs, *Indian Family Defense: A Bulletin of the Association on American Indian Affairs* 2 (Summer 1974).

16 *Indian Family Defence* 2 (Summer 1974): 1.

17 *Indian Family Defence* 2 (Summer 1974): 1. In the spirit of comparative history, in a recent discussion with a First Nations friend, he also recalls hiding under the bed as a child with his siblings when the social worker knocked on the door if they were absent from school.

18 Such stories can be read in publications such as Miller, *Shingwauk's Vision*; Jacobs, *White Mother to a Dark Race*.

19 Andrew Armitage, *Comparing the Policy of Aboriginal Assimilation: Australia, Canada, and New Zealand* (Vancouver: UBC Press, 1995), 110.

20 Submission: National Indian Health Board Indian Child Welfare Act, hearing before the Unites States Senate Select Committee on Indian Affairs, Fifty-Fifth Congress, First Session, on S. 1214 (Washington: 1977), 320.

21 Steven Unger, ed., *The Destruction of American Indian Families* (New York: Association on American Indian Affairs, 1977), 2–8.

22 Joseph Westermeyer, "The Ravage of Indian Families in Crisis," in Unger, *Destruction of American Indian Families*, 53.

23 A growing body of literature is beginning to balance out the representation of Native American women. Long overdue, women's roles and power within their own communities are coming to light to challenge the Euro-American stereotypes of the "squaw" or "Indian princess." Laura F. Klein and Lillian A. Ackerman, eds, *Women and Power in Native North America* (Norman: University of Oklahoma Press, 1995), 5.

24 Mary Ellen Kelm, "Diagnosing the Discursive Indian, Medicine Gender and the 'Dying Race,'" *Ethnohistory* 52, no. 2 (Spring 2005): 390.

25 American Association on Indian Affairs, *Indian Family Defense* 2 (Summer 1974).

26 This topic is examined in greater detail in Jane Lawrence, "The Indian Health Service and the Sterilization of Native American Women," *American Indian Quarterly* 24, no. 3 (Summer 2000): 400–19.

27 Lawrence, "Indian Health Service."

28 Randi Cull, "Aboriginal Mothering under the State's Gaze: Motherhood," in *"Until Our Hearts Are on the Ground": Aboriginal Mothering, Oppression, Resistance and Rebirth*, ed. D. Memee Lavell-Harvard and Janette Corbiere Lavell (Toronto: Demeter, 2006), 153; Kline, "Complicating the Ideology of Motherhood," 306; Monture, "Vicious Cycle."

29 Devon A. Mihesuah, "Commonality of Difference: American Indian Women and History," in *American Indians in American Indian History, 1870–2001: A Companion Reader*, ed. Sterling Evans (Westport, CT: Praeger, 2002), 168.

30 Statement of Raymond V. Butler, acting department commissioner of Bureau of Indian Affairs, Indian Child Welfare Act of 1977, hearing before the United States Select Committee on Indian Affairs, 95th Congress, 1st Session, on s. 1214 to Establish Standards.

31 ARENA submission: Mary Joe Fales, project director, Indian Child Welfare Act of 1977, hearing before the United States Select Committee on Indian Affairs, 95th Congress, 1st Session, on s. 1214 to Establish Standards for the Placement of Indian Children in Foster or Adoptive Homes, to Prevent the Breakup of Indian Families, and for Other Purposes (Washington: United States Government Printing Office, 1977).

32 ARENA submission.

33 Hearings before the United States Select Committee on Indian Affairs, 95th Congress, 1st Session, on s. 1214, to Establish Standards for the Placement of Indian Children in Foster or Adoptive Homes, to Prevent the Breakup of Indian Families, and for Other Purposes (Washington: United States Government Printing Office, 1977), 539.

34 Hearings before the United States Select Committee on Indian Affairs.

35 Hearings before the United States Select Committee on Indian Affairs.

36 Title II, s 201 (a), Indian Child Welfare Act of 1978: An Act to Establish Standards for the Placement of Indian Children in Foster and Adoptive Homes, to Prevent the Breakup of Indian Families and for Other Purposes.

37 Bradford Morse, *Indian Tribal Courts in the United States: A Model for Canada?* (Saskatoon: University of Saskatchewan Law Centre, 1980), 3–21.

38 Morse, *Indian Tribal Courts in the United States.*

39 Dippie, *Vanishing American*, 309–22.

40 Nichols, *Indians in the United States and Canada*, 250–1.

41 For a discussion on the origins of the blood quantum and definitions of Indian tribal membership, see Paul Srpuhlan, "A Legal History of Blood Quantum in Federal Indian Law to 1935," *South Dakota Law Review* 51, no. 1 (2006): 1–50.

42 Srpuhlan, "Legal History of Blood Quantum," 35.

43 See Palmater, *Beyond Blood*, 19. Palmater makes the argument that while Canadian Indian legislation doesn't have "blood quantum" requirements per se, it nonetheless sets up a "notional blood quantum allocation" that discriminates against Indigenous women and their descendants; and also Kirsty Gover, *Tribal Constitutionalism: States, Tribes, and the Governance of Membership* (Oxford: Oxford University Press, 2010).

44 A succinct discussion of Indigenous women's political strategies in Canada is Joanne Barker, "Gender, Sovereignty, and the Discourse of Rights in Native Women's Activism," *Meridians: Feminism, Race, Transnationalism* 7, no. 1 (2006): 127–61.

45 Compulsory enfranchisement of women who married non-Indigenous men, introduced in 1951, s 12 (1) (b); women lost the right to live on a reserve, to treaty benefits, and to inherit reserve land; Royal Commission on

Indigenous Peoples, *Report of the Royal Commission on Aboriginal People*, vol. 1, *Looking Forward, Looking Back* (Ottawa: Supply and Services, 1996), 313.

46 For a discussion of the impact of government policy on identity, see Bonita Lawrence, *"Real" Indians and Others: Mixed-Blood Urban Native Peoples and Aboriginal Nationhood* (Lincoln: University of Nebraska Press, 2004); Lee, "'Because Our Law Is Our Law'"; and Palmater, *Beyond Blood*.

47 D. Memee Harvard Lavell and Jeannette Corbiere Lavell, "Aboriginal Women vs Canada," in Lavell-Harvard and Corbiere Lavell, *"Until Our Hearts Are on the Ground,"* 188.

48 Harvard Lavell and Corbiere Lavell, "Aboriginal Women vs Canada," 190. Indigenous women eventually had their status restored through Bill C-31 in 1985, although unfortunately this has not resolved issues of exclusion or solved issues of gender discrimination. For a discussion of the women who have had their status returned, see Katrina Srigley, "'I Am a Proud Anishinaabekwe': Issues of Identity and Status in Northern Ontario after Bill C-31," in *Finding a Way to the Heart: Feminist Writings on Aboriginal and Women's History in Canada*, ed. Robin Jarvis Brownlee and Valerie J. Korinek, 241–59 (Winnipeg: University of Manitoba Press, 2012).

49 One good discussion of their perspectives is Green, *Making Space for Indigenous Feminism*.

50 Renée Elizabeth Mzinegizhigo-kwe Bédard, "An Anishinbaabe-kwe Ideology on Mothering and Motherhood," in Lavell-Harvard and Corbiere Lavell, *"Until Our Hearts Are on the Ground,"* 66 and 73–4; Jo-Anne Fiske, "Carrier Women and the Politics of Mothering," in *Rethinking Canada: The Promise of Women's History*, 4th ed., ed. Veronica Strong-Boag, Mona Gleason, and Adele Perry (Don Mills, ON: Oxford University Press), 242, states that extended families in Carrier communities of matrilocal kinship units of three to four generations are the strongest economic unit.

51 Jo-Anne Fiske, "Boundary Crossings: Power and Marginalization in the Formation of Canadian Indigenous Women's Identities," *Gender and Development* 14, no. 2 (July 2006): 247.

52 See also Auger, "North Ojibwe."

53 Hawthorn, Cairns, and Tremblay, *Survey of the Contemporary Indians of Canada*, 61.

54 For an overview of the origin and intent of the White Paper, Miller, *Skyscrapers Hide the Heavens*. The reaction of First Nations on the Prairies was a swift and furious rejection of the Trudeau and Chrétien policy to repeal the Indian Act and gradually eliminate the treaty obligations of the government. See Harold Cardinal, *The Unjust Society* (Edmonton: M.G. Hurtig, 1969).

55 Miller, *Skyscrapers Hide the Heavens*, 284.

56 Joyce Green, "Balancing Strategies: Aboriginal Women and Constitutional Rights in Canada," in *Making Space for Indigenous Feminism*, ed. Joyce Green (Winnipeg, MB: Fernwood Publishing, 2007), 140.

57 On 2 December 1980, Marlene Pierre-Aggamaway and Donna Phillips, representing the Native Women's Association of Canada, testified before the Joint Committee on the Constitution http://www.cpac.ca/en/programs/cpac-special/episodes/51315054.

58 Innes, *Elder Brother and the Law of the People*.

59 Teresa Nahanee, "Dancing with a Gorilla: Indigenous Women, Justice and the Charter," in *Indigenous Peoples and the Justice System: Report of the National Round Table on Indigenous Justice Issues* (Ottawa: Minister of Supply and Services, 1993), 19. This argument is also made by Palmater, *Beyond Blood*.

60 Canadian Indian Lawyers Association, Summary of Proceedings, National Workshop on Indian Child Welfare Rights, March 1981.

61 Clem Chartier to Steven Unger, 19 December 1980, box 75, folder 3, Canadian Indian Child Welfare, 1973–1984, American Association on Indian Affairs Collection, Seeley G. Mudd Manuscript Library, Princeton University.

62 Appendix C, excerpts from Spallumcheen Indian Band By-Law, No. 2-1980, in Johnston, *Children and the Welfare System*, 138.

63 Mercredi and Chartier, "Status of Child Welfare Services for the Aboriginal Peoples of Canada."

64 Section 3 (a), Spallumcheen By-law no. 2-1980, Johnston, *Children and the Welfare System*, 138.

65 By-Law s. 10 (7), Johnston, *Children and the Welfare System*, 138.

66 Johnston, *Children and the Welfare System*, 107.

67 The Blackfoot Band in Alberta signed a tri-partite agreement in 1975, and the Manitoba Indian Brotherhood signed an agreement with the federal and provincial governments in 1982 establishing a framework to extend autonomy to bands in southern and central Manitoba. This agreement was preceded by the Dakota-Ojibway Child and Family Services Agreement of 1981, Canada's first Child and Family Services Society run completely by Aboriginal peoples; Johnston, *Children and the Welfare System*, 106–20; see also Carrière, *Aski Awasis/Children of the Earth*.

68 Mercredi and Chartier, "Status of Child Welfare Services."

69 Mercredi and Chartier, "Status of Child Welfare Services."

70 Mercredi and Chartier, "Status of Child Welfare Services."

71 Kent McNeil, *Indian Child Welfare: Whose Responsibility? Report No. 1* (Saskatoon: University of Saskatchewan Native Law Centre, 1981).

72 McNeil, *Indian Child Welfare*, 4.

73 McNeil, *Indian Child Welfare*, 11.

74 Marv Hendrikson, executive director, Treaty Indian Policy Secretariat, to Duane Adams, deputy minister, Saskatchewan Social Services, 9 February 1982, file 10.10.1. Indian/Native Issues, R-1655, Department of Social Services, SAB.

75 Indian Child Welfare Agreement Signed, file 10.10.1, Indian/Native Issues, R-1655, Department of Social Services, SAB.

76 Indian and Northern Affairs Canada, Child Welfare Program Policy, 1 May 1982, Preamble, file 10.10.1 Indian/Native Issues, R-1655, Department of Social Services, SAB.

77 Indian and Northern Affairs Canada, Child Welfare Program Policy.

78 Revised Family Services Policy Statement, 10 May 1982, file 10.10.1 Indian/Native Issues, R-1655, Department of Social Services, SAB.

79 Harvey Stalwick, Lavina Bitternose, Yvonne House Thomas, and Peter Brook, "Reform as the Creation of New Usages: 1982–1985: Synopsis of the Taking Control Project," in *Perspectives on Social Services and Social Issues*, ed. Jacqueline S. Ismael and Ray J. Tomlinson (Canadian Council on Social Development), Selections from the Proceedings of the Second Conference on Provincial Welfare Policy held at the University of Calgary, 1–3 May 1985, 223.

80 Stalwick et al., "Reform as the Creation of New Usages," 224.

81 Stalwick et al., "Reform as the Creation of New Usages," 227.

82 Executive director, Regional Services Division, to Dianne Anderson, director Federal-Provincial Arrangements Branch, 29 March 1982, Re: Resolutions from the Working Together Conference 1982, file 10.10.1. Indian/Native Issues, R-1655, Department of Social Services, SAB.

83 "Resolution D: Need for Indian child custody courts on reserves for the purpose of Indian governments to make policy decisions regarding the future care and adoption of our Indian people in Sask. Reponses of the Department of Social Services: positive goal, interested in hearing further results of the two projects. We would be interested in discussing such an approach with bands in this province that feel able to undertake such responsibilities." Executive director to Anderson, 29 March 1982.

84 Family and Children Services – General File Dates: 1980–90, file E6575-1, acc. E-1998-01236-0, RG 10, Pacific Regional Services, LAC.

85 *Indian Head Woolsey News*, "Minister Says Inquiry Not Necessary," 13 July 1983.

86 Patricia A. Smith, minister of social services, to Grant Devine and members of the Cabinet, memorandum, Cabinet Agenda Item re: The Family Services Act: Review of the Child Protection Services, 27 June 1983, file 10.5.3., Family Services Act Review, R-1655, Department of Social Services, SAB.

87 Henry Bartel, Conference of Mennonites in Canada, to Minister Patricia A. Smith, 24 June 1983, file 14, Family Services Act Review, R-1156, Gordon Dirks fonds, SAB.

88 Patrick Johnston to Minister of Social Services Patricia A. Smith, 6 July 1983, file 14, Family Services Act Review, R-1156, Gordon Dirks fonds, SAB.

89 "Child Welfare Inquiry," press release, 30 June 1983, file 10.5.3, Family Services Act Review, coll. R-1655, Department of Social Services, SAB.

90 Minister of Social Services Gordon Dirks to Paul Meagher, chairman, and members of the Caucus Committee, memorandum re: Review of the Family Services Act, 3 August 1982, file 10.5.3. Family Services Act Review, coll. R-1655, Department of Social Services, SAB.

91 Dirks to Meagher and members of the Caucus Committee, 3 August 1982.
92 Minister of Social Services Patricia A. Smith to Paul Meagher, chairman, Caucus Health and Social Services Committee, memorandum re: Discussion Paper – Family Services Act, 6 July 1983, file 10.5.3, Family Services Act Review, coll. R-1655, Department of Social Services, SAB.
93 Linda D. Lock, "Custom Adoption and Its Implications on the Breakdown of the Indian Culture," 15 April 1983, Saskatoon, SK: Native Law Centre University of Saskatchewan, file 10.5.3, Family Services Act Review, coll. R-1655, Department of Social Services, SAB, 5.
94 Lock, "Custom Adoption," 5.
95 Lock, "Custom Adoption," 48.
96 Gordon Dirks, Minister of Social Services, address to the Peyakowak Committee on the FSA, 14 September 1983, file 10.5.3, Family Services Act Review, coll. R-1655, Department of Social Services, SAB.
97 *Saskatoon Star Phoenix*, "Advisory Council Meetings Set," 13 October 1983.
98 Dirks, address to Peyakowak Committee.
99 Jenni Mortin, "Advisory Council Hears Conflicting Advice," *Saskatoon Star Phoenix*, 5 November 1983.
100 *Saskatoon Star Phoenix*, "Dirks Doesn't Envision Conflicts in Act," 1 November 1983.
101 *Regina Leader Post*, "Extended Foster Family Home Discussed," 8 November 1983.
102 *Saskatoon Star Phoenix*, "Indians Seek Child Welfare Control," 3 November 1983.
103 "Indian Control of Indian Child Welfare" echoed an earlier policy paper submitted to the federal government following the White Paper by the National Indian Brotherhood, "Indian Control of Indian Education" (Ottawa: National Indian Brotherhood, 1972).
104 "Indian Control of Indian Child Welfare": A Report by the Health and Social Development Commission, Federation of Saskatchewan Indian Nations, Vice-Chief Melvin Isnana, executive member in charge, December 1983, 1.
105 "Indian Control of Indian Child Welfare."
106 *Saskatoon Star Phoenix*, "Moratorium Said Pending on Indian Child Adoption," 21 October 1983.
107 Minister's Advisory Council on Child Protection, *Family Services Act Review*, submitted to Gordon Dirks, February 1984.
108 All recommendations, from Minister's Advisory Council on Child Protection, Family Services Act Review, submitted to Gordon Dirks, February 1984.
109 Other jurisdictions that reviewed their child welfare legislation at this time included Alberta (Bill 105), Ontario (Child and Family Services Act of Ontario, 1984), Manitoba (Manitoba Child and Welfare Services Act), and British Columbia; Minister's Advisory Council on Child Protection, 4.

110 Youngwolfe, "Miyo-Ohpikāwasowin," 2.
111 Youngwolfe, "Miyo-Ohpikāwasowin," 47.

Conclusion

1 The change in focus from outright assimilation to integration is documented by Shewell, *"Enough to Keep Them Alive."* For the Indigenous
perspective on this enforced political assimilation, see James Sákéj Youngblood Henderson, "Sui Generis and Treaty Citizenship," *Citizenship Studies*
6, no. 4 (1 December 2002): 415–40, https://doi.org/10.1080/136210202200
0041259.
2 Shewell, *"Enough to Keep Them Alive"*; this change is also explored by
Chupik-Hall, "'Good Families Do Not Just Happen.'"
3 This aspect of Native-newcomer relations has been explored by gender
and queer historians such as Gary Kingsman, *The Regulation of Desire:
Homo and Hetero Sexualities* (Toronto: Black Rose Books, 1996); and Carter,
Importance of Being Monogamous; and in the United States by Nancy Cott,
Public Vows: A History of Marriage and Nation (Cambridge, MA: Harvard
University Press, 2002); and John Demilio and Estelle Freedman, *Intimate
Matters: A History of Sexuality in America* (Chicago: University of Chicago
Press, 1997), see especially chap. 5, "Race and Sexuality."
4 Tobias, "Protection, Civilization, Assimilation"; and Martin Cannon, "The
Regulation of First Nations Sexuality," *Canadian Journal of Native Studies* 18,
no. 1 (1998): 1–18.
5 This point is also made by Fiske, "Political Status of Native Women," 334.
6 This aspect of the heterosexual relationship, female dependency, has been
termed the "patriarchal necessity" by feminist scholar Dorothy C. Miller,
Women and Social Welfare: A Feminist Analysis (New York: Praeger, 1990).
7 Gleason, *Normalizing the Ideal*, documents the increasing focus on psychological discourses of motherhood and delinquency in the post-war period
that pathologized immigrant and Aboriginal mothers in new and perva-
sive ways.
8 "Joint Submission of Canadian Association of Social Workers and Canadian Welfare Council to the Senate-Commons Committee on Indian Affairs," Section: Housing, January 1947, 4.
9 "Joint Submission of Canadian Association of Social Workers and Canadian Welfare Council," 6.
10 The connection between colonization and ill health of Indian peoples in
Canada has been documented by Lux, *Medicine That Walks*; and more
recently by Daschuk, *Clearing the Plains*, 177. He looks especially at the
prevalence of tuberculosis among Indian people on the plains and the poor
housing and conditions on reserves that were never properly addressed,
leading to current health crises. The connection between colonization and
ill health in British Columbia also detailed by Kelm, *Colonizing Bodies*.

11 "Joint Submission of Canadian Association of Social Workers and Canadian Welfare Council," 2.

12 Dyck, *What Is the Indian Problem?*, 3. The concept of the "Indian problem" has its origins in the earliest contacts between Europeans and First Peoples. According to Dyck, "Discussions of the Indian 'problem' revolve around the deep-rooted belief that perceived differences between Indians and other Canadians constitute a regrettable situation that needs to be remedied," Dyck, 1. The remedies that have been applied over the course of contact represent the underlying belief that with just the correct combination of guidance and knowledge, First Nations and Métis people will join the Canadian polity as another colourful tile in the mosaic without a distinct political voice.

13 Two academic works published in this period applied this analysis that provided an authoritative gloss to justify popular sentiment. See Stanley, *Birth of Western Canada*, for a portrayal of the Métis as backward and archaic, resisting the inevitable expansion of modernity. Also Marcel Giraud, *Les métis canadien* (Saint-Boniface, MB: Editions du Blé, 1984), documented the origins of the Métis people as a regressive example of the failure of racial mixing, and an example of inevitable dominance of Anglo-Protestant civilization; these interpretations held sway until the 1970s.

14 The process by which many Prairie Métis ended up living in road allowance communities has not been fully explored by academic historians.

15 White, "Restructuring the Domestic Sphere," examines the period up to 1930 when the state attempted to refashion Indian women to replicate the feminine roles in Euro-Canadian society. Women were encouraged by white women field matrons and Indian agents to cook bread rather than bannock, live in homes with more than one room, and improve housekeeping skills. Women were often portrayed as negligent in their housekeeping duties and responsible for the high rates of TB on reserves rather than placing the blame on lack of adequate medical facilities or federal policies that gutted reserves of economic opportunities.

16 White, "Restructuring the Domestic Sphere," 13.

17 Phillip Hepworth, *Foster Care and Adoption in Canada*, 93.

18 Hepworth, *Foster Care and Adoption in Canada*, 119.

19 Hepworth, *Foster Care and Adoption in Canada*, 183.

20 *Iskwew*, Saskatchewan Native Women's Movement Newsletter, May 1975.

21 Cull, "Aboriginal Mothering under the State's Gaze," 153.

22 For a better understanding of the impact of violence on the lives of Indigenous women and children, see Anne McGillivray and Brenda Comansky, *Black Eyes All of the Time: Intimate Violence, Aboriginal Women, and the Justice System* (Toronto: University of Toronto Press, 1999).

23 There are locations where Indigenous adoption is recognized and practised, such as Nunavut, British Columbia, and Alberta. Yellowhead Tribal Services Agency in Alberta has developed an award-winning custom adoption program that boasts a 100 per cent success rate in that there have been no adoption breakdowns in 100 cases. Cindy Blackstock, "Supporting

First Nations Adoptions," submission to Standing Committee on Human Resources, Skill and Social Development and the Status of Persons with Disabilities, December 2010, http://www.fncaringsociety.com/sites /default/files/13.FNCFCS-Supporting-First-Nations-Adoption-Dec2010 .pdf; see Marilyn Poitras and Norman Zlotkin, "An Overview of the Recognition of Customary Adoption in Canada," prepared for the Saskatchewan First Nations Family and Community Institute, 15 February 2013. Zlotkin and Poitras recommend that the government of Saskatchewan make changes to adoption legislation to enable customary adoption to have the same legislative weight as provincial adoption, 4.

24 Youngwolfe, "Miyo-Ohpikāwasowin." A recent report by the representative for children and youth in British Columbia has looked at the failure of social welfare agencies in British Columbia and Saskatchewan to provide proper oversight to ensure the safety of a small girl placed on reserve in her grandfather's care. A convicted criminal battling with additions, he and his spouse abused the child while acting as foster parents. The report looks not only at the individual factors but the systemic problems with Indian child welfare in Canada. Representative for children and youth, "Out of Sight: How One Indigenous Child's Best Interests Were Lost between Two Provinces: A Special Report," September 2013, https://cwrp.ca /publications/out-sight-how-one-aboriginal-childs-best-interests-were -lost-between-two-provinces.

25 Barbara Ann Atwood, *Children, Tribes, and States: Adoption and Custody Conflicts over American Indian Children* (Durham, NC: Carolina Academic Press, 2010).

26 Minister of Indigenous Services Jane Philpot announced on 30 November that the government of Canada plans to co-develop national Indigenous child welfare legislation with Inuit, Métis and First Nations to address the over-representation of Indigenous children, the harms of the Sixties Scoop, and work towards creating a new relationship with Indigenous peoples. Mia Rabson, "Jane Philpott Says Child Welfare Law Will Keep More Indigenous Families Together," *Huffpost*, 30 November 2018, https://www. huffingtonpost.ca/2018/11/30/jane-philpott-says-child-welfare-law-will-keep-more-indigenous-families-together_a_23605585/

27 Truth and Reconciliation Commission of Canada, *Truth and Reconciliation Commission of Canada: Calls to Action* (Manitoba Truth and Reconciliation Commission of Canada, 2015), http://trc.ca/assets/pdf/Calls_to _Action_English2.pdf.

Epilogue

1 McLeod, *Cree Narrative Memory*, 54.
2 James Grierson MacGregor, *Peter Fidler, Canada's Forgotten Surveyor, 1769–1822* (Toronto: McClelland and Stewart, 1966).
3 Paget Code, "Les autres Métis: The English Métis of the Prince Albert settlement 1862–1886" (MA thesis, University of Saskatchewan, 2008), 35.

4 Thanks to Cheryl Troupe for kindly sharing her copy of these petitions. Prince Albert Petitions, 15 January 1878, in "Papers and Correspondence in Connection with the Half-breed Claims and Other Matters Relating to the North-West Territories," Canada, *Sessional Papers*, vol. 13, Third Session of the Fifth Parliament, 48 Victoria, 1885 (no. 116), 29–31.

5 Petitions, Sessional Papers 116, 1885.

6 Razack, *Dying from Improvement*.

7 Razack, *Dying from Improvement*, 8.

8 Razack, *Dying from Improvement*, 176.

9 Robert Alexander Innes and Kim Anderson, eds, *Indigenous Men and Masculinities: Legacies, Identities, Regeneration* (Winnipeg: University of Manitoba Press, 2015), 7.

Appendix

1 Robert G. Doucette, *The Archival Resource Guide for Aboriginal Issues* (Saskatoon, SK: Gabriel Dumont Institute, 2009), 49–50.

Bibliography

Primary Sources

Interviews

B., E. Interview by Allyson Stevenson. Melfort, SK, 19 September 2012.

B., R. Interview by Allyson Stevenson. Melfort, SK, 19 September 2012.

Bishop, Peter, and Nora Cummings. Interview by Ron Laliberte. 28–9 February 2004. Interview 11. *Virtual Museum of Métis History and Culture.* Gabriel Dumont Institute, Saskatoon, SK, PDF.

Cummings, Nora. Interview by Allyson Stevenson. Saskatoon, SK, 3 May 2012.

Doucette, Robert. Interview by Allyson Stevenson. Saskatoon, SK, 10 October 2012.

Durocher, Jim, and Sinclair, Jim. Interview by Ron Laliberte, 17 April 2004. *Virtual Museum of Métis History and Culture.* Gabriel Dumont Institute, Saskatoon, SK, PDF.

Nippi, Peter. Interview by Allyson Stevenson. Kinistin, SK, 21 February 2011.

Pelletier, Henry. Interview by Joanne Greenwood. Regina, 19 March 1978. *Virtual Museum of Métis History and Culture.* Gabriel Dumont Institute, Saskatoon, SK, PDF File.

Pelletier, Isadore. 23 November 2000. Virtual Museum of Métis History and Culture. Gabriel Dumont Institute, Saskatoon, SK, video.

Pitzel, Julie. Interview by Allyson Stevenson. Prince Albert, SK, 16 October 2012.

W., G. Interview by Allyson Stevenson. Melfort, SK, 19 September 2012.

Wilson, Vickie. Interview by Allyson Stevenson. Prince Albert, SK, 3 October
    2012.

Newspapers

Iskwew: Saskatchewan Native Women's Movement Newsletter, 1975.
New Breed Magazine, 1970–85.
Regina Leader Post, 1965–85.
Saskatoon Star Phoenix, 1965–85.

Government Documents

Statutes, Regulations, and Court Cases

Statutes of Canada

Act to Amend the Indian Act. SC 1919–20, c 50 (19-11 Geo V)
Indian Act, 1927
Indian Act, 1951, c 29, s 1

Saskatchewan Statutes

Act Respecting the Welfare of Children, 1946
Adoption of Children Act, 1922

Statutes of the United States

Select Committee on Indian Affairs, 95th Cong., 1 1977. *Indian Child Welfare
    Act of 1977*: Hearing before the United States Senate, H.R. Rep. No. 1386, at
    9 (1977).
U.S. Senate Report. 1977. Hearing on s. 1214 before the Senate Select Commit-
    tee on Indian Affairs. 95th Congress, 1st Session, 43.

Archival Series

Anglican Church Archives, Prince Albert, SK
    Marriage Register
Government of Saskatchewan
    Record of Registration of Death, Province of Saskatchewan
Library and Archives Canada (LAC), Ottawa
    Census of Canada, 1891, 1901, 1906 (NWT), 1911, 1916 (Prairie Provinces) 1921
    Department of Citizenship and Immigration, Indian Affairs Branch, RG 10
    Department of Indian Affairs, RG 10, Black Series
    Department of Indian Affairs, RG 10, Red Series

Department of Indian Affairs and Northern Development, RG 10
Department of the Interior, RG 15
Department of Justice, RG13
Homestead Grant Registers, R190-75-1-E
Mudd Manuscript Library, Princeton University Archives
   Association on American Indian Affairs Records
Prince Albert Historical Society Archives
   James Isbister File
   1878 Prince Albert Settlement Special Survey
Saskatchewan Archives Board (SAB), Regina
   Government Records Series
      Department of Natural Resources
      Department of Social Welfare
      Department of Social Services
      Department of Social Welfare and Rehabilitation Branch
      Indian and Métis Department
   Homestead Records
   Honourable Gordon Dirks Fonds
   Human Resources Development Agency
   Manuscript Series
      Saskatchewan Native Women's Movement
   Premier T.C. Douglas Fonds
Social Welfare History Archives, University of Minnesota
   Child Welfare League of America Papers

Printed Government Documents

Canada. Department of Citizenship and Immigration. Indian Affairs Branch. *Annual Reports*, 1950–1965.
– Department of Indian Affairs. *Annual Reports*, 1945–1980.
– Minutes of Proceedings and Evidence, 1946–1948.
– Special Joint Committee of the Senate and the House of Commons Appointed to Examine and Consider the Indian Act. Fourth Report [final report], June 22, 1948.
Saskatchewan. Documents and Articles about Métis people. Pamphlet "Métis" Pamphlet Collection. Saskatchewan Legislative Library, 1972.
– Government Publications, Department of Social Welfare and Rehabilitation, *Annual Reports*, 1944/45–1965.
– Government Publications. Department of Welfare, *Annual Reports*, 1966–75.

Printed Primary Sources

Adams, Howard. *Prison of Grass: Canada from a Native Point of View*. Toronto: Fifth House, 1975.

Association on American Indian Affairs. "The Destruction of Indian Families."
    Indian Family Defense 1 (Winter 1974): 1–2.

– "Senate Probes Child Welfare Crisis." *Indian Family Defense* 2 (Winter 1974):
    1–6.

Battel, Mildred E. *Children Shall Be First: Child Welfare Saskatchewan, 1944–64.*
    Regina: Saskatchewan Department of Culture and Youth Local History
    Program, 1979.

Byler, W. "Removing Children: The Destruction of American Indian Families."
    Civil Rights Digest 94 (Summer 1977): 19–27.

Campbell, Marie. *Halfbreed.* Toronto: McClelland and Stewart, 1973.

Campbell, Marie, and Sherry Farrell Racette. *Stories of the Road Allowance
    People.* Saskatoon: Gabriel Dumont Institute, 2010.

Cardinal, Harold. *The Unjust Society.* Edmonton: M.G. Hurtig, 1969.

Chartier, Clem. *Summary of Proceedings: National Workshop on Indian Child Wel-
    fare Rights, Canadian Indian Lawyers Association, Indian Child Welfare Rights
    Workshop 1981.* Regina, SK: National Workshop on Indian Child Welfare
    Rights, 1981.

Child Welfare Review Panel. "For the Good of Our Children and Youth:
    A New Vision, a New Direction." 2010. https://cwrp.ca/publications/
    saskatchewan-child-welfare-review-panel-report-good-our-children-and-
    youth.

Dales, Alice. "Closing a Children's Institution in Saskatchewan." *Canadian
    Welfare* 30, no. 6 (1954): 39–43.

Douglas, T.C. "The Problems of the Subnormal Family." MA thesis, McMaster
    University, 1933.

Erasmus, Peter. *Buffalo Days and Nights.* Calgary: Fifth House, 1999.

Ethelton Sunset Club. *Ethelton Pioneers.* Ethelton: Ethelton Sunset Club,
    1976.

Fanshel, David. *Far from the Reservation: The Transracial Adoption of American
    Indian Children.* Metuchen, NJ: Scarecrow, 1972.

Hawthorn, H.B., H.A.C. Cairns, and M.A. Tremblay. *A Survey of the Contempo-
    rary Indians of Canada: A Report on Economic, Political, Educational Needs and
    Policies.* Ottawa: Indian Affairs Branch, 1966–7.

Isnana, Melvin. *Indian Control of Indian Child Welfare: A Report by Federation of
    Saskatchewan Indian Nations Health and Social Development Commission WMC
    Associates Firm.* Regina, SK: Federation of Saskatchewan Indian Nations
    Health and Social Development Commission, 1983.

Lamontangne, B., and the Prince Albert Historical Society. *The Voice of the
    People: Reminiscences of the Prince Albert Settlement's Early Citizens, 1866–1895.*
    Prince Albert, SK: Prince Albert Historical Society, 1985.

Lyslo, A. "Adoptive Placement of American Indian Children with Non-Indian
    Families," part 1, "The Indian Adoption Project." *Child Welfare: Journal of the
    Child Welfare League of America* (May 1961).

– "Adoptive Placement of Indian Children." *Catholic Charities Review* 512
    (1967): 23–5.

– "The Indian Adoption Project: An Appeal to Catholic Agencies to Participate." *Catholic Charities Review* 48, no. 5 (1964): 12–16.
– *The Indian Adoption Project – 1958 through 1967: Report of Its Accomplishments, Evaluation and Recommendations for Adoption Services to Indian Children.* New York: Child Welfare League of America, 1968.
– *1966 Year End Summary of the Indian Adoption Project.* New York: Child Welfare League of America, 1967.
– *Suggested Criteria to Evaluate Families to Adopt American Indian Children through Indian Adoption Project.* New York: Child Welfare League of America, 1962.
Manitoba Review Committee on Indian and Métis Adoptions and Placements. *"No Quiet Place": Final Report to the Honourable Muriel Smith, Minister of Community Services.* Winnipeg, MB: Manitoba Community Services, 1985.
– *Transcripts and Briefs: Public Hearings, Special Hearings, Briefs.* Winnipeg: Manitoba Community Services, 1985.
Mercredi, Ovide. *The Status of Child Welfare Services for the Indigenous Peoples of Canada: The Problem, the Law and the Solution.* Regina, SK: Indian Child Welfare Rights Conference, 1981.
National Indian Brotherhood. *Indian Control of Indian Education.* Ottawa: National Indian Brotherhood, 1972.
Saskatchewan Minister's Advisory Council on Child Protection. "Child and Family Services Act 1973 Review, Submitted to Gordon Dirks, Minister of Social Services." Regina: Council, 1984.
Shore, J.H. "Destruction of Indian Families: Beyond the Best Interests of Indian Children." *White Cloud Journal* (Summer 1978): 12–16.
Stalwick, Harvey, Lavinia Bitternose, Yvonne House Thomas, and Peter Brook. "Reform as the Creation of New Usages: 1982–1985. Synopsis of the Taking Control Project." In *Perspectives on Social Services and Social Issues,* edited by Jaqueline S. Ismael and Ray J. Thomlison, 223–36. Canadian Council on Social Development. Selections from the Proceedings of the Second Conference on Provincial Welfare Policy held at the University of Calgary, 1–3 May 1985.
Symington, D.F. "Métis Rehabilitation." *Canadian Geographical Journal* 46, no. 4 (April 1953): 128–39.
Unger, Steven, ed. *The Destruction of American Indian Families.* New York: Association of American Indian Affairs, 1977.
Valentine, V.F. "Some Problems of the Métis of Northern Saskatchewan." *Canadian Journal of Economics and Political Science* 20, no. 1 (February 1954): 89–95.
Wright, Jim. "Experiment with Métis." *Saskatoon Star Phoenix,* 21 September 1949.

Secondary Sources

Aboriginal Justice Implementation Commission. The Justice System and Aboriginal People. Chapter 14, "Child Welfare." 2001. http://www.ajic.mb.ca/volumel/chapter14.html.

Adams, David Wallace. *Education for Extinction: American Indians and the Board-ing School Experience, 1875–1928*. Lawrence: University of Kansas, 1995.

Adams, Marie Adams. *Our Son, a Stranger: Adoption Breakdown and Its Effect on Parents*. Montreal and Kingston: McGill-Queen's University Press, 2002.

Albers, Patricia. "Autonomy and Dependency in the Lives of Dakota Women: A Study in Historical Change." *Review of Radical Political Economics* 17, no. 3 (1985): 109–34.

Alberta. "Sixties Scoop Apology." 28 May 2018. Alberta.ca/ SixtiesScoopApology.

Allen, Richard. "The Social Gospel as the Religion of the Agrarian Revolt." In *Riel to Reform: A History of Protest in Western Canada Saskatoon*, edited by George Melnyk, 138–48. Calgary: Fifth House Publishers, 1992.

Anderson, Kim. *Life Stages and Native Women: Memory, Teachings, and Story Medicine*. Critical Studies in Native History 15. Winnipeg: University of Manitoba Press, 2011.

Anderson, Kim, and Bonita Lawrence, eds. *Strong Women Stories: Native Vision and Community Survival Life Stages and Native Women: Memory Teachings, and Story Medicine*. Winnipeg: University of Manitoba Press, 2011.

Anderson, Mark Cronlund, and Carmen L. Robertson, *Seeing Red: A History of Natives in Canadian Newspapers*. Winnipeg: University of Manitoba Press, 2011.

Anuik, Jonathan. "Métis Families and Schools: The Decline and Reclamation of Métis Identity in Saskatchewan, 1885–1980." PhD diss., University of Saskatchewan, 2009.

Ariès, Phillipe. *Centuries of Childhood: A Social History of Family Life*, Translated by Robert Baldick. New York: Vintage Books, 1962.

Armitage, Andrew. *Comparing the Policy of Indigenous Assimilation: Australia, Canada and New Zealand*. Vancouver: UBC Press, 1995.

Atwood, Barbara Ann. *Children, Tribes, and States: Adoption and Custody Con-flicts over American Indian Children*. Durham, NC: Carolina Academic Press, 2010.

Auger, Donald J. "The Northern Ojibwe and Their Family Law." PhD diss., York University, 2001.

Augustus, Camilla Charity. "Métis Scrip." http://scaa.sk.ca/ourlegacy/es-says/OurLegacy_Essays_07_Augustus.pdf.

– "Mixed Race, Legal Space: Official Discourse, Indigeneity, and Racial Mix-ing in Canada, the US and Australia, 1850–1950." PhD diss., University of Saskatchewan, 2013.

Axtell, James. *The Pleasures of Academe: A Celebration and Defense of Higher Learning*. Lincoln: University of Nebraska Press, 1998.

– "The White Indians of Colonial America." *William and Mary Quarterly*, 3rd ser., 32, no. 1 (January 1975): 55–88.

Balcom, Karen. "The Logic of Exchange: The Child Welfare League of Amer-ica, the Adoption Resource Exchange Movement, and the Indian Adoption Project, 1958–1967." *Adoption and Culture* 1, no. 1 (2007): 1–65.

– *The Traffic in Babies: Cross-Border Adoptions and Baby Selling between the United States and Canada, 1930–1972*, Studies in Gender and History. Toronto: University of Toronto Press, 2011.

Baldassi, Cindy L. "The Legal Status of Aboriginal Customary Adoption across Canada: Comparisons, Contrasts and Convergences." *University of British Columbia Law Review* 39 (2006): 63.

Barker, Joanne. "Gender, Sovereignty, and the Discourse of Rights in Native Women's Activism." *Meridians: Feminism, Race, Transnationalism* 7, no. 1 (2006): 127–61.

Barman, Jean. "Aboriginal Women on the Streets of Victoria: Rethinking Transgressive Sexuality during the Colonial Encounter." In *Contact Zones: Aboriginal and Settler Women in Canada's Colonial Past*, edited by Katie Pickles and Myra Rutherdale, 205–27. Vancouver: UBC Press, 2005.

– "Taming Indigenous Sexuality: Gender, Power and Race in British Columbia, 1850–1900." In *In the Days of Our Grandmothers: A Reader in Indigenous Women's History in Canada*, edited by Mary-Ellen Kelm and Lorna Townsend, 270–300. Toronto: University of Toronto Press, 2006.

Barron, F.L. "The CCF and the Development of Métis Colonies in Southern Saskatchewan during the Premiership of TC Douglas." n.d. http://www3.brandonu.ca/library/cjns/10.2/barron.pdf.

– *Encyclopedia of the Great Plains Indians*, s.v. "Poundmaker."

– *Walking in Indian Moccasins: The Native Policies of Tommy Douglas and the CCF*. Vancouver: UBC Press, 1997.

Barrera, Jorge. "Indigenous Child Welfare Rates Creating 'Humanitarian Crisis' in Canada, Says Federal Minister." CBC News, 2 November 2017. https://www.cbc.ca/news/indigenous/crisis-philpott-child-welfare-1.4385136.

Bartholet, Elizabeth. *Family Bonds: Adoption and the Politics of Parenting*. Boston: Houghton Mifflin, 1993. *Indigenous Feminism*.

Bédard, Renée, and Elizabeth Mzinegizhigo-kwe. "An Anishinbaabe-kwe Ideology on Mothering and Motherhood." In *"Until Our Hearts Are on the Ground,"* edited by Memee Lavell-Harvard and Janette Corbiere-Lavell. Toronto: Demeter, 2006.

Berebitsky, Julie. *Like Our Very Own: Adoption and the Changing Culture of Motherhood, 1851–1950*. Lawrence: University of Kansas Press, 2001.

Biolsi, Thomas. "The Birth of the Reservation: Making the Modern Individual among the Lakota." *American Ethnologist* 22, no. 1 (February 1995): 28–53.

Blackstock, Cindy. "Supporting First Nations Adoptions." Submission to Standing Committee on Human Resources, Skill and Social Development and the Status of Persons with Disabilities, December 2010. http://www.fncaringsociety.com/sites/default/files/13.FNCFCS-Supporting-First-Nations-Adoption-Dec2010.pdf.

Bolt, Christine. *American Indian Policy and Reform: Case Studies of the Campaign to Assimilate the American Indians*. London: Allen and Unwin, 1987.

Bombay, Amy, Kim Matheson, and Hymie Anison. "Intergenerational Trauma: Convergence of Multiple Processes among First Nations People in Canada." *International Journal of Indigenous Health* 5 no. 3 (November 2009): 6–47.

Borrows, John. *Canada's Indigenous Constitution*. Toronto: University of Toronto Press, 2010.

– *Recovering Canada: The Resurgence of Indigenous Law*. Toronto: University of Toronto Press, 2002.

Briggs, Laura. "Mother, Child, Race, Nation: The Visual Iconography of Rescue and the Politics of Transracial and Transnational Adoption." *Gender and History* 15, no. 2 (August 2003): 179–200.

– *Somebody's Children: The Politics of Transnational and Transracial Adoption*. Durham NC: Duke University Press, 2012.

British Columbia Representative for Children and Youth. "Out of Sight: How One Indigenous Child's Best Interests Were Lost between Two Provinces: A Special Report." September 2013. https://cwrp.ca/publications/out-sight-how-one-aboriginal-childs-best-interests-were-lost-between-two-provinces.

Brownlie, Robin. *A Fatherly Eye: Indian Agents, Government Power, and Indigenous Resistance in Ontario, 1918–1939*. Don Mills, ON: Oxford University Press, 2003.

– "Intimate Surveillance: Indian Affairs, Colonization, and the Regulation of Aboriginal Women's Sexuality." In *Contact Zones: Aboriginal and Settler Women in Canada's Colonial Past*, edited by Katie Pickles and Myra Rutherdale, 160–78. Vancouver: UBC Press, 2005.

Brownlie, Robin, and Valerie J. Korinek, eds. *Finding a Way to the Heart: Feminist Writings on Indigenous and Women's History in Canada*. Winnipeg: University of Manitoba Press, 2012.

Buckley, Helen. *From Wooden Ploughs to Welfare: Why Indian Policy Failed in the Prairie Provinces*. Montreal and Kingston: McGill-Queen's University Press, 1992.

Burley, David G. "Rooster Town: Winnipeg's Lost Métis Suburb, 1900–1960." *Urban History Review* 42, no. 1 (2013): 3–25.

CBC News. "Apology Coming but No Money for Sixties Scoop: Sask. Premier Brad Wall." 24 June 2015. https://www.cbc.ca/news/canada/saskatchewan/apology-coming-but-no-money-for-sixties-scoop-sask-premier-brad-wall-1.3126003.

Cahn, Naomi R., and Joan H. Hollinger, eds. *Families by Law: An Adoption Reader*. New York: New York University Press, 2004.

Canadian Institute of Health Research, Natural Sciences and Engineering Research Council of Canada, and Social Sciences and Humanities Research Council of Canada. *Tri-Council Policy Statement: Ethical Conduct for Research Involving Humans*. 2010.

Cannon, Martin. "First Nations Citizenship: An Act to Amend the Indian Act (1985) and the Accommodation of Sex Discriminatory Policy." *Canadian Review of Social Policy* (2006): 40–71.

– "The Regulation of First Nations Sexuality." *Canadian Journal of Native Studies* 18, no. 1 (1998): 1–18.

Cardinal, Harold. *Treaty Elders of Saskatchewan: Our Dream Is That Our Peoples Will One Day Be Clearly Recognized as Nations*. Calgary: University of Calgary Press, 2000.

Carp, E. Wayne. *Adoption in America: Historical Perspectives*. Ann Arbor: University of Michigan Press, 2002.

Carrière, Jeannine, ed. *Aski Awasis/Children of the Earth: First Peoples Speaking on Adoption*, Fernwood Basics. Black Point, NS: Fernwood Publications, 2010.

– "The Role of Connectedness and Health for First Nation Adoptees." PhD diss., University of Alberta, 2005.

Carrière, Jeannine, and Cathy Richardson. "From Longing to Belonging: Attachment Theory, Connectedness and Aboriginal Children in Canada." In *Passion for Action in Child and Family Services: Voices from the Prairies*, edited by Ivan Brown and Donald Michael Fuchs, 49–68. Regina: Canadian Plains Research Centre, 2009.

Carrière, Jeannine, and Susan Scarth. "Aboriginal Children: Maintaining Connections in Adoption." In *Putting a Human Face on Child Welfare: Voices from The Prairies*, edited by I. Brown, F. Chaze, D. Fuchs, J. Lafrance, S. McKay, and S.T. Prokop, 203–21 (Prairie Child Welfare Consortium and Centre for Excellence for Child Welfare, 2007).

Carrière, Jeannine, and Susan Strega. *"Walking This Path Together": Anti-Racist and Oppressive Practice in Child Welfare*. Halifax: Fernwood Publishing, 2009.

Carter, Sarah. "Categories and Terrains of Exclusion: Constructing the 'Indian Woman' in the Early Settlement Era in Western Canada." *Great Plains Quarterly* 13 (Summer 1993): 147–61.

– *Capturing Women: The Manipulation of Cultural Imagery in Canada's Prairie West*. Montreal and Kingston: McGill-Queen's University Press, 1997.

– *The Importance of Being Monogamous: Marriage and Nation Building in Western Canada to 1915*. Edmonton: University of Alberta Press, 2008.

– *Lost Harvests: Prairie Indian Reserve Farmers and Government Policy*. Montreal and Kingston: McGill-Queen's University Press, 1993.

Chuchryk, Patricia. *Women of the First Nations*. Winnipeg: University of Manitoba Press, 1994.

Chupik-Hall, Jessa. "'Good Families Do Not Just Happen': Indigenous People and Child Welfare Services in Canada, 1950–1965." MA thesis, Trent University, 2001.

Clark, D. Anthony Tyeeme. "Decolonization Matters: Featured Review Essay." *Wicazo Sa Review* 22, no. 1 (2007): 101–18. https://muse.jhu.edu/article/215459.

Clatworthy, Stewart J. *Native Economic Conditions in Regina and Saskatoon*. Edited by Jeremy Hull. Winnipeg: Institute of Urban Studies University of Winnipeg, 1983.

Clibbon, Jennifer. "First Nations Child Advocate Wins 1st Battle with Ottawa on Services." CBC News, 19 April 2012. http://www.cbc.ca/news/canada/first-nations-child-advocate-wins-1st-battle-with-ottawa-on-services-1.1149966.

Code, Paget. "Les autres Métis: The English Métis of the Prince Albert Settlement 1862–1886." MA thesis, University of Saskatchewan, 2008.

Cook, Ramsay. *The Regenerators: Social Criticism in Late Victorian English Canada.* Toronto: University of Toronto Press, 1985.

Cott, Nancy F. "Afterword." In *Haunted by Empire: Geographies of Intimacy in North American History,* edited by Ann Laura Stoler, 469–72. Durham, NC: Duke University Press, 2006.

– *Public Vows: A History of Marriage and the Nation.* Cambridge, MA: Harvard University Press, 2000.

Critchlow, Donald T., and Charles H. Parker, eds. *With Us Always: A History of Private Charity and Public Welfare.* Lanham, MD: Rowman and Littlefield, 1998.

Cull, Randi. "Aboriginal Mothering under the State's Gaze: Motherhood." In *"Until Our Hearts Are on the Ground": Aboriginal Mothering, Oppression, Resistance and Rebirth,* edited by D. Memee Lavell-Harvard and Janette Corbiere Lavell. Toronto: Demeter, 2006.

Daniels, Harry W. *The Forgotten People: Métis and Non-Status Indian Land Claims.* Edited by Native Council of Canada. Ottawa: Native Council of Canada, 1979.

Daschuk, James. *Clearing the Plains: Disease, Politics of Starvation, and the Loss of Indigenous Life.* Regina, SK: University of Regina Press, 2013.

Davis, May J. "Adoptive Placement of American Indian Children with Non-Indian Families: Part II." *Child Welfare* (June 1961).

DeMallie, Raymond. "Kinship and Biology in Sioux Culture." In *North American Indian Anthropology: Essays on Society and* Culture, edited by Raymond J. DeMallie and Alfonso Ortiz, 125–46. Norman: University of Oklahoma Press, 1994.

Demilio, John, and Estelle Freedman. *Intimate Matters: A History of Sexuality in America.* Chicago: University of Chicago Press, 1997.

Demos, John. *Unredeemed Captive: A Family Story from Early America.* New York: Alfred Knopf, 1994.

Dippie, Brian. *The Vanishing American: White Attitudes and U.S. Indian Policy.* Lawrence: University Press of Kansas, 1982.

Dobbin, Murray. *The One-and-a-Half Men: The Story of Jim Brady and Malcolm Norris, Métis Patriots of the Twentieth Century.* Vancouver: New Star Books, 1981.

– "Prairie Colonialism: The CCF in Northern Saskatchewan, 1944–1964." *Studies in Political Economy* 16 (1985): 7–40.

Dornstauder, Frank, and David Macknak. "100 Years of Child Welfare Services in Saskatchewan: A Survey." http://sasw.in1touch.org/uploaded/web/CW/100-ChildWelfarePaper.pdf.

Doucette, Robert G. *The Archival Resource Guide for Indigenous Issues*. Saskatoon, SK: Gabriel Dumont Institute, 2009.

Dubinsky, Karen. *Babies without Borders: Adoption and Migration across the Americas*. Toronto: University of Toronto Press, 2010.

Dyck, Erica. *Facing Eugenics: Reproduction, Sterilization, and the Politics of Choice*. Toronto: University of Toronto Press, 2013.

Dyck, Noel. *What Is the Indian "Problem": Tutelage and Resistance in Canadian Indian Administration*. Edited by Memorial University of Newfoundland. St John's, NL: Institute of Social and Economic Research Memorial University of Newfoundland, 1991.

Eberts, Mary. "Victoria's Secret: How to Make a Population of Prey." In *Indivisible: Indigenous Human Rights*, edited by Joyce Green, 144–66. Halifax: Fernwood, 2014.

Emberley, Julia V. "The Bourgeois Family, Indigenous Women, and Colonial Governance in Canada: A Study in Feminist Historical and Cultural Materialism." *Signs* 27, no. 1 (Autumn 2001): 58–85.

Fessler, Ann. *The Girls Who Went Away: The Hidden History of Women Who Surrendered Children for Adoption in the Decades before Roe v. Wade*. New York: Penguin, 2006.

First Nations Caring Society. "Information Sheet: The Canadian Human Rights Tribunal on First Nations Child Welfare (Docket: T1340/7708)." July 2014. Accessed November 23, 2014, http://fncaringsociety.com/all-news.

Fiske, Jo-Anne. "Boundary Crossings: Power and Marginalization in the Formation of Canadian Indigenous Women's Identities." *Gender and Development* 14, no. 2 (July 2006): 247–58.

– "Carrier Women and the Politics of Mothering." In *Rethinking Canada: The Promise of Women's History*, 4th ed., edited by Veronica Strong-Boag, Mona Gleason, and Adele Perry, 235–48. Don Mills, ON: Oxford University Press, 2004.

– "The Political Status of Native Women: Contradictory Implications of Canadian State Policy." In *In the Days of Our Grandmothers: A Reader in Indigenous Women's History*, edited by Mary-Ellen Kelm and Lorna Townsend, 336–66. Toronto: University of Toronto Press, 2006.

Fixico, Donald Lee. *Rethinking American Indian History*. Albuquerque: University of New Mexico Press, 1997.

– *Termination and Relocation: Federal Indian Policy, 1945–1960*. Albuquerque: University of New Mexico Press, 1986.

Foucault, Michel. *The History of Sexuality*. New York: Vintage Books, 1980.

Fournier, S., and E. Crey. *Stolen from Our Embrace: The Abduction of First Nations Children and the Restoration of Indigenous Communities*. Vancouver, BC: Douglas & McIntyre, 1997.

Fraser, D.C. "Sask. Government to Issue Apology for Sixties Scoop on Jan. 7." *Regina Leader-Post*, 17 December 2018. https://leaderpost.com/news/saskatchewan/the-saskatchewan-government-will-issue-an-apology-for-the-sixties-scoop-on-jan-7.

Gabriel Dumont Institute. *The Story of the Crescent Lake Métis: Our Life on the Road Allowance*. Saskatoon, SK: Gabriel Dumont Institute, 2002.

Gailey, Christine Ward. *Blue Ribbon Babies and Labors of Love: Race, Class and Gender in U.S. Adoption Practice*. Austin: University of Texas Press, 2010.

Galloway, Gloria. "Métis Say They Should Not Have Been Left Out of '60's Scoop Compensation." *Globe and Mail*, 10 October 2017. https://www.theglobeandmail.com/news/politics/metis-say-they-should-not-have-been-left-out-of-sixties-scoop-compensation/article36536782/

Gilbert, Larry. *Entitlement to Indian Status and Membership Codes in Canada*. Scarborough, ON: Carswell, 1996.

Gilchrist, L. "Aboriginal Street Youth in Vancouver, Winnipeg and Montreal." PhD diss., University of British Columbia, 1995.

Giraud, Marcel. *Les métis canadien*. Saint-Boniface, MB: Editions du Blé, 1984.

Glasbeek, Amanda, ed. *Moral Regulation and Governance in Canada: History, Context and Critical Issues*. Toronto: Canadian Scholar's Press, 2006.

Gleason, Mona. *Normalizing the Ideal: Psychology, the School, and the Family in Postwar Canada*. Toronto: University of Toronto Press, 1999.

Green, Joyce, ed. *Making Space for Indigenous Feminism*. Winnipeg: Fernwood, 2007.

– "Sexual Equality and Indian Government: An Analysis of Bill C-31 Amendments to the Indian Act." *Native Studies Review* 1 (1985): 81–95.

Gover, Kirsty. *Tribal Constitutionalism: States, Tribes, and the Governance of Membership*. Oxford: Oxford University Press, 2010.

Grier, Emily. "Indigenous Children in Limbo: A Comment on Re *R.T.*" *Saskatchewan Law Review* 68 (2005): 435–53.

Harness, Susan Devan. *Mixing Cultural Identities through Transracial Adoption: Outcomes of the Indian Adoption Project (1958–1967)*. Lewiston, NY: Edwin Mellen, 2008.

Harris, Cole. *Making Native Space: Colonialism, Resistance, and Reserves in British Columbia*. Vancouver: UBC Press, 2002.

Henderson, James Sákéj Youngblood. *First Nations Jurisprudence and Aboriginal Rights: Defining the Just Society*. Saskatoon, SK: Native Law Centre, University of Saskatchewan, 2006.

– "Sui Generis and Treaty Citizenship," *Citizenship Studies* 6, no. 4 (December 2002): 414–40.

Hepworth, H. Philip. *Foster Care and Adoption in Canada*. Ottawa: Canadian Council on Social Development, 1980.

Herman, Ellen. *Kinship by Design: A History of Adoption in the Modern United States*. Chicago: University of Chicago Press, 2008.

Hinton, Alexander Laban, Andrew Woolford, and Jeff Benvenuto. *Colonial Genocide in Indigenous North America*. Durham, NC: Duke University Press, 2014.

Hostbjor, Stella. "Social Service to the Indian Unmarried Mother." *Child Welfare* (May 1961): 7–9.

Hoye, Bryce. "Manitoba Premier Greg Selinger Apologizes for Sixties Scoop." CBC News, 17 June 2015. https://www.cbc.ca/news/canada/manitoba/manitoba-premier-greg-selinger-apologizes-for-sixties-scoop-1.3118049.

Huck, Nicole. "Merchant Law Firm Launches Class-Action Lawsuit for '60s Scoop' Adoptees." CBC News, 9 February 2015. https://www.cbc.ca/news/canada/saskatchewan/merchant-law-firm-launches-class-action-lawsuit-for-60s-scoop-adoptees-1.2949635.

Hudson, Pete, and Brad McKenzie. "Child Welfare and Native People: The Extension of Colonialism." *Social Worker* 49, no. 2 (Summer 1981): 63–88.

Iacovetta, Franca. *Gatekeepers: Reshaping Immigrant Lives in Cold War Canada*. Toronto: Between the Lines, 2006.

Information Services Corporation of Saskatchewan, ISC, https://www.isc.ca/Pages/default.aspx, Saskatchewan. https://www.saskatchewan.ca/government/public-consultations/help-inform-the-sixties-scoop-apology.

Innes, Robert Alexander. *Elder Brother and the Law of the People: Contemporary Kinship and Cowessess First Nation*. Winnipeg: University of Manitoba Press, 2013.

– "Historians and Indigenous Genocide in Saskatchewan." Shekon Neechie: An Indigenous History Site, 21 June 2018. https://shekonneechie.ca/2018/06/21/historians-and-indigenous-genocide-in-saskatchewan/.

Innes, Robert Alexander, and Kim Anderson, eds. *Indigenous Men and Masculinities: Legacies, Identities, Regeneration*. Winnipeg, MB: University of Manitoba Press, 2015.

Jacobs, Margaret D. *A Generation Removed: The Fostering and Adoption of Indigenous Children in the Post-War World*. Lincoln: University of Nebraska Press, 2014.

– "Remembering the Forgotten Child: The American Indian Child Welfare Crisis of the 1960s and 1970s." *American Indian Quarterly* 37, nos. 1–2 (Winter/Spring 2013): 136–59.

– *White Mother to a Dark Race: Settler Colonialism, Maternalism, and the Removal of Indigenous Children in the American West and Australia, 1880–1940*. Lincoln: University of Nebraska Press, 2009.

Jamieson, Kathleen. *Indian Women and the Law in Canada: Citizens Minus*. Ottawa: Advisory Council on the Status of Women, 1978.

Jennissen, Therese. *One Hundred Years of Social Work : A History of the Profession in English Canada, 1900–2000*. Waterloo, ON: Wilfrid Laurier University Press, 2011.

Johnson, A.W. *Dream No Little Dreams: A Biography of the Douglas Government of Saskatchewan, 1944–1961*. Toronto: University of Toronto Press, 2004.

Johnston, Patrick. *Native Children and the Child Welfare System*. Toronto: James Lorimer, 1983.

Jones, Andrew, and Leonard Rutman. *In the Children's Aid: J.J. Kelso and Child Welfare in Ontario.* Toronto: University of Toronto Press, 1981.

Jones, Merry Bloch. *Birthmothers: Women Who Have Relinquished Babies for Adoption Tell Their Stories.* Chicago: Press Review, 1993.

Kan, Sergei, ed. *Strangers to Relatives: The Adoption and Naming of Anthropologists in Native North America.* Lincoln: University of Nebraska Press, 2001.

Keewatin, Darin. "An Indigenous Perspective on Custom Adoption." MSW thesis, University of Manitoba, 2004.

Kelm, Mary Ellen. *Colonizing Bodies: Indigenous Health and Healing in British Columbia, 1900–1950.* Vancouver: UBC Press, 1996.

– "Diagnosing the Discursive Indian, Medicine Gender and the 'Dying Race.'" *Ethnohistory* 52, no. 2 (Spring 2005): 371–406.

Kelm, Mary Ellen, and Lorna Townsend, eds. *In the Days of Our Grandmothers: A Reader in Indigenous Women's History in Canada.* Toronto: University of Toronto Press, 2006.

Kingsman, Gary. *The Regulation of Desire.* Montreal: Black Rose Books, 1996.

Kirk, H. David. *Adoptive Kinship: A Modern Institution in Need of Reform,* rev. and enlarged ed. Brentwood Bay, BC: Ben-Simon Publications, 1985.

– *Exploring Adoptive Family Life: The Collected Adoption Papers of H. David Kirk.* Edited by B.J. Tansey. Brentwood Bay, BC: Ben-Simon Publications, 1988.

– *Shared Fate: A Theory and Method of Adoptive Relationships.* Port Angeles, WA: Ben-Simon Publications 1984.

Klein, Laura F., and Lillian A. Ackerman, eds. *Women and Power in Native North America.* Norman: University of Oklahoma Press, 1995.

Kline, Marlee. "Child Welfare Law, 'Best Interests of the Child Ideology,' and First Nations." *Osgoode Hall Law Journal* 30, no. 2 (1992): 375–425.

– "Complicating the Ideology of Motherhood: Child Welfare Law and First Nation Women." *Queen's Law Journal* 18 (1993): 306–42.

Kovach, Margaret. *Indigenous Methodologies: Characteristics, Conversations, and Contexts.* Toronto: University of Toronto Press, 2009.

Krieken, Robert. "Rethinking Cultural Genocide: Aboriginal Child Removal and Settler-Colonial State Formation." *Oceania* 75, no. 2 (2004): 125–51. https://doi.org/10.1002/j.1834-4461.2004.tb02873.x.

Kunzel, Regina. *Fallen Women, Problem Girls: Unmarried Mothers and the Professionalization of Social Work, 1890–1945.* New Haven, CT: Yale University Press, 1993.

LaRocque, Emma. "The Colonization of a Native Woman Scholar." In *In the Days of Our Grandmothers: A Reader in Indigenous Women's History,* edited by Mary-Ellen Kelm and Lorna Townsend, 397–406. Toronto: University of Toronto Press, 2006.

Lavell-Harvard, Memee, and Janette Corbiere-Lavell, eds. *"Until Our Hearts Are on the Ground": Indigenous Mothering, Oppression, Resistance and Rebirth.* Toronto: Demeter, 2006.

Lawrence, Bonita. *"Real" Indians and Others: Mixed Blood Urban Native Peoples and Indigenous Nationhood.* Lincoln: University of Nebraska Press, 2004.

Lawrence, Jane. "The Indian Health Service and the Sterilization of Native American Women." *American Indian Quarterly* 24, no. 3 (Summer 2000): 400–19.

Lee, Damien. "'Because Our Law Is Our Law': Considering Anishinaabe Citizenship Orders through Adoption Narratives at Fort William First Nation." PhD diss., University of Manitoba, 2017.

Leslie, John F. "Assimilation, Integration or Termination? The Development of Canadian Indian Policy, 1943–1963." PhD diss., Carleton University, 1999.

Leupp, Francis E. *The Indian and His Problem.* New York: Anro, 1971. First published 1910 by Charles Scribner's Sons (1910).

Levine, Philippa. *Gender and Empire.* Oxford History of the British Empire Companion Series. Oxford: Oxford University Press, 2007.

Lock, Linda D. "Custom Adoption and Its Implications on the Breakdown of the Indian Culture." Saskatoon, SK: Native Law Centre University of Saskatchewan, 1983.

Loo, Tina. "Africville and the Dynamics of State Power in Postwar Canada."*Acadiensis* 39, no. 2 (Summer/Autumn 2010): 23–47.

Lutz, Harmut, ed. *Howard Adams: Otapawy: The Life of a Métis Leader in His Own Words and Those of His Contemporaries.* Saskatoon, SK: Gabriel Dumont Institute, 2005.

Lutz, John. *Makuk: A New History of Indigenous White Relations.* Vancouver: UBC Press, 2008.

Lux, Maureen K. *Medicine That Walks: Disease, Medicine and Canadian Plains Native People, 1880–1940.* Toronto: University of Toronto Press, 2001.

Macdougall, Brenda. *One of the Family: Métis Culture in Nineteenth Century Northwestern Saskatchewan.* Vancouver: UBC Press, 2010.

MacGregor, James Grierson. *Peter Fidler, Canada's Forgotten Surveyor, 1769–1822.* Toronto: McClelland and Stewart, 1966.

Mandelbaum, David Goodman. *The Plains Cree: An Ethnographic, Historical and Comparative Study.* Edited by University of Regina. Regina: Canadian Plains Research Centre, University of Regina, 1979.

Massie, Merle. *Forest Prairie Edge: Place History in Saskatchewan.* Winnipeg: University of Manitoba Press, 2014.

Maurice, J.M. "De-spiriting Aboriginal Children: Aboriginal Children during the 1960s and 1970s Child Welfare Era." PhD diss., University of Toronto, 2003.

McCallum, Mary Jane Logan. *Indigenous Women, Work, and History, 1940–1980.* Critical Studies in Native History, 16. Winnipeg: University of Manitoba Press, 2014.

McClintock, Anne. *Imperial Leather.* New York: Routledge, 1995.

McGillivray, Anne, and Brenda Comansky. *Black Eyes All of the Time: Intimate Violence, Indigenous Women, and the Justice System.* Toronto: University of Toronto Press, 1999.

McIvor, Sharon. "Indigenous Women's Rights as 'Existing Rights.'" *Canadian Woman Studies* 15 (Spring/Summer 1995): 34–8.

McKay, Ian. "The Liberal Order Framework: A Prospectus for a Reconnais-
    sance of Canadian History." *Canadian Historical Review* 81, no. 4 (2009):
    616–78. https://doi.org/10.3138/chr.81.4.616.
McLeod, Neal. *Cree Narrative Memory: From Treaties to Contemporary Times.*
    Saskatoon, SK: Purich Publishing, 2007.
McLeod, Thomas H., and Ian McLeod. *Tommy Douglas: The Road to Jerusalem.*
    Edmonton, AB: Hurtig Publishers, 1987.
McMaster, Gerald. "Colonial Alchemy: Reading the Boarding School Experi-
    ence." In *Partial Recall*, edited by Lucy Lippard, 76–87. New York: New
    York, 1992.
McNeil, Kent. *Indian Child Welfare: Whose Responsibility? Update 1984.* Saska-
    toon, SK: University of Saskatchewan Native Law Centre, 1981.
Medicine, Bea. "American Indian Family: Cultural Change and Adaptive
    Strategies." *Journal of Ethic Studies* 8, no. 4 (Winter 1981): 13–23.
Mihesuah, D.A. "American Indian Identities: Issues of Individual Choices and
    Development." *American Indian Cultures and Research Journal* 22 no. 2 (2007):
    193–226.
– "Commonality of Difference: American Indian Women and History." In
    American Indians in American Indian History, 1870–2001: A Companion Reader,
    edited by Sterling Evans. Westport, CT: Praeger, 2002.
Mihesuah, D.A., and Angela Cavender, eds. *Indigenizing the Academy: Trans-
    forming Scholarship and Empowering Communities.* Lincoln: University of
    Nebraska Press, 2004.
Miller, Dorothy C. *Women and Social Welfare: A Feminist Analysis.* New York:
    Praeger, 1990.
Miller, J.R. "From Riel to the Métis." *Canadian Historical Review* 69, no. 1
    (March 1998): 1–20.
– "Owen Glendower, Hotspur, and Canadian Indian Policy." In *Sweet Promises:
    A Reader in Indian-White Relations.* Toronto: University of Toronto Press, 1996.
– *Shingwauk's Vision: A History of Native Residential Schools.* Toronto: University
    of Toronto Press, 1996.
– *Skyscrapers Hide the Heavens: A History of Native-Newcomer Relations in Canada.*
    4th ed. Toronto: University of Toronto Press, 2017.
–, ed. *Sweet Promises: A Reader on Indian-White Relations in Canada.* Toronto:
    University of Toronto Press, 1991.
Millions, Erin. "Ties Undone: A Gendered and Racial Analysis of the 1885
    Northwest Rebellion in the Saskatchewan District." MA thesis, University
    of Saskatchewan, 2004.
Milloy, John. *A National Crime: The Canadian Government and the Residential
    School System, 1879–1986.* Winnipeg: University of Manitoba Press, 1999.
Mills, Sean. *The Empire Within: Postcolonial Thought and Political Thought in
    Sixties Montreal.* Montreal and Kingston: McGill-Queen's University Press,
    2010.

Mitchinson, Wendy. *Giving Birth in Canada, 1900–1950*. Toronto: University of Toronto Press, 2002.

Monture, Patricia. "'A Vicious Cycle': Child Welfare and First Nations." *Canadian Journal of Women and the Law* 3 (1989–90): 1–17.

Morgensen, Scott Lauria. "Theorizing Gender, Sexuality and Settler Colonialism: An Introduction in Settler Colonial Studies." *Settler Colonial Studies* 2, no. 2 (2012): 2–22.

Morse, Bradford W. *Indian Tribal Courts in the United States: A Model for Canada?* Saskatoon, SK: Native Law Centre, 1980.

– *Indigenous Children and the Social Welfare State in Canada: An Overview*. Saskatoon, SK: University of Saskatchewan Library, 1985.

– *Indigenous Peoples and the Law: Indian, Métis and Inuit Rights in Canada*. Don Mills, ON: Oxford University Press, 1991.

Mosby, Ian. "Administering Colonial Science: Nutrition Research and Human Biomedical Experimentation in Indigenous Communities and Residential Schools, 1942–1952." *Social History* 46, no. 91 (May 2013): 145–72.

Nahanee, Teresa. "Dancing with a Gorilla: Indigenous Women, Justice and the Charter." In *Indigenous Peoples and the Justice System: Report of the National Round Table on Indigenous Justice Issues*. Ottawa: Minister of Supply and Services, 1993.

National Aboriginal Health Organization (NAHO). "Six Principles of Métis Health Research: Ethical Principles to Guide the Métis Centre in Its Work." www.naho.ca/Métiscentre (site discontinued).

Nichols, Roger. *Indians in the United States and Canada: A Comparative History*. Lincoln: University of Nebraska Press, 1998.

Nicholson, L. "Native People and the Child Welfare System: A Study in Multi-Generational Experience." MA thesis, University of Toronto, 1996.

Nurse, Andrew. "Tradition and Modernity: The Cultural Works of Marius Barbeau." PhD diss., Queen's University, 1997.

Nuttgens, S. "Life Stories of Indigenous Adults Raised in Non-Indigenous Families." PhD diss., University of Alberta, 2004.

O'Byrne, N.C. "No Other Weapon Except Organization": The Métis Association of Alberta and the 1938 Metis Population Betterment Act. *Journal of the Canadian Historical Association / Revue de la Société historique du Canada* 24, no. 2 (2013): 311–352. https://doi.org/10.7202/1025081ar.

O'halloran, Kerry. *The Politics of Adoption: International Perspectives on Law, Policy & Practice*, vol. 41. Dordrecht: Springer Netherlands, 2006.

Online Cree Dictionary. www.creedictionary.com.

Owram, Doug. *Promise of Eden: The Canadian Expansionist Movement and the Idea of the West, 1856–1900*. Toronto: University of Toronto Press, 1992.

Paisley, Fiona. "Childhood and Race: Growing Up in the Empire." In *Gender and Empire*, edited by Philippa Levine, Oxford History of the British Empire Companion Series. Oxford: Oxford University Press, 2007.

Palmater, Pamela. *Beyond Blood: Rethinking Indigenous Identity*. Saskatoon, SK: Purich Publishing, 2011.

Pannekoek, Frits. "Métis Studies: The Development of a Field and New Directions." In *From Rupert's Land to Canada: Essays in Honour of John E. Foster*, edited by Theodore Binnema, Gerhard Ens, and R.C. McLeod, 111–28. Edmonton: University of Alberta Press, 2001.

Perry, Adele. *On the Edge of Empire: Gender, Race and the Making of British Columbia, 1849–1871*. Studies in Gender and History. Toronto: University of Toronto Press, 2001.

Peterson, Jacqueline, and Jennifer S.H. Brown, eds. *The New Peoples: Being and Becoming Métis in North America*. Winnipeg: University of Manitoba Press, 1985.

Pettipas, Katherine. *Severing the Ties That Bind: Government Repression of Indigenous Religious Ceremonies on the Prairies*. Winnipeg: University of Manitoba Press, 1994.

Phillips, D.W., R.J. Raphael, D.J. Manning, and J.A. Turnbull, eds. *Adoption Law in Canada: Practice and Procedures*. Toronto: Carswell Thomson Professional Publishing, 1995.

Pitsula, James. "The Saskatchewan CCF Government and Treaty Indians, 1944–64." *Canadian Historical Review* 71, no. 1 (1994): 21–52.

– "The Thatcher Government in Saskatchewan and the Revival of Métis Nationalism, 1964–71." *Great Plains Quarterly* 17, no. 3 (1997): 213–35.

– "The Thatcher Government in Saskatchewan and Treaty Indians, 1964–1971: The Quiet Revolution." *Saskatchewan History* 48, no. 1 (1996): 3–17.

Plant, Byron King. "The Politics of Indian Administration: A Revisionist History of Intrastate Relations in Mid-Twentieth Century British Columbia." PhD diss., University of Saskatchewan, 2009.

Poitras, Marilyn, and Norman Zlotkin. "An Overview of the Recognition of Customary Adoption in Canada." Prepared for the Saskatchewan First Nations Family and Community Institute, 15 February 2013.

Pratt, Mary Louise. *Imperial Eyes: Travel Writing and Transculturation*. London: Routledge, 1992.

Quiring, David M. *Colonialism in Northern Saskatchewan: Battling Parish Priests, Bootleggers, and Fur Sharks*. Vancouver: UBC Press, 2004.

Ray, Arthur J., J.R. Miller, and Frank Tough. *Bounty and Benevolence: A History of Saskatchewan Treaties*. Montreal and Kingston: McGill-Queen's University Press, 2000.

Razack, Sherene. *Dying from Improvement: Inquests and Inquiries into Indigenous Deaths in Custody*. Toronto: University of Toronto Press, 2015.

– "Gendered Racial Violence and Spatialized Justice: The Murder of Pamela George." In *Race, Space and the Law: Unmapping White Settler Society*, edited by Sherene Razack, 91–130. Toronto: Between the Lines, 2002.

Reder, Deanna. "Âcimisowin as Theoretical Practice: Autobiography as Indigenous Intellectual Tradition in Canada." PhD diss., UBC, 2007.

Rifkin, Mark. *When Did Indians Become Straight: Kinship, the History of Sexuality and Native Sovereignty*. New York: Oxford University Press, 2011.

Rogers-Black, Mary. "Effects of Adoption on the Round Lake Study." In *Stranger to Relatives: The Adoption and Naming of Anthropologists in Native North America*, edited by Sergei Kan, 99–118. Lincoln: University of Nebraska Press.

Rooke, Patricia T., and R.L. Schnell. *Discarding the Asylum: From Child Rescue to the Welfare State in English-Canada 1800–1950*. Lanham, MD: University Press of America, 1983.

Royal Commission on Indigenous Peoples. *Report of the Royal Commission on Indigenous Peoples*. Vol. 1, *Looking Forward, Looking Back*. Ottawa: Supply and Services, 1996.

Rutherdale, Myra, and Katie Pickles, eds. *Contact Zones: Indigenous and Settler Women in Canada's Colonial Past*. Vancouver: UBC Press, 2006.

Sangster, Joan. "Criminalizing the Colonized: Ontario Native Women Confront the Criminal Justice System, 1920–60." *Canadian Historical Review* 80, no. 1 (1999): 32–60.

– *Regulating Girls and Women: Sexuality, Family and Law in Ontario, 1920–1960*. Don Mills, ON: Oxford University Press, 2001.

Scarth, Susan. "Aboriginal Children: Maintaining Connections in adoption." In *Putting a Human Face on Child Welfare: Voices from the Prairies*, edited by I. Brown, F. Chaze, D. Fuchs, J. Lafrance, S. McKay, and S.T. Prokop, 203–21. Prairie Child Welfare Consortium and Centre for Excellence for Child Welfare, 2007.

Schneider, David Murray. *American Kinship: A Cultural Account*. Englewood Cliffs, NJ: Prentice-Hall, 1968.

Scofield, Gregory A. *Thunder through My Veins: Memories of a Métis Childhood*. Toronto : HarperFlamingo Canada, 1999.

Scott, James C. *Seeing Like a State: How Certain Schemes to Improve the Human Condition Have Failed*. Yale Agrarian Studies. New Haven, CT: Yale University Press, 1998.

Sealey, D. Bruce, and Antoine S. Lussier. *The Métis: Canada's Forgotten People*. Winnipeg, MB: Pemmican Publications, 1975.

Shevall, Michael. "A Canadian Paradox: Tommy Douglas and Eugenics." *Canadian Journal of Neurological Sciences* 29 (2012): 35–9.

Shewell, Hugh. *"Enough to Keep Them Alive": Indian Welfare in Canada, 1873–1965*. Toronto: University of Toronto Press, 2004.

– "'What Makes the Indian Tick?' The Influence of Social Sciences on Canada's Indian Policy, 1947–1964." *Histoire Sociale/Social History* 34, no. 67 (1 May 2001): 133–67.

Simon, R.J., and H. Alstein. *Transracial Adoption*. New York: John Wiley & Sons, 1977.

Simon, R.J., H. Alstein, and Sarah Hernandez. *Native American Transracial Adoptees Tell Their Stories*. Lanham, MD: Lexington Books, 2008.

Sinclair, Raven. "All My Relations: Native Trans-Cultural Adoption: A Critical Case Study of Cultural Identity." PhD diss., University of Calgary, 2007.

Sinha, V., and A. Kozlowski. "The Structure of Aboriginal Child Welfare in Canada." *International Indigenous Policy Journal* 4, no. 2 (2013). http://ir.lib.uwo.ca/iipj/vol4/iss2/2.

Smith, Andrea. *Conquest: Sexual Violence and American Indian Genocide*. Cambridge, MA: South End, 2005.

Smith, Keith D. *Liberalism, Surveillance and Resistance: Indigenous Communities in Western Canada, 1877–1927*. Edmonton, AB: Athabasca, 2009.

Smith, Linda Tuhiwai. *Decolonizing Methodologies: Research and Indigenous Peoples*. London: Zed Books, 2013.

Smyth, David. "Isbister, James." in *Dictionary of Canadian Biography*, vol. 14 (1911–1920). http://www.biographi.ca/en/bio/isbister_james_14E.html.

Solinger, Rickie. *Beggars and Choosers: How the Politics of Choice Shapes Adoption, Abortion, and Welfare in the United States*. New York: Hill and Wang, 2001.

– *Pregnancy and Power: A Short History of Reproductive Politics in America*. New York: New York University Press, 2005.

– *Wake Up Little Susie: Single Pregnancy and Race Before Roe v. Wade*. 2nd ed. London: Routledge, 2000.

Sprague, D.N. *Canada and the Métis, 1869–1885*. Waterloo, ON: Wilfrid Laurier University Press, 1988.

Sprague, D.N., and R.P. Frye. *The Genealogy of the First Métis Nation: The Development and Dispersal of the Red River Settlement, 1820–1900*. Winnipeg, MB: Pemmican Publications, 1983.

Srigley, Katrina. "'I Am a Proud Anishinaabekwe': Issues of Identity and Status in Northern Ontario after Bill C-31." In *Finding a Way to the Heart: Feminist Writings on Aboriginal and Women's History in Canada*, edited by Robin Jarvis Brownlie and Valerie J. Korinek, 241–59. Winnipeg: University of Manitoba Press.

Srpuhlan, Paul. "A Legal History of Blood Quantum in Federal Indian Law to 1935." *South Dakota Law Review* 51, no. 1 (2006): 1–50.

Stanley, G.F.G. *The Birth of Western Canada: A History of the Riel Rebellions*. Toronto: University of Toronto Press, 1992.

Stevenson, Allyson. "The Adoption of Frances T: Blood, Belonging, and Aboriginal Transracial Adoption in Twentieth-Century Canada." *Canadian Journal of History* 50, no. 3 (2015): 469–91.

– "Karen B. and Indigenous Girlhood on the Prairies: Disrupting the Images of Indigenous Children in Adoption Advertising in North America." In *Children's Voices from the Past: New Historical and Interdisciplinary Perspectives*, edited by Kristin Moruzi, Nell Musgrove, and Carla Pascoe Leahy, 159–90. Cham: Palgrave Macmillan, 2019.

Stoler, Ann Laura. *Carnal Knowledge and Imperial Power: Race and the Intimate in Colonial Rule*. Berkeley: University of California Press, 2002.

– *Race and the Education of Desire: Foucault's History of Sexuality and the Colonial Order of Things*. Durham, NC: Duke University Press, 1995.

– "Tense and Tender Ties: The Politics of Comparison in North American History and Post-Colonial Studies." *Journal of American History* 88, no. 3 (December 2001): 829–65.

Stone, Linda. *Kinship and Gender: An Introduction.* 2nd ed. Boulder, CO: West-view, 2000.

Stonechild, Blair, and Bill Waiser. *Loyal till Death: Indians and the Northwest Rebellion.* Markham, ON: Fifth House, 2010.

Strange, Carolyn. *Toronto's Girl Problem: The Perils and Pleasures of the City, 1880–1930.* Toronto: University of Toronto Press, 1995.

Strong-Boag, Veronica. *Finding Families, Finding Ourselves: English Canada Encounters Adoption from the Nineteenth Century to the 1990's.* Don Mills, ON: Oxford University Press, 2006.

– *Fostering Nation: Canada Confronts Its History of Childhood Disadvantage.* Waterloo, ON: Wilfrid Laurier University Press, 2011.

Swain, Shurlee, and Margot Hillel. *Child, Nation, Race and Empire: Child Rescue Discourse, England, Canada and Australia, 1850–1915.* Manchester: Manchester University Press, 2010.

Swidrovich, Cheryl Marlene. "Positive Experiences of First Nations Children in Non-Indigenous Foster or Adoptive Care: De-constructing the 'Sixties Scoop.'" MA thesis, University of Saskatchewan, 2004.

Swift, Karen. *Manufacturing "Bad" Mothers: A Critical Perspective on Child Neglect.* Toronto: University of Toronto Press, 1995.

Thompson, K. "The History of the Adoption Myth: Adoption Policies in Saskatchewan." MA thesis, University of Regina, 1999.

Timpson, Joyce. "Four Decades of Child Welfare Services to Native Indians in Ontario: A Contemporary Attempt to Understand the Sixties Scoop in Historical, Socioeconomic and Political Perspective." PhD diss., Wilfrid Laurier University, 1993.

Tobias, John L. "Protection, Civilization, Assimilation: An Outline History of Canada's Indian Policy." In *As Long as the Sun Shines and Water Flows: A Reader in Canadian Native Studies,* edited by Ian A.L. Getty and Antoine S. Lussier, 29–38. Vancouver: University of British Columbia Press, 1983.

Truth and Reconciliation Commission of Canada. *Canada's Residential Schools: The History, Part 2, 1939–2000. The Final Report of the Truth and Reconciliation Commission of Canada.* Vol. 1. Montreal and Kingston: McGill-Queen's University Press, 2015.

– *Final Report of the Truth and Reconciliation Commission of Canada.* Vol. 1: *Summary: Honouring the Truth, Reconciling for the Future.* Ottawa: Truth and Reconciliation Commission of Canada, 2015.

– *Truth and Reconciliation Commission of Canada: Calls to Action.* (Manitoba Truth and Reconciliation Commission of Canada, 2015). http://trc.ca/assets/pdf/Calls_to_Action_English2.pdf.

Tuck, Eve, and Marcia McKenzie. *Place in Research: Theory, Methodology and Methods.* New York: Routledge, 2015.

Turner, Dale. *This Is Not a Peace Pipe: Towards a Critical Indigenous Philosophy*. Toronto: University of Toronto Press, 2006.

Turner, Tara. "Re-Searching Métis Identity: My Métis Family Story." PhD diss., University of Saskatchewan, 2010.

Turpel, Mary Ellen. "Patriarchy and Paternalism: The Legacy of the Canadian State for First Nations Women." *Canadian Journal of Women and the Law* 6, no. 1 (1993): 174–92.

Tyler-May, Elaine. *Homeward Bound: American Families in the Cold War Era*. New York: Basic Books, 1988.

Valverde, Mariana. *The Age of Light, Soap and Water: Moral Reform in English Canada, 1885–1925*. Toronto: McClelland and Stewart, 1991.

Van Kirk, Sylvia. *Women in Fur Trade Society, 1670–1870*. Winnipeg, MB: Watson and Dwyer, 1999.

Venne, Sharon. *Indian Acts and Amendments, 1868–1975: An Indexed Collection*. Saskatoon: University of Saskatchewan, Native Law Centre, 1981.

– "Understanding Treaty 6: An Indigenous Perspective." In *Aboriginal and Treaty Rights in Canada: Essays on Law, Equity and Respect for Difference*, ed. Michael Asch, 173–207. Vancouver: UBC Press, 1997.

Veracini, Lorenzo. "Introducing Settler Colonial Studies." *Settler Colonial Studies* 1 (2011): 1–12.

Waiser, Bill. *Saskatchewan: A New History*. Calgary, AB: Fifth House, 2005.

– *A World We Have Lost: Saskatchewan before 1905*. Markham, ON: Fifth House Books, 2016.

Wall, D. "Joseph Francis Dion." https://www.ualberta.ca/~walld/dion.html.

Walmsley, Christopher. *Protecting Indigenous Children*. Vancouver: UBC Press, 2005.

Ward, M. *The Adoption of Native Canadian Children*. Cobalt, ON: Highway Book Shop, 1984.

Weaver, Sally. *Making Canada's Indian Policy: The Hidden Agenda, 1968–1970*. Toronto: University of Toronto Press, 1981.

Wegar, Katerina. *Adoption, Identity and Kinship: The Debate over the Sealed Birth Records*. New Haven, CT: Yale University Press, 1997.

Westermeyer, Joseph. "The Ravage of Indian Families in Crisis." In *The Destruction of American Indian Families*, edited by Steven Unger. New York: Association on American Indian Affairs, 1977.

White, Pamela Margaret. "Restructuring the Domestic Sphere: Prairie Indian Women on Reserves: Image, Ideology and State Policy." PhD diss., McGill University, 1987.

Wolfe, Patrick. "Settler Colonialism and the Elimination of the Native." *Journal of Genocide Research* 8, no. 4 (December 2006): 387–409.

– *Traces of History : Elementary Structures of Race*. London: Verso Books, 2016.

York, Geoffrey. *The Dispossessed: Life and Death in Native Canada*. Toronto: Little, Brown, 1992.

Youngwolfe, Denali. "Miyo-Ohpikāwasowin – Raising Our Children in a Good Way: Disrupting Indigenous Child Removal Systems through Kinship Care in Northern Saskatchewan." MA thesis, University of Saskatchewan, 2017.

Index

Page numbers in *italics* indicate a figure; page numbers in **bold** indicate a table

North Dakota, 151
Notley, Rachel, 16
Nova Scotia, 182
nuclear family: adoption and, 50, 108, 150–1; Euro-Canadian view of, 20, 31, 52, 53, 54, 55, 59, 73, 139, 226; importance of home, 150; Indigenous kinship and, 43, 154; Indigenous people and, 50, 114, 119, 226; Métis and, 166, 211; residential schools and, 20, 114; social work professionals promoting, 132, 139, 150
Nuremburg Race Laws of 1935, 75

Ojibway, 41, 209
Ontario, 128, 182
Ostrander, J.P.B., 125

Parr, V.M., 125
patriarchy, 40, 64–5, 122, 139, 142, 210
Pelletier, Henry, 80
Pelletier, Isadore, 83–4
Peter S—— case, 57–8
Peyakowak Committee, 200, 202, 215, 217, 218–20, 223
Piapot, 161
Pitsula, Jim, 24, 159, 180
Plains people, 21
poor health, 20–1, 61, 70, 228, 229. See also ill health
Poundmaker, 48–9
poverty: government solutions to, 22, 24, 87, 161, 211, 226; Indigenous solutions to, 5, 145, 214; living with, 27, 52, 64, 133, 144, 155, 167–8, 226; Métis and, 68–9, 74–5, 81, 97, 167–8, 229; not acknowledged by Adopt Indian and Métis, 161; over-representation of Indigenous children in the child welfare system due to, 9, 107, 137, 226; overview, 20–5; racialized, 21, 44, 67, 138; rationalized by government, 61; as reason to

remove children, 9, 20, 145, 148, 155; unwed mothers and, 145, 153, 154; whitewashing of, 168; white women to provide solution to, 153
Prairie First Nations, 23
public inquiries, 69, 200–1, 218–19, 224
Punnichy, Saskatchewan, 88, 89
putative father, 95, 103, 131, 141, 228

Quebec, 182
Quiring, David, 25, 26

Racette, Vicki, 178
racism: in Adopt Indian and Métis ads, 167–8, 178, 180–1; best interests of the child concept and, 31–2; biopower and, 28; child removal and, 31; decolonization and, 27; as justification for marginalization, 148; Lavell lawsuit, 209–10; product of economics, 180; social reform and, 29; structured by liberalism, 32; toward Métis, 27, 68, 74–5. See also attitudes (racial)
Razack, Sherene, 237
Recollect boarding school, 17–18
Regional Conference on Social Welfare, 91
rehabilitation defined, 74. See also Métis
reproduction: attempted regulation of Métis, 79; decolonization and, 232; Douglas focus on, 77–8; legislation and, 39, 166; national building and, 40; women-centred cultural approach to, 51–3
residential schools: adoption and, 57; as child welfare institutions, 22, 118; correlation to numbers in child welfare system, 144; education and, 7, 17, 18, 19–20, 41, 230; ill health in, 21; Indian Act, 18; logic of, 42; nuclear family and, 20, 114; overview of, 17–18; social work professionals critical of, 114–15;

STUDIES IN GENDER AND HISTORY

General Editors: Franca Iacovetta and Karen Dubinsky